AMERICAN LITERATURE AND THE UNIVERSE OF FORCE

Ronald E. Martin

AMERICAN LITERATURE AND THE UNIVERSE OF FORCE

... This leads us to undertake an account of the idea of Force in general. This is the great conception which, developed in the early part of the seventeenth century from the rude idea of a cause, and constantly improved upon since, has shown us how to explain all the changes of motion which bodies experience, and how to think about all physical phenomena; which has given birth to modern science, and changed the face of the globe; and which, aside from its more special uses, has played a principal part in directing the course of modern thought, and in furthering modern social development. It is, therefore, worth some pains to comprehend it.

C. S. Peirce, "How to Make Our Ideas Clear,"
Popular Science Monthly, 1878

All things are an exchange for fire, and fire for all things, even as wares for gold, and gold for wares.

Heraclitus

Duke University Press   Durham, North Carolina   1981

Library of Congress Cataloging in Publication Data

Martin, Ronald E., 1933–
    American literature and the universe of force.

    Bibliography: p.
    Includes index.
    1. American literature—History and criticism.
2. Naturalism in literature.   3. Literature and
science.   4. Philosophy in literature.   I. Title.
PS169.N38M3   810'.9'12   81-7806
ISBN 0-8223-0451-1 (cloth)   AACR2
ISBN 0-8223-0579-8 (paper)

This book is dedicated to Viola Wendt, *Emerita Professor of* English, *and* Jacob Van Tuinen, *Emeritus Professor of Philosophy, of Carroll College, Waukesha, Wisconsin, in appreciation of their thoughtful and stimulating teaching and fine examples of character.*

CONTENTS

ACKNOWLEDGMENTS

THIS STUDY has been nearly thirteen years in the making, and I have received valuable help, support and encouragement at every stage of the work. I would like to acknowledge, first of all, the University of Delaware, which contributed to this book in many ways, giving me two sabbatical leaves, two summer grants, a typing grant, some student assistance and a little released time, as well as the trust and the leeway I needed to work on a major project for all that time without requiring me to demonstrate my scholarly worth in frequent small projects. The four chairmen my department has had over these years, Paul Cundiff, Edward Rosenberry, Charles Bohner, and Zack Bowen, have been instrumental in gaining and channeling the University's support for this project. Edward Lurie has been both supportive, as director of the University's Center for Science and Culture, and informative, as a historian of American science. I would also like to acknowledge the support of the American Council of Learned Societies which, by awarding me a Grant-in-Aid in 1967, gave me invaluable encouragement.

I carried out my research at the University of Delaware Morris Library, the Library of Congress, the New York Public Library, the Massachusetts Historical Society, and the Cambridge University Library, and I appreciate both the accessibility of these collections and the helpfulness of the librarians. My student research assistants in the early stages of the project, Gordon Henderson, Gary Mullinax, and Charlotte Godfrey, deserve recognition for their careful and useful work. The final preparation of the manuscript for submission was done extraordinarily well by Rita Beasley, for which I am extremely grateful. Donald Pizer and Peter Shaw both offered very helpful suggestions about the completed manuscript. And finally and most of all, I thank my wife Barbara, whose intelligence, attentiveness and concern have infused and inspired this project at every stage, from the first long discussions of its largest issues to the copy-reading of its last comma; that sharing is a finer thing than any book can be.

University of Delaware:
Department of English, and
Center for Science and Culture

INTRODUCTION

THE IDEA that reality was in essence a system of forces was widely popular and influential in America around the turn of the century. Its spread was a new movement in thought, originating in mid-nineteenth-century science and rapidly extending its manifestations, explicit and implicit, throughout American culture. The views associated with what I call "the universe of force" appeared not only in the usual media of scientific and philosophical discussion, but in newspapers and novels, in letters and diaries, in speeches, sermons, and boardroom exhortations. A whole generation of Americans was in fact reared on emerging scientism and the "Synthetic Philosophy" of Herbert Spencer. Americans as eminent and various as Andrew Carnegie, John Fiske, Jack London, and Henry Ward Beecher embraced this brave new synthesis, and those who did not were virtually put on the defensive by it. As John Dewey said in looking back on Spencer's influence in America, "He has so thoroughly imposed his idea that even non-Spencerians must talk in his terms and adjust their problems to his statements."[1]

The movement is gone now as such, the concept of a force-universe leaving only scattered residues in our language and literature, our sociology, and our popular physics, but it deeply infused turn-of-the-century American culture and literature, it played an important part in shaping our twentieth-century scientific culture, and it is unquestionably significant for its lessons in the history of our modes of thought. For all those reasons, the effort to understand the complex story of the universe of force is, to echo C. S. Peirce's words, clearly "worth some pains."

The following is a study, then, of the origins, transmission, and uses of this historically important concept in our culture. I examine the concept of a force-universe as it appears in science, philosophy, and imaginative literature, from its origination as a loosely defined but extraordinarily fruitful premise in the science of the 1840s, through its elaboration (even as it was becoming increasingly obsolete in science) by Spencer and like-minded metaphysicians into a rationalistically magnificent universal system, and ultimately in the heydey of its public acceptance, to its incorporation (even as metaphysics itself was dying) by Henry Adams, Frank Norris, Jack London, and Theodore Dreiser, variously and individualistically, into the fabric of literary works they hoped would stand as timeless. At every stage of transfer of the concept from one discipline to the next there was cultural lag, misunderstanding, and distortion to the point of redefinition, but, strangely, there was often new discovery too. It is an intricate and revealing phase of our intellectual and artistic past, and I intend to give it careful and genuinely interdisciplinary scrutiny, not merely following a straightforward chain of influences through the history of thought, but studying each successive articulation of the universe of force in the context of its own time, culture, and discipline. Only in this way, I feel, can we approach the complex significances of the whole episode.

THE CONCEPT of force came to scientific prominence in the early and mid-nineteenth century, as the base concept in the "discovery" of one of modern science's most important theories, the law of the conservation of energy. This law was first formulated in the 1840s as the Law of the Conservation of Force, and, curiously, it was discovered virtually simultaneously by perhaps a dozen widely separated scientists, each taking a somewhat different route. They tended to think of force as inherent in or acting upon physical nature wherever motion or change occurred (and in this they were undoubtedly influenced by the term's varied and fertile vernacular tradition). Especially in conversion phenomena, where motion was converted into heat, for example, or chemical reaction into electricity, they believed that what they were observing was the transformation of an entity—force—from one form to another; and as they began to be able to quantify these correlations and see consistency in the rates of exchange, they felt confirmed in the intuition they had had from the beginning: that, as was the case with the already established theory of the conservation of matter, the total quantity of force in the universe was unchanging, that force could neither be created nor destroyed. It was an enormous inductive leap, but its payoff was enormous too, as the Law of the Conservation of Force provided the theoretical framework for a rush of scientific activity which yielded dramatic results, especially in the correlation of previously separate branches of science. Even biology and psychology were greatly stimulated by the inclusion of their phenomena in the overall picture of universal conservation. It was an exciting era of scientific discovery, and I argue that the very protean vagueness of the term *force* played a part in the formulation and amazingly productive application of the idea of universal conservation. Scientists generally soon refined their terminology, in the 1850s substituting the term *energy* for the somewhat more ambiguous *force*, and gradually coming to rely more on mathematical and less on verbalized articulation, coming to question the habit, as old as philosophy itself, of assuming the actual existence of such a metaphysical entity as "force." In twentieth-century science *force* has had little importance other than as a purely relational concept in mechanics, but the effects on science, language, and culture of those heady days of the Law of the Conservation of Force were far-reaching and long-lasting.

The English philosopher Herbert Spencer came of age intellectually in this milieu of burgeoning science and the conservation of force and, personally disinclined toward religion, he experienced the rationalist's equivalent of an epiphany when he conceived a cosmic scheme based on a combination of what he called "the persistence of force" and an equally idiosyncratic concept of evolution (contemporaneous with Darwin's but independent of it). "Force" was the fundamental element of Spencer's universe, and he envisioned force's innate and peculiar pattern of evolution (and devolution) as the pattern of universal process, whether it be in the formation of the solar system, the industrialization of nineteenth-century Europe, or the development of artistic style. Spencer, an extremely dedicated man, produced dozens of volumes which taken together fulfill to a surprising extent his ambition of applying his vision of force evolution to every area of human knowledge. Seen retrospectively, his contribution seems in fact to have been to pick up the philosophical preconceptions of force-oriented science and elaborate them into a comprehensive model of the universe, although in his own mind he felt he was describing the real and absolute order of things knowable. It is ironic that he did it at a time when scientific thought had largely bypassed both his method and his basic concept of force. Although his works were obsolete in their "first principles" and unsophisticated method virtually from the moment of their publication, they are still impressive today in their scope and painstaking thoroughness, and it is not difficult to empathize with the vast number of his American contemporaries who, attuned to his partly metaphysical, partly scientific style of thought (and themselves perhaps less than wholly sophisticated in epistemological matters) saw in Spencer's "Synthetic Philosophy" a convincing description of the universe and its processes.

In late nineteenth-century America, then, universe-of-force ideas were promoted and endorsed by philosophers, scientists, ministers, journalists, and others, and, despite trenchant criticism by several of our best thinkers, widely adopted. The extent of the ideas' influence can be traced in the field of imaginative literature, and that literature can be better understood when viewed in the light of this connection, because although literary artists are often highly and subtly aware of the intellectual currents of their day, the special and specific demands of their craft often work counter to any such sweepingly general theory of reality, and the tension thus produced is not only revealing about the culture that spawned it, but is interesting—esthetically and intellectually—in itself. When Henry Adams, for example, attempts in *The Education of Henry Adams* to study his society and times using terminology, theories, and even structural forms derived from the scientific and social force-lore of his times, or when Frank Norris launches a trilogy aimed at representing the impact of the colossal "force of the wheat" on farmers, speculators, and consumers, they are showing the influence of the universe of force, to be sure, but, more interestingly, they are struggling with these physics-born concepts in the full contexts of their creative imaginations, where the rationalistic truth or falsity, currency or obsolescence of individual concepts matter far less than the quality of the intuition, esthetic sense, and whole symbolic vision they are able to embody in particular works. It seems ironic that imaginative writers should have tried to build timelessly with conceptual materials that were fallible and obsolete; it is beyond irony that they succeeded.

Although the fact was not at all evident to its turn-of-the-century proponents, the universe of force is, of course, a purely conceptual universe. That it is indeed a metaphysical notion based on a specific theory of nineteenth-century physical science is worth a moment's consideration at the outset so that the broadest significance of the study can be ascertained. The concept of force is nonempirical; despite appearances, it is an arbitrary concept, possessing no special relationship to reality. The term *force* is essentially figurative in all its uses, and in its functions of explaining relationships underlying experience it carries along with it implications of mechanistic and inevitable causality. This is, of course, expressive of the mind-set of most of the science of its age—materialistic, deterministic, reductive, and absolute. As a whole approach to reality, a system that describes the universe in terms of forces differs from traditional metaphysical systems in that it is nonanthropomorphic and nontheological; its fundamental patterns come not from man's own qualities or ideals but from his conception of the laws of the behavior of physical objects. New in substance, in that it was rooted in science and scientific rationalism, yet old in approach, in that it was conceived and articulated in terms of metaphysical entities, laws, and absolutes, the universe of force is a peculiar sort of transitional landmark in Western thought.

A number of scientists of the 1840s previsioned force-metaphysics in highly optimistic terms: a universe so based would be both totally accessible to man's intellect and utterly beautiful in its rational intricacy. Spencer and the force-oriented philosophers showed the moral goodness of this rational intricacy and located in its processes humane ideas of ethical progress and (principally in American versions) the will of a benevolent and personal god. But it remained for imaginative writers—notably Henry Adams, Frank Norris, Jack London, and Theodore Dreiser—to sense and begin to articulate the human significance of the starkly mechanistic basis of this view. In their works we get the first clear intimations of how depressing, amoral, and absurd the universe can appear to man in certain nontraditional, nonanthropomorphic conceptual frameworks; they give us our first strong taste of naturalistic alienation.

In addition, the universe-of-force viewpoint was of a piece with some of the Western world's most pernicious social practices and theories at the turn of the century. Force-thinking generally rationalized racism, class superiority, imperialism, the acquisition of wealth and power, and veneration of the "fittest." Explicitly a philosophy of inevitable and benevolent progress, of an evolutionary hierarchy in which some individuals or societies are by nature superior because of their higher organization or greater concentration of power, it meshed only too neatly with the rampant forms of Social Darwinism and helped to obscure from otherwise responsible men the obligation and even the possibility of social reform. Furthermore it tended to be socially deterministic, fatalistic; if life were structured and controlled by forces, what significance could individual or social responsibility possibly have? The universe-of-force conception justified a power-hungry, imperialistic society, and those thinkers and writers who attempted to stand against such a society's callousness, exploitation, and greed often found themselves at odds with their own concept of the very nature of physical reality.

These problem areas of determinism and social inequity seem to have bothered Spencer and the philosophers but little—in a metaphysical framework, in the balance with higher abstract good, social injustice and individual insignificance were temporary, lesser evils, relatively easily accommodated. For scientists too, the nature of their discipline tended to take them away from such conflicts. But for the imaginative writers, whose commitment was neither to usable science nor to metaphysical consistency, the anguish was less concealable. Their allegiance to a philosophical pattern was often at odds with their more immediate perceptions, emotions, and ideals, and their works, in directly involving their immediate human responses, clearly represent, and in some cases place in revealing perspective, these contemporary contradictions and tensions. The universe of force was for all thinkers a paradigm which in some ways liberated and in some ways limited thought; in the moral and social realms works of imaginative literature especially show this mixed effect, and at times even show an author's awareness of it.

One of the fascinating aspects of an interdisciplinary study such as this is the comparative view it can give of the ways in which various disciplines discover, use, and develop a concept. Science, philosophy, and literature use language in somewhat different ways: their explanations are somewhat differently constituted, and their metaphors have somewhat different functions. They also develop different criteria of evidence and "proof," and different means of deriving implications, subconcepts, or corollaries. In a way, force is force when a scientist, a philosopher, and a literary artist discuss the subject with one another, and in a way it is not. They do to some extent understand one another, but one might be professionally concerned with the quantitative causal relationships between physical bodies, another might deduce a benevolent universal process, and the third deeply sense the circumstantial violation of an individual person's moral autonomy. Interestingly, the value of the concept employed within one disciplinary framework is not necessarily limited by its value in any other. As we shall see, an obsolete, discredited, and maybe even misunderstood concept of physics can indeed yield discovery in the field of literature. Disciplines interact awkwardly but fruitfully. These themes will claim some attention in the pages to follow, especially in the crucial regard of the humanistic employment of nonhumanistic knowledge.

IN STUDYING an intellectual movement that had its impulse deep in human nature and its origins distant in human history, that grew on two continents, flourished for almost a hundred years, and permeated virtually every area of human culture, an author must resign himself to severe and arbitrary exclusions or never see the end of his labor. The whole story of the concept of the universe of force in Western culture includes not only its backgrounds, development, and transmission, but the individual people who created it and found that it did or didn't suit them, the times and milieus in which they did their work, the intellectual disciplines through which they developed their insights, and the effects of their thought on their world. Given so broad a field, many of my exclusions had to follow from limitations of my own knowledge and capacity; for what was within my range or could conveniently be gotten there, selectivity followed from my sense of what was most significant in the developing structure of the idea of the universe of force.

In somewhat more specific terms, the inclusions and exclusions which my approach entails are as follows. The history of the development and transmission of the concept of the universe of force, being both fully accessible and absolutely necessary to the study—its backbone, in fact—has been treated thoroughly and centrally. Of the concept's many formulations and repudiations I have chosen those that seemed most representative and revealing. I have tried to reconstruct the historical universe of force here, relying on actual usages and direct influences and especially not yielding to the temptation to designate anything as "force" that was not so designated by the people of that day. Their usage of the term was indeed broad, but characteristically related to ideas of mechanical correlation, universal conservation, Spencerian evolution, and the like, and I have tried to let their usages and thought patterns dictate my selectivity. Of course there were other kinds of deterministic, transcendental, and energy-oriented ideas in the air in the late nineteenth century, but I have largely foregone discussion of them in order to focus on the direct line of influence I am identifying.

I have not had the space to go very extensively into the lives of the people who created and contributed to the universe of force. The times and milieus of these people and their ideas are if anything even more difficult to be both economical and truthful about, but here I could often exclude a great deal and rely both on my readers' general cultural knowledge and on the already large number of books offering historical views of the period to fill in the background. On the subject of the particular disciplines through which the force-universe concepts were developed, I felt that I had to be explicitly didactic. Because our tendency is to simplify intellectual history and to imply that a particular idea is the same idea wherever it occurs, I felt it necessary to emphasize each discipline as a separately integrated context of meaning and method that both affects and is affected by the new idea.

In treating the effects of universe-of-force concepts in human experience, I have normally confined myself to experience in science, philosophy, and literature. The concepts had other interesting and far-reaching implications—in the social, political, and religious spheres, for instance. I allude to such implications occasionally, but I have generally (and perhaps arbitrarily) thought of them as beyond the bounds of my project. The heaviest emphasis in the book falls on the imaginative literature and the effects in it of the scientific and philosophic ideas; to me this is the most interesting and enlightening aspect of the subject.

I do not intend to discount the importance of the large body of valuable scholarly and critical opinion about the figures and works I discuss, but in the interest of getting on with a very long story I have not joined critical frays along the way nor comprehensively anticipated objections to my views. Similarly, I have not systematically acknowledged ideas relatable in some way or other to my own, except in the causes of making my points clear or discharging the obligations of direct intellectual indebtedness.

Briefly, such are the principles of selectivity by which I have tried to reduce the whole story of the universe of force to the point of manageability. I mean the book to offer new insight into America in transition. The concept of a force-universe was, I maintain, an important and influential factor in the increasingly secular, scientific American culture of the turn of the century. To shed light on this period by studying the multifarious constituents and effects of this concept is my basic aim, and beyond that, to use this particular historical context to better understand human mentality. Thus I mean to reveal a complex cultural situation, not just trace a linear development. For this purpose I would like to have the study regarded as a kind of idea-novel, with the universe-of-force concept as a changeable protagonist—not very admirable or easy to identify with—followed through a number of inconclusive episodes which illustrate no single theme and teach no single lesson, unless it is the broadest and simplest one of all—that man can never know enough.

AMERICAN LITERATURE AND THE UNIVERSE OF FORCE

PROLOGUE: VERNACULAR *FORCE*

THE TERM *force* had a rich vernacular tradition before its articulation as a central concept of the science of mechanics. This vernacular tradition continued to support and affect the term as it was extended from mechanics into the burgeoning fields that later came to be called thermodynamics and energetics, and subsequently to support it as it was carried into all areas of science, indeed, by this route into all areas of systematic knowledge. Surveying the vast array of historical uses of *force*, the *Oxford English Dictionary* not only shows that its applications in physical science were preceded by three hundred or more years of popular use with a wide variety of meanings, but explicitly states that as a term in physics *force* was "used in various senses developed from the older popular uses."[1] Our preliminary concern, then, before we consider *force*'s amazing career in nineteenth-century thought, is with the popular usages that exerted so much influence over scientific conceptualization.

As early as the fourteenth century, judging from the *O.E.D.* listings, *force* had a varied and complex set of significations, ranging from nature's strength to man's moral fortitude. Deriving from the Latin *fortis* (strong), as early as 1300 it was used to designate, as an attribute of a living being, "physical strength, might, or vigour," and "as an attribute of physical action or movement: strength, impetus, violence, or intensity of effect." Examples the *O.E.D.* offers include, from c. 1400, *Ywaine and Gawain*, "With hir force sho hasted so fast that sho overtook him at the last," and from Dampier's *Voyages* of 1697, "The Sea falls with such force on the shore." The power or might possessed by a ruler is another of *force*'s earliest significations, often specifically in reference to military power, an armed force. Another of its earliest meanings was strength or power as specifically exerted upon an object or a person, this use carrying connotations of necessity, constraint, coercion, and even of violence. Thus, Milton's use in *Paradise Lost* (1667), "To work in close design, by fraud or guile, What force effected not," or Defoe's in *The True-Born Englishman* (1701), "The Bad with Force they eagerly subdue." Individuals could also have the subjective sense of being under the constraint or compulsion of a nonmaterial force, as in Wolsey's 1690 statement (in the *London Gazette*), "It was a very unfortunate Force, which the soldiers . . . put upon me, to burn the Town." And in another sense, *force* could at that time also refer to an inner, mental, or moral strength equivalent to fortitude or resistance: "Force is an other vertue by the whiche a man undertaketh to do or suffer for the love of god these thynges strange and harde" (*Ord. Crysten Men*, 1502).

Sixteenth-century accretions, generally more abstract and more specialized applications of these same sorts of meanings, augmented the idea of the power of moral or nonmaterial factors to influence man ("Mine appetite of lesse force then mine affection," Lyly, *T. Watson's Centurie of Love*, 1582), and added the idea of the power to convince by rational means. The binding power of a law is thus spoken of as "the force of a law," and the "force" of a word, a statement or a document is a designation of its real import or precise meaning (as in Steele's "The Examination of the Force of the Particle *For*," *Tatler* no. 58). From the sixteenth century onward the term is also used to mean the "peculiar power resident in a thing to produce special effects," as in Shakespeare's "On whose eyes I might approue This flowers force in stirring loue" (*Mids. N.*, 1590).

Even in this highly simplified version of the history of the term, then, there are crosscurrents of physical and metaphysical significations and among them are implications that force might be inherent in people or things, might be characteristic of them and their effects, that it might be necessitous in its operation, that it might be menacing or heroic, that it might be intentional and even rational. If the "force" represented in all these pre- and extrascientific significations were to be conceived of as a single thing manifested in these various ways, the metaphysical implications would be stupendous: Force would be a thing of pure efficaciousness, indwelling and universal, not unlike a deity.

Strictly speaking, of course, force is in no sense an actual, verifiable thing but a nonempirical concept, a habit of expression we often fall into when we refer to relationships or attributes of things or people. It is nonetheless a powerfully vivid and suggestive concept, one which seems specific, personal, and immediate. It certainly *seems* as if force were experienced directly, and this peculiarity of the term is an important factor in its extensive elaboration in the nineteenth century. In 1800 no less than now, it seems rooted in every individual's personal experience. I force something, something forces me: the experience of force seems immediate and undeniable. The term asserts something about causation—something was made to *happen*—and something about necessity—something was *made* to happen. If I push an object across the top of my desk, I have a paradigmatic "force" situation. I am clearly aware that the object moves because I push it, and aware that it cannot not move unless my force ceases or is opposed by some greater one. I am aware of my intentions and my expenditure of energy as well as my effect on the object. When I feel "forced" in some way, I feel like I think that pushed object might feel. One of our most typical linguistic habits is to refer to such events as transactions in force. By so speaking, however, we create at least verbally a new entity, which, if we happen to be a bit naive about the relationships of our words to realities, might seem to be an entity operative in other kinds of situations, possibly even throughout the whole universe of process.

When from an objective standpoint I see a thing move another thing, my natural tendency is to regard the situation analogically, as if it were the same as my personal experience of pushing or being pushed by something. The apparent causation, the apparent necessity, the apparent expenditure of effort are present to my perception, and possibly, if I am not alert to the "otherness" of things, even the teleological intention. Prior to anyone's objective perception of "force," in other words, is their strong and immediate and kinesthetic sense of effort and will, which naturally tends to shape, anthropomorphically, any other use to which they put the designating word.

The nineteenth-century elaborations of the concept of force are, of course, hightly sophisticated in figurative, analogical, definitional, and even mathematical terms, but so strong is the anthropomorphic, holistic impulse in human thought that every use of the concept tended to echo other uses of it and set resonating a great metaphysical diapason which could take even a cautious, methodical, and well-respected scientist into rhapsody over the force-interconnectedness of all things.

1. NINETEENTH-CENTURY SCIENCE AND THE CONSERVATION OF FORCE

> We in vain struggle to escape from these ideas; if we ever do so, our mental powers must undergo a change of which we at present see no prospect.
>
> William Grove, *The Correlation of Physical Forces*, 1850 edition

The universe was thoroughly and intricately modeled as a system of forces by scientists in the 1840s in what they then conceived of as the Law of the Conservation of Force. This chapter is the story of the construction of that model, the complex and peculiar concept of force which provided its basis, the amazing and productive expansion of that idea into all areas of the natural sciences, and then universal force's sudden obsolescence as it was replaced by the concept of energy and repudiated in the development of a more sophisticated and critical sense of the nature of scientific thought.

Several interesting general ideas about nineteenth-century science and human understanding grow out of this segment of the study. First of all, it is obvious that cultural factors—notably philosophical assumptions about the regularity and purposefulness of God's universe, and the semantic backgrounds of the term force—*were crucially operative in the "discovery" of this scientific theory. Experimentation was also crucial, but it is clear that the scientists discovered what they were culturally ready to discover, that scientific creativity in this instance was as much a matter of ingeniously applied* a priori *intuition as it was a matter of empirical observation and inductive conclusion-drawing. Science was a less specialized and technical, more generally philosophical field in the early nineteenth century than it has since become, and scientists more generally expected that their bench work would follow from and shed light upon metaphysical truth in some fairly direct way. Their thought tended to be of a piece, regardless of what level of abstraction they were on, so the interinvolvement of scientific and nonscientific thought was a matter of course; indeed that very distinction is a somewhat blurred and arbitrary, retrospective one.*

The career of force *also suggests some revealing things about nineteenth-century science's growing capacity to refine scientific concepts and to understand their nature, and these developments have enormous significance in the history of thought. The concept of the conservation of force may have come into science as an intuitive insight, based in metaphysics and linguistic usage as well as in science, but its elaboration, critical analysis, and ultimate rejection were accomplished by intellectual means that were distinctively scientific. The increasing mathematization of scientific thought was one important factor in the struggle to clarify this concept, but of more significance for this study was the gradual development of the philosophy of science as a critical discipline.*

Viewed as a study in semantics, the career of force *in nineteenth-century science may be best understood in terms of a tension between expanded application and precise usage, between metaphor and denotation. Metaphoric expansion was sudden and extreme, and it yielded strikingly constructive new insights about the interconnection of phenomena. Expanding the mechanical concept of "moving force" so that it shared an identity with the "forces" of light, heat, magnetism, electricity, chemical affinity, and so forth enabled scientists to construct an explanatory framework by which, for example, the sun's rays, the formation of coal, the chemistry of combustion and vaporization, the pressure of steam on a piston, and the motion of a locomotive could all be viewed as a single chain of conversions of force. Expansion of the term in this way was semantically imprecise and to a great extent empirically unwarranted, but it did enable scientists to regard these diverse phenomena as parts of an interconnected whole, the connections of which were then subject to experimentation, empirical verification, quantification, and use.*

Certain intuitions and their applications can be brilliant, but the physical world is finally under no compulsion to conform to the contours of human thought, and rampant metaphoric expansion of the concept of force into explanations of all physical processes was bound to introduce into science many potentially distracting elements of the vernacular usages, elements that would have to be excised if science's precise and verifiable relationship to the physical world were to be maintained. It was tempting to assume, for example, that a term such as force *had a real and existential referent, that there was a real underlying force which sometimes took the guise of motion, sometimes heat, sometimes gravitation, and so forth. The fact that force seemed to be a common kinesthetic experience served, of course, to reinforce this reification. This reifying habit of thought has been termed "naive realism." It was a common habit in the nineteenth century (as we shall see in considering such thinkers as Hermann von Helmholtz), and directly related to the influence of the vernacular.*

There were other ways too in which vernacular language could divert or inhibit scientific thought: there were always the risks that the linguistic structure which commonly existed as a kind of field around the term would be regarded as part of the reality-structure of the phenomenon the term was supposed to designate, or that the connotations of the vernacular term would be spuriously imported into scientific thought. The linguistic field of the term force is made up of the agent (the force), an object acted upon, and generally a source of the agent, and a direction or perhaps even a purpose to the action; thus the nineteenth-century scientist easily was led, through designating some event as the action of a force, to assume that some other element or elements of the implied linguistic structure were also elements in the event. Likewise, such vernacular connotations of force as those intimating strength, causal relatedness, resistance, and necessity tended to shape or affect the meaning of the scientist's observations as he extended the concept to ever wider applications. Thus if science were to preserve its essential precision of concept and method, the time of careful and analytical definition had to come.

In terms of its effect upon science and upon the whole culture, one of the most crucial aspects of the use of the concept of force is its intermingling with the concept of cause. A number of scientists used the terms force and cause virtually synonymously in the early nineteenth century. At that time mechanical forces were conceived of as measurable, predictable entities which changed direction or even form at consistent rates, and in the everyday experience of a scientist they were real, necessitous, and usually purposive. Causes, of course, were everywhere; a scientist automatically assumed that every event had a cause and that equal causes always produced equal effects, although he may well have been aware that since David Hume's analysis of causality he could not ascribe objective necessity to causal relationships. But if every force is a cause and every cause can be regarded as a force, forces are then everywhere, in all processes of the universe, and equivalent to their resultants no matter how indirect the correlation, and causes are necessitous and essentially analyzable as phenomena of motion or the "moving force" of mechanics. Viewed by these lights, the Law of the Conservation of Force seems to be a semantic redundancy, a recasting in terms of force of science's a priori but indispensable assumption of the universal proportionality of cause and effect. To the nineteenth-century scientists, however, the Law of the Conservation of Force embodied their discovery of the fundamentally rational and quantifiable consistency in things.

Enthusiastic optimism was the least of the emotions many of them felt in contemplating the universal mechanism, although this optimism did not prevail as the whole culture's response. The scientists saw the universe operating with a rational consistency which was beautiful to behold, but they saw with increasing excitement that the key to this consistency was accessible to man. The laws of the simple forces were the fundamental laws of the entire universe, and equipped with an understanding of them, scientists might well be on the *brink of absolute understanding of all phenomena, past, present, and future. Ironically the brink they would come to sooner was the brink of cultural shock and the widespread rejection of science and its vision of the universe as a deterministic machine. But science grows not only through brilliant synthetic intuitions but through clearsighted critical reexaminations (some of them brilliant intuitions too) of its own methods and terms, and to a great extent the critical reexamination of science refined the philosophical and cultural ramifications as well, so that force could be separated from cause, and cause separated from necessity, and mechanistic cosmic determinism could ultimately be seen as a semantic rather than a natural phenomenon. In this respect the definition stage did more than purify science—it freed the culture of its most threatening philosophical vision.*

Seen from the perspective of a later century, the situation is rife with irony. The "Law" of the Conservation of Force seems to have been implicit all along in the language and assumptions of nineteenth-century science, yet its "discovery" was one of the major theoretical advances of the century, indeed providing the basis for our science of energetics. Though its formulation was based on questionable use of language, notably the indiscriminately metaphorical use of the term force, *the history of science shows few periods of quicker and surer progress; and the progress, it must be acknowledged, was a direct result of the very indiscriminacy of the procedure. The irony ought to warn us to go slowly in our judgment; because we can in our hindsight enumerate the factors that led to this strange "discovery," let us not undervalue the insight and ingeniousness—what in any humanistic field we would call "inspiration"— that was involved in relating together the various uses and possibilities of the concept of force, thereby unifying the sciences, establishing a theoretical base which, though subsequently modified, is still fundamental to our understanding of the natural world, and in the process creating a whole new rationalistic conception of the universe, a universe of force.*

THE NINETEENTH-CENTURY theory of the universal conservation of force had its roots in the intellectual traditions and habits of the preceding two centuries—to be sure, in the highly developed science of mechanics, which had arrived at several clear and usable definitions of *force* (or its correlates, *vis, kraft,* or *forza*), but equally important, in the wide variety of vernacular usages and in the time's basically metaphysical habit of mind, which tended to cast ideas in absolutistic if not outrightly metaphysical or theological terms. The clear tendency of these early traditions was to suggest force as a fundamental and pervasive entity in physical processes and to intimate its universality and conservation. The scientific reputability of the specific term in mechanics was to serve, then, to give the expanded general term greater credibility.

In the seventeenth and eighteenth centuries the concept of force figured prominently in the formation of the problems of what we now call classical mechanics. The term *force* was applied in studies of rectilinear and curvilinear motion, impact, free fall, the inclined plane, celestial gravitation, inertia, simple machines, and other such phenomena. Theoretical discussion focused on such issues as whether the force of a moving body was inherent or external; whether what seemed to be action-at-a-distance (such as gravitation) was essentially metaphysical or really a matter of mechanical causation like the impact of particles; whether the basic phenomenon of force was impact, free fall, curvilinear motion, or the lever; whether, indeed, all force was a single entity, two-fold (the "living force" of motion and the "dead force" of weight or position, or perhaps "natural" and "violent" force) or manifold. Mathematical description was developed for many of the phenomena of mechanical physics, and several laws of matter and motion were clearly and usably defined; the articulation of mechanics in the seventeenth and eighteenth centuries was a very imaginative, creative, and subsequently valuable development in Western thought, and metaphysical inquiries into the absolute natures of force, matter, and motion were integral to it.

In his extremely useful book on the concept of force in early mechanics, *Force in Newton's Physics*, Richard S. Westfall summarizes the concept of force of Galileo (1564–1642), pointing out that this pioneer of the science made frequent and consistent use of the term *forza* in analyzing the action of simple machines. Galileo's paradigmatic idea of force was that which was applied to one end of a lever to move the weight at the other end. Galileo denied the metaphysical assumption that a body in motion requires the continued action of a mover, and spoke rather of its "*forza*"; still, he was not beyond speaking of the *forza* (strength) of a horse, or even the *forza* of a discourse or of truth. And Galileo did not classify gravity as a force (as would later scientists, to great advantage), but, in keeping with his intellectual heritage, as a natural tendency.[1] He did a great deal to shape what was later to become a very sophisticated science of mechanics, but it is clear that he was limited by some of his metaphysically or linguistically based approaches.

Another of the very important early shapers of mechanics was René Descartes (1596–1650), in whose conceptions the universe itself was a great rational mechanism. He used the term *force* in a great many ways, and probably, Westfall suggests, thus effected its adoption as a central concept in dynamics. Descartes attempted to discriminate between different types of force, such as moving force and tension; he sometimes used the term in senses which were quantifiable; and he sometimes related it to change of motion (all of which practices were subsequently to be productive directions of development in the use of the term). But his basic concept of moving force (as something that a body has, rather than something that acts upon it) was unquantifiable, and his liberal use of analogous and metaphorical senses of the term, speaking of the "force" of light or even of a particular medicine, the "force" of a man, the sun's "force," the soul's "force," and so forth, put his concept beyond any possibility of clear scientific definition. Virtually any power would be a "force" in Descartes' mind, even a concept close to the later concept of energy.[2] This foreshadowing of energetics is more than a mere coincidence, however: it is seminal. Descartes also had a concept of the regular proportionality of cause and effect and a theory that the total amount of motion in the universe was always uniform; the universal conservation of force/energy was implicit here, and at least conceptually adumbrated a good while before its "discovery."

Max Jammer in his book *Concepts of Force* notes this pre-nineteenth-century tendency to anticipate the conservation of energy, and quotes Gottfried Wilhelm Leibniz's (1646–1716) statement that "according to my opinion, the same force and vigour remain always in the world, and only passes from one part of matter to another, agreeably to the laws of nature." Leibniz's opinion followed from his religious conviction that since God had created the universe perfectly, no special intervention was required to maintain its energy and motion.[3] Leibniz conceived of force as *vis viva* or "moving force," and, repudiating Descartes's identification of the quantity of motion (*mv*) with force, he established mv^2 as the measure of force, and force as the basic element of mechanics.[4] His attempt to discriminate between "living force" and "dead force," and his perception that perpetual motion devices were impossible because of the force lost through friction were both steps in the direction in which physics was to go, but his contributions to the science of mechanics, as Westfall points out, were to a large extent determined by his metaphysical theory, by his perception of all motion and change as dynamistic, the result of purposeful forces within things which lead them regularly and systematically through their stages.

> *Every passion of a body is spontaneous or arises from an internal force, though upon an external occasion.* . . . It is the nature of created substance to change continually following a certain order which leads it spontaneously (if I may be allowed to use this word) through all the states which it encounters, in such a way that he who sees all things sees all its past and future states in its present.[5]

Behind Leibniz's thought an anthropomorphic metaphysics provides an important conceptual base for scientific insight into the physical world, influential both in eighteenth-century mechanics and nineteenth-century energetics.

Beyond question, prior to the nineteenth-century the man who did the most to determine the course of physical science, to put it on a basis which was fundamentally both mathematical and empirical, was Isaac Newton (1642–1727). He shunned Leibniz's metaphysical dynamism by conceiving of force as an external cause of change of motion rather than as a property of a moving body. Force was a measurable relationship, then, rather than an entity or property which was only verbally conceivable, although, as Mary B. Hesse points out in her book, *Forces and Fields*, he still assumed the absolute reality of these forces.[6] During a lifetime of studying and theorizing about physical processes, Newton attempted to arrive at some discriminations between types of forces, identifying at one point three distinct types (inherent force, centripetal force, and resistance) and later adding three others (the force of motion, exerted force, and impressed force), although, as Westfall points out, each of the types of force has a different explanatory function, and they are by no means entirely compatible.[7] Newton still yearned for philosophical unity, however; he hoped to see the single pattern that underlay the universe's various physical processes, and he sensed that it would be a pattern of force. In his preface to *Principia Mathematica* (1686), he stated, after a discussion of gravitation and celestial mechanics:

> I wish we could derive the rest of the phenomena of nature by the same kind of reasoning from mechanical principles, for I am induced by many reasons to suspect that they all may depend upon certain forces by which the particles of bodies, by some causes hitherto unknown, are either mutually impelled towards one another, and cohere in regular figures, or are repelled and recede from one another. These forces being unknown, philosophers have hitherto attempted the search of nature in vain; but I hope the principles here laid down will afford some light either to this or some truer method of philosophy.[8]

In their development of the theory of mechanics, Galileo, Descartes, Leibniz, and Newton (among others) brought science a long way from the simple and comprehensive metaphysics that had earlier prevailed. Earlier beliefs no longer seemed viable as explanations—Aristotle's belief, for example, that continued motion required continuous application of force, and the related idea of Aquinas and other early Christian philosophers that God was the sustainer of all motion, and even (in some versions) that angels propelled the planets in their spheres. Newton's laws of motion—de-anthropomorphized, quantifiable, verifiable, functional—were a different order of explanation; yet they still implied such metaphysical absolutes as universal force.

Conceptually immanent, the theory of force conservation might be said to have beem empirically triggered. In the early days of the industrial revolution there was enormous incentive for engineers and scientists to develop and im-

movement is a gambit I plan to respectfully decline, referring the reader to the works of scholars such as Gillispie and Kuhn, qualifying prior treatments of this phase of scientific history only by insisting on the adoption of the usage of the 1840s, the expression "conservation of force" which, although perhaps less immediately meaningful to the modern audience of historians of science, still is better representative of the broad, somewhat various, and indiscriminate conceptual routes by which scientists came to the principle of the conservation of energy. This established, my plan is to look into the nature and structure of this new universal system by studying the theories of three prominent conservationists, James Prescott Joule, William Grove, and Hermann von Helmholtz, chosen not because I mean to rank them as the preeminent scientists of the movement, but because their thought involves some of the more representative and revealing elaborations of the concept *force*.

JAMES PRESCOTT JOULE (1818–1899), an English physicist with one of the earliest claims on the "discovery" of the conservation of force, arrived at the grand theory by way of traditional British empiricism and equally traditional religious faith. He was a practical and scrupulous man of science with, generally, little concern with broader aspects of theory. His collected papers show him to be very empirically minded, focusing his attention on concrete and particular matters such as determining the specific heat of various bodies and experimenting with different kinds of machines, with batteries, and with other electrical phenomena. Rarely does he mention subjects more general than the mechanical theory of heat. His approach to conservation-of-force theory came through specific experiments with conversion phenomena, and he is justifiably famous for establishing (with amazing accuracy) a quantitative mechanical equivalent for heat. As he explained in a popular lecture,

> Heat, living force, and attraction through space . . . are mutually convertible into one another. In these conversions nothing is lost. The same quantity of heat will always be converted into the same quantity of living force. We can therefore express the equivalency in definite language applicable at all times and under all circumstances. Thus the attraction of 817 lb. through the space of one foot is equivalent to and convertible into, the living force possessed by a body of the same weight of 817 lb. when moving with the velocity of eight feet per second, and this living force is again convertible into the quantity of heat which can increase the temperature of one pound of water by one degree Farenheit.[12]

The idea seems prosaic in the atomic age, but it was a very practical and careful piece of work in its day (the actual equivalent has since been established at 772 ft. lbs.), and in terms of imagination and scientific theory it established for the first time a quantified "correlation" which could confirm the intuition of universal conservation.

Joule's basic concept of force is what he calls variously "mechanical force," "living force," or "the force of bodies in motion," or occasionally, using Leibniz's term, "*vis viva.*" His measure of force was mv^2, and his principal concern was its transformation into heat. Joule was a cautious man who resisted enthusiasm and saying or even implying more than he could warrant, but the spirit of the times caught up with him. In a pioneering statement in 1843 about the convertibility of mechanical force and heat he spoke guardedly of a given quantity of heat which "is equal to, and may be converted into," a certain quantity of "mechanical force" (156). In 1845 he spoke of "the mechanical equivalent of heat" as a relational factor, but using the term *vis viva* for mechanical force, he tried also to calculate the amount of *vis viva* that existed *in matter* judging from its temperature (202, 204–205). Later, by 1847, he claimed not only that there was an equivalence of moving force, attraction through space, heat (and, he even suggests, light), but that "heat must . . . consist of either living force or of attraction through space" (273). And in 1849 he stated, approvingly,

> In 1834 Dr. Faraday demonstrated the "Identity of the Chemical and Electrical Forces." This law, along with others subsequently discovered by that great man, showing the relations which subsist between magnetism, electricity, and light, have enabled him to advance the idea that the so-called imponderable bodies are merely the exponents of different forms of Force. (300)

As he moved in the direction of viewing force as an underlying metaphysical absolute, theological ideas tended to appear in his statement, at least in those aimed at a popular audience:

> We might reason, *à priori*, that such absolute destruction of living force cannot possibly take place, because it is manifestly absurd to suppose that the powers with which God has endowed matter can be destroyed any more than that they can be created by man's agency; but we are not left with this argument alone, decisive as it must be to every unprejudiced mind. (268–269)

Thus he introduces a discussion of conversion phenomena in a popular essay of 1847. Later in that same essay he traces the transfer of living force and heat throughout the whole system of the universe, saying,

Behold, then, the wonderful arrangements of creation. . . . Indeed the phenomena of nature, whether mechanical, chemical, or vital, consist almost
entirely in a continual conversion of attraction through space, living force,
and heat into one another. Thus it is that order is maintained in the universe—nothing is deranged, nothing ever lost, but the entire machinery,
complicated as it is, works smoothly and harmoniously. And though, as in
the awful vision of Ezekiel, "wheel may be in the middle of wheel," and
every thing may appear complicated and involved in the apparent confusion and intricacy of an almost endless variety of causes, effects, conversions, and arrangements, yet is the most perfect regularity preserved—the
whole being governed by the sovereign will of God. (271, 273)

The logical leap for Joule, then, from individual conversions to universal conservation ultimately is made by the leap of faith. The nineteenth-century scientist, in his broadest generalizations, essentially uses the patterns of religious
thought which are part of his cultural heritage. Moments of rhapsody are rare
in Joule's writing, however, and scarcely could affect the integrity of his scientific work. A considerable number of conservation theorists had, in the years
between 1843 and 1847, gone a good deal farther than Joule in these statements, which fact undoubtedly reinforced his own metaphysical enthusiasm.

Joule's countryman, William Robert Grove (1811–1896), another of the
"discoverers" of force conservation, was a more original and adventurous
theorist who in addition had some critical sense about scientific and philosophic terminology. Although he is little recognized now, Grove distinguished
himself in two careers in his lifetime; as a jurist he rose to the position of
justice of the high court, and as a scientist his achievements brought him the
royal medal and election to the vice-presidency of the Royal Society. His principal scientific investigations were carried out in the fields of electricity and
magnetism, and he invented the powerful gas voltaic battery which bears his
name. His claim as discoverer is warranted by his broadly ranging essay, "On
the Correlation of Physical Forces," first given as a lecture in 1842, which,
printed the next year and reprinted at least seven times by 1874, became one
of the most influential statements of conservation theory. Today it is interesting
in two ways. A widely researched study of forces and survey of their various
relations, it presents a clear and enthusiastic picture of the state and direction
of scientific inquiry of the mid-nineteenth century; and hedging and self-criti-
cal in its terminology, it is an inexpert and in some ways pioneering effort in
scientific semantics and epistemology. Grove's reissues of the essay often were
also revisions, in which he incorporated recent advances in science and modifications in terminology—to suit critics, perhaps, but certainly to reflect a
growing awareness of the fallibility of contemporary scientific language. His

attempt to maintain his essay as a kind of compendium of up-to-date scientific thought broke down in 1874, however, as he admitted in the sixth English edition that "physical science has moved on far too quickly for me to follow it."[13]

As Grove reflected on his own experiments with conversion phenomena and as he studied the work of other scientists, he was increasingly impelled to conclude that some form of force was behind all phenomena, that its essence was motion, that its function was causal, and that it was conserved in the universe. The pattern of such thought is that of traditional metaphysics—force the creator and sustainer, omnipresent, omnipotent, and eternal—but Grove was thoroughly convinced, consciously at least, that scientific language should be limited to the verifiable, the quantifiable and the relational, that it should leave the essences, ultimate causes, and deterministic ideas of causal necessity to metaphysics and theology. His language betrayed him, and he knew it. Repeatedly he was led to a metaphysical conclusion only to reject it and bemoan the lack of nonmetaphysical words and linguistic patterns: "We in vain struggle to escape from these ideas; if we ever do so, our mental powers must undergo a change of which we at present see no prospect."[14]

Grove tries to say that force is the key to all process in the universe and that it is universally conserved, at the same time trying not to say that force is a real entity or that it is the same thing as simple causal necessity. His sensitivity to problems of language and epistemology makes him sound like a faltering theorist but gives him special interest for us. In his very explanation of the purpose of his essay we can see the conscious imprecision:

> The position which I seek to establish in this Essay is, that the various affections of matter which constitute the main objects of experimental physics, *viz.*, heat, light, electricity, magnetism, chemical affinity, and motion, are all correlative, or have a reciprocal dependence, that neither, taken abstractedly, can be said to be the essential cause of the others, but that either may as a force produce any of the others: thus heat may mediately or immediately produce electricity, electricity may produce heat; and so with the rest, each merging itself as the force it produces becomes developed: and that the same must hold good of other forces, it being an irresistible inference that a force cannot originate otherwise than by generation from some antecedent force or forces.[15]

In a later version of this passage he revises "either may as a force produce any of the others" to say "either may produce or be convertible into, any of the others," deleting the entity "force" and making the relationship more indefinite; and he substitutes "a force cannot originate otherwise than by *generation* from some *antecedent* force or forces" with "otherwise than by *devolution* from some *pre-existing* force or forces," [16] attempting, probably, to blur the necessitous causality implied in "generation" from an "antecedent," since there is no necessity implied in "pre-existing," and "devolution" sounds somewhat vaguer and more like a possibly autonomous action than "generation." However, even in the revised version the terminological substitutions for the verb "cause"—"are correlative," "have a reciprocal dependence," "produce," "are convertible into," "become developed," and "devolve from"—remain only a set of ineffective euphemisms. Their total effect is to hint ambiguously at the idea of cause, rather than to establish the idea of some different kind of relationship between phenomena. Grove is continually and unsuccessfully looking for some sort of relational concept to substitute for the metaphysical concept of necessitous cause.

His reliance on the ambiguous concept of "correlation" enmeshes him even deeper in it, however. He tries to define *correlation* in terms of mental relationships—"The term Correlation . . . strictly interpreted, means a necessary mutual or reciprocal dependence of two ideas, inseparable even in mental conception: thus, the idea of height cannot exist without involving the idea of its correlate, depth; the idea of parent cannot exist without involving the idea of offspring" [17]—but he soon carries his definition into the realm of physical reality ("one arm of a lever cannot be depressed without the other being elevated—the finger cannot press the table without the table pressing the finger"), and by the time he is finished he is defining *correlation* in terms of simple necessitous causation as he at first had been unwilling to do: "The sense I have attached to the word correlation, in treating of physical phenomena, will, I think, be evident from the previous parts of this essay, to be that of a reciprocal production; in other words, that any force capable of producing another, may, in its turn, be produced by it." [18]

Grove does confront the problem of causality directly in the essay, however. At one point in the later editions he cites David Hume's landmark critique of the concept of causality (all we can assert is sequence in time, not necessitous relationships, Hume established). At another moment Grove tries, somewhat confusingly, to deal with the Humian perspective, stating that

> instead of regarding the proper object of physical science as a search after essential causes, I believe it ought to be, and must be, a search after facts and relations—that although the word Cause may be used in a secondary and concrete sense, as meaning antecedent forces, yet in an abstract sense it is totally inapplicable; we can not predicate of any physical agency that it is abstractedly the cause of another. (15)

And he also warned against believing that force was the simple and adequate explanation it was often taken to be:

We must guard against supposing that we know essentially more of the phenomena by saying they are produced by something, which something is only a word derived from the constancy and similarity of the phenomena we seek to explain by it. . . . No further insight into why the apple falls is acquired by saying it is forced to fall, or it falls by the force of gravitation. (21)

His concept of force was such that he found it impossible to talk about it without the animism, the reification, the determinism of the vernacular concept, so strong were the conventional patterns of language and thought. Unlike Joule, whose concept of force was at least initially rooted in quantitative measurements, Grove began with an essentially verbal, unquantitative concept from an earlier type of mechanics: "The term force . . . in its limited sense may be defined as that which produces or resists motion." He went on to enlarge this definition to "that active principle inseparable from matter which is supposed to induce its various changes." Yet he attempted to draw back from the implications of his vernacular usage, and stress the point that force was not really an observable entity: "We do not see force—we see motion or moving matter," he says, and goes on to define force as an abstract term standing for that which is alike in such phenomena as a strung bow, a stretched and released piece of rubber, a falling apple. But despite his struggle to view force as a mental abstraction, a relational concept rather than a real and causative entity, his very patterns of thought and language forced him back into the more common and traditional usages and views. He asserts that when we observe a body in motion we do not see any force, but rather, "all we know or see is the effect," thus implying an identification of force with cause; in describing the tension within the structure of a strip of glass or of elastic, he claims that "every particle of the caoutchouc or glass must be acting and contributing to resist or arrest the motion of the mass of matter appended to it. It is difficult, in such cases, not to recognize a reality in force" (20–22).

Grove uses "affection of matter" as synonymous with *force*, in keeping with his definition of force as that which affects or induces changes in matter. The body of his essay on the correlation of physical forces studies each of these "affections of matter" in its individual nature and its correlations with each of the other "affections": motion, heat, electricity, light, magnetism, chemical affinity, and other modes of force (including catalysis, cohesive attraction, and aggregation). These carefully explained conversions are the heart of his essay, and they comprise an impressive body of circumstantial evidence for universal conservation, showing as they do a complex network of connections of force. For Grove the law of conservation is a dependable and awesome principle of the universe—"Neither matter nor force can be created or annihilated," he asserted—although he is clear that strictly speaking it has not yet been fully established by science: "The great problem which remains to be solved, in regard to the correlation of physical forces, is [the] establishment of . . . equivalents of power, or [the] measurable relation to a given standard" (199).

As is necessary to any quantifiable scheme of universal conservation, Grove had a concept of "tension" or "static force," a descendant of the concept of "dead force" and a forerunner of "potential energy." Each force seems to have had a static mode which Grove explains in terms such as the following: "Dynamic electricity and magnetism are themselves motion, and . . . permanent magnetism, and Franklinic electricity, are static conditions of force bearing a similar relation to motion which tension or gravitation do" (187). Grove's sense of "static force" was essentially mechanical in nature and was obviously strongly influenced by the kinetic theory of heat:

> As in the case of friction, the gross or palpable motion, which is arrested by the contact of another body, is subdivided into molecular motions or vibrations, which vibrations are heat or electricity, as in the case may be; so the other affections are only matter moved or molecularly agitated in certain definite directions. (186–187)

Although "potential energy" would in a few years become a sophisticated and indispensable concept in energetics, its earliest formulations like Grove's "static force" were clearly mechanical conceptions of subdivided or stored "moving force."

He repeatedly suggests, in fact, that all the "affections of matter" might turn out to be a single force, might reduce, ultimately, to motion. Again the patterns of language and thought determine conclusions, in this case conclusions having the absolutism of metaphysics and the parsimony of mechanics. But Grove is one of the few force conservationists, indeed one of the few scientists of his age, to recognize that the universe was not necessarily exclusively explainable in terms of matter, motion, and force, that indeed the whole force-conservation paradigm had certain social and cultural origins and no special sanction from the natural universe—that it was, after all, only an explanatory model:

> Whether it be that, on account of our familiarity with motion, we refer other affections to it, as to a language which is most easily construed and most capable of explaining them; whether it be that it is in reality the only mode in which our minds, as contradistinguished from our senses, are able to conceive material agencies; certain it is, that all hypotheses hitherto framed to account for the varied phenomena of nature have resolved them into motion. . . . In vain has the mind hitherto sought to comprehend, or the tongue to explain, natural agencies by other means than by motion. In all these hypotheses, matter and motion are the only conceptions.[19]

Grove was trying, in an age of naive realism, to carry out simultaneous inquiries into physical reality and the nature of scientific conceptualization. He was not very successful and his personal influence was not very great. However, he clearly recognized the powerful pull of existing patterns of thought on the formation of scientific theory, and his cries of dismay in recognizing his helplessness in that sway are invaluable.

Hermann Ludwig Ferdinand von Helmholtz (1821–1894), another of the "discoverers" of the Law of Conservation of Force, was a man of considerably more scientific importance than Grove and considerably broader grasp of theory than Joule. Trained first in medicine and natural science, he was a surgeon in the Prussian army before becoming a professor, first of physiology and later of physics, at several distinguished German universities. He published definitive studies on physiology and the physics of vision and on the physiology of hearing in relation to acoustics and music, as well as important studies in chemistry, magnetism, electricity, and mechanics, but of most importance in our present context is the early work that brought him to international prominence, first published in his 1847 book *Über die Erhaltung der Kraft* and afterwards reexamined in a number of scientific and popular essays. As Gillispie points out, Helmholtz brilliantly employed the concepts and formulae of mechanics and Carnot's pioneering concepts of thermodynamics to arrive at a definition and formula of the conservation of force. His concept of potential energy was subtler and less mechanical than Grove's, and it enabled him to formulate the principle of conservation in such a way that it could become a cornerstone of the nascent science of energetics. Helmholtz's prose statement of the principle (translated into English) says:

> In all cases of the motion of free material points under the influence of their attracting and repelling forces, the intensity of which depends solely upon distance, the loss in tensional force [what was later called potential energy] is always equal to the gain in vis viva [later, kinetic energy], and the gain in the former is always equal to the loss in the latter. Hence, *the sum of the tensional forces and vires vivae present is always constant.* In this more general form, we can call our law *the principle of the conservation of force.*[20]

And in a later rephrasing he states,

> We may express the meaning of the law of conservation of force by saying that every force of nature, when it effects any alteration, loses and exhausts its faculty to effect the same alteration a second time. But while, by every alteration in nature, that force which has been the cause of this alteration is exhausted, there is always another force which gains as much power of producing new alterations in nature as the first has lost. Although, there-

fore, it is the nature of all inorganic forces to become exhausted by their own working, the power of the whole system in which these alterations take place is neither exhausted nor increased in quantity, but only changed in form.[21]

Ingenious though he was in making new conceptualizations out of old theories, Helmholtz seemed well satisfied with the old thought patterns. He had little epistemological sophistication and showed none of the anguish and constraint Grove exhibited in dealing with the language of mechanics. He discussed force as if it were a real entity, analyzable as either "*vis viva*" or "tension" and fundamental to all processes in the universe. He speaks for example, of "the *vis viva* of the sun's rays."[22] He labored in his several conservation essays to establish links between particular chemical, electrical, magnetic, and thermal phenomena on a basis of force, and he viewed the explanatory possibilities of the law of force conservation as universal and boundless: "We will, therefore, make use of our law to glance over the household of the universe with respect to the store of force, capable of action, which it possesses" (230), he states, and goes on to show the conservation of force operating in such constructs as the Nebular Hypothesis of the formation of the solar system, in the geological theory of the formation of the earth's crust by cooling, in the biological theory of the dependence of all life on the force of the sun, in the theory of the action of ocean tides, and in other areas, including the question of the permanence of the solar system.

Not only did Helmholtz regard force as a real entity underlying the structure and processes of the universe, but, unlike Grove, he was unencumbered by epistemological considerations and straightforwardly affirmed the single identity of force and cause. Clearly the naive commonsense realist, he explains (here in a late popular essay) that "our desire to *comprehend* natural phenomena, in other words to ascertain their *laws*, thus takes another form of expression—that is, we have to seek out the *forces* which are the *causes* of the phenomena."[23]

Clearly the concept of cause haunted all of the force conservationists and informed their terminology whether like Helmholtz they wanted it to, or like Grove they did not. Yet for purposes of arriving at the theory of universal energy conservation, the connection of force and cause was more an advantage than a handicap. The idea of causation, ambiguously combined with the concept of moving force, enabled theorists to universalize "force" and seemingly shorten the leap from particular force-transferences to a generalized law of nature. Certainly all of the early conservation theorists used the concept of force-as-cause either consciously or unconsciously, most of them simply affirming the connection, as did Helmholtz. J. R. Mayer, another of the discoverers of force conservation, stated baldly that "forces are causes" and proceeded to derive a theory of conservation of force from the proposition that the cause is always equal to the effect. Mayer classified causes as "material" (matter) and "immaterial" (forces) and saw both kinds of causes as by nature indestructible and convertible.[24] Michael Faraday too defined force in terms of cause:

> The word "force" is understood by many to mean simply "the tendency of a body to pass from one place to another," which is equivalent, I suppose, to the phrase "mechanical force". . . . What I mean by the word "force," is the *cause* of a physical action; the source or sources of all possible changes amongst the particles or materials of the universe.[25]

As Helmholtz saw it, if forces are both actual and universally caused, the implications for science are clear: "The ultimate aim of physical science must be to determine the movements which are the real causes of all other phenomena, and to discover the motive powers on which they depend; in other words, to merge itself into mechanics."[26] Viewed within his historical context it is not difficult to understand Helmholtz's optimism about a universe of force—it is rational, describable, and to a great extent humanly controllable. Man had the tools: "Physical-mechanical laws are, as it were, the telescopes of our spiritual eye, which can penetrate into the deepest night of time, past and to come" (243); and he could look forward to using these "telescopes" to arrive at absolute knowledge of the workings of the universe: "The work of science will have been completed only when phenomena have been traced back to the simple forces, and when it can be shown also that the given account is the only possible one admitted by the phenomena. Then this would have been proven to be the necessary way of interpreting nature, and it would be the one to which objective truth should be ascribed."[27] Viewed from our own time, across the abysses of *fin-de-siècle* pessimism, deterministic naturalism, and nihilism, from an age of computerization, behavior control and economic imperialism, Helmholtz's confidence seems incredibly naive and ironic. A universe reducible to "the simple forces" would prove in time to be a philosophical nightmare.

Once it was announced to the world by Joule, Grove, Helmholtz, and its other "discoverers," the Law of the Conservation of Force spread like wildfire throughout all branches of science in the mid-nineteenth century. Even those life scientists whose basic orientation was not mechanistic could see exciting possibilities in the scope and methods of force-conservation theory. The German chemist and biologist Justus von Liebig (1803–1873) was one of the first to study biological phenomena as part of the universal system of forces. He was an important pioneering investigator of the subjects of animal heat and the interrelationships between the animal and vegetable kingdoms, which he saw in broad terms of force correlations. Living nature, he felt, was part of the universal correlation and conservation of forces; force transmitted from the sun to vegetation was, when consumed by animals, translated into animal heat and motion, and then, through death and decomposition, cycled back into chemical forces which were returned to earth and the vegetable kingdom. Although he saw all living forms as participating in such force-relationships, Liebig was never willing to admit that life itself was reducible to mechanics. He remained a vitalist, although this left him open to much criticism in his day.[28] Also he never stressed causal inevitability in the transference of forces in the living world, playing down the element of determinism which was by then clearly implied in the force-conservation categories.

Similarly the English physiologist and psychologist William B. Carpenter, although not a thoroughgoing mechanist, was convinced that the existence of real forces was revealed to us cognitively by our "sense of effort,"[29] and he employed force-conservation concepts in theorizing about the connections of the phenomena of life and mind:

> It is difficult to see that the dynamical agency which we term will is more removed from nerve-force on the one hand than nerve-force is removed from motor force on the other. Each, in giving origin to the next, is itself expended or ceases to exist *as such*, and each bears, in its own intensity, a precise relation to that of its antecedent and its consequent.[30]

So rapid and thorough was the spread of the force-conservation paradigm that the German physiologist and psychologist Wilhelm Wundt was prompted to exclaim in the 1870s that

> the view that has now become dominant, and is ordinarily designated as the mechanical or physical view, has its origin in the causal conception long prevalent in the kindred departments of natural science, which regards nature as a single chain of causes and effects wherein the ultimate laws of causal action are the laws of mechanics. Physiology thus appears as a branch of applied physics, its problem being a reduction of vital phenomena to general physical laws, and thus ultimately to the fundamental laws of mechanics.[31]

The theory of the conservation of force induced a similar restructuring of all the sciences. This sudden, revolutionary flurry opened a myriad of new opportunities, notably in widening the contexts and elaborating the interconnections of the sciences and in moving scientific thought away from the simple materialism that had earlier explained phenomena in terms of hypothetical substances such as caloric and phlogiston and toward explanations in terms of subtler abstractions such as those of mechanics and, later, energetics. But the force-conservation paradigm had definite limitations, most of them associated with the ambiguous term *force*, which, meaning everything from human will to mv^2, first served its function as an inspiration to scientists to expand the bounds of their former thought, but later needed to be precisely and operationally defined—rather than merely being metaphorically extended—if it were to represent a demonstrable and usable scientific concept. Philosophically too, science would hardly be able to operate from a base so simply mechanical.

THERE WAS some criticism of the looser applications of the concept of force even from some of the most enthusiastic proponents of force conservation. We have earlier seen Grove's hesitancy in applying some of the force terminology, and at the same time J. R. Mayer pointed out that in mechanics scientists tended to use the concept *force* in two disparate senses, which introduced considerable confusion into that discipline. "On the one hand," he says, "it denotes every push or pull, every effort of an inert body to change its state of rest or of motion; . . . on the other hand, . . . the product—or half-product—of the mass into the square of the velocity, is named 'force.'"[32] John Tyndall was another conservationist who recognized and objected to the number of different types of phenomena referred to as *force*. He cited "gravity" and "living force," "poles," and "tensions," "the force of heat and of magnetism," among others, "all of which terms have been employed more or less loosely by writers on physics."[33] Tyndall, writing in the mid-1860s is able to resolve the difficulty of the 1840s by relying on the recently developed concept of energy, which of course is the theoretical construct recognized by modern science and about which more will be said later.

Opponents of the concept of universal force played an increasingly important part in the scientific discussion of this issue in the mid- and late nineteenth century. As early as the late 1840s the German physiologist Emil DuBois-Reymond criticized the habit of regarding force as the cause of motion, pointing out that this idea was little more than a primitive analogy,

> . . . nothing but an abstruse product of the irresistible tendency to personification which is impressed upon us; a rhetorical device, as it were, of our brain, which snatches at a figurative term, because it is destitute of any conception clear enough to be literally expressed. . . . What do we gain by saying it is reciprocal attraction whereby two particles of matter approach each other? Not the shadow of an insight into the nature of the fact. But strangely enough, our inherent quest of causes is in a manner satisfied by the involuntary image tracing itself before our inner eye, of a hand which gently draws the inert matter to it, or of invisible tentacles, with which the

particles of matter clasp each other, try to draw each other close, and at last twine together into a knot.[34]

The Scottish physicist and mathematician Peter Guthrie Tait, in a well-known and controversial essay, "On Force" (1869), attacked the concept of force more broadly: "We read constantly of the so-called 'Physical Forces'—Heat, Light, Electricity, etc.,—of the 'Correlation of the Physical Forces'—of the 'Persistence or Conservation of Force.' To an accurate man of science all this is simply error and confusion."[35] Tait indicts the broad and careless use of the term *force* in popular expressions such as *the force of habit, the force of example*, and so forth and in scientific use such concepts as *accelerating force, living force, centripetal force* and so forth, and he decided of such usage that "this, alone, serves to give a preliminary hint that ... there is probably *no such thing* as force at all! That it is, in fact, merely a convenient expression for a certain 'rate.'"[36] Tait insisted that the only meaningful definition of *force* for science was rate-change of momentum, and that phenomena of mechanics that supposedly display the action of force really show us no force and no causal relationship, but only a "transference, or a tendency to transference, of what is called energy from one portion of matter to another."[37] Thus Tait too finds his way out of the difficulty of defining force through reference to the newly emerged concept of energy.

At mid-century a great many scientists recognized or at least felt that the concept of force was radically overextended; its use in referring to that which is consistently conserved in all physical processes was too various, vague, and inclusive, and, for scientific purposes, then seen to be out of keeping with the longstanding concept of mechanical force, itself clearly not conserved in the universe. The concept of universal force in science was ready to collapse of its own weight and complexity when the term *energy* was introduced in the early 1850s and quickly supplanted it in the framework of conservation theory. Historian J. T. Merz identifies the first use of the term *energy* in something like the modern sense as that of the English physicist Thomas Young, who at the beginning of the nineteenth century used *energy* to stand for *living force*, mv^2 of a moving body.[38] In 1852, however, William Thomson, Lord Kelvin, used *energy*—meaning the power to perform work—as a substitute for the ambiguous term *force*, and other scientists were quick to follow. Scottish physicist William Rankine introduced the term *potential energy* in 1853, thereby casting the force conservationists' concepts of *tension, falling force, static force*, or *dead force* in the terminology of energetics. The term *kinetic energy*, signifying what the force conservationists called *living force* or *vis viva*, was first used in an article by Kelvin and P. G. Tait in 1862.[39] Thus the First Law of Thermodynamics was articulated as the Law of the Conservation of Energy, the principle that the sum total of kinetic and potential energy in the universe always remains constant. The concept of force became largely obsolete, essentially replaced by a newer, more usable concept after a decade of supremacy in science. It might be noted that, although free of *force*'s prior significations in mechanics, *energy* is itself no less metaphorical and anthropomorphic—but that is another story.

Even the optimistic philosophical overtones of the concept of the conservation of force, Joule's belief in "the wonderful arrangements of creation" where "nothing is deranged, nothing ever lost" and Helmholtz's faith in the comprehensible economy of "the simple forces," were drowned out by the resonances of the Second Law of Thermodynamics—the law of entropy and the dissipation of energy, formulated in the 1850s by German mathematical physicist Rudolph Clausius and by Kelvin. Focusing on the small amount of energy which is dissipated in every conversion process (like the heat which is diffused into the atmosphere by a steam engine), the Second Law shows that although the absolute quantity of energy in the universe is constant, an increasing amount of it becomes unusable by man. Entropy increases; the differentials between heat and energy levels, upon which our ability to do work depends, gradually and inevitably tend to equalize; change is irreversible. Popular scientific and pseudoscientific writing took on a new romantically dire tone at the end of the century in the shadow of this new construct, predicting the death of the sun and the final decline of all energy into the sea of entropy. If the First Law of Thermodynamics could nurture a romantic enthusiasm of an optimistic sort, the Second Law certainly appealed to a romantic pessimism, some effects of which we shall see subsequently in this study.

Concurrent with science's freeing itself from the metaphysical concept of force, it was developing a critical understanding of the nature of scientific "knowledge" such that the conservation of force would be the last metaphysical paradigm widely accepted by scientists as an absolute description of reality. In the closing decades of the nineteenth century such men as Ernst Mach in Germany, Henri Poincaré in France, Karl Pearson in England, and Chauncey Wright in the United States particularly strove to eliminate metaphysical thinking from science. They brought to fulfillment the epistemological ideas of Hume and Kant which were only intuitive in Joule and only tentative and inconsistent in Grove; in the process they contributed to the foundations of the discipline of philosophy of science. As a result of developments in scientific epistemology such as revised the idea of the nature of *force*, science was able to free itself from the traditional semantic sloughs, like the reification, the obtruding connotations, and the assumptions of causal necessity that had afflicted the thought of the early force conservationists.

Mach's contribution is especially important in the present context since through his definitive work in mechanics he most deeply affected the scientific uses of the term *force*. In 1868 he redefined *force* as a purely relational expression as part of his revision of mechanics (and indeed of all science) along phenomenological lines. Force was not an absolute entity because indeed science knew no absolute entities whatever; all it knew were hypothetical constructs more or less closely related to direct sense impressions; its statements were not about reality but about phenomena. Forces were thus entirely dispensable to Mach "because [in the words of Buchdahl] they failed to have the logical features of elements of sensation and thus were not sufficiently ultimate."[40] "Force [in the words of Jammer] was only a name to signify the product of mass and acceleration, and any other name . . . would have done as well."[41]

In the time since the late 1860s when Mach propounded his ideas scientists have generally found it unfruitful to frame their concepts as if they were merely statements about phenomena, but the reorientation of scientific thinking which Mach helped to initiate—toward regarding its concepts as hypothetical constructs concerning relations, rather than as absolute truths about real substances and causal necessities—has proved very fruitful. Indeed, the distinguished philosopher of science Ernst Cassirer regarded it as one of the great achievements of nineteenth-century thought.[42] Its influence was cerainly great, and its effect on force theory was devastating.

In its wake the twentieth-century thinker can now recognize that (as Albert Einstein and Leopold Infeld point out) "physical conceptions are recreations of the human mind and not however it may seem uniquely determined by the external world."[43] Scientific ideas have complex roots, not only in the physical world but in the history of science and mathematics, in the conditions and ideas current in the scientist's culture and in the individuality and even the eccentricity or neuroticism of the scientist himself. Before he begins a particular scientific investigation, a scientist has a conception of what is significant, what is worth observing, what knowledge is worth having, and it is in that conception that the extrascientific influences abound. Philosophers of science see the course of science as determined not only by what Max Jammer calls "the somehow fortuitous sequence of experimentation and observation,"[44] but also, in the words of Robert S. Cohen, "We, as self-conscious and society-conscious thinkers, recognize that the sources of creative scientific theory—the ideas, analyses, visions of models, formal systems, experimental devices and so forth—may exist in any aspect of human experience whatsoever; and we are receptive to the notion that all human events, even creative acts, have their genesis in other ascertainable parts of human culture."[45]

Arbitrary and man-oriented in its origin, scientific theory is also recognized as tentative and relative in its nature. Scientists' conceptions are not final. Contemporary philosophers of science Philip P. Wiener and Aaron Noland put it that "recent philosophies of science (as held by scientists themselves) support Kant's view that the investigator of nature is helped or guided by conceptual structures or models but reject the idea that there is any finality or certainty which the mind may legitimately impose on nature."[46] Another, A. d'Abro, says the scientist now thinks of his theories as "progressive approximations," always open to revision or supercedence.[47] Liberated then, from the metaphysical absoluteness of earlier theorists, the twentieth-century scientist has freer reign in inventing new theoretical frameworks, in posing alternative theories, in living with inconclusive or contradictory constructs. In the classic example, the question whether light is actually made up of waves or particles is a metaphysical one on which the scientist need take no position; absolute essences are no concern of his, and he finds both wave theory and particle theory useful for explaining phenomena of light, although the two are in some ways logically incompatible.

In the light of such radical revision of science and the philosophy of science the ideas of universal force and its conservation are, of course, archaic and unthinkable. They were, in retrospect, very convenient for science for a very short time, but they are now definitely part of our metaphysical past. Today "force" is in no way recognized as an entity by science; it is a mere relational expression meaning "the space rate of change of energy."[48] Some physicists still use the term *force* informally as a generic term referring to whatever begins or modifies motion or change, but force so conceived is not thought of as a real entity and has no status as a scientific concept.

Even the cultural residues of metaphysical force, as dire and durable as they have proved to be in the twentieth century, are susceptible to the modern sense of the nature of scientific thought and usage. In terms of cultural impact, one of the most pervasive and oppressive consequences of nineteenth-century science and its theory of force conservation was the force-cause-determinism chain it forged out of mechanics and metaphysics. In the late nineteenth and early twentieth centuries, thinkers and writers were, as we shall see, still struggling with an idea of necessitous causation in the natural and human worlds which was based on scientific thought patterns and paradigms that were by then already obsolete. Western man's basically metaphysical habit of mind, combined with a cultural lag between scientific thought and much contemporary philosophy and literature, accounts for a good deal of end-of-the-century deterministic pessimism. The view of the universe as a deterministic machine could not, of course, prevail even in the light of nineteenth-century critiques of the naive "commonsense" conception of necessitous causality which have already been discussed. Twentieth-century philosophers of science, continuing along the lines of reasoning of Hume, Mach, Poincaré, and Pearson, reject, as

R. B. Braithwaite says, "the view that there is anything objective in causal necessity over and above constant conjunction."[49] Simple experience is an inadequate guide to the understanding of causal phenomena because, as Ernst Cassirer has pointed out,

> What this experience customarily takes for *one* thing, for an undivided whole subsisting in itself, is in truth very heterogeneous and multiform, an exceedingly intricate composite, not so much of things as of conditions. We must follow these conditions one by one and resolve them into their elements, if we want to attain to genuine, scientifically useful causal judgments.[50]

Consequently the causal principle should be considered "a proposition concerning cognitions," not "one concerning things and events" (Cassirer) in which deterministic necessity is foregone in favor of "logical necessity" (Braithwaite) or "potential predictability" (Rudolph Carnap).[51]

Thus through the critical study of method and epistemology science was able to clarify its concepts and largely free itself from the metaphysical imprisonment of the force-cause-determinism chain. Perhaps no other set of ideas shows the particular value of the philosophy of science so clearly, because what was once taken to be a deterministic universal force-machine, omnipotent, omnipresent, and eternal, is now revealed to have been a mental construct, based upon naively metaphysical thought-patterns. Determinism is not a cosmic fate-spectre but a manner of speaking.

It has always been our tendency to interpret the nonhuman in terms of the human, to recreate the universe mentally out of the rational and emotional elements of our own mind, and then believe in the objective reality of the resulting picture. In its great nineteenth-century struggle to control its own anthropocentrism science has at least developed a methodology and a critical epistemology. Physical science is still the human study of the nonhuman, but enormous progress can be made in understanding this universe, given the fullest sort of recognition of that condition.

2. HERBERT SPENCER'S UNIVERSE OF FORCE

> The sole truth which transcends experience by underlying it is thus the persistence of force. This being the basis of experience must be the basis of any scientific organization of experiences. To this an ultimate analysis brings us down, and on this a rational synthesis must build up.
>
> Herbert Spencer, *First Principles*, 1862

It is ironic but not at all surprising that the concept of force should be glorified into cosmic philosophy in the latter nineteenth century. Even as a concept in mechanics its origin had been largely metaphysical, and, despite the fact that it had come under increasing suspicion and attack in the 1850s and 1860s, if a scientist as careful as Joule could have used it to make a leap from the mechanical equivalent of heat to "the wonderful arrangements of creation," or one as brilliant as Helmholtz could see the possibility of explaining all things in the universe by reducing them to "the simple forces," the invitation was probably more than a scientifically inclined, philosophically minded man could resist.

Of course neither philosophy nor science was then regarded as a separate discipline as it is today, with the critical integrity of a "discipline" and a special, necessary, preprofessional course of training. Anyone's broadest generalizations could be regarded as "philosophy." One might philosophize in ignorance of the epistemological challenges to amateur metaphysics offered by Hume and Kant, and might adopt concepts from philosophy or science without much regard for their denotative accuracy, but with the implicitly metaphysical groundwork supplied by nineteenth-century science one had only to translate scientific conceptions and preconceptions into the framework of traditional philosophical discourse to be well on the way to constructing a system which was gratifyingly inclusive and one which seemed to have behind it all the authority of modern science.

Herbert Spencer (1820-1903) was more than any other man responsible for building such a system on the basis of the concept of force. The system which he termed his "Synthetic Philosophy," is one of the last and most impressive attempts in Western philosophy to describe the nature of the universe in absolute and all-inclusive terms, and its working-out in his writings is a monu-

ment to his almost unparalleled qualities of ambition and diligence. Five major works—First Principles, The Principles of Biology *(2 vols.),* The Principles of Psychology *(2 vols.),* The Principles of Sociology *(3 vols.), and* The Principles of Ethics *(2 vols.)—as well as numerous other studies, essays, and reviews, develop his principles and carry their implications into virtually every area of human knowledge. Inquiring into everything from astronomy to zoology, from local banking laws to the religions of mankind, from literary style to railroad operation or salt-cellar design, Spencer tried to explain and unite all knowable phenomena.*

Spencer was fiercely individualistic about his work, insisting on the originality and independence of his thought, disclaiming influences, and admitting ignorance of other men's ideas and impatience with their writings. "The only indebtedness he recognized," quotes one biographer, "was 'the indebtedness of antagonism.' "[1] Yet for all his protestations there is a casual, often unintentional eclecticism about Spencer, not wholly unlikely in a thinker who prides himself on being ignorant of other men's thought. He was extraordinarily sensitive to ideas, especially the scientific ideas that were "in the air" in the midnineteenth century.

The two ideas he was most specifically attracted to were the theory of force conservation and the development hypothesis, the broadly based forerunners of the nineteenth century's two great scientific generalizations, the laws of energy conservation and evolution. Out of these two grand conceptions Spencer built an even grander one, a universe visualized as gradually but with mechanical inevitability realizing and perfecting itself, a universe of evolutionary force. His main technique for the discovery and elaboration of his concepts was the uninhibited extension of the concept force *and the scientific theories of force, conservation, development, and evolution to every application that could be imagined. (Scientists had "discovered" and applied the law of force conservation in a similar manner, but the range of their application of their concepts was narrow compared to Spencer's and their methods of verifying their insights were generally empirical and experimental unlike his, which were primarily ratiocinative.) There is a kind of ingenious naiveté about the way in which he builds his system, although he did not suppose that he could present it as an eternal map of reality; the ultimate reality is The Unknowable, he admitted, and all we can humanly consider are the observable manifestations of it. There was no doubt in his mind, however, that the true, comprehensive, and only way of understanding these observable manifestations was through his version of force evolution. Since he openly assumed that the whole order of the knowable universe had awaited, throughout the whole of intellectual history, his accurate and comprehensive description, he had no qualms whatever in seeing even his more idiosyncratic metaphors as the nearest ap-*

proach man could make to absolute reality. To the motif of naive realism—treating one's mental constructs as if they were unquestionably representative of objective reality—Spencer added a tendency toward what we can call naive absolutism—treating one's general vision as if it were eternally and comprehensively true.

Yet even for all that, he was a man of great breadth and scientific erudition, a complex Victorian whom we are here taking on in his weakest suit. The Herbert Spencer one tends to construct for an epistemology lesson—the one who, with no real awareness of the relationships between words, concepts, and physical events, built the last of the great metaphysical systems on an analogy with mechanics, the one who should have given more credence to some of his critics and had less absolute confidence in the products of his own mind—represents, really, only one of the many possible versions of the historical Herbert Spencer. There is, alternatively, the Herbert Spencer American culture now rather singlemindedly perceives, the casebook Social Darwinist, whose all-out advocacy of the theory of laissez faire *was such an intellectual boon to the robber barons and an impediment to social justice at the end of the century. Today Herbert Spencer is generally no more to us than an object lesson in socioeconomic morality. The historical Herbert Spencer was also, however, notable as a founder of the science of sociology, a shaper of the science of psychology, a political theorist, a civic-minded and articulate participant in many contemporary debates on particular societal issues, and of course an advocate of the theory of evolution; he had the respect and friendship of many of the most notable people of the century, including Thomas Henry Huxley, George Eliot, Charles Darwin. No single, simple vision of the man and his achievement can be comprehensive, finally, or entirely fair.*

Even the Synthetic Philosophy, the principal product of his complex mind, has many aspects. There is no question about the skill with which he gathers and presents data, draws conclusions, or argues his points. He had a genius for manipulating, classifying, and recalling large bodies of facts, for perceiving complex affinities, for organizing and articulating a clear and forceful exposition. Put aside some basic considerations of semantics and epistemology, and Spencer is a highly persuasive philosopher with a system that can rival any for convincingness, breadth, and complexity. Ambition and diligence, secondhand scientific theory and ratiocinative ingeniousness: these are the main ingredients of the Synthetic Philosphy. The unified vision of reality which is their end product is both magnificent and absurd.

SPENCER'S PLAN in building his Synthetic Philosophy was first to establish the general laws by which the universe operated, its First Principles, and then to apply these Principles in explaining and unifying all fields of specific knowledge. As he saw it, the first and fundamental task of philosophy was to arrive at "knowledge of the highest degree of generality," [2] and this was done by further generalizing the generalizations of science. In Spencer's words,

> The truths of philosophy thus bear the same relation to the highest scientific truths that each of these bears to lower scientific truths. As each widest generalization of science comprehends and consolidates the narrower generalizations of its own division, so the generalizations of philosophy comprehend and consolidate the widest generalizations of science. . . . It is the final product of that process which begins with a mere colligation of crude observations, goes on establishing propositions that are broader and more separated from particular cases, and ends in universal propositions. (113)

He saw himself as an unconventional thinker, breaking with traditional philosophy not in terms of ends but in terms of means. Indeed he might seem to us like an early philosopher of science, analyzing and systematizing the assumptions and implications of scientific theory, if it were not for the fact that his syntheses include a great deal more than pure scientific generalization. His own metaphysical predilections and ambitions and his own linguistic habits subverted his method, and the resulting system is, though based in scientific theory, idiosyncratic in structure.

He arrived at his "highest degree of generality," the theory of cosmic force evolution, by ascending through successive levels of generality largely by means of metaphor. Choosing certain theories from specific sciences to begin with, he metaphorically extended their applicability over a much wider field and established them as intermediate-level laws of process. In the right sort of combination these laws would comprise an exhaustive, scientifically based compound formula of knowable reality.

Spencer's methods can readily be observed in the case of the discovery that he regarded as the crucial initial step in the formation of the Synthetic Philosophy, the discovery of the "law" that all things progress from homogeneity to heterogeneity.[3] Having previously decided that, biologically, the lower orders of animals were composed of fewer, simpler, and more independent parts while the higher orders of animals were composed of more complex and mutually dependent parts, and, sociologically, that societies progressed from the uniform to the multiform,[4] when Spencer came across the theory of the Estonian embryologist Karl Ernest von Baer, that individual organisms developed from initial homogeneity to heterogeneity, he felt he had found the key to universal process. Baer's convenient formulation, extended beyond the realm of embryology, beyond even the realm of the individual organism, could comprehend development of any sort anywhere in the universe. Universal process, then, was for Spencer progress from homogeneity to heterogeneity. That his terms had rather different significations when applied to, say, a developing embryo and a developing society seemed not to have concerned Spencer, in the full flush of his discovery of cosmic law. What impressed him was that the words seemed to cover all situations of change in the cosmos and that he himself was the father of the law.

Of course Spencer was running with the current of his times in attempting to describe the universe in a framework of development. One of the great general movements in nineteenth-century thought was the movement toward the description of reality in terms of process or even progress rather than in terms of fixed classifications or essences. In the throes of this movement not only was the century developing a popular awareness of social and economic progress, but its scientists were arriving at important and influential theories by studying reality from the standpoint of development. Darwin is, of course, the most notable case in point. By mid-century a number of developmental theories were well-known: in geology, the uniformitarian theory promulgated by Sir Charles Lyell (the earth has come to its present composition through the gradual operation of the same sorts of forces that are now operating); in biology, Lamarck's idea of nature's tending toward perfection and complexity, and his theory of use-inheritance (characteristics which have been acquired or changed in the organization of an organism are transmitted to its offspring); and in astronomy, Laplace's nebular hypothesis (the solar system has evolved from a nebula by processes of condensation, centrifugal force, and cooling). Philosophy too had its evolutionary leanings well before there was a theory of evolution. Most notably there was Auguste Comte, who, attempting to discover the laws behind social and intellectual phenomena, developed his Law of the Three States, which asserted that the human mind naturally passed through three stages in attempting to develop any branch of knowledge: the Theological, in which causal reference was made to the volition of some supernatural being; the Metaphysical, in which abstract force or essence is the causal referent; and finally the Positivistic, in which phenomena were regarded as phenomena and explained only in terms of their relationships. Herbert Spencer, above all else a man of his times, had read Lyell in 1840, through Lyell had been introduced to Lamarck's theory[5] (which he was to uphold throughout his life), had worked out a lengthy defense of the nebular hypothesis at that stage of his career,[6] and in 1853–1854 had studied Comte (whose influence he was to spend the rest of his life denying).[7] Thus he was bound to feel that it was of utmost importance to locate the law "that unifies the successive changes which sensible existences, separately and together, pass through" (243); his "highest degree of generality" was sure to be developmental.

But the nineteenth-century impulse toward theories of development and the more specific metascientific applications of the Baer formula still did not provide the metaphysician with the whole kernel of his system. Development occurred, it was clear, and to Spencer it seemed that it always occurred in the same way, no matter where or in what medium it took place. But the formula was like a subjectless predicate until he found some basic underlying sameness in things which would warrant the fact that everything underwent the same course of development. Exactly what was it that developed? He turned to the basic physics which had flourished when he had been teaching himself science in the forties and early fifties and decided it was force.

Although the fact has been overlooked, Spencer was very specifically acquainted with the work of the force conservationists and powerfully influenced by them in the building of the Synthetic Philosophy. In *First Principles* he cites the work of Mayer, Joule, Grove, and Helmholtz, he repeats some of their findings, and he adopts their generalizations in his system. In one account he admitted that he knew of the scientific world's preoccupation with "the Conservation of Force" at the time when he tended "to seek for ultimate physical principles as keys to complex phenomena,"[8] and in another account he states,

> There had become familiar to me the doctrine of the Conservation of Force, as it was then called—in those days a novelty; and with this was joined in my mind Sir William Grove's doctrine of the correlation of the physical forces. Of course these universal principles ranged themselves alongside the two universal principles I had been recently illustrating [as aspects of the change from the simple to the complex]—the instability of the homogeneous and the multiplication of effects.... There naturally arose the thought—these various universal truths are manifestly aspects of one universal transformation.... Evidently these universal laws of force to which conforms this unceasing redistribution of matter and motion, constitute the *nexus* of [the] concrete sciences—express a community of nature which binds them together as parts of a whole. And then came the idea of trying thus to present them.[9]

In this way the question "What evolves?" was answered to Spencer's satisfaction; the universal laws became formulated as "universal laws of force."

Again it is a process of metaphorical expansion—here of an entire scientific theory—by which Spencer arrives at his universal. Although at particular moments in his application of the term *force* he sometimes shows a good deal of semantic caution, the full working-out of what he calls his First Principles finally involves him in asserting or implying that everything which could conceivably be designated as force, is force, and that everything which cannot be so designated is ultimately reducible to force. Beginning with a scientific term, Spencer not only applies it in every vernacular sense, but he adds ingenious applications of his own, intending all the while that it retain the status in reality which the science of the 1840s seemingly granted it. Spencer not only uses *force* to refer to the cause of motion or of change of motion, to energy (both kinetic and potential) and to our sense of effort or resistance. Additionally, he asserts, "our experience of *force* is that out of which the idea of matter is built" (141), "experiences of forces variously correlated are those from which our consciousness of space is abstracted" (140), and he makes a similar claim for our consciousness of time. And since the concept of motion is made up of our concepts of matter, space, and time, "and since, as we have seen, these are severally elaborated from experiences of *force* as given in certain correlations, it follows that from a further synthesis of such experiences the idea of motion is also elaborated" (142). Not only are such seeming absolutes really effects of force but so too are all phenomena, all data of the senses—even thought and consciousness itself.

> We come down then finally to force, as the ultimate of ultimates. Though space, time, matter and motion, are apparently all necessary data of intelligence, yet a psychological analysis . . . shows us that these are either built up of, or abstracted from experiences of force. . . . Deeper down than these, however, are the primordial experiences of force, which, as occurring in consciousness in different combinations, supply at once the materials whence the forms of relations are generalized and the related objects built up. . . . Though no single impression of force so received could itself produce consciousness (which implies relations between different states), yet a multiplication of such impressions, differing in kind and degree, would give the materials for the establishment of relations; that is, of thought. And if such relations differed in their forms as well as in their contents the impressions of such forms would be organized simultaneously with the impressions they contained. Thus all other modes of consciousness are derivable from experiences of force; but experiences of force are not derivable from anything else. (143–144)

With its partly physical, partly psychological basis, *force* is an even broader notion than all causality (although causality is central to it); its nearest synonym is *reality*. Spencer himself practically makes the identification between *force* and *reality* in his use of the concept of *persistence* as the definitive test of reality. As he says, "By reality we mean *persistence* in consciousness. . . . The real, as we conceive it, is distinguished solely by the test of persistence; for by this test we separate it from what we call the unreal" (136). And he later completes the identification:

> There must exist some principle which, as being the basis of science, cannot be established by science. All reasoned-out conclusions whatever must rest on some postulate. . . . We cannot go on merging derivative truths in those wider and wider truths from which they are derived, without reaching at last a widest truth which can be merged in no other or derived from no other. And whoever contemplates the relation in which it stands to the truths of science in general, will see that this truth transcending demonstration is the persistence of force. (166)

In the context of physics, of course, *the persistence of force* meant roughly the same thing as *the conservation of energy* (although Spencer, in later editions of *First Principles*, explained that he preferred his terms because *force* seemed [of course!] more inclusive than *energy*, could even include the concept of "the space-occupying kind of force" [163], and *persistence* seemed to have fewer anthropomorphic connotations for him than *conservation*, which he thought implied "a conserver and an act of conserving" [162]). It was scientific proof of his principles, then, that heat was really molecular motion, that motion could be transformed into heat at a definite, consistent rate as Joule had shown, and that all the various forms of physical forces correlated with each other consistently, as Grove, Helmholtz, and others had shown. In Spencerian language, "the relations among forces persist" too, and this principle could be taken as the same thing as the uniformity of law in the universe.

When Spencer undertook the description of physical reality in terms of development, early conservation theory offered no general support; until Kelvin later showed with the Second Law of Thermodynamics that the only progress inherent in energetics was progress toward entropy, conservation theory merely treated the *redistribution* of force in the universe. Spencer saw this redistribution as necessarily orderly and directional; it evolved entities that were maximally integrated, heterogeneous, stable, and adapted.

With his peculiar combination of the theories of force conservation and "development," Spencer was able to unify not only the science of his day, but all knowledge, in a single formula. It is a bizarrely elaborate formula, its mechanical consistency is a masterpiece of philosopher's art, and its myriad proofs and illustrations, from almost every phase of human experience, give it a naive though overwhelming convincingness. Its first element was "the progressive integration of matter and concomitant loss of motion," which Spencer asserted is evidenced by "existences of all orders" (266). Astronomically, for example, the theory Spencer upheld and argued for throughout his career, the nebular hypothesis, illustrated this aspect of Spencerian evolution in that it described the solar system as having gradually concentrated from a nebulous ring. Geologically he saw as evidence of integration of matter and loss of motion not only the formation of the earth's crust from molten and vaporous elements, but also the very nature of igneous and sedimentary processes. Biologically he saw the processes of the absorption of nutriment and of maturation as evidences in individual organisms, while the gregarious tendencies of certain species evidenced an even broader sort of integration of matter and loss of motion. In human society too he pointed out how aggregates tended to form larger aggregates, whether on a tribal or a pan-European scale, and how the internal integration of a social unit increased with its size (like a city with its publishers' district, its corn-merchants' district, its banking district, and so forth). He saw language as developing according to his principle in the way that more highly developed languages tended to have shorter words for common objects (the Anglo-Saxon *steorra* and *mona* became the English *star* and *moon*); the very development of science to ever-larger generalizations was another sort of evidence; industry tended to develop single machines that did many tasks, and factories themselves became well-integrated units; the history of art shows a progressive increase in compositional unity, the history of music shows a growth from simple repetitious chants to complex and unified melodies, and the history of literature shows a development from simple episodic narrative to a complex integration of plot, character, and moral relations. Thus the "progressive integration of matter and concomitant loss of motion" is observable for Spencer in all processes, given his extremely flexible application of the terms *matter* and *motion*.

The second element of Spencer's formula for evolution was the progression from homogeneity to heterogeneity, sometimes termed "progressive differentiation." He pointed out how the nebular hypothesis accounted for the differentiation of the various planets from an originally homogeneous whole, how the cooling of the earth led to the "deposition of all solidifiable elements contained in the atmosphere and finally to precipitation of the water and separation of it from the air" (287), and how (in copious, specific detail) "the history of every plant and every animal, while it is a history of increasing bulk is also a history of simultaneously increasing differences among the parts" (289). Civilized man has evolved a more complex nervous system, claims Spencer, and this also helps to illustrate progressive differentiation, as does the tendency of societies to differentiate classes and functions and (in a clear echo of Comte) to separate the religious and secular spheres as they became more developed. The development of language has, correspondingly, been in the direction of greater variety of grammatical structures, more different parts of speech and so forth, while the history of esthetics shows how mural decoration differentiated into the separate arts of painting and sculpture, how music, poetry, and dance differentiated, and how the use of multipurposed literary form such as scripture developed into the later use of heterogeneous genres by authors.

The third element of the evolutionary formula was the progression from what he called an indefinite state to a definite one. For this element too (not entirely separable from the ideas of integration and differentiation, of course) Spencer cited copious confirming instances. The nebular hypothesis is again a prime one: according to it, bodies and systems had become increasingly more definite, and planetary space-relations and force-relations increasingly more settled and mathematizable. Geologically, the later developments in the formation of the earth were such things as the establishment of clearly defined mountain ranges. Living organisms showed an increasing definiteness of parts and functions in their embryonic development, and whereas protozoa were indefinite in shape, higher forms were more definite. Social relations are more settled and definite in a civilized group than in a savage society, he asserted, language tends to have a progressively more specialized and definite vocabulary, and science has clearly progressed from the indefiniteness of its early concepts. The development of the industrial arts was a development in the exact application of tools to needs, and the art of painting showed a progress from indefiniteness to a "more precise rendering of appearances of objects" (328). Even vague and ambiguous myth had given way to exact and definite history.

For the completion of his basic formula for evolution Spencer felt he needed to establish that, while these aforementioned changes are taking place in things, the motion of those things undergoes concomitant changes, dissipating and becoming more integrated, heterogeneous, and definite. Again he offers an array of illustrations, beginning with the nebular hypothesis and extending to such examples as that of the progressively more integrated, purposeful, and complex "motion" that results as a child learns to speak, and that of the increased order, interdependence, and heterogeneity of the motion of soldiers in a modern army as compared with the chaotic homogeneousness of an intertribal fray.

Again we must note that Spencer's use of language is the principal factor in the development of the system—the "motion" of a child's speech, the "motion" of an army in battle, the "motion" of the history of painting and the "motion" of the solar system are really examples of strained and figurative usage rather than of any uniformity of phenomena in the objective world. Similarly *integration*, *heterogeneity*, and *definiteness*, like his fundamental term *force*, expand, shift in meaning, and apply in oblique and metaphorical ways in order to fulfill the abstract and *a priori* needs of the universal conception. Thus the two most strikingly convincing aspects of Spencer's exposition—its sense of exhaustive empirical validation and its aura of rational precision—are merely linguistic illusions, induced by arbitrary usage and nomenclature.

Spencer's completed formula for evolution is as follows: "Evolution is an integration of matter and concomitant dissipation of motion; during which the matter passes from an indefinite incoherent homogeneity to a definite coherent heterogeneity; and during which the retained motion undergoes a parallel transformation" (343). Spencer is very insistent that the entire system has been deduced from the fact of the persistence of force; thus it would seem to be founded on the bedrock of scientific reality. He also insists that evolution is a single omnipresent phenomenon which he has, for convenience of discussing, analyzed into separate manifestations: "There are not several kinds of evolution having certain traits in common, but one evolution going on everywhere after the same manner" (472). Thus the system also has a unifying comprehensiveness.

As elaborate and terminologically complex as his statement of the formula is at this point, evolution's implications are still not explained to Spencer's satisfaction. There are four other principles (corrolaries, alternative explanations, prior laws—Spencer isn't clear which) to be established, also in Spencer's characteristic terminology. The first of these principles he calls "the instability of the homogeneous," and is a necessary law of nature if evolution is to operate in the direction of heterogeneity the way he says it does. "The condition of homogeneity is a condition of unstable equilibrium" (347) he asserts, borrowing the phrase "unstable equilibrium" from mechanics and applying it to a great number of phenomena from the cosmic to the microscopic levels. (The earth was homogeneous when it was incandescent, he asserts, and its cooling into heterogeneity was inevitable because of the instability of that former state.) The second supporting principle is that of "the multiplication of effects"; as he explains it, "When a uniform aggregate is subject to a uniform force . . . its constituents, being differently conditioned, are differently modified . . . [and there are] unlike changes simultaneously produced on the various parts of the incident force" (373). This principle is the "law" that underlies the phenomenon of differentiation, of course, and it is exemplified in multifarious detail (like the basic fact that, in mechanics, two bodies colliding multiply the motion into various effects of sound, air vibration, heat, possibly fracture and incandescence, and so forth). The third supporting principle, that of "segregation," is one used to explain the phenomena of increasing integration and definiteness, and it is one which is not founded on a law of mechanics, although it is mechanically visualized. "Segregation" is the "local integration which accompanies local differentiation" (397), the gathering together of like elements of a disintegrating homogeneous whole. Spencer conceives of this as happening in complex combinations of both forces and matter which are homogeneous, heterogeneous, or mixed, and he exemplifies it exhaustively (the uniform force of the autumn wind tends to segregate the dead leaves in a tree and separate them from those still alive; emigrants tend to live together in a new country, and so forth).

The final supporting principle is that of "Equilibration," the concept of the "impassable limit" toward which evolution progresses. Spencer sees two kinds of equilibrium, an *"equilibrium mobile"* in which opposing forces are temporarily counterbalanced, and a "complete equilibrium" in which the end of all evolution has been achieved and there is no motion at all. The moving equilibrium is evidenced in such things as the balance of centrifugal and centripetal forces in an orbiting comet, in the adaptation of a living organism to changes in its environment, and in "moral adaptation . . . which is a continual approach to equilibrium between the emotions and the kinds of conduct necessitated by surrounding conditions" (437). The "complete equilibrium," on the other hand, seems even to Spencer like "omnipresent death": "For the present it must suffice that the proximate end of all the transformations we have traced is a state of quiescence" (445). But, he adds, in one of several of his transcendent evasions of the negative implications of his force-determinism, there well might be "an equilibration of a far wider kind" (464) beyond anything we can foresee as proximate; and meanwhile in the developing, integrating, adapting stage of our universe "we finally draw from [the theory] a warrant for the belief, that evolution can end only in the establishment of the greatest perfection and the most complete happiness" (448).

Thus Spencer exceeds Helmholtz, Grove, and the other conservationists in optimism, just as he exceeded them in metaphysical inclusiveness and semantic elasticity. The conservationists were excited merely by the effectiveness of their newly discovered scientific approach and by the intricately organized universe it revealed. Their faith in the goodness of things was implicit. Spencer's theory of evolution contains all the consolations offered by the scientific theorists and in addition it explicitly promises "the greatest perfection and the most complete happiness" as the goal of all the universe's intricately organized changes. Not only is the machine-universe good, it is programmed for eventual perfection.

According to Spencer, cosmic evolution stood within two larger conceptual frameworks, one being the rhythmic alternation of evolution and dissolution, and the other being the epistemological distinction between the knowable and the unknowable. Neither larger framework substantially affected the pseudo-scientific optimism of the theory of evolution, however.

Spencer felt that evolution itself necessarily implied a counter-cycle of dissolution, although the idea seems to have come as a kind of afterthought. In *First Principles* (after the first edition, at least) he speaks belittlingly of the necessity of discussing a phase of dissolution "to complete the argument." In an essay on how he formulated his Synthetic Philosophy he recalls how he came across the ideas of equilibration and dissolution; the long statement is worth repeating because it shows how an intuitive philosopher operates totally at the mercy of his words.

> I have a dim recollection that, referring to the general process of transformation set forth in "Progress: its Law and Cause," which had been the topic of conversation (during an afternoon call at Huxley's), Tyndall put to me the question—"But how does it all end?" or some question to that effect. I cannot now remember whether the answer was given forthwith or whether it came only after reflection; but my impression is that up to that time I had not considered what was the outcome of this unceasing change to a state ever more heterogeneous and ever more definite. It needed only to ask the question, however, to bring the inevitable answer, and the chapter on "Equilibration" was the result. And then, in pursuance of the same line of thought, embodying itself in the question—"What happens after equilibration is completed?" there came the reply, "Dissolution." This was at once recognised as complementary to Evolution, and similarly universal.[10]

The idea of dissolution was a part of Spencer's scheme from the beginning, but not until the second edition of *First Principles* did it receive a full chapter's discussion, and even there it is forlornly underdeveloped, overwhelmed by ten chapters entirely devoted to evolution: "Not indeed that we need to dwell long on dissolution [he allows], which has none of those various and interesting aspects which evolution presents . . . " (449).

As a process, dissolution is merely evolution in reverse. When an equilibrium had been reached, some outside force would tend to unstabilize it and start a movement of dissolution, resolving matter into motion, organization into chaos, definiteness into indefiniteness. Thus are societies broken down and driven back into anarchical masses, solar systems dissipated back into nebulae, and the highly differentiated parts of living organisms dissolved after death back into inchoate matter. Spencer is able to cite examples of the process but he is unable to present an effective explanation of its mechanics. His ingenuity all tended the other way; his discussion of biological death and decay in such characteristic terms as the absorption of motion and the transformation of the motion of aggregates into the motion of units seems not only forced but grotesquely super-rationalistic.

The cyclical process of evolution and dissolution is complex at any given moment, Spencer thought—some local dissolution occurs in periods of predominant evolution and vice-versa—and he used this very complexity as reassurance that misfortune (according to a human scale of values) could never prevail. Not only could local dissolution (death, social discord, or such) be transcendently viewed as part of a constructive, evolutionary cosmic phase, but also the final, death-like cosmic equilibrium would logically be expected to disintegrate (on the principle that "the entire process of things as displayed in the aggregate of the visible universe is analogous to the entire process of things as displayed in the smallest aggregates" [464]), so that after a limited period of dissolution, the universe would surely get another journey to perfection and happiness.

The largest framework of *First Principles*, the distinction between "the Unknowable" and "the Knowable," was set up by Spencer because he was worried that "I should be charged with propounding a purely materialistic interpretation of things" if ultimate metaphysical and theological questions were not dealt with in the Synthetic Philosophy.[11] Spencer willingly admitted that religion and theology never "recommended themselves" much to him, but he felt the need to give them some legitimate place within his system if only for the purpose of reaching his audience. In itself the theory of the Unknowable is unoriginal and unimportant, but its significance to his readership was enormous. Ironically and to Spencer's great dismay, many critics responded solely or principally to "the Unknowable" in criticizing his system, seeing in it the red flag of an objectionable and assailable agnosticism. On the other hand, to Spencer's uncritical American following (as we shall see in later chapters), it seemed to bridge the most dangerous chasm of the age, that between science and religion, and thus it constituted the highest possible recommendation for the entire Synthetic Philosophy.

Since religious beliefs and sentiments are evidenced by mankind in all times, climates, and societies, Spencer reasoned, they must have some correspondence with an absolute reality. This is his grudging allocation to religion; just how grudging it is was overlooked by his American disciples, but its basic tenor is really unmistakable: "Thus, however untenable may be any or all the existing religious creeds, however gross the absurdities associated with them, however irrational the arguments set forth in their defense, we must not ignore the verity which in all likelihood lies hidden within them. The general probability that widely spread beliefs are not absolutely baseless, is in this case enforced by a further probability due to the omnipresence of the beliefs" (13).

As Spencer saw it, the problem with the religious approach to absolute reality was that the absolute existed on too high a plane of generality for man to correlate his conceptions of it with actuality; and additionally, "we habitually mistake our symbolic conceptions for real ones; and so are betrayed into countless false inferences" (23). Quoting the epistemology of Sir William Hamilton (culled, he admits from Henry Mansel's *Limits of Religious Thought*

[33]), Spencer claims that the human mind can know only "*the limited and conditionally limited*," and that anything infinite or absolute is simply beyond it, "unknowable" (63). This is true of scientific as well as of religious thought: "Ultimate religious ideas and ultimate scientific ideas alike turn out to be merely symbols of the actual, not cognitions of it" (58). Thus, of the ultimate essence of the universe nothing can be known by any means; man must content himself with indefinite but genuine apprehensions of it. His proper study is the finite world of things in their relationships. Even force itself is ultimately inscrutable, Spencer at one point admits, its essential nature and mode of operation beyond human knowing, although its concrete manifestations may be studied and their relationships described in generalizations.

THE 1862 publication of *First Principles* was only the first step in the grand plan that Spencer had decided upon in 1858, to show the various aspects of the "one universal transformation . . . [and] to treat astronomy, geology, biology, psychology, sociology and social products, in successive order from the evolution point of view." [12] In fulfilling his Synthetic Philosophy he wrote multivolume works on biology, psychology, sociology, and ethics, completing the project in 1896, sixteen years after his expected completion date. He never began the works on astronomy and geology, feeling, as one biographer states, that the workings of Evolution in those areas were "more obvious and less in need of exposition" than in the others. [13]

Each of his works on specific fields is compendious and individualistic, aimed at including all classes of phenomena in considerable detail and accommodating them totally to the language and categories of the First Principles. Spencer employed a research assistant to compile details and he used several authoritative acquaintances (such as T. H. Huxley and Sir Joseph Hooker for the biology volumes) as technical advisers on the fields. He was characteristically independent regarding other men's theories in each of the works, relying on those he knew of when they suited his purposes, and ignoring them otherwise. Thus the works are too idiosyncratic to be of much value to the particular fields, although some of Spencer's evolutionary-force-oriented insights are credited by some authorities as contributions. The four specific works comprising the Synthetic Philosophy are worth considering here if only briefly, to show the convincing consistency and grandiose scope of this vision.

The Principles of Biology was published in 1864, two years after *First Principles*, and it is obviously a direct application of the Spencerian evolutionary formula. Life is defined as a moving equilibrium, a continually adjusting balance between external and internal forces; growth is the integration of matter;

development is the change from homogeneity to heterogeneity; living forms, both individuals and species, tend to increase in complexity, interdependence, integration, and differentiation—the terms are familiar from *First Principles*, the treatment is highly systematic, and the examples are myriad. Beyond the terms of *First Principles* but running parallel to them are several other key ideas. The essential element in life, Spencer felt, is a dynamic element which is ultimately unknowable but which reveals its existence in observable manifestations (the ultimately unknowable universal force is obviously the prototype of this idea). He also added to his earlier theories the idea that the factors tending to preserve the race were necessarily antagonistic to the factors tending to preserve and develop the individual. Along these lines, he saw individualism as an evolutionary goal, as the force taken from reproduction was expended in individuation in the higher forms of life. Spencer consequently saw our biological future in optimistic, anti-Malthusian terms, as the human race evolved toward minimal death- and reproduction-rates and an existence that offered the individual the greatest amount of life at the least expense.

The relationship of Spencer's theories, both general and biological, to Darwin's evolutionary theory epitomizes the gradually widening difference between scientific and metaphysical thought in the mid-nineteenth century. The two great evolutionists formed their theories independently of each other, although they were aware of each other's work and Spencer finally incorporated Darwin's ideas of variation and natural selection into the Synthetic Philosophy. Spencer was the first to publish on evolution: his ideas about universal progress and the Development Hypothesis were published in his essay "Progress: Its Law and Cause" in 1857; and they drew an acknowledgment from Darwin, dated November 25 [1858]:

> Your remarks on the general argument of the so-called Development Theory seem to me admirable. I am at the present preparing an abstract of a larger work on the changes of species; but I treat the subject simply as a naturalist, and not from a general point of view; otherwise, in my opinion, your argument could not have been improved upon, and might have been quoted by me with great advantage.[14]

Darwin's "abstract," *On the Origin of Species*, was published in 1859, and in it Darwin did not quote Spencer nor did he aspire toward his "general point of view," striving rather to describe as specifically as possible the processes by which species change and to use empirical evidence to reduce as much as possible the chasmal inductive leap required by his radical theory of natural selection. Spencer, meanwhile, operating like a metaphysician rather than a scientist, set as his main goal the unification of all knowledge under his own reality formula, which happened also to be evolutionary. Biology was not the sole ground of his theory but instead a crucial application. To keep our sense of the chronological relationship clear we should note that the prospectus of the Synthetic Philosophy appeared, after Darwin's *Origin*, in 1860, and *First Principles* appeared in 1862.

Spencer's specific ideas about biological evolution are either deduced directly from his general formula for evolution or they are borrowed. In a strict sense Spencer was no biological thinker at all. As Hugh Elliot has pointed out, before Spencer was influenced by Darwin his only conception of a biological factor in evolution was Lamarck's idea of the inheritance of acquired characteristics, an idea soon generally rejected by biologists but always stoutly upheld by Spencer as the main factor in the evolutionary changes in the higher forms of life.[15] When Darwin's theory of natural selection was published, Spencer strove to accommodate it in the Synthetic Philosophy, announcing in a letter to his father on May 27, 1864, that "only yesterday I arrived at a point of view from which Darwin's doctrine of 'Natural Selection' is seen to be absorbed into the general theory of Evolution as I am interpreting it"; that is, organic evolution could at last be "exhibited as resulting from the redistribution of matter and motion everywhere and always going on."[16] Natural Selection is renamed "Indirect Equilibration" in Spencer's *Biology*, or more picturesquely, "The Survival of the Fittest"; according to it, a particular individual of a species survives because its inner, adaptive forces can accommodate the various outer forces and changes of force and sustain the moving equilibrium that is life. Thus is Spencer able to assert the priority and inclusiveness of his evolutionary formula in biology; generally it has been of little use to that science.

The Principles of Psychology was first published in one volume in 1855, several years before Spencer formulated his evolutionary theory and his plan for its applications, and he later revised and expanded it and brought it out in 1870–1872 as volumes four and five of the Synthetic Philosophy. The first edition had been distinctly preevolutionary and derivative; the associationist school of psychological thought (including James Mill, John Stuart Mill, and Alexander Bain) viewed the mind in terms of the associative relationships of its sensations, ideas, feelings, memories, and so forth, and Spencer's early one-volume *Psychology* was, to quote Edwin G. Boring's *A History of Experimental Psychology*, "simply another associational psychology, although by a very great man."[17] The second edition, however, with the addition of the evolutionary perspective, was an important and original contribution to psychology.[18] (Again, as with the early conservationists' application of the loose term *force*, scientific progress seems to have resulted from the use of a fallible concept.)

Spencer's second edition of the *Psychology* takes the position that there is an unknowable, ultimate, dynamic element in mind (another ultimate unknowable), and to understand the knowable elements of it we need to see it in developmental terms. The nervous system evolved from inchoate cellular material; feelings or mental processes are compounded from simpler psychic elements; and just as instinct is inherited habit, so too are conscious perception, memory, and reason developed in accord with the laws of cosmic evolution and in response to the increasing heterogeneity of the rest of the habitat. The mind is an important factor in the adjustment of inner and outer relations that constitutes life, and the laws of its development promise humanity ever-increasing happiness and fulfillment. Again, as in his biological theory, Spencer's optimism depends on Lamarck's questionable theory of the inheritance of acquired characteristics, as he perceived the attainments of one generation as transmitted in a literally hereditary way to the next. The level of intelligence in the civilized world is consistently increasing, he felt, because of structural modifications in the human nervous system produced by the increased mental activity of each successive generation.

Spencer concluded his *Psychology* with a study of the psychological aspects of social and ethical behavior. The social and ethical areas seemed to be the most attractive to him; certainly he tended to culminate his theories in them as being the points of greatest complexity and concern. Psychologically, he ranked sympathy and "sociality" high on the evolutionary scale, linking sympathy to intelligence and gregariousness to conditions of individual freedom from fear and insecurity. The only factors preventing the attainment of the "highest social sentiments"[19] were man's predatory impulses and his regressive capacity to segregate the areas of his affection and disaffection; war-making confounded utopian social evolution. Likewise (and this is a rare kind of admission in Spencer, who usually viewed war and industrial development as antithetical) he allowed that there was inevitably also an ethical retardation in industrial development:

> Beyond this checking of the sympathies which the antagonisms of societies have necessitated and still necessitate, there has been a checking of them consequent on the struggle for existence within each society. Not only does this struggle for existence involve the necessity that personal ends must be pursued with little regard to the evils entailed on unsuccessful competitors; but it also involves the necessity that there shall be not too keen a sympathy with that diffused suffering inevitably accompanying this industrial battle. Clearly if there were so quick a sympathy for this suffering as to make it felt in anything like its real greatness and intensity life would be rendered intolerable to all.[20]

In the psychology of individual morality Spencer saw an evolutionary scale ranging (and progressing) from egoism to altruism. From a beginning point in

pure egoism, individuals (and societies too) developed "ego-altruistic" sentiments, that is, genuine ethical feelings based on the pleasure-pain nexus of
social rewards and punishments. A fuller and finer level of development was
reached when the individual was motivated by altruism, a product of intelligence and sympathy, and the opposite of egoism.

The *Psychology* is somewhat less concerned with applying the First Principles than is the *Biology*, and there is certainly far less of the heavy analogizing of psychological and mechanical phenomena that occurs in *First Principles*. The *Psychology* also surprisingly makes only infrequent and minor
mention of Darwinian evolution.

To a great many people today Spencer is best known as a sociologist, and it
is probably in this area that the special applications of his evolutionary theory
had the greatest effect. He published the three-volume *The Principles of Sociology* in several segments from 1876 to 1896, contributing to the infant science an evolutionary perspective, a method (a forerunner of modern struc-
tural-functional analysis),[21] an enormous fund of categorized information
about cultures all over the world (culled from his multivolume *Descriptive
Sociology*, then in progress), and, probably as a result, a great deal of prestige.
Charles Horton Cooley later admitted, "I imagine that nearly all of us who
took up sociology between 1870, say, and 1890 did so at the instigation of
Spencer." [22]

The Principles themselves are developed predominantly along the lines of
force-evolution, although with a heavy admixture of some other predilections
of Spencer's, like his individualism, his dislike of governmental control or restraint, and his abstract humanitarianism. Although he saw the study of sociology as separable into "social statics" and "social dynamics," importing
those categories directly from mechanics, he begins his social analysis with the
biologically derived idea that society is like an organism, and that sociology
therefore has to deal with a kind of "Super-Organic Evolution." Although
Spencer was clearly aware of significant ways in which societies and organisms
differed, he felt it was illuminating to notice that both followed the same laws
in that they both grew in mass and at the same time increased in complexity,
integration, and interdependence. They both had similar systems, the railroads
and routes of commerce like the vascular system, the regulative functions of
society like the systems of nerves and muscles, to cite two examples. Like the
life of an organism, society's life was a moving equilibrium, a balance of inner
and outer forces.

Social evolution was now for Spencer not merely what it had been in *First
Principles*, a development from simple to complex, homogeneous to heterogeneous, and so forth; he saw it primarily (and even somewhat fervently) as a
progress from militarism to industrialism. The first major stage in the evolu-

tion of a society had to be the bridling of individual egoism in the interests of filling social needs; this was a stage of maximum government and was necessarily coercive, authoritarian, and, since the first needs were for defense, militaristic. The militaristic society, Spencer thought, would be at war much of the time, require the subordination of the individual to the state, and operate internally primarily by means of fear and even brutality to preserve itself. This hateful stage would ultimately evolve, however, into an industrial stage where authority would be considerably weakened and the prosperity brought by industrial development would bring security, peace, and progressively increasing individual liberty. In the industrial society men would eventually come to participating voluntarily, even philanthropically, and would be capable of governing themselves with a minimum of institutional restraint. Individual liberty was both an ethical and an evolutionary goal of society for Spencer. It was his ultimate belief, sanguine and moral, that

> the ultimate man will be one whose private requirements coincide with public ones. He will be that manner of man who, in spontaneously fulfilling his own nature, incidentally performs the functions of a social unit; and yet is only enabled so to fulfill his own nature by all others doing the like.[23]

He was not so naively optimistic as to see social evolution as simple linear progress however; not only would that have been empirically unsound, but it would not have jibed with the universal evolution he depicted in *First Principles* as being complex, rhythmically intermixed with the process of dissolution. There was no doubt in his mind, however, that absolute change was in the direction of social improvement and that some day human society would be totally integrated, harmonious, and free.

Looking ahead for a moment at the subsequent social function of this theory of social evolution, neither Spencer's humanitarian idealism nor his attempt to qualify the concept of automatic progress would prevent it from being used by the proponents of *laissez-faire* capitalism to rationalize even the most egregiously exploitive and monopolistic practices and their perpetrators. Spencer's "Survival of the Fittest" was too easily translated into "dog eat dog," his concept of "man . . . spontaneously fulfilling his own nature" simply stretched to cover the "root, hog or die" type of capitalistic individualism. His idea of minimizing governmental restraints on free enterprise and evolutionary progress was to American capitalism a useful philosophical and political tool. Some of the most influential proponents of his social theory were, in his own terms, far less highly evolved ethically than he assumed they would be. As a result, a posterity finely attuned to questions of social justice has given Spencer the derogatory label of Social Darwinist in response to this crucial shortcoming of his social insight.

The bulk of the *Sociology* is devoted to the function and evolution of social institutions—domestic, political, ecclesiastical, professional, and industrial. In those individual elements of society as well as in society as a whole the developmental tendency is toward both coherent heterogeneity and individual liberty. An example of this which secondarily implies Spencer's whole attitude toward religion is his treatment of ecclesiastical institutions. Religion itself Spencer saw as arising out of fear of dead ancestors and desire to propitiate them. The earliest forms of ecclesiastical organization revolved around tribal chiefs who, in addition to their roles as secular rulers, led the tribe in the worship of the deified spirits of prior chiefs, usually in totemic forms. Gradually, as societal differentiation took place, the chief and priest functions separated, and polytheism developed towards monotheism as one of the gods would tend to excel the others in importance and number of followers. Religious institutions developed like political institutions: at first maximally coercive, monolithic, based on fear; later becoming more heterogeneous and offering more individual freedom. In a free industrial society, religion too would be free, individual, and in no way connected to the state; the earlier belief in a demanding and anthropomorphic god would give way to an appreciation of the unknowable causal force behind phenomena, a faith which would be rational and congenial with science.

Spencer published *The Principles of Ethics* in two volumes in 1892 and 1893 and with it was able to reach the culminating point of the Synthetic Philosophy and to articulate his theories in an area of deepest concern for him. In 1878 he wrote, "Since the whole system was at the outset, and has ever continued to be, a basis for a right rule of life, individual and social, it would be a great misfortune if this, which is the outcome of it all, should remain undone," [24] and in a period of illness in the late seventies, deeply fearing that he might be unable to complete his work, he began *The Data of Ethics* to establish his evolutionary approach to the subject in a way that could at least be continued by others. The *Data* was published in 1879 and later included as the first segment of the completed *Principles* in the nineties.

The ethical system that culminated the Synthetic Philosophy was an evolutionary utilitarianism. It was evolutionary in the terms established in *First Principles*: ethics are the adjustment of acts to ends and of the individual to his surroundings; ethical behavior, occurring only on the highest evolutionary level, is itself highly developed in terms of heterogeneity, definiteness, coherence; like the rest of the universe man's moral development tends towards an equilibrium in which (Spencer's optimism again being foremost) "the individual has no desires but those which may be satisfied without exceeding his proper sphere of action, while society maintains no restraints but those which the individual voluntarily respects."[25] Spencer's ethics were utilitarian in viewing conduct in terms of its aims and positing as the highest possible aim "the greatest totality of life in self, in offspring, and in fellow men."[26] The ethical world operated on a pleasure-pain nexus, but one in which pleasures were differentiated qualitatively on a hierarchical scale.

Spencer is a pure rationalist in his ethics, everywhere viewing human behavior in terms of rational means and goals; thus he feels that improvement in understanding necessarily tends to bring improvement in morality. Additionally (and this is his most farfetched adaptation of Lamarck) Spencer claimed that each man inherited some of the moral instincts and even some of the particular moral principles of his forebears. Moral progress toward utopian equilibrium was, like other types of progress, structured mechanically into the universe and hereditarily into mankind. Spencer expected there would be a bit of backsliding and hypocrisy, but that man would gradually move toward higher and higher sorts of goals. The first evolutionary step was primitive man's postponement of an immediate gratification in the interest of some greater future benefit; civilized man would gradually develop altruistic responses to more remote goals, such as the good of society; and totally civilized man in the full flower of knowing would act so as to realize the most impersonal and abstract ethical goods.

Of course moral and social evolution were indivisible. Man's fullest life could only be realized in a mutually cooperative community such as the free industrial society Spencer envisioned. The state's power over the individual needed to be limited to the administration of justice; militarism and excessive government were antithetical to evolved moral good. Competition in the industrial society ought to be totally free but freely tempered by altruistic motives; in the absence of militarism a larger social solidarity would be achieved and competition would ultimately decline in amount and importance. Meanwhile, however, it would be imperative to avoid interfering with natural selection and upsetting the relationship between capability and survival. Beneficence should be a fundamental attribute of the good society, Spencer felt, and it involved individual helping, sharing, and almsgiving, as well as respecting the basic freedom of others in exercising one's own, but any attempt to institutionalize exemptions from natural selection would create more misery for later generations than it would prevent in the present. Thus, individual misfortune could always be written off on the long-term balance sheet of the universe of force.

The cosmic sweep and ultimacy of his ideas never inhibited Spencer's minute didacticism, and the *Ethics* clearly illustrates the fact that virtually nothing was beneath his regard. He has his say about such matters as the use of alcohol, the proper amount of rest, the function of the Poor Laws, the right of bequest and so forth, airing his opinions on every imaginable "ethical" matter and subsuming it all under the authority of the laws of the universe of force. One feels a kind of megalomania here, hears the voice of a man in touch with the ultimate, conscientiously setting to rights the entire human universe, a man for whom not a sparrow could fall but its reasons would be known and its lesson clear.

THE WHOLE Synthetic Philosophy is clearly the product of a highly receptive, yet highly idiosyncratic mind. It is a colossal compendium of nineteenth-century ideas—force-conservation, development, use-inheritance, *laissez-faire* economics, associationism, utilitarianism, the nebular hypothesis. There are gleanings from Grove, Comte, Lamarck, Baer, Hamilton, Lyell, Mill, Darwin, and numerous others, but the ideas are selected for their compatibility with the First Principles. They are abridged, altered, or extended to accommodate the universal context, and they are applied in almost all cases as if they were eternal truths rather than the hypothetical scientific, social, or ethical theories which in fact they are. The scientific aura of Spencer's thought is actually illusory; his method is that of metaphysics. Likewise the sense of breadth and inclusiveness his system gives one through its hypermundane, repetitious particularity of detail is illusory. Although George Santayana could appreciate Spencer's effort to "describe the world of our daily plodding and commerce," seeing it as superior to the attempt of most other philosophers to find "a refuge from it in some contrasted spiritual assurance,"[27] it is still true, as Hugh Elliot pointed out, that Spencer was attuned only to those facts that supported his ideas, and gives only "the appearance of an encyclopaedic knowledge and of genuine induction."[28] Spencer's "refuge" is a pseudoscientific rationalism which, rather than directly encountering daily reality, projects a rather specialized model of it.

Spencer used language idiosyncratically and arbitrarily in building his system. He was the very epitome of naive realism, believing that his words infallibly stood for real things and that the relationships between words represented relationships between things. The nature and operation of his universe were thus dictated by the linguistic logic of his terminology and syntax, as surely as "force" "evolves" or "evolution" has its "devolution." Language was for him a simple paradigm of reality.

Similarly, he received his own perceptions, apprehensions, and ideas absolutely uncritically. The outer world existed essentially as he perceived it, he felt, and "persistence of force" essentially meant "force's persistence in con-

sciousness." His naive realism was more elaborate than that of the early scientists, but no less naive. Since his own mind was oriented toward rationality
and causality, he saw those aspects as self-evident essentials of the universal
system itself—force moved through plenitudinous evolutionary cause-effect
transactions toward a logically foreseeable ultimate state. Yet not only did
human rationality present the universe with its pattern for the process of evolution, human hopes and needs provided the pattern for its ends. The universe
was a deterministic machine that labored ceaselessly for human fulfillment and
happiness. The "higher forms" of evolutionary development—specialized, integrated, self-sufficient, individualistic, libertarian—always looked oddly like
Herbert Spencer himself.

The ultimate basis of the Synthetic Philosophy would in fact seem to be
Spencer's own egocentrism. It is shown not only in his unbounded trust in his
own words, his own perceptions and his own values, not only in his intoler-
ance of criticism and his hostility to alien ideas, but in what must strike us as
the unmitigated hubris of his whole undertaking. His assumption that the
whole of universal process, human thought, and human history, should have
remained obscure for aeons, waiting for him to come along and make final
sense out of it is what invites negative judgment, although such hubris is neither rare nor quite so conspicuous among other thinkers of his age. In his
Autobiography, describing the minor revisions he had made in *First Principles*
in 1867, he concludes, "I was about to add that the final phase of Evolution—
equilibration—was now illustrated by the arrival at an equilibrium between
the conception and the phenomena: a balance such that the order of ideas was
no longer to be disturbed by the order of the facts." [29] A grain of humility
dissuades him from claiming the absolute perfection of his system, but his very
willingness to suggest it reveals the extent of his naive and egotistical absolutism.

His autobiography is an interesting document in itself, and it presents the
creation of the Synthetic Philosophy as the defining event of his lifetime, similar to the discovery of faith in a religious autobiography, except that Spencer
himself created the faith and he saw himself in no state of sin or ignorance
before the great discovery. He composed *An Autobiography* in 1889, when at
sixty-nine he felt virtually unfit to work on anything else, but disciplining "a
constitutional lack of reticence," he withheld publication during his lifetime
and even prefaced his manuscript with an apology for the "provoking necessity that an autobiography should be egotistic." [30] He scrupulously avoided
public displays of egotism in his autobiography as he did in his life, but its
twelve-hundred-forty-eight pages clearly testify to the importance to the world
of the Synthetic Philosophy's creation. The autobiography is artless, repeti-
tiously particular, and stuffily analytical, and whatever tension builds in its

enumeratively chronological structure comes from its anticipation of the "discovery" of the complex law of force-evolution. The first of the two volumes builds loosely toward that moment from the earliest adumbrations in the forties through its gradual increments in the next decade, interspersed with information about Spencer's publications, recreations, friendships, and health (always a matter of scrupulous concern); the second volume details the story of the Synthetic Philosophy, tracing again (and again!) what Spencer called "the filiation of ideas" that led to its inception, and describing the grand conceptual program and his fulfillment of it over the next several decades. The later portions are anticlimactic accounts of travel, revisions, and increasing invalidism, with none of the excitement of intellectual discovery of the earlier portions. At sixty-nine he saw his law of force evolution as itself momentously growing out of an evolutionary process, and concurrently as the central, determining element in his own life—all his traits and background experiences feeding into it, and his calling, his life's work and his stature growing out of it. We will later find interesting parallels in a number of autobiographical and semiautobiographical works by American writers—works like Theodore Dreiser's autobiography, his novel *The "Genius"* and Jack London's novel *Martin Eden*—which use the (second-hand) discovery of Spencer's philosophy in a similar way. Spencer's theory of the universe of force thus shaped life stories other than his own.

SCIENTIFIC CRITIQUES of expanded uncritical uses of the term *force* were, of course, available to Spencer, but his sensitivity to physical science dated back to the 1840s when the terminology of science formed and confirmed his metaphysical vision. Critiques such as those by Ernst Mach and Spencer's own countryman, Peter G. Tait, removed the scientific basis from the general use of the term *force* in the 1870s, and in 1892 Karl Pearson (in what must have been a mood of exasperation) still felt he had to lecture a largely inattentive world that Spencer "uses force without special definition in the following senses: (i) As cause of change in motion; (ii) as a biological process; (iii) as a name for kinetic energy; (iv) as a name for potential energy; (v) as a general name for physical sense-impressions, such as light and heat, etc.!"[31] Furthermore, no one attuned to science in the 1850s could have been unaware of the abandonment of the broad term *force* in favor of *energy*, or of the formulation of the Second Law of Thermodynamics, which, as Gillispie recently put it, was "[totally] damaging to the cosmic historicism of Herbert Spencer. . . . For the ineluctable increase of entropy in the universe precisely contradicts this liberal tendency in things."[32] Spencer's friend Thomas Henry

Huxley campaigned against the metaphysical use of the term *force*,[33] and an exchange of letters between John Tyndall and Spencer shows the former trying unsuccessfully to convince his friend that "the conservation of energy" is more accurate scientific usage than "the persistence of force," but what was adequate for science was not adequate for the pseudoscientific Synthetic Philosophy, and Spencer politely rejected the correction as inappropriate.[34]

The weaknesses of his grand system were known and pointed out to him, but he was able, in his own mind, to overcome or overlook any and all criticism. With the Synthetic Philosophy in full bloom he had stronger needs than the need for scientific validity, and—as friends found out when they tried to correct him, even in minor questions of terminology—he thought of himself as virtually infallible. Also it was unfortunately the case that criticism which was soundly based in science or epistemology was all but drowned out by the welter of less instructive responses, ranging from rank adulation to virulent personal invective and dominated by the theistic outcry against Spencer's nearly godless universe; his closed-mindedness to criticism was perhaps not totally unjustified.

One of the important lessons of Spencer, finally, is that the philosopher, social theorist, or such who employs a concept from physical science needs a full, complex, and up-to-date comprehension of that concept and how it is used in its discipline or he is only making a metaphor. There is, of course, a kind of utility in new metaphoric uses of a borrowed concept: it often generates valuable new approaches and ideas which can eventually become part of the nonmetaphoric theoretical framework of that discipline, much the way that psychology and sociology benefited from Spencer's figurative force-evolution. This metaphoric regeneration of existing disciplines is indeed probably the principal contribution to the history of thought by both Herbert Spencer and the concept of force. The process is creditably valid only when the borrower is aware of the metaphoric nature of the process, however, and doesn't assume that his theory is grounded in physical reality because physical science has supplied him with his key term.

SPENCER WAS NOT the only philosopher to envision a universe of force, although he was far and away the one with the greatest American influence and reputation. The starting assumptions for a metaphysical force-system were in the air, and acknowledgment of several of Spencer's fellow philosophers is necessary in order to avoid oversimplifying the intellectual background at this point.

Ludwig Büchner (1824–1899) was a German physicist-philosopher whose work, *Kraft und Stoff* was widely reprinted throughout the Western world. It was his view that force and matter are essentially the same thing, that the universe is essentially monistic and deterministic, and that the agnostics' idea of "the unknowable" is a theistic surrogate. Ernst Haeckel (1834–1919) was a German zoologist-philosopher whose book, *The Riddle of the Universe at the Close of the Nineteenth Century* (1900) had considerable American popularity and a strong effect on Jack London. Haeckel was an outspoken monist, rigorously opposed to theological and teleological ideas, who founded his philosophy on the "Law of Substance" which "establishes the eternal persistence of matter and force" and on the "Law of Evolution" which establishes that "the world is nothing else than an eternal evolution of substance."[35] Haeckel was a promoter of Spencer's works in Germany, and his philosophy can be approximately characterized as a cross between Büchner's and Spencer's. Wilhelm Ostwald (1853–1932) was a German chemist-philosopher who, in his work *Vorlesungen über Naturphilosophie* (1902), also put forth a physically based monistic system, but he was strongly aware of the limitations of mechanical explanations and described the universe in terms of energy and the differentials in its levels. All three monists are essentially determinists like Spencer, and all three insist that man is not comprised of special mind- or soul-substance which is different from the rest of the universe.

3. THE AMERICANIZATION OF THE UNIVERSE OF FORCE

> He [Spencer] was in fashion once, therefore he filled a need. Our fashion is not more respectable than any other. If a man has his time of being in fashion he has all that anyone has, and has proved his claim to be a force shaping the future.
>
> Justice Oliver Wendell Holmes to Harold Laski, August 24, 1924

The universe of force had an extraordinary impact in America. Principally in its Spencerian formulation—indissoluably tied to the theory of evolution—not only did it become a factor to be reckoned with in American science, philosophy, and religion, but it penetrated to levels of the American population never before reached by any formal philosophy save Christianity. The phenomena of its Americanization—the responses it got and the resistances it encountered, the uses, adaptations, and alterations it experienced, the institutions and mechanisms by which it was propagated—constitute a complex picture and one which is quite revealing of the character of American society in the last quarter of the nineteenth century.

A number of American philosophers, several of them men of some eminence in their day, propounded evolutionary force systems; generally these systems were more or less imitations of Spencer's, they were developed in language which was even broader, vaguer, and more metaphorical than Spencer's, and they were, if anything, more naively absolutistic than the Synthetic Philosophy. John Fiske's system is a conspicuous case in point: in the vastnesses of his Cosmic Philosophy the concepts of force and evolution become broader still, more indiscriminately figurative and more metaphysical than they were for the master. Fiske is even more at the mercy of his language and hopes than Spencer was, and Fiske is probably the best of the American force-philosophers.

Interestingly, American universe-of-force philosophers all tended to impel the tradition in the same directions: toward optimism and toward theism. Their naive use of language and their epistemological innocence gave them a good deal of freedom in conceptualizing the universe, and they used this freedom to affirm that, according to the best and most up-to-date science and philosophy, man and society were good and automatically evolving toward perfection, and God was Force or at least the Mover of forces that expressed His will in the universe. If a man were worried about the injustices of capitalistic industrialism or about the weakening of religion in its conflict with science, the American universe-of-force philosophies seem to have been especially constructed to provide explicit and absolute reassurance. It is an odd phenomenon to have a deterministic, physics-and-biology-based system used in the cause of concepts of human ideality and immanent divine benevolence, but the universe of force did function that way in America. Of course in a way the Americans were only extending Spencer's own ideas—that the universe's progress was toward human values such as individualism, altruism, and peace, and that the absolute truth behind phenomena was a mysterious Unknowable (the very use of a noun and a capital letter already endowing it with transcendent entitihood)—but they elaborated his philosophy with their own very special Godly slant.

Evolutionary force-philosophy filled a specific need in America, and it was taken up widely and avidly. A great many Americans who were not philosophers, seeing in the universe of force a belief that explained the nature of their society—the industrialization, the competition, the unremitting change and growth—were reassured to know that this state of affairs was not only inevitable but it was right, that these were God's ways, although they were less mysterious than they were thought to be in less scientific times. Spencer became far more popular and influential here than he was in England or Europe, selling a half-million books in America, an unprecedented sale for a philosopher. Similarly John Fiske's compendious Outlines of Cosmic Philosophy *went to twenty printings between 1874 and 1900, and numerous other books and even series of books discussing science, philosophy, religion, nature, society, or man from a universe-of-force viewpoint were published and widely circulated. Even today there is ample evidence of this great scientific awakening gathering dust in attics and second-hand bookstores all over America.*

Enthusiastic advocacy of the "new views" (as they were called by Edward Livingston Youmans, probably their most energetic and effective disciple) even shaded off into what we can only call "promotion." Subscriptions were widely sold for forthcoming works of Herbert Spencer, and, in 1882, for a banquet to honor him in person; the Appletons' publishing house launched The Scientific Monthly *to bring the "new views" to a wider public, and followed with "The International Scientific Library," a fifty-volume series of classics of this modern movement; even the nonprofit Brooklyn Ethical Association turned its ambitious lecture series on the topic of (basically Spencerian) evolution into a set of inexpensive proselytizing reprints. And there were sermons and speeches and articles in the popular press which interpreted and fostered the "new views" and extended them to various popular topics.*

The intellectual quality of that part of the discussion which came down to the lay American public in the Sunday supplement features and the hometown lecture series was, of course, a further and final debasement of Helmholtz's dream of order. In the popular consciousness, all Joule's empirical and mathematical precision, all Spencer's ingeniously exhaustive metaphysical rationalizing, all Fiske's anxious pseudoscientific yearning for divine reassurance were distorted, finally, into such ideas as those of man's magnificent control of the "forces" of nature, the mysterious operation of occult "forces," the "forces" that attest to a life after death for man, and the benevolent determinism of the "forces" that shape and change society. Americans with untrained minds— perhaps like Theodore Dreiser, people also with powerful imaginations— would encounter seminal ideas of the universe of force, then, on this lowest level.

On the level of the best in formal American thought, however, there was a highly developed philosophical tradition which was fully capable of maintaining perspective on the universe of force even in the 1860s, before the days of its popularity. Opposition was variously based, of course, but that which is most crucial in the present context is based in criticism of the habits of thought and language which the universe of force represents. Among the critics, Chauncey Wright, J. B. Stallo, and William James all confronted Spencerianism and the universe of force in some direct, full, and complex way, developing, in fact, their own critical perspectives—indeed even their basic approaches to thought—in the encounter. The immediate cultural impact of these critical thinkers was not great, but it is essentially their guidelines that we follow today; finally the greatest contribution of the universe of force to American philosophy may have been to sharpen its critical awareness and to free it from the absolutism and the naive realism that the notion itself represents. For purposes of perspective I have chosen to begin the episode of the Americanization of the universe of force with these critics; viewed in this order the whole vast movement seems (as indeed it was) an anachronism, a study in cultural lag, a great irony in the history of American thought.

TO JUDGE only by the Americanization of the universe of force, America in the latter nineteenth century would seem to have been a country that was pervasively religious, thoroughly optimistic, highly enterprising, and intellectually naive. A strong faith in God, in science, in contemporary American civilization and in progress was in evidence as American thought and the universe of force underwent the mutual modifications that made for happy compatibility. The naiveté in that process shows most clearly in the obliviousness of the many Spencerian enthusiasts to the critical approaches to knowledge that were then developing in science and philosophy and to their very articulate American advocates. The universe of force would finally prove to be a dead end in philosophy, and, despite and to some extent prior to the great popularity of the concept, several American thinkers were clearly aware of its weakness and transciency. There were a wide variety of possible American approaches to this insight; Chauncey Wright, J. B. Stallo, and William James, for example, arrived at similar ideas about the universe of force, although they came to them from somewhat different directions. Wright was keenly aware of scientific method and tended to look for pragmatic usability in evaluating concepts; Stallo, a bit more abstractly oriented, reacted strongly against the simplistic metaphysic implied in so much of physical science; and James strongly felt the inadequacy of any merely rationalistic system for representing the rich diversity of human mind and experience.

Chauncey Wright (1830–1875), the Northampton, Massachusetts mathematician and philosopher, published as early as 1865 a thoroughgoing and sound critique of Spencer's ideas. Wright was not a career academician (although at various times he was a lecturer at Harvard in Philosophy, Psychology, and Mathematical Physics) and the writings he produced in his short lifetime are only a miscellaneous collection of articles, reviews, and letters, but he was extremely influential in his associations with C. S. Peirce, William James, Oliver Wendell Holmes, Jr., and others in the so-called "Metaphysical Club," and he is regarded as seminal to the formulation of one of America's most distinctive contributions to Western thought, the philosophy of pragmatism. Wright was an extraordinarily clear thinker, well grounded in scientific logic, who became an important figure in American philosophy without writing books or instructing disciples.

Wright was a critic of metaphysical systems rather than a builder of them, aligning himself with sceptics and empiricists against the teleological tendency of nineteenth-century thought. A strong admirer of Darwin, he allowed for no wider application of evolutionary theory than Darwin could scientifically warrant: "Progress and development, when they mean more than a continuous proceeding, have a meaning suspiciously like what the moral and mythic instincts are inclined to—something having a beginning, a middle, and an end—an epic poem, a dramatic representation, a story, a cosmogony."[1] If some cosmic generalization were called for, Wright preferred the concept of "cosmic weather"—that is, a flux of "countermovements" with no discernible purpose or tendency. He was profoundly aware of the degree to which human desires tended to shape our ideas and perceptions, and he saw the progress of modern science as mankind's gradual shift away from "subjective motives" (which anthropocentrically developed theologies and cosmic philosophies according to human needs) toward "objective motives" (which built up a body of reliable knowledge through curiosity and a rational discipline).[2] William James once wrote of Wright, by way of tribute, that "never in a human head was contemplation more separated from desire."[3] In "The Philosophy of Herbert Spencer," a review of eight of Spencer's works in the April 1865 *North American Review*, Wright repeatedly links Spencer's ideas with the outworn subjective style of philosophizing, despite their surface claim to consideration as new and scientific. Early in the essay Wright disparages Spencer's assumed omniscience:

> The Synthetic Philosophy [is] an inconceivable undertaking—we will say nothing of the impossibility of any one man's acquiring adequately all the knowledge requisite for the successful accomplishment of such an undertaking as Mr. Spencer has proposed for himself.

He also insists that Spencer had no first-hand scientific experience whatever, borrowing all his findings and misunderstanding the basic nature of scientific method and theory (448). In pointing this out he foreshadows not only later scientific epistemology but pragmatism as well:

> Mr. Spencer applies a method for the ascertainment of ultimate truths, which a positivist would regard as correct only on the supposition that the materials of truth have all been collected, and that the research of science is no longer for the enlargement of our experience or for the informing of the mind. . . . Nothing justifies the development of abstract principles in science but their utility in enlarging our concrete knowledge of nature. The ideas on which mathematical Mechanics and the Calculus are founded, the morphological ideas of Natural History, and the theories of Chemistry are such working ideas—finders, not merely summaries of truth. (436)

Wright sees another pernicious result of Spencer's lack of acquaintance with real science in his unwitting teleological bent. He sees Spencer as wanting to derive his evolutionary theory from empirically based scientific fact, but actually imposing on selected scientific phenomena his own subjective sense of order, at root a vision of progress and ultimately a reflex of man's moral feelings rather than a legitimate objective inference (450–451).

Wright points out that Spencer was subjectively selective in his utilization of scientific ideas and irresponsibly vague in his use of them. Not only did Spencer tend to avoid basic physics, for example, and build his theory on special problems such as the nebular hypothesis and the relation of physical forces to organic life, but he also seriously distorted the ideas in the process of elaborating his cosmic theory: "To all the ideas which he adopts from science he adds a new sense, or rather a vagueness, so as to make them descriptive of as much as possible" (458). Thus the definiteness and utility is gone out of them in their new context and they become "corrupting and misleading ideas" (457).

Wright notes that the concept of force was one of those most abused by Spencer: "This word is used in mathematical mechanics in three different senses, but fortunately they are distinct. They are not here fused together, as they are by Mr. Spencer, into one vague expression of what nobody in fact knows anything about" (458). Wright sees that as Spencer vaguely groups phenomena together as manifestations of "the persistence of force" (assuming, for example, that mechanical and chemical "forces" are transferrable and conserved despite the fact that "chemical forces are not mathematically comprehended and are therefore utterly unknown" [459], and further assuming that universal laws may be applied confidently in areas where there is neither mathematical nor experimental justification), his use of the term has little to do with any scientific theory: "His principle seems to us to bear a much closer resemblance to the old metaphysical 'Principle of Causality,' or the impossibility of any change in the quantity of existence (whatever this may mean); and it also seems to us as profitless" (460). Thus Chauncey Wright, well on his way to articulating a sound scientific epistemology, emphasizing the utility rather than the absolute truth of scientific concepts, repeatedly classifies Spencer as a reactionary metaphysician who uses scientific concepts irresponsibly.

Johann Bernhard Stallo (1823–1900) attacked universe-of-force concepts more broadly than did Wright, focusing not merely on Spencer but on the whole conceptual framework of science and scientific philosophy in his 1881 book *The Concepts and Theories of Modern Physics*. Like Wright he was not a philosopher or scholar by profession: although he taught for a while (German, physics, chemistry, and mathematics) he made his major achievements as a jurist in Cincinnati. Unlike Wright he was not really in close communication with other important thinkers of his day: his influence was more diffuse and his thinking at times more eccentric.

In 1881 there was very little precedent for the type of book that *The Concepts and Theories of Modern Physics* was intended to be, although since that time the genre has flourished with the philosophy of science. Stallo explains that his book is "designed as a contribution, not to physics, nor, certainly, to metaphysics, but to the theory of cognition. . . . Its tendency is throughout to eliminate from science its latent metaphysical elements, . . . the insidious intrusion into the meditations of the man of science of the old metaphysical spirit."[4] Stallo sees the most insidious of these intrusions in the fundamental fact that "modern physical science aims at a mechanical interpretation of all the phenomena of the universe. It seeks to explain these phenomena by reducing them to the elements of mass and motion and exhibiting their diversities and changes as mere differences and variations in the distribution and aggregation of ultimate and invariable bodies or particles in space" (49). He terms this implicit philosophy the "atomo-mechanical theory" and shows in numerous quotations (like several of those of Joule, Grove, and Helmholtz which appear in Chapter 1, above) how this metaphysical theory is a part of scientists' thinking about the nature of science itself. For example, he quotes Kirchoff as saying in 1865, "The highest object at which the natural sciences are constrained to aim, but which they will never reach, is the determination of the forces which are present in nature, and of the state of matter at any given moment—in one word, the reduction of all the phenomena of nature to mechanics" (51–52).

The basic relation of thoughts to things was not recognized, Stallo insists, even among scientific thinkers. "Metaphysical thinking," he says, "is an attempt to deduce the true nature of things from our concepts of them," and four "radical errors of metaphysics" had, in the evolution of thought, become so basic to men's thinking as to be termed "structural fallacies of the intellect." The "radical errors" include the mistaken assumptions that every concept has a real thing which corresponds to it, that more general concepts preexist the less general and evolve or derive them, that the genesis of concepts corresponds to the genesis of things, and that relationships in the world are always relationships between absolute entities (159–160).

The atomo-mechanical view grew out of such errors, Stallo shows, and his critique of the concept of force on this basis is especially telling, because the reification of force is precisely an example of the naive attribution of real, independent, and even prior reality to a conceptual invention. Stallo concludes, in this crucial case, that

> force is not an individual thing or entity that presents itself directly to observation or to thought, but . . . it is purely an incident to the conception of the interdependence of moving masses. . . . Otherwise expressed, force is a mere inference from the motion itself under the universal conditions of reality, and its measure and determination lie solely in the effect for which it is postulated as a cause; it has no other existence. (186)

In his introduction to the second edition of his book (1884), Stallo briefly singles out Spencer as one whose theories amount to a "substantialization of force" and he shows how Spencer's account of gravitation is naive and unacceptable (37–38).

Stallo's contribution to "the theory of cognition" was considerable; his book alerts scientific thinkers to their responsibility to be critical about their assumptions, and it offers a model of systematic analysis of scientific concepts. In his vigorous expunging of metaphysical ideas, Stallo sometimes forced himself into too critical a position, however. His campaign against the hard little atoms of the atomo-mechanists left him unable to accept any kind of atomic theory, and he had similar shortcomings in respect to his opposition to the kinetic theory of gasses and Riemannian geometry. Yet by and large his critical ideas were sound and timely. Anyone who read Stallo's book would never again find a comfortable refuge in naive realism, as we shall see in considering Henry Adams.

William James (1842–1910) read and fell under the influence of *First Principles* in the early sixties, but soon afterwards freed himself of this spell with the aid of his friend C. S. Peirce, who, himself one of the earliest opponents of the general use of the concept *force*, definitively pilloried it in his 1878 essay "How to Make Our Ideas Clear"[5] as a glaring case in point of the unclear and unwarranted use of what should have remained a clearly definable term in mechanics. James for the rest of his life maintained toward Spencer and the universe of force an attitude of creative antagonism. He used Spencer's books in his courses at Harvard, often in order to contend with them, and he wrote a number of reviews and rebuttals of Spencer's published ideas; in effect (according to James's distinguished biographer, Ralph Barton Perry), "he acquired a sense of his own philosophical power through feeling so confidently, and seeing so clearly, that Spencer was wrong."[6]

The Jamesian perspective is especially advantageous for viewing the inadequacies of Spencerianism. James came to philosophy from the biological sciences and psychology, so he had background in areas of special concern for Spencer, but with the important difference that James was a practicing scientist in these fields. Additionally, James saw the universe as multifarious, spontaneous, and open—as ultimately irreducible to a system or a theory, especially to a deterministic "block universe" theory. He denied the absoluteness of human rationality, allowing, in the search for truth, for the unavoidable and legitimate operation of feelings and attitudes, and recognizing the tentative, anthropocentric nature of truth. Like Wright he was also, as we are about to see, a careful semanticist.

James's fullest and final critique of Spencer and his system appeared in a review of Spencer's autobiography in 1904, and in it he used the personal focus provided by the autobiography to get at the shortcomings of the Synthetic Philosophy. "Greatness and smallness surely never lived so closely in one skin together,"[7] James asserts as an opening evaluation, and he relates Spencer's habits of thought, some avowed in the autobiography and some implicit, to the resulting system. Crediting Spencer with full measures of such traits as dedication, erudition, and civic conscience, James still sees him as excessively rationalistic, fault-finding, and closed to the ideas of others.

He gives a queer sense of having no emotional perspective, as if small things and large were on the same plane of vision, and equally commanded his attention. . . . One finds no twilight region in his mind, and no capacity for dreaminess or passivity. All parts of it are filled with the same noonday glare, like a dry desert where every grain of sand shows singly, and there are no mysteries or shadows. (100)

James says that this "noonday glare" of rationalism, combined with a total lack of self-doubt, not only led Spencer to overlook a good deal of the richness and subtlety of experience, but to reject any ideas not directly applicable to his system.

Spencer's mind was so narrowly systematized, that he was at last almost incapable of believing in the reality of alien ways of feeling. The invariable arrogance of his replies to criticisms shows his absolute self-confidence. Every opinion in the world had to be articulately right or articulately wrong,—so proved by some principle or other of his infallible system. (101)

Thus the monotony, the dry literalness, the "tone of pedantic rectitude" of Spencer's writings is both deeply expressive of his own personality and indicative of the worst shortcomings of his vision of reality.

James had long been a critic of Spencer's concepts of mind and the relation of mind to life. In two articles of the late seventies, "Remarks on Spencer's Definition of Mind as Correspondence" and "Spencer's *Data of Ethics*,"[8] he objects to Spencer's disregarding of the religious, esthetic, emotional aspects of the mind and reducing it to its cognitive and adaptive—that is, its survival—functions. This was too narrow a view of human life for James who claimed that a person so constituted would be an "earthly incarnation of prudence" with a "monotonously narrow passion for self-preservation."[9] He also insists that evolutionary theory in itself is insufficient to generate ethical theory and that subjectivity and personal bias are unavoidable factors, Spencer himself being a case in point, his own theories notwithstanding. James states, "In Germany especially the 'struggle for existence' has been made the baptismal formula for the most cynical assertions of brute egotism; with Mr. Spencer the same theories have bred an almost Quakerish humanitarianism and regard for peace."[10]

James regarded Spencer's *First Principles* as "almost a museum of blundering reasoning" (104). Although he gave Spencer the credit "of having been the first to see in evolution an absolutely universal principle" (103), he shows him to be a philosopher who "aims at a purely mechanical explanation of Nature" (105). Spencer's law of evolution can at best be classified as a "statistical law"—"such laws prophesy the real future *en gros*, but they never help us to predict any particular detail of it"—and its value, a direct function of its exactness and its consistency, is notably debased because "his terms are vagueness and ambiguity incarnate" (105).

James is eloquent on the subject of Spencer's vagueness. Spencer's idea of "definiteness" is vitiated by the fact that "definite things, in his book, finally appear as *things that men have made separate names for*" rather than having some independent characteristic of definiteness. And quite typically "integration" is impossibly comprehensive, including, among other phenomena,

> the contraction of the solar nebula, the formation of the earth's crust, the calcification of cartilage, the shortening of the body of crabs, the loss of his tail by man, the mutual dependence of plants and animals, the growth of powerful states, the tendency of human occupations to go to distinct localities, the dropping of terminal inflexions in English grammar, the formation of general concepts by the mind, the use of machinery instead of simple tools, the development of "composition" in the fine arts, etc., etc.

One can only conclude that "it is obvious that no one form of motion of matter characterizes all these facts" (106).

Spencer's central concept of force James regards as especially vague. Trying to interpret "the persistence of force" drives James virtually to exasperation:

> By this Spencer sometimes means the phenomenal law of conservation of energy, sometimes the metaphysical principle that the quantity of existence is unalterable, sometimes the logical principle that nothing can happen without a reason, sometimes the practical postulate that in the absence of any assignable difference you must call a thing the same. This law is one vast vagueness, of which I can give no clear account. (107)

Terms such as *mental force* and *social force* James regards "special vaguenesses"—undefinable, and, in spite of all Spencer's insistence to the contrary, inconceivable as being correlatable with mechanical force: "Mr. Spencer himself is a great social force; but he ate no more than an average man, and his body, if cremated, would disengage no more energy" (107).

James finally judged Spencer to be a personal enigma, "a figure unique for quaint consistency," an "inimitable blend of small and vast mindedness, of liberality and crabbedness" (107). His judgment on the concept of force, the concept that Spencer attempted to apotheosize, had been delivered years earlier in 1880:

> The physicist knows nothing whatever of force in a non-phenomenal sense. Force is for him only a generic name for all those *things* which will cause motion. A falling stone, a magnet, a cylinder of steam, a man, just

as they appear to sense, *are* forces. There is no supersensible force *in* or *behind* them. Their force is just their sensible pull or push, if we take them naturally, and just their positions and motions if we take them scientifically. If we aspire to strip off from Nature all anthropomorphic qualities, there is none we should get rid of quicker than its "Force." [11]

THE TIDE of the times was not, however, running with men of critical perspicacity. Foremost in the minds of a great many thinkers, including some of the most widely known and circulated, were the immense philosophical possibilities of science and its theories of evolution and the "simple forces." Exploring those possibilities and bringing them into accord with the established truths by which men lived became the philosophical order of the day. In fact the strongest motive of American thought of the late nineteenth century was to reconcile science and religion; strangely enough the universe of force became the vehicle for this reconciliation in the minds of many. Despite the fact that its patriarch, Herbert Spencer, was by his own admission a secular man to whom "supernaturalism in whatever form, had never commended itself," [12] his American disciples, differently inspired, made it into a model of the universe that had a place for God just as it had a place for science, and thus justified the ways of both. It was a time of system building and transcendent reconciliation in America, and the universe of force became an influential pattern for the philosophers who built the systems.

John Fiske (1842–1910)—scholar, historian, ultra-Spencerian propounder of the "Cosmic Philosophy"—filled, from the 1870s to the end of the century, the role of arch-reconciler, of apologist for God, American progress, and the evolution of force in American philosophy, although he seems to have grown into it through stages of sincere, personal, and sometimes agonizing questing. He was a thinker of little originality or imagination, but, like Spencer, he explored with great care and intensity his vision of the universe of force. Of all the American force-philosophers Fiske had the clearest mind and the most diligent approach.

He was still a student at Harvard when he had an experience of a sort soon to become a familiar motif in American culture: he discovered Herbert Spencer and suddenly saw the whole world in a new way. "I have had an 'intellectual drunk' over it," he wrote to his mother. [13] The discovery not only liberated him for the time being from his conservative religious upbringing, but it also helped him discover his calling, to be a philosopher like Spencer.

It was as a historian that Fiske came to the universe of force. Having a humanistic background (very unlike Spencer's technical engineering background), he was especially attuned to those aspects of the cosmic system that had to do with human affairs, and notably with the development of Western society, culture, and ethics. The scientific (and the pseudoscientific) parts of the Synthetic Philosophy he was for the most part inclined to take on faith. It was a very great faith, too, because historian Fiske strongly believed that the persistence of force and its evolutionary corollaries constituted a set of laws that could comprehensively explain the course of human affairs.

He was a practitioner of what has come to be called "scientific history"; along with British historian Henry T. Buckle and several Americans such as George Bancroft, Brooks Adams, and (somewhat ambiguously and dubiously, to be sure) Brooks's brother Henry (see Chapter 4), Fiske was part of what retrospectively seems to have been a "movement" among nineteenth-century historians to write history that was thematically based upon a general scientific or metascientific principle. Of course "scientific history" could not have been scientific in any real sense. It was really only another example, like that of Spencer's philosophy, of the extension of the theories and terminology of science into a different discipline, another metaphoric process which could result in nothing like absolute understanding, since the crucial questions— which scientific principle applied, and to which historical phenomena—were solved by the predisposition of the individual historian rather than by the historical events themselves. The suppositions of "scientific history" were never closely examined in its day, but the movement was nevertheless shortlived.[14]

When he was only nineteen, Fiske had already shown his leanings toward "scientific history" in an extended review he wrote of Henry T. Buckle's influential *History of Civilization in England*; that Buckle meant to provide "for the history of man something equivalent, or at all events analogous, to what had been effected by other inquirers for different branches of natural science,"[15] Fiske approved, but he was far from satisfied with Buckle's exemption of moral and intellectual matters from the ordinary laws of history. Spencer's law of evolution, superior for Fiske because it was both science-based and wholly inclusive, was ever after to supply the central theme of Fiske's "scientific history." The course of history meant "progress," as he was to explain later, and progress meant Spencer's evolution of force:

> If I may cite my own experience, it was largely the absorbing and over-mastering passion for the study of history that first led me to study evolution in order to obtain a correct method. When one has frequent occasion to refer to the political and social *progress* of the human race, one likes to know what one is talking about.[16]

Fiske's method of history-writing is summarized clearly by Milton Berman in his valuable biography: "To Fiske the function of the historian was to shape a narrative that would make clear the underlying philosophical principles which explained the events of history. These principles he knew in advance; he drew them from his previous study of Spencer and the Anglo-Teutonic school of historians. He saw no need for research and depended on previous histories for details." [17] What well might seem to be a self-confirming tendency in this method is borne out in the vision of human history it yields; again I quote Berman, who succinctly states, "He drew a picture of the United States as the peak of an evolutionary process which operated through history to produce the free democratic republic that emerged from the Revolution and which in the future would produce a world republic led by 'Anglo Saxons' bringing peace and prosperity to the entire globe." [18] Like Spencer's philosophy, Fiske's history mirrored its author. Cosmic evolution culminated in his own culture.

But what seemed to Fiske the pinnacle of human history might well look to us like the vision of a dangerously complacent world racism, a potential justification for "Anglo-Saxon" domination of the world. The theme of evolutionary racism is an important one in late nineteenth-century thought, and one that in some minds was linked to the universe of force. In studying Frank Norris's ideas we shall see another example of this union of Saxonism and force evolution; for the present occasion this cursory summary of Fiske's approach to the discipline of history need only indicate something about the tendencies and quality of his thought and the objectivity of "scientific history."

Fiske was never anything but generously candid about his intellectual debt to Spencer, and on the basis of that acknowledgment of discipleship a strong and durable long-distance relationship developed. In a letter to Spencer in 1864 Fiske set the terms:

> The influence of your writings is apparent alike in every line of my writings and every sentence of conversation. So inextricably have they become intertwined with my own thinking, that frequently on making a new generalization, I scarcely know whether to credit myself with it or not.[19]

In that same year, responding to an early article of Fiske's which applied Spencerian principles to philology, Spencer commended his "power of independent thought." [20] Later, responding to Fiske's treatment of society in the series of lectures that would be incorporated in *Outlines of Cosmic Philosophy*, which predated his own *Principles of Sociology*, Spencer confessed to him, with only slightly hedged generosity, "You have to some extent forestalled me in the elaboration of the doctrine of Evolution under its sociological aspects." [21] And in recalling his 1882 visit to America in his autobiography Spencer recognizes Fiske as "one who had done so much as an expositor of the Synthetic Philosophy," and therefore, "was the first to whom attention was due."[22]

Fiske was always willing to say unreservedly that Spencer was the greatest philosopher in the world, and in formulating his own philosophy in his influential and encyclopedic *Outlines of Cosmic Philosophy* (2 vols., 1874) he paid Spencer the further compliment of massive borrowing and imitation. In Fiske's mind, presumably, the basic nature of cosmic evolution was absolutely known and described by Spencer; there was no need to search for other ways to understand the universe's first principles. His preface acknowledges the fact that his *Outlines* contains barely enough original matter so that "it can no longer be regarded as a mere reproduction of Mr. Spencer's thoughts,"[23] but at the same time it promised to prove that "the hostility between Science and Religion, about which so much is talked and written, . . . is purely a chimera of the imagination," that "while knowledge grows and old beliefs fall away and creed succeeds to creed, nevertheless that Faith which makes the innermost essence of religion is indestructible" (xii). There is no better paradigm of the intentions of the philosophical Americanization of the universe of force.

Fiske's *Outlines* grew out of a set of lectures attacking Comte, and its first eleven chapters (all of Part I, "Prolegomena") reproduce those arguments against the predecessor whom Spencer was so fervent about repudiating. Fiske, acting as "Spencer's bulldog," resolves questions of epistemology, the test of truth, and causality, among others, in this section, giving all philosophy a Spencerian rather than a Comtean orientation and superceding the latter's "Positivism" with his own "Cosmism." One of Fiske's favorite generalizations was about the nature and direction of progress, and in Part I of *Outlines* he (typically) rejects Comte's theory that human history has progressed through three basic stages—the mytho-religious, the metaphysical, and the Positivistic-scientific—insisting that there is only one vast and continuous development from "Anthropomorphism" to "Cosmism."

Fiske saw human progress as rooted in universal Evolution, and Evolution follows from the persistence of force. Part II of his work ("Synthesis") posits all of the basic Spencerian categories in straight Spencerian language. Matter is indestructible, motion is continuous, and force is persistent; the homogeneous is unstable, effects of forces multiply, and dissolution is (at least hypothetically) the stage after evolution. The Spencerian definition of evolution is quoted, illustrated, and applied. Fiske, a bit uncertain about scientific theory and terminology, sticks safely to second-hand illustrations. Astronomic and geologic applications he borrows from Spencer and from other scientific popularizers, and his treatment of "The Sources of Terrestrial Energy" is a watered-down version of popular ideas about the correlation and conservation of forces. For categories and illustrations of organic evolution he relies principally on Darwin. Unlike Spencer who, starting without doctrinal religious preconceptions did not feel specially challenged by the doctrine of special creation, Fiske is much concerned to argue it down. Essentially, however, Fiske's concept of biology is Spencerian rather than Darwinian or post-Christian or anything else, as, considering the question of natural selection under the heading of "Equilibriation," he follows the master in applying the paradigm of pseudophysics to this aspect of the living world:

> Thus with the increase of the organism in heterogeneity, definiteness, and coherence, its environment increases in heterogeneity and presents more definite and coherent relations to which the organism must adjust itself. And in this way the heterogeneous, definite, and coherent activity of the organism is again enhanced. (II, 72)

Fiske's substantive deviations from Spencer were slight. Besides his overall emphasis on progress and his pervasive concern with religious questions, Fiske's own contributions were matters of extensions, elaborations, and peripheral insights. He took (and received) a good deal of credit for originally propounding a theory of the evolutionary function of the length of infancy, which stated that creatures of a higher degree of evolutionary complexity required a longer period of infancy, and correlatively, parental affection which was deeper and more enduring. In terms of scientific legitimacy this idea was no more (though certainly no less) than a likely hunch, and Fiske, untrained in science and ultimately interested in a bigger game, shrugged off the problem of validation as being virtually self-evident:

> The prolongation of infancy accompanying the development of intelligence, and the correlative extension of parental feelings, are facts established by observation wherever observation is possible. (II, 344)

In the discussion of society—the one Spencer admitted "to some extent forestalled" him—Fiske uses his typical approach on virtually virgin ground, applying Spencer's general formula and shortcutting any real scientific validation. Following a brief discussion of social change, he asserts that "the evolution of society, no less than the evolution of life, conforms to that universal law of evolution discovered by Mr. Spencer" (II, 209), and goes on to elaborate what he calls the "Law of Progress":

> *The Evolution of Society is a continuous establishment of psychical relations within the Community, in conformity to physical and psychical relations arising in the Environment; during which, both the Community and the Environment pass from a state of relatively indefinite, incoherent*

homogeneity to a state of relatively definite, coherent heterogeneity; and during which, the constituent Units of the Community become ever more distinctly individuated. (II, 223–224; Fiske's italics)

Like Spencer, Fiske saw social progress occurring specifically in terms of the development of societies away from militarism and toward industrialism, a gradual amelioration of the intrasocietal struggle for survival, and in all ways *"the continuous weakening of selfishness and the continuous strengthening of sympathy"* (II, 201; Fiske's italics).

Fiske differed from Spencer in the extent of his trust in the automatic operation of natural mechanism in the social sphere. He did not share Spencer's interest in reform, as limited as that was, but urged his readers that progress occurred regardless of man's efforts and often even in spite of them, and that man's appropriate reaction to societal imperfections was one of patient, confident submission:

> Science is teaching us that the method of evolution is that mill of God, of which we have heard, which, while it grinds with infinite efficacy, yet grinds with wearisome slowness." [24]

In Fiske's view of society, the rich and powerful man, the captain of industry, was a heroic figure, an example of the highest point of human evolution to date, and Fiske explicitly celebrated him as such.[25] Later in his life (Berman suggests), his actual responses to the conditions accompanying increased industrialism and to the men who profited from them grew increasingly less favorable.[26] Whatever crucial paradox brewed within him was never confronted in his public writing, however, and Fiske remained an apologist for the capitalist and the God of Progress.

Fiske's ethical theory, like his social theory, was a derivative system centered in fact around the idea of automatic progress. Using the pleasure-pain nexus of the Utilitarians and Spencer's definition of life as adjustment, he viewed pleasure as following from the perfect adjustment of inner to outer relations, while pain followed from some lack of adjustment (II, 331–332). Along with the Utilitarians he claimed that greater pleasure than the purely personal could be derived from behavior that benefited family, community or humanity. Evil, then, was neither a metaphysical entity nor a part of man's makeup but was merely a temporary state of maladjustment, the rectifying of which is an automatic tendency of a benevolent (and oddly fatherly) universal mechanism:

> To be delivered from evil, we must avoid the mal-adjustments of which evil is the consequence and the symptom. . . . The reverent follower of science perceives the truth of the paradox that the infliction of pain is sub-

servient to a beneficent end. "Pervading all nature, he sees at work a stern discipline, which is a little cruel, that it may be very kind." (II, 461–462; Fiske does not identify the source of his quotation.)

Ultimately, Fiske leaves no doubt that his system is theologically based, and in this he departs most clearly and widely from Spencer's (fundamentally agnostic) position. He insists that "our Cosmic Philosophy is based upon the affirmation of God's existence, and not upon the denial of it, like irreligious Atheism, or upon the ignoring of it, like non-religious Positivism" (II, 377), maintaining, nevertheless, a position he termed "Cosmic Theism," as opposed to "Anthropomorphic Theism" with its person-God and special providence. He was far more concerned with the demythologization of philosophy than was Spencer, who could view conventional religion with detachment and disdain, and he was extremely anxious to offer his readers the extraordinary assurance that morality and its essential religious basis were unchanged in his system:

> In the grand equation between duty and action, the substitution of scientific for theological symbols involves no alteration of ethical values. And thus in casting aside the mythologic formulas in which religious obligation was formerly symbolized, we do but recognize the obligation as more binding than ever. (II, 468)

Fiske's wedding of traditional Christianity and pseudoscientific determinism was one of those vast, unstable, impossibly hopeful syntheses that are preserved, even only temporarily, by shifting definitions, backtracking explanations and the sheer force of will and rhetoric. In discussing religious matters in the culminating section of his *Outlines* he (as a scientific man) continually cautions his readers against misuse of his word-symbols to arrive at an oversimplified identification of the scientist's force and the religionist's God:

> To the scientific inquirer, the terms "matter" and "force" are mere symbols which stand *tant bien que mal* for certain generalized modes of Divine manifestation: they are no more real existences than the x and y of the algebraist are real existences. The question as to identifying Deity with Force is, therefore, simply ruled out. (II, 430)

Yet sometimes even this distinction is presented in the form of a credo, with a credo's connotative effect: "*There exists a* POWER, *to which no limit in time or space is conceivable, of which all phenomena, as presented in consciousness, are manifestations, but which we can know only through these manifestations*" (II, 415; Fiske's italics). And in moments of devout enthusiasm he (as a religious man) far exceeds the intent of his own caution:

What is this wondrous Dynamis which manifests itself to our consciousness in harmonious activity throughout the length and breadth and depth of the universe, which guides the stars for countless ages in paths that never err, and which animates the molecules of the dew-drop that gleams for a brief hour on the shaven lawn,—whose workings are so resistless that we have naught to do but reverently obey them, yet so infallible that we can place our unshaken trust in them, yesterday, to-day, and for ever? When, summing up all activity in one most comprehensive epithet, we call it Force, we are but using a scientific symbol, expressing an affection of our consciousness, which is yet powerless to express the ineffable Reality. To us, therefore, as to the Israelite of old, the very name of Jehovah is that which is not to be spoken. Push our scientific research as far as we may, pursuing generalization until all phenomena, past, present, and future, are embraced within a single formula;—we shall never fathom this ultimate mystery, we shall be no nearer the comprehension of this omnipresent Energy. Here science must ever reverently pause, acknowledging the presence of the mystery of mysteries. Here religion must ever hold sway, reminding us that from birth until death we are dependent on a Power to whose eternal decrees we must submit, to whose dispensations we must resign ourselves, and upon whose constancy we may implicitly rely. (II, 444)

Even in such a rhapsody as this he makes a minor effort to keep his terminology clear ("we are but using a scientific symbol"), and he can in another context later recognize the semantic paradox he has all along faced ("that a Positive mode of philosophizing is impracticable, and that we can never get entirely rid of all traces of anthropomorphism" [II, 449]), but there can be little doubt that at times in Fiske's mind, Spencer's Unknowable, the ur-force, takes on godly qualities. His naming it "Dynamis" is itself revealing here too, being at once a quasi-scientific and quasi-mythological adaptation.

In the decade following the publication of *Outlines of Cosmic Philosophy* Fiske's ideas underwent an essential though not unforseeable change. As the years passed by, as the theological outcry against evolution cooled, and as personal difficulties tended to increase for him, the American evolutionist (the term is his, self-applied) rediscovered purpose and design in the evolving universe, and spoke more and more of a personal God and the immortality of the individual soul. Not that he abandoned Spencer or Darwin or a theory of cosmic evolution at least remotely based on the theories and findings of science, but he tended to reinterpret them in the light of his newly rediscovered ancient truth, and to refer seldom to "Force" or "The Unknowable" and often to "God." By the mid-eighties, in such works as *The Destiny of Man, Viewed in the Light of his Origin* and *The Idea of God as Affected by Modern Knowl-*

edge, he saw his principal task as a setting forth of the "outlines of a theory of religion," in which his earlier works were "simply wayside studies preliminary to the undertaking of this complicated and difficult task." [27] He did not feel he had substantially altered his ideas, and probably he hadn't: granted the wide parameters of his language in *Outlines* and its irrepressible theological inclinations, he could change his intent from a preponderantly Positivistic to an avowedly religious one without explicitly contradicting himself.

Spencer was careful never to speak of a teleological purpose in the evolutionary process, and Fiske had followed him in this in his *Outlines*, but he confessed in 1885 to having felt that his Cosmic Philosophy was incomplete in its lack of "the teleological element," and explained of his realization that "when, after long hovering in the background of consciousness, it suddenly flashed upon me two years ago, it came with such vividness as to seem like a revelation." [28] He set to work reinterpreting in this light not only his own earlier ideas (admitting that the only hints of teleology he could find in his *Outlines* were sadly underdeveloped), but those of his mentors as well: "According to Darwinism, the creation of Man is still the goal toward which Nature tended from the beginning. Not the production of any higher creature, but the perfecting of Humanity, is to be the glorious consummation of Nature's long and tedious work." [29] At this stage he misrepresents Darwin mightily, but he forestalls any objections with statements implicitly backed by his own reputation as an "evolutionist": "The Darwinian theory, properly understood, replaces as much teleology as it destroys. . . . The doctrine of evolution does not allow us to take the atheistic view of the position of man." [30] For Fiske finally the law of evolution is the means by which God brings things about, the expression, in time, of His immanence and will. The "perfecting of Humanity" is His ultimate purpose, and to achieve this, evolution in the future would take on a whole new aspect: "Henceforth, in short, the dominant aspect of evolution was to be not the genesis of species, but the progress of Civilization." [31] Even personal immortality was a likely adjunct to purposeful Cosmic progress. "Has all this work [of evolution] been done for nothing?" he queries rhetorically. [32]

Thus Fiske's later version of the cosmos is a reversion to centering the entire universe and all its processes around the hopes and needs and fears of man— and not even those of all mankind so much as those of nineteenth-century, middle-class, Harvard-educated, Christian-inclined, progressive, democratic American man. An important but in some ways awkward step in the completion of this man-centered vision was the reanthropomorphization of God. Although in the seventies he had loudly denounced anthropomorphism in religion, in 1885 Fiske hedgingly attempted a reconciliation with it:

We may hold that the world of phenomena is intelligible only when regarded as the multiform manifestation of an Omnipresent Energy that is in some way—albeit in a way quite above our finite comprehension—anthropomorphic or quasi-personal.[33]

He argues at this stage that "since . . . our notion of force is purely a generalization from our subjective sensations of effort overcoming resistance, there is scarcely less anthropomorphism lurking in the phrase 'Infinite Power' than in the phrase 'Infinite Person,'"[34] using a clear perception to rationalize a muddy conclusion; and he further alleges, enlisting preeminent authority in the cause of his persuasion, that Herbert Spencer, "the greatest philosopher of modern times, the master and teacher of all who shall study the process of evolution for many a day to come," showed that "the divine energy which is manifest throughout the knowable universe is the same energy that wells up in us as consciousness."[35] (The idea is recognizable as Spencer's, although the term "divine energy" is clearly Fiske's.) Whatever potential existed in the concept of force to help man discover the otherness of the universe is jettisoned by Fiske in his need for the reassurance of a personal, anthropomorphic God. He will not allow "force" to have "a mode of action distinguishable from that of Deity,"[36] and he enthusiastically affirms that "the infinite and eternal Power that is manifested in every pulsation of the universe is none other than living God. . . . God is in the deepest sense a moral Being. The everlasting source of phenomena is none other than the infinite Power that makes for righteousness."[37]

In sum, despite all his explanations and pseudoreconciliations, Fiske's scientific ideas are little more than window dressing for his essentially religious cosmos; the ideas of force and God have been merged. His version of the Spencerian world picture is more metaphoric, more metaphysical, and more mythic than the original and less clear and consistent. His close friendship with Chauncey Wright seems to have benefited his thinking not at all, and his sojourn in the realms of science and "Positivism" ultimately produced for him only a spurious popular reputation as an expert on matters scientific, so that his metaphysics of American progress and his final turning to God would seem, in the minds of the complacent or unwary, to have the authority of the best and most recent human knowledge. John Fiske is now remembered not as a thinker at all but as an influential popularizer of the ideas of his day, and this judgment of posterity seems just; too anxious to reconcile, he reached too soon for the all-comprehending, all-reassuring solution that would quiet the questionings and controversies without searching their depths.

JOHN FISKE'S was the most thoroughly developed and elaborate version of the universe of force that America was to produce, but its tenor and quality were typical of numerous other philosophies of the seventies, eighties, and nineties. Spencerian force-evolution was both the pattern and the inspiration for a motley school of American philosophers, who, enthused about the broadest, vaguest ideas of force, God, evolution, progress, providence, and ideality, presented America with their visions of a force-reconciled universe. Religion and science were happily fused. Through the thought of the period ran a strong strain of sunny determinism.

In their backgrounds the American exponents of the universe of force were as different as the church and the laboratory, but they uniformly lacked not only a critical understanding of the nature of their words but even a systematic discipline wherewith to get one. They were naive realists who unconsciously assumed that reality conformed to the lines of their language and concepts. Four examples can make this clear as well as demonstrate both typical and ingenious American versions of the universe of force. The first of them, that of Lyman Abbot, eminent Congregational minister and author of *The Evolution of Christianity* (1892), represents the simplest of all approaches to reconciling religion and science—scientific theories are merely translated into conventional religious terms and the conflict is at an end. In Abbot's conception, the universe of force is God's universe, plain and simple: the forces that science sees in all phenomena are actually divine immanence, evolution is God's design, the Bible is a record of spiritual evolution, and Christ was born on earth "in order to 'evolve the latent divinity' in man." Abbot's book affirms that "there is a God in history as there is a God in nature—a God who is working out some great design among men, as there is a God who is working out great designs through all material and mechanical phenomena." [38]

A philosophy identical to Abbot's in effect and only slightly more elaborate in language and approach was that of Benjamin Martin (1816–1883). A minister himself until 1852 and subsequently a professor of psychology at the University of the City of New York, Martin wrote on many subjects, most notably contributing to the antislavery issue, but his 1871 book, *The Natural Theology of the Doctrine of the Forces*, is a landmark example of the naive synthesis of an optimistic faith in God and a hazy understanding of "the doctrine of the forces." Beginning with the idea of the correlation and conservation of the forces and the generalization that "each phenomenon is an intelligible result of some modified operation of the one great and universal Force of Nature," [39] he finds God through science in the awesome power of the forces of atoms and in the regularity of the inverse square law of gravitational attraction. Scientists have not yet defined "force" adequately, Martin claims, because the idea is "metaphysical rather than physical, . . . one of these universal ideas which belong of necessity to the intellectual furniture of every human mind" (721, 722). Also, since the only force with which we are immediately acquainted is that of our own mind, other forces that become known to us do so presumably "from" mind too, Martin reasons, as he proceeds analogically from a vague version of the idea of our sense of effort as our primary experience of "force" to the uplifting conclusion that the Universal Force "has all the characteristics of an intelligent and spiritual nature, like that of the human mind" (727). From there an easy step takes him to the doctrine that the Universal Force is a person, has a moral nature, and so forth.

A system that is fuller and more elaborate—though really no more profound—was worked out by Joseph LeConte (1823–1901), a doctor of medicine and a former student of Agassiz, and later a geologist and a professor of science at the University of California (where Frank Norris was one of his students—see Chapter 5). Of his role in reconciling science and religion LeConte was quite clear and proud; summing up in his autobiography what he saw as the distinctively American contribution to evolutionary theory he asserts that

> the role of Lamarck was to introduce evolution as a scientific theory; that of Darwin to present the theory in such wise as to make it acceptable to and accepted by the scientific mind; that of Huxley to fight the battles of evolution and to win its acceptance by the intelligent popular mind; that of Spencer to generalize it into a universal law of nature, thereby making it a philosophy as well as a scientific theory. Finally, it was left to American thinkers to show that a materialistic implication is wholly unwarranted, that evolution is entirely consistent with a rational theism and with other fundamental religious beliefs. My own work has been chiefly in this direction. . . . I began this line of thought in 1871, and believe, and therefore claim, that I was the pioneer in this reaction against the materialistic and irreligious implication of the doctrine of evolution.[40]

The lack of discrimination here between several very different theories of evolution is a fair representation of LeConte's philosophical thinking, but he was an influential and in many ways typical figure of his day. His principal nontechnical works, *The Correlation of Physical, Chemical and Vital Force* (1859), *Religion and Science* (1874), *Evolution and Its Relation to Religious Thought* (1888), and his autobiography (1903, posthumous) demonstrate his Spencerian outlook and his anxious concern to bring the revolutionary new theories of science into accord with traditional Protestant Christianity.

LeConte's system begins with the concept of force, but in such a naive and wishful manner as to make Spencer seem a careful semanticist in comparison:

There are two poles of existence, without the recognition of which philosophy is impossible; they may be variously represented as matter and force, or matter and spirit, or Nature and God. Matter is essential *inertness*, spirit is essential *activity*. The very origin of our notion of force is, I believe, the consciousness of our own mental energy. Matter reveals itself to our senses, but energy, or force, only to our consciousness. We then extend it to external Nature.

What then is force, or the universal energy of Nature? It is an effluence from the person of Deity pervading the universe—an effluence closely connected with Him, yet distinct from His person. . . . The Divine Spirit, brooding upon the primal chaos, communicated to it an influence, an energy, a life, call it what you like, which became the force of evolution of the cosmos and still controls and maintains its beautiful order.[41]

LeConte sees the universe arranged in increasingly more honorific planes of force:

As there are several planes of material existence, raised one above the other—mineral kingdom, vegetable kingdom, animal kingdom—so there are several planes of force raised one above the other, viz., physical force, chemical force, vital force, spiritual force.[42]

Yet everything in the universe seems to be made by God to move across these coexistent planes: "All forces, by progressive dynamic individuation, are on the way toward entity or personality, but fully attain that condition only in man."[43] who attains "completed individuality—separation from the all-pervading forces of Nature."[44]

Evolution, then, is defined as "progressive change, according to certain laws, and by means of resident forces."[45] The laws of evolution are those of (Spencerian) differentiation, of universal progress, and of cyclical movement within universal progress (in the way, for example, that the reptilian age rose and fell, giving way to the mammalian age). Thus LeConte's evolution is of force and by force, through levels and within them, moving because of the intentions of a personal God and "by means of resident forces" toward the condition of independent human selfhood. Like the other American force-philosophers, LeConte had as his ultimate, deeply felt goal emotional reassurance rather than trustworthy generalization, and he was at some pains to establish that, since Nature is the handwriting of God, science is "the study of the modes of operation of the first cause" and is therefore subsumable as a branch of religion rather than standing opposed to it.

Abbot had merely translated vaguely understood scientific categories into the dominant and more familiar religious terminology; Martin had attempted to thrust theological terms and categories (as transcendent and self-evident truths) into an essentially scientific description of the experiential world; LeConte, just a little more original and sophisticated, had tried to include both science and religion in an eclectic blend of idealistic metaphysical concepts. All of them used conventional language very loosely and uncritically in their system-building. A somewhat different approach was taken by Edward Drinker Cope (1840–1897), an eminent paleontologist and evolutionist who attempted to describe a fully reconciled universe of force by (at least in part) coining his own language.

Cope's version of the universe of force, detailed in his book *Primary Factors in Organic Evolution* (1896), is not merely warmed-over and theologized Spencer but is the result of eclectic study and eccentric reflection. He analyzes the universal process of evolution in terms of "energies," but his conception is really another articulation of the universe of force, as is clear from his definitions ("the term energy is used to express the motion of matter")[46] and from his usages (in the process of evolution "a once simple energy becomes specialized into specific energies, each of which, once established, pursues its mode of motion in opposition to all other modes not more potent than itself" [480]).

Cope's individuality comes out in his strange elaboration of the universe of force as a thoroughly vitalistic system. Human mind and will were absolutes to him; he tended to find their counterparts everywhere in organic nature and to assert unequivocally the primacy of such factors in the process of evolution: "The doctrine of evolution may be defined as the teaching which holds that creation has been and is accomplished by the agency of the energies which are intrinsic in the evolving matter, and without the interference of agencies which are external to it" (1). There are really two basic and opposing forms of energy, Cope insists, "those which tend away from, and those which tend toward, the phenomena of life." He terms the former, all the physical and chemical forces, "Catagenetic," and the latter, the vital, "Anagenetic" (475). Spencer's definition of evolution as the integration of matter and dissipation of motion works only for inorganic phenomena, Cope claims, since "in organic anagenesis there is absorption of energy," not dissipation (476). The catagenetic energies tended toward entropy, Cope claimed, in keeping with the Second Law of Thermodynamics, but anagenetic energy was clearly superior to the catagenetic, since "in spite of the mechanical destructability of its physical basis (protoplasm), and the ease with which its mechanisms are destroyed, it successfully resists, controls, and remodels the catagenetic energies for its purposes" (478).

Cope gave the term "Bathmism" to what he saw as the special growth-force in the anagenetic process. Modifications of bathmic energy constituted evolution, and such modifications could take place on either a molar or a molecular scale ("physiogenesis" and "kinetogenesis," Cope termed them). Cope had always been concerned to locate the *originative* forces of evolution. Dissatisfied both with Spencer's posited generalities like "the instability of the homogeneous" and with Darwin's emphasis on the process of natural selection, which only eliminated and did not create variations, and as yet unaware of Mendel's concept of heredity, Cope relied on the questionable theories of Lamarck and an analogy drawn from thermodynamics to supply him with the sought-after explanation. The result was ingenious but unfortunate. Lamarck's theory of the inheritance of acquired characteristics had a dim future and was under heavy attack by many biologists well before Cope's *Primary Factors* staked everything on it in 1896. Beyond that, Cope's theory of transmission of characteristics—"the most rational conception of this inheritance of structural characteristics is the transmission of a mode of motion from the soma to the germ cells" (480)—is a metaphorical and unworkable extension of the force-conservationist's standby, the theory of heat as molecular motion.

Perhaps the most bizarre feature of Cope's system is the function of consciousness or sensibility (he uses the terms synonymously, as he does "energy" and "motion") in evolution. Life is *energy directed by sensibility, or by a mechanism which has originated under the direction of sensibility*" (513; Cope's italics), he asserts, making it sound a good deal like the indwelling energy that motivates evolution has free will and makes conscious choices. His anthropomorphic vitalism is even more clearly revealed when he asserts of catagenesis that "primitive energy was and is conscious, and that all unconscious forms of energy, whether 'vital' or non-vital have been derived from it by a process of retrograde metamorphosis."[47] Mind is prior to matter, the vision and the desire of the indwelling sensibility anticipating and causing the form of the protoplastic material; inert matter once had sensibility but now has fallen into mindlessness (the first stage of which process is termed "cryptopnoy").

Cope suggested the existence of a "general mind" which was prior to individual minds, and he, like LeConte, viewed the prospects of the human race in terms that suggest human deification:

> Moral will power then represents the highest attribute of mind, whether greater or lesser, and we must suppose that it has, like other mental functions, a correspondingly peculiar molecular basis. And it must be the creator of this basis under the general law of the limited control of mind over physical energy. It seems eminently reasonable that the development of will in man should eventuate in the production of a type of energy similar in kind to that which expresses will in Deity, and that it should be persistent in the one case as it is in the other.[48]

Despite Cope's considerable contributions to the science of paleontology, his evolutionary metaphysic can only be regarded as ingeniously quaint. With his language he attempted to reconcile science and religion, not by subsuming one under the terminology of the other as Fiske and Abbot tried to do, but by going to neutral ground and coining a new set of terms, a Greek-derived jargon which in itself, he presumably hoped, enlisted him in neither camp. But beneath the jargon his philosophical vision is simply and basically no more than an all-encompassing belief in man's powers and in the ideality of his destiny, expressed through neo-Lamarckian biological theory and a radical anthropomorphization of the universe of force.

The American force-cosmists were all relatively inexperienced philosophers, ignorant of the highly developed epistemological approaches of their countrymen Wright, James, and Stallo, and anxious to unify science and religion and view their universe in some single, simple, reassuring way. They wanted to be scientific, evolutionary, to utilize the latest learning in their thought, but they were deeply imbued with theism, optimism, teleology, and individualism, and their approaches were self-reflectively anthropomorphic. What they essentially accomplished was to warp and modify both the traditional religious ideas and the promising but in some ways disquieting new scientific theories until both seemed to be saying the same thing. The process itself was neither new nor distinctively American—several of Newton's followers in seventeenth-century England, particularly Ralph Cudworth and Henry More, were quick to bring the master's concepts of force and motion into line with the traditional concept of God's will[49]— but the American philosophers, in reaching their new and progress-oriented accommodation, were clothing with their optimism, their traditional faith, and their good will a conception of the universe that was born of mechanical physics and that remained not only mechanistic, but inescapably deterministic. And by the time of the conception's widest appeal in the eighties and nineties, it was no longer tenable scientifically at all.

IT WOULD be difficult to exaggerate the extent to which Spencer and the universe of force affected the popular imagination in America. The range of Spencer's influence was unprecedented in American culture, and the content of his ideas and the style of his philosophical approach colored the thinking of many Americans for many decades after he was "discovered" in the 1860s.[50] As early as the early 1860s the Spencerian ranks included such culturally influential people as the Reverend Henry Ward Beecher, George Ripley (who had organized the Brook Farm experiment), Ephraim Whitman Gurney (a Harvard professor and later Dean of Faculty), George Litch Roberts (a Boston patent lawyer), Reverend William Rounseville Alger (a Unitarian clergyman and author of theological works), John W. Draper (the author of *The History of the*

Intellectual Development of Europe), Daniel Appleton and his son (partners of the Appleton publishing house), and Manton Marble (editor-owner of *The New York World*).[51] And in time, with the impetus of such advocacy, Spencerianism spread into every important area of American cultural life. It was taught in a number of universities, expounded in public lectures, preached from pulpits, and written about in books, magazines, journals, and newspapers in the last third of the nineteenth century.

Even among nonsupporters of Spencer we can see a measure of his influence in the recognition he frequently received in contemporary letters, memoirs, and studies, acknowledgments like that of Justice Oliver Wendell Holmes, who wrote in 1895 (in a letter to the wife of Sir Frederick Pollock),

> He is dull. He writes an ugly uncharming style, his ideals are those of a lower middle class British Philistine. And yet after all abatements I doubt if any writer of English except Darwin has done so much to affect our whole way of thinking about the universe.[52]

John Dewey is another who gave Spencer a grudgingly respectful tribute:

> He presents the achieved culmination of ideas already in overt and external operation. He winds up an old dispensation. Here is the secret of his astounding success, of the way in which he has so thoroughly imposed his idea that even non-Spencerians must talk in his terms and adjust their problems to his statements.[53]

Among the outright supporters of Spencer, his great influence is apparent in the profuse and grandiose tributes. For example, a Fiske essay cites Spencer's system as "that system of philosophy which marks the highest point to which the progressive intelligence of mankind has yet attained."[54] Editor-publisher Henry Holt's book of reminiscences cites Spencer for his contributions in unifying the great scientific laws and bringing the categories of evolution into popular consciousness, and estimates his importance as equal to or greater than Aristotle's.[55] Reverend Beecher ranked him as the "ablest thinker of them all, and the ablest man that has appeared for centuries,"[56] and Daniel Greenleaf Thompson, in a published lecture on Spencer states that "without disparaging these really worthy Greeks [Plato and Aristotle] who would be considered good philosophers, as philosophers go in our time, and who, it must be remembered, were far better than they used to run in earlier days, I do not hesitate to aver that the subject of this sketch, for instance, is much greater than either of them."[57]

The daring note of amateur profundity in Thompson's statement is typical of a great deal of Spencer's American support, as the Synthetic Philosophy penetrated to levels of the culture never before significantly reached by abstract ideas. William James recognized this phenomenon and cited it as an important achievement by Spencer:

> Misprised by many specialists, who carp at his technical imperfections, he has nevertheless enlarged the imagination, and set free the speculative mind of countless doctors, engineers, and lawyers, of many physicists and chemists, and of thoughtful laymen generally. He is the philosopher whom those who have no other philosopher can appreciate.[58]

Just how large and diverse this group of "thoughtful laymen" was can be inferred from the list of subscribers to the banquet held in Spencer's honor on November 11, 1882, during what was to be his only visit to this country.[59] These are the people whose commitment or at least interest was great enough that they would put down their good money and then spend an entire evening listening to speeches by and about a philosopher. Subscribers prominent in business and finance included Andrew Carnegie, Cyrus W. Field (merchant and capitalist), Chauncey Depew (lawyer for the New York Central Railroad and later its president), Morris K. Jesup (banker), Rowland G. Hazard (wool manufacturer), Abram S. Hewitt (iron manufacturer and congressman, later mayor of New York), and Matthias N. Forney (inventor and designer of locomotives). Those prominent in law and politics included (as well as Hewitt), Carl Schurz, Elihu Root (corporation lawyer and later Secretary of War), Benjamin H. Bristow (later Treasury Secretary), John Bigelow (minister to France, editor of the works of Benjamin Franklin), William M. Evarts (Secretary of State), Andrew H. Green (New York City Park Commissioner and Comptroller), and William D. ("Pig Iron") Kelley (protectionist Philadelphia congressman). The press was represented by New York editors Horace White (*Evening Post*), Parke Godwin (*Commercial Advertiser*), William H. Hurlbert (*World*), Charles A. Dana (*Sun*), and reporter Junius Henri Browne (*Tribune*); magazine journalism by Edwin L. Godkin (*Nation*), and William C. Church (*Galaxy; Army and Navy Journal*); and publishing by several of the Appletons, Henry Holt, and D. Van Nostrand. Clergyman subscribers included, in addition to Henry Ward Beecher, Minot J. Savage (Unitarian), Charlton T. Lewis (Methodist), Lyman Abbot (Unitarian and later Congregational), and R. Heber Newton (Episcopal). Representing the sciences, Henry Draper (astronomy), Samuel H. Scudder (entomology), Othniel Marsh (paleontology), and D. Cady Eaton (botany) were among those enrolled, as well as members of the medical profession Fessenden N. Otis (physician and medical text writer), William T. Lusk (obstetrician), Edward C. Spitzka (neurologist, psychiatrist), Abraham Jacobi (pediatrician), William A. Hammond (neurologist, Surgeon-General), and Morris H. Henry (physician-surgeon and founder of *The American Journal of Syphilography and Dermatology*). Sociologists William G. Sumner and

Lester Ward, economist Henry W. Farnam, and educators Norman A. Calkins (author on primary school teaching), and Vincenzo Botta (professor of Italian at New York University) also subscribed, as did representatives of the arts E. C. Stedman (poet), Calvert Vaux (landscape architect), Richard M. Hunt (architect), John Q. A. Ward (sculptor), and Albert Bierstadt (painter). The list seems like a cross-section of prominent Americans of 1882; behind them the less prominent "thoughtful laymen" of Spencerianism must have been legion.

It is not that Spencer was a dramatic or entertaining speaker; indeed Youmans (with every inclination to be charitable) reports that "his speech, which was delivered in low, conversational tone, and without gesture, betrayed his extreme physical weakness."[60] Spencer himself felt it was flat and uninspiring, and judging from the printed text it was. Spencer lectured the Americans on their national excesses of ambition and overwork, pointing out that civilization and the Anglo-Saxon heritage were imperiled here by a way of life in which "the satisfaction of getting on, devours nearly all other satisfactions." The drawing power had to be in the Synthetic Philosophy and the fame of its author rather than in his person or his style. It was likewise with his books—very long, exhaustingly detailed tomes with a flat and uninspiring style, yet an amazing total American circulation of around a half million.

The Spencer boom coincided with a vast explosion of knowledge in popular American culture, notably scientific and pseudoscientific knowledge. The experience portrayed in London's *Martin Eden* and Dreiser's *The "Genius"*—of an uneducated or self-educated man discovering a science-oriented cosmic philosophy and understanding his life and integrating his mind on its unfailing basis—constituted a familiar and emotionally potent image in this age. A great number of Americans were awakening intellectually, stirred by the controversies over evolution, over new social ideas and problems, and over the relationship of science and religion; and when they awoke, the first and most imposing system of ideas they saw was the Synthetic Philosophy or something very like it.

The nation was undergoing an educational and cultural revolution, and many of the institutions and organizations that substantially contributed to it were the ones that advocated and publicized the universe of force. The most prominent of them in the publishing field were the Appleton publishing company (of which more will be said later), *The New York World*, and *Arena* magazine. Manton Marble's editing of the *World* provided, as early as the late sixties, a wide popular forum for the "new" Spencerian views, which Marble himself shared and willingly spread. *Arena*, especially under B. O. Flower's editorship in the early nineties, consistently attempted to establish a broadly favorable attitude toward the "new" knowledge,[61] and to use universe-of-force categories in a number of varied popular topics of the day ranging from science itself to "spiritual evolution" and even occultism. *Arena* was also notable for its nationwide organization of study clubs.[62]

Among numerous lecture-and-discussion groups, the Brooklyn Ethical Association was outstanding in the energy and dedication of its educational effort and in its inclination toward Spencerianism and the universe of force. Its watchword was "Evolution," and its tone was pedagogic, almost reverent, as is shown in the introduction to its *Evolution: Popular Lectures and Discussions*:

> Evolution: the word is in every mouth. . . . Even in its biological aspects, the doctrine of Evolution is seen to touch the greatest problems of religion and philosophy—of origin and destiny. . . . Evolution, reaching backward takes hold upon the great cosmic problems of the birth and growth of worlds, the nature of Matter and Spirit, the relation of the phenomenal Universe to its efficient Cause. Reaching forward, it touches and illuminates the pressing problems of ethics and sociology, offering to the careful student wise instruction for his guidance in all the practical affairs of life.
>
> Evolution, it is said, is not a philosophy, it is not a religion—"it is only a method." But it is a *universal* method; the discovery and formulation of its law as applied to all the processes of organic, social and intellectual development, constituted the widest generalization of science.

The numerous BEA lecturers in the late eighties and nineties took a popularizing approach and followed, according to their lights, their topic of evolution into myriads of connections—scientific, religious, and even artistic. Most of the lecturers were not notable people in the history of American thought or letters—the likes of Lewis George Janes, Sylvan Drey, Daniel Greenleaf Thompson, and John W. Chadwick were the principal contributors—but occasionally a Cope or a Fiske would offer a contribution. The impact of this organization was immeasurably increased when it decided to publish its lectures in inexpensive form both singly and in collections. Even Herbert Spencer himself saw the advantages of that scheme in spreading the evolutionary force gospel, and he wrote the Association in commendation that it was

> gratifying to me both on personal and on public grounds. The spread of the doctrine of Evolution, first of all in its limited acceptation and now in its wider acceptation, is alike surprising and encouraging; and doubtless the movement now to be initiated by the lectures and essays set forth in your programme will greatly accelerate its progress—especially if full reports of your proceedings can be circulated in a cheap printed form. The mode of presentation described seems to me admirably adapted for popularizing evolution views, and it will, I think, be a great pity if the effect of such a presentation should be limited to a few listeners in Brooklyn.[63]

In addition to such efforts as the BEA's, two individual author-lecturers deserve singling out in this account for functioning in effect as one-man promotional institutions for the universe of force. The first is John Fiske himself, who through tireless lecturing and voluminous writing—witness, for example, the pieces collected in his *Darwinism and Other Essays* (1888), *Excursions of an Evolutionist* (1889), and *A Century of Science and Other Essays* (1899)— became a leading educator of the American public in the new views. The second was Edward Livingston Youmans, a principal organizer of the 1882 Spencer banquet (and editor of its published proceedings), who also had been the editor and introducer of the crucial 1864 collection of scientific essays by Helmholtz, Grove, Mayer, and others, *The Correlation and Conservation of the Forces*, the book which, if we can judge by the tone of its introduction, was ostensibly calculated to become the bible of the universe of force. There is a great deal more to the story of Youmans's complex and influential activities on behalf of the universe of force, however; he had great energy and great promotional ability (though not a profound or original mind), and at times in viewing his career we may well detect the zeal of the philosophical convert shading off into the ambitiousness of the business promoter.

It all seems to have begun in 1861 when Youmans influenced the Appletons to publish Spencer's *Education*. According to Grant Overton's account, "Youmans fairly bounded into the President's office one day with the news that he had discovered a great philosopher." [64] Youmans had not been officially connected with Appleton's but from this point on he became their agent in dealing with Herbert Spencer, contracting the *Education* and negotiating the publication of each of the philosopher's subsequent works as he brought them to completion. Appleton's was extremely scrupulous in paying royalties, even in the absence of an international copyright agreement, and, as Spencer's American sales in time considerably outran his English sales, it was undoubtedly the Appleton connection that kept him solvent. At one point in 1865 when Spencer's perennial lack of funds threatened to terminate his work on the Synthetic Philosophy, Youmans personally helped raise $7,000 to keep him going. [65] Youmans's contribution to the universe of force thus went beyond mere advocacy: acting as personal friend and financial adviser to Spencer and as publisher's representative and inside consultant to Appleton's he, in a way, really enabled it to be formulated.

His advocacy must not be underestimated, however. From the sixties onward he lectured on Spencer, reviewed his works, and recommended the Synthetic Philosophy in every context he could. He also wrote and edited other works pertaining not just to Spencer but to the universe of force and its societal and cultural extensions. The aforementioned *The Correlation and Conservation of the Forces* is one important example, and another is his *The Culture*

Demanded by Modern Life (1867), in which he collected essays by Tyndall, Huxley, and others and put them in the context of an educational imperative to modern man to understand and apply the generalizations of science.

Throughout his campaign to win acceptance for the universe of force, Youmans thus seems to have worked not only to get the "new" views expressed in the public forum but also to get them reviewed, referred to, popularized, and cross-referenced. As an important part of this campaign he persuaded Appleton's to found *Appleton's Journal* in 1867, intended as a popular magazine focusing on Spencer, Darwin, and the new science and philosophy in general. Not very successful, the *Journal* was followed in 1872 by the Youmans-edited *Popular Science Monthly*, about which Richard Hofstadter has pointed out,

> The monthly was surprisingly well received, considering the difficulty of some of its subject matter, and soon sold eleven thousand copies a month. There, next to more sensational sketches designed to satisfy common curiosity—"Great Fires and Rainstorms," "Hypnotism in Animals," "The Genesis of Superstition," "Earthquakes and their Causes"—were learned articles on the philosophy of science, laudatory sketches of leading scientists, discussions of the reconciliation between science and religion, polemics against obscurantism, and reports on the latest progress of research. Edited on a high level and followed faithfully by a substantial body of readers, the monthly was the signal journalistic accomplishment of the scientific revival.[66]

It was also a key instrument in the propagation of the universe of force and the promotion of the Appletons' books on the subject.

More grandiose still, Youmans persuaded Daniel Appleton to begin in 1871 the "International Scientific Library" which would, under his editorship, "contain the best work of every important scientific thinker of the day in all countries."[67] This meant that Youmans dealt with the likes of Darwin, Tyndall, Buckle, Huxley, and Haeckel and produced a series of fifty volumes, each published simultaneously in America and Europe. The series was a resounding success. A landmark in the popularization of science, it gave added publicity and authenticity to universe-of-force ideas; and not-so-incidentally the Youmans-Appleton team had attained a hegemony in an important new area of publishing. As Henry Holt, a rival publisher, would later ruefully recall of Appleton's, "Youmans became the scientific adviser of the house, and brought it so many of the important books on the great questions of that epoch, as to place the house first on those subjects, and the rest nowhere."[68] Although the widespread promulgation of the universe of force was essentially sincere and spontaneous (there can be no doubt that Youmans was a true believer), we still might have an uneasy sense of foreboding in view of the fact that popular

America's great conversion to a "scientific" philosophy coincided with a promotional campaign of considerable scope and sophistication.

As one might expect, the popularizations of the new knowledge and the universe of force varied extremely in quality. A number of them—notably many of the contributions to The International Scientific Library, to the *Popular Science Monthly*, and to *The Correlation and Conservation of the Forces*—were cogent and informative; a greater proportion of the popularizations, however, were written by inexperienced thinkers and poor writers whose enthusiasm was their only saving grace. Many of the *Arena* articles and many sermons and Brooklyn Ethical Association addresses are of this quality. At their worst, such writings produced sheer misinformation and superstition out of the universe of force. For example, A. B. Richmond, in his *Arena* article "Is There a To-Morrow for the Human Race?"[69] first reconstructs human history out of a misunderstanding of Fiske or Spencer—

> the first lesson taught to primal man by the senses was: that the physical universe was composed of matter and force, and dull indeed would have been the intellect that could not recognize this fact in every moving thing. Centuries passed and it became an established scientific fact that there was an intelligence in this force that directed the movements of atoms in accordance with formulated designs

—then he uses this amazing universe-of-force construction in conjunction with several accounts of mystic experiences he has had with mediums to conclude that there is indeed an occult intelligence behind the universe and that the human race can indeed look forward to an afterlife, a "to-morrow." Popularizers frequently associated the universe of force with spiritualism; usually the treatments were less bizarre than Richmond's, although no less anxious to reassure. In this vein Lewis Janes writes, in a Brooklyn Ethical Association contribution, "The Scope and Principles of Evolution Philosophy,"

> to speak of "the philosophy of Evolution," . . . is not without warrant. We may well term it, with John Fiske, a "cosmic philosophy," since it is universal in its scope and application; or with Mr. Spencer, a "synthetic philosophy," since, like the founder of Christianity, it comes not to destroy but to fulfill, discovering the mesh of truth which resides in each antagonistic system, and by a new and deeper synthesis combining them into a harmonious and perfect whole.[70]

And in such debauches of reconciliation of science and religion not only was the arrival of the Synthetic Philosophy regarded as a kind of Second Coming, but evolutionary force itself tended to be deified. John W. Chadwick, another of the lights in the BEA, in attempting to explain the new scientific philosophy's sense of teleology, rhapsodizes,

> It is a teleology of dynamics, of tendencies. It is immanent in the universe as its omnipresent thought and life, not external to it as that of a mechanical Creator, working in material alien to or other than himself. Here is no aimless drift, destructive of all fates and aspirations of religion, but a tide that sweeps forever through the universe of matter and of man in the direction of the True, the Beautiful, the Good.[71]

And in the mode of rhapsody (which has always had a peculiar conjunction with the universe of force), one of the most popularly moving statements was Youmans's reverential tribute to the law of the conservation of force in his introduction to *The Correlation and Conservation of Forces*:

> The law characterized by Faraday as the highest in physical science which our faculties permit us to perceive, has a far more extended sway; it might well have been proclaimed the highest law of *all* science—the most far-reaching principle that adventuring reason has discovered in the universe. Its stupendous reach spans all order of existence. Not only does it govern the movements of the heavenly bodies, but it presides over the genesis of the constellations; not only does it control those radiant floods of power which fill the eternal spaces, bathing, warming, illumining and vivifying our planet, but it rules the actions and relations of men, and regulates the march of terrestrial affairs. Nor is its domain limited to physical phenomena; it prevails equally in the world of mind, controlling all the faculties and processes of thought and feeling. The star-suns of the remoter galaxies dart their radiations across the universe; and although the distances are so profound that hundreds of centuries may have been required to traverse them, the impulses of force enter the eye, and impressing an atomic change upon the nerve, give origin to the sense of sight. Star and nerve-tissue are parts of the same system—stellar and nervous forces are correlated. Nay more; sensation awakens thought and kindles emotion, so that this wondrous dynamic chain binds into living unity the realms of matter and mind through measureless amplitudes of space and time.
>
> And if these high realities are but faint and fitful glimpses which science has obtained in the dim dawn of discovery, what must be the glories of the coming day? If indeed they are but "pebbles" gathered from the shores of the great ocean of truth, what are the mysteries still hidden in the bosom of the mighty unexplored? And how far transcending all stretch of thought that Unknown and Infinite Cause of all to which the human spirit turns evermore in solemn and mysterious worship![72]

TO COMPLETE the picture, we need to consider the effect of Spencerianism and the universe of force on social thought in America, although many of its aspects have been very carefully studied by other scholars in other contexts. I do not plan to repeat their findings here, but to focus on those aspects related to the Americanization of the universe of force, referring the reader to the much fuller treatment presented in such standard studies of the period as Richard Hofstadter's *Social Darwinism in American Thought*, Stow Persons' *Evolutionary Thought in America*, Henry Steele Commager's *The American Mind*, and Merle Curti's *The Growth of American Thought*.

In America, Spencer's influence on sociology was very great in the late nineteenth century. Simon Patten (*The Theory of Social Forces*, 1896) and Franklin Giddings (*The Elements of Sociology*, 1898) worked this vein, and William Graham Sumner, the author of *Folkways* (1906) and probably America's most prominent sociologist, was an outspoken and somewhat individualistic Spencerian. Sumner viewed social change (such as the development and alteration of folkways) as deterministic and nonvolitional, a kind of natural selection of social patterns; he accepted Spencer's mechanistic and evolutionary concepts of society, and like Fiske he made a point of stressing the futility of man's attempt to reform society—"The Absurd Effort to Make the World Over" is the title and the burden of an essay he published in 1894. He rejected, however, the belief of both Fiske and Spencer that social evolution moved ineluctably in the direction of the greatest human happiness. In recognizing the determinism and rejecting the wishful and gratuitous optimism of the Spencerian system, Sumner came closer than most others to understanding its true implications, and produced in the process a much less appealing social philosophy.

On the level of popular discussion, however, much American social thought of the eighties and nineties was motivated by a desire to justify the socioeconomic arrangements within the system and to sanction—as "Progress"—the particular course which change was taking. Ideas of Spencer, Fiske, and Sumner were easily adapted to this use. The same first principles which gave Spencer and Fiske their reassurance that universal evolution naturally produced increasingly higher levels of moral good, and the same concepts by which Sumner maintained that human evolution was ineluctable and reform either futile or counterproductive were ideas that could easily be turned to justifying any sort of competitive or monopolistic capitalism, any measure of exploitation or imperialism, any level of social inequality. Personal wealth, uninhibited individualism, strength and even racial superiority were glorified in the popular discussion of social issues. Scientific and up-to-date philosophy seemed to indicate that it was both inevitable and morally right that the rich and powerful lead America and that America lead the world. The ideas of Spencer, Fiske, and Sumner were thus very appealing to the American financiers and industrial magnates, men such as Andrew Carnegie, Cyrus Field, Chauncey Depew, Morris Jesup, and Abram Hewitt, those patrons of the Spencer testimonial banquet, who could feel themselves personally and morally vindicated in the Synthetic and Cosmic Philosophies.[73] Frequently the businessman's discovery of a philosophy of self-justification struck him with the force of a religious inspiration, as exemplified by publisher Henry Holt who said that when he read *First Principles* "my eyes opened to a new heaven and a new earth," and by Carnegie for whom, after reading Darwin and Spencer, "light came in a flood and all was clear."[74] In the popular imagination, the universe of force thus in several ways became part of the intellectual superstructure of the romance of American capitalism.

THE UNIVERSE-OF-FORCE views, widely available in American culture in the latter nineteenth century, conceived in various forms and addressed to audiences of various levels of education and intellectuality, had, philosophically, something for nearly everybody. In the last analysis their popularity is attributable to the fact that they could be so many things for so many people. The Americanized universe of force could present and unify all the findings of modern science, explain the workings of the universe in terms of simple commonsense causality, rationalize progress (including industrial exploitation and international imperialism), and offer a scientifically based ethical and social philosophy. It could also offer the reassurance that a more-or-less unknowable God was behind all force and processes, mechanical, human, or cosmic, and that man and his civilization were the ultimate achievements of the evolution of the universe. Whatever the particular values a person might derive from an Americanized universe-of-force philosophy, he could have the assurance that his beliefs were based upon absolute scientific bedrock and were in accord with the highest religious truths as well.

Virtually lost in the tide of reassurance and reconciliation in the seventies and eighties were, first of all, any sense that this was a deterministic mechanical system, and secondly, any recognition that it lacked a feature vital to most prior American belief-systems, an emphasis on moral freedom and individual responsibility. In time the real implications of the belief in a universe of force became more evident and far more burdensome. The widespread pessimism of the next generation was, as Vernon Parrington has pointed out, a consequence of the crumbling of the benevolent determinism of the Synthetic Philosophy.[75] As we are about to see, a number of creative writers of the period struggled desperately with the problem of the individual in this universe of large-scale evolutionary forces—was he free and potentially heroic or a mere victim of forces beyond his control? Did his actions, his fate, even matter?

4. HENRY ADAMS: INTIMATIONS OF THE ABSURD IN THE UNIVERSE OF FORCE

> The game was singularly simple, ... but never played out successfully by any artist however great.
>
> Henry Adams to Barrett Wendell, March 12, 1909

In turning now to a consideration of the specific relationships of American literature and the universe of force, we begin with Henry Adams (1838–1918) who, of all the literary artists to become involved with universe-of-force concepts, was undoubtedly the most original, the most self-aware, and the most esthetically sophisticated. He was also the most competent intellectually: a highly educated, highly literate, complex man of many interests, he kept himself abreast of contemporary culture, especially in science, philosophy, politics, and art, in a way that few American writers of any period have been able and willing to do. The combination of his literary originality and his complex intellectuality make him a fascinating though a difficult figure to study in regard to the universe of force.

Adams was always interested in the large, abstract philosophical questions about the nature and direction of human life. He focused most of his intellectual attention upon building a world view, but judging from his works and his correspondence he never got it satisfactorily and permanently built. His later works are increasingly dark in tone (as is the case with his contemporary, Mark Twain), and an increasing sense in them of the lack of acceptable answers is accompanied by an increasing semiantagonistic preoccupation with science and "force" and by increasingly daring experiments with intellectual hypothesis, metaphor, and literary form. His quest was admittedly a failure, although a stimulating and challenging endeavor.

His exposure to the concept of the universe of force came at the highest intellectual levels. No reader of Sunday supplements or attender of Chautauqua lectures, he learned scientific philosophy from the scientists and philosophers themselves—he read Kelvin, Faraday, Darwin, Spencer, Ostwald, Willard Gibbs, Karl Pearson, Henri Poincaré, and J. B. Stallo; he knew Lyell, Agassiz, Clarence King, and belonged to the Metaphysical Club with Chauncey

Wright and John Fiske. His relationship to the universe of force was as diverse as his exposure to it: no mere disciple of Spencer, no yearner after simple metaphysical reassurance and having, finally, little faith in rationality and human progress, he challenged it as much as he espoused it. In fact, as we shall see, given the nature of his mind and art it is often difficult to determine what Adams's espousal of an idea consists of or signifies.

The very complexity of the tone of Adams's own writings, their rhetoric of indeterminacy, may well to some extent follow from the dilemma inherent in late nineteenth-century science, for if one turned to the study of that science for the answers to very large and troubling metaphysical questions, one was likely to get either universal determinism or epistemological relativity—the world was a locked mechanical system or it was ultimately unknowable and could be visualized only in terms of hypothetical phantoms—and neither of these two conceptions was at all satisfying or reassuring to a man of metaphysical imagination. As a thinker and writer Adams was increasingly haunted by them both, however; and further, as the twentieth-century world itself seemed to him to be going to hell in almost all other respects as well, tones of pessimism, irony, and absurdism engulfed his works. What saved his intellectual vision, where indeed it was saved, was his art.

A historian (and a distinguished one) early in his writing career, he viewed reality from the omniscient, objective perspective of the conventional historian, flirting with "scientific history" (such as Fiske had a great hankering for) in his History of the United States during the Administrations of Jefferson and Madison *(1884–1891), and even directly forecasting it in* The Tendency of History *(1894) and* A Letter to American Teachers of History *(1910). To his twin literary masterpieces, however—*Mont-Saint-Michel and Chartres *(1904) and* The Education of Henry Adams *(1907)—he brought none of the posited omniscience of the scientific historian, but brought, rather, a sense of the relativity, the impermanence, and the fallibility of human perspective. This sense, created by his use of limited, subjective, fallible narrators, gives these books both the candor of eyewitness testimony and the added complexity of insight into the cultural, psychological, and emotional aspects of human perception itself. Thus, out of the very materials of his metaphysical uncertainty Adams built works of enduring value. Additionally, through the imaginative use of language he was able to take what were deterministically conceived of as the fundamental entities of the universe—forces—and from them create complex cultural symbols such as the Virgin and the dynamo, comprising man's values and yearnings as well as the mechanical evolution of civilization. And furthermore, with his sophisticated grasp of literary form, he was able to use force's laws, states, and correlations as structural patterns for works founded on the discovery of or the contention with the universe of force. Far from having his* *artistic imagination dominated or stymied by the universe of force, hopelessly deterministic or relativistic though he knew that conception to be, Adams was able to use its constituents in the construction of a literary vision far richer and more lasting than any of its scientific or philosophical originals.*

FEW MEN of his time had a range of background and experiences comparable to Henry Adams's. Grandson and great-grandson of presidents of the United States, independently wealthy and educated at Harvard (1854–1858) and in Europe (1858–1860), he served in the sixties as private secretary to his father who was a congressman and subsequently minister to Great Britain, as foreign correspondent to several newspapers, and as freelance writer on political and historical subjects. In the 1870s he taught medieval history at Harvard, edited the *North American Review*, and continued to write on history and current affairs, publishing a biography of Albert Gallatin in 1879. In the eighties he wrote two novels, *Democracy* and *Esther* (for anonymous publication), a biography of John Randolph, and the *History of the United States during the Administrations of Jefferson and Madison*—his major historical work and a landmark in American history writing. The suicide of his wife in 1885 was a blow he recovered from with much difficulty. He traveled a good deal in the nineties, most notably to Japan and the South Seas, gathered material for a history of Tahiti (*Memoirs of Arii Taimai*, 1902), and presided over the American Historical Association, usually from a distance. Among his personal friends were a number of the most interesting and accomplished people of the day, such as statesman John Hay and artist Oliver LaFarge. At the turn of the century, in *Mont-Saint-Michel and Chartres* (1904) and *The Education of Henry Adams* (1907), he experimented with a new literary form, an original type midway between historical and imaginative writing. Later, in the last stages of his life and authorship he wrote a biography (1911) of his recently deceased friend, George Cabot Lodge, and a pair of bleak essays which problematically applied scientific theory directly to the study of history, and he worked desultorily at revising *The Education*. Then too, throughout this diverse career Adams attached himself to a variety of other concerns from the esthetics of stained glass to the family lives of his many friends. His was a full and cosmopolitan and very productive life.

By the time that he was searching the scientific literature of the late nineteenth century for the answers to his largest questions, Adams had already been an intellectual maverick for a good while. His needs were nothing unusual, but his dissatisfaction with what had satisfied other men was. He wanted "unity" and he wanted "truth"—knowledge that was both metaphysical and absolute—and, disillusioned with traditional philosophy and theology, he looked for it in what seemed to be the most likely area, modern science. His was a temperamental need but a complex one. Like Fiske he sought some kind of religion or reasonable surrogate which was specifically compatible with the modern scientific world; unlike him, Adams would not accept any vast and easy semantic accommodations.

When he plunged into scientific study it was with a keen eye for contradictions and complications; searching for unity he courted multiplicity, probably relishing the debunkers and bafflers among scientific writers more than the synthesizers and reconcilers. His correspondence, his library and his marginalia indicate that he read them all, however. His library, now in the Massachusetts Historical Society, includes his annotated copies of such scientific texts and popularizations as Despaux's *Cause des Énergies Attractives*, Findlay's *The Phase Rule and its Applications*, Hertz's *Electric Waves*, Houston and Kennelly's *Magnetism*, Lodge's *Modern Views of Electricity* and *Electrons . . .*, Lucien Poincaré's *La Physique Moderne, son Évolution*, Balfour Stewart's *The Conservation of Energy* (in French), and Trowbridge's *What Is Electricity?* It also includes works of scientific philosophy, such as *The Positive Philosophy of Auguste Comte*, Hans Dreisch's *The Science and Philosophy of the Organism*, Ernest Haeckel's *The Riddle of the Universe* (in French), Spencer's *First Principles* and Alfred Wallace's *Man's Place in the Universe*; and antithetically, it also included works analyzing and criticizing science and scientific philosophy such as Karl Pearson's *The Grammar of Science*, Henri Poincaré's *La Science et l'Hypothèse* and the French translation of J. B. Stallo's *Concepts and Theories of Modern Physics*. It is an interesting conglomeration, and Adams's relationship to it is at best ambivalent. Down through the years his marginalia have two characteristic themes: a querulous bafflement in the face of science's refusal to claim universality and finality for its theories, and, almost conversely, an emphatic delight (almost as if he were vindicated) in any sign of uncertainty, confusion, or contradiction, admitted or manifested by a scientific writer. Science may have been the most likely place to find Truth in the late nineteenth century, but what Adams found was ultimately unsatisfying, unreassuring, uncertain, or unclear.

His immersion in the morass of scientific Truth was gradual, and the evidences of universe-of-force thinking in his early writings are sporadic and minor, but these first phases of his education clearly set the stage for his later struggle with science and force. In the early period of Adams's authorship, the period from the early 1860s when he was serving as secretary to his father to the late eighties when he was publishing his *History of the United States . . .*, he was at his most optimistic as a thinker and writer. He was, however, already deeply attracted to scientific theory and method (and their application to social and historical questions), and he already tended to think about universal process in terms of mechanistic determinism. That he was acquainted with Spencer's ideas is indisputable. As Adams's biographer Ernest Samuels shows, Spencer was much talked about in the London intellectual circles in which Adams moved in the sixties, and Adams in a review written in the early seventies acknowledged Spencer as being of comparable stature to Darwin.[1] Additionally, Adams's library contained an 1882 edition of *First Principles*, and his 1910 *Letter to American Teachers of History* is by his own admission at least partly intended to refute Spencer.[2] The men whom Samuels cites as being the strongest early influences on him, Comte, Buckle, and Spencer, all tended to move him in the direction of radical new ways of thinking by stressing the millenial prospects of man's increasing scientific knowledge, the universal applicability of scientific method, and the view that physical laws are basic to all phenomena. Of course the emotional tenor of the writings of these three thinkers is basically optimistic, in keeping with the vision of progress which was characteristic of the mid-nineteenth century and the prospects of the complete scientific description of the universe which had been enthusiastically anticipated by Joule, Helmholtz, and Laplace. But incipient in this mechanistically based scientific determinism was the pessimism of the end of the century, and nobody reflects the working-out of its implications better than Henry Adams. In a letter to his brother Charles written during the Civil War he stated:

> The truth is, everything in this universe has its regular waves and tides. Electricity, sound, the wind, and I believe every part of organic nature will be brought some day within this law. But my philosophy teaches me, and I firmly believe it, that the laws which govern animated beings will be ultimately found to be at bottom the same with those which rule inanimate nature, and as I entertain a profound conviction of the littleness of our kind, and of the curious enormity of creation, I am quite ready to receive with pleasure any basis for a systematic conception of it all. Thus (to explain this rather alarming digression) as sort of experimentalist, I look for regular tides in the affairs of man, and of course, in our own affairs. In every progression, somehow or other, the nations move by the same process which has never been explained but is evident in the ocean and the air. On this theory I should expect at about this time, a turn which would carry us backward.[3]

From early statements like this we can see that not only was Adams fairly close to a Helmholtzian or a Spencerian position in the sixties, but (as shall be seen in what follows) the basic pattern of his thought changed very little in the next fifty years, despite his efforts to change it and despite an enormous shift in tone which made the little touch of cyclical pessimism at the end of this quotation into the governing spirit of all his thought.

The first scientific-philosophical battlegrounds on which Adams tested his developing beliefs were biology and geology; the occasion was his writing of a review of a newly revised edition of Lyell's *Principles of Geology* in 1868. Darwin's theory of evolution and Lyell's uniformitarian theory of geologic formation themselves came as ambitious attempts to understand, in terms of scientific causality rather than of revealed theology, how the world came to be the way it is; both asserted the slow and systematic operation of scientific law. Adams was not at all unwilling to forego traditional, scripture-oriented thought on these matters, favoring greatly the scientific approach combined with the vast generalization. (One of Comte's ideas that most appealed to Adams was that scientists should try to generalize more widely lest they stick at the level of specifics and never see high-level laws.)[4] But although Adams was inclined toward Darwinism and Lyellism in the 1860s, he later turned away from them because he felt more convinced by a rival scientific theory— the catastrophism of his friend Clarence King and his former Harvard professor Agassiz.[5] Adams's ultimate rejection of both evolution and uniformitarian geology counted strongly in his ultimate attitude toward modern science and supplied an important theme in *The Education*.

As Adams was, in the seventies, serving as Assistant Professor of Medieval and American History at Harvard, and becoming a writer of history too, his scientific and philosophic ideas couldn't help but influence his work as historian. He had the theory and practice of Buckle to encourage him to put the study of history on a scientific basis and to discover the human equivalent of the universal laws of physical phenomena, and there are inklings of this "scientific history" in his early work, although they are as yet undeveloped. The form this tendency would later take was, as William Jordy shows, clearly foreshadowed in 1876 in a review in the *North American Review* of Holst's *Constitutional and Political History of the United States*:

> The people of the United States, as they pass further and further from the vital struggles which characterize this first period of their national history, are quite right in believing that, above all the details of human weakness and corruption, there will appear in more and more symmetry the real majesty and force of the national movement. If the historian will only consent to shut his eyes for a moment to the microscopic analysis of personal motives and idiosyncrasies, he cannot but become conscious of a silent pulsation that commands his respect, a steady movement that resembles in its mode of operation the mechanical operation of Nature herself.[6]

This attention to the "silent pulsation that commands respect" is an element that becomes increasingly important as Adams's career as a writer develops, but it was not yet a dominant element when he was writing *The History of the United States during the Administrations of Jefferson and Madison* (1884–1891).

The scholar searching for the conceptual roots of Adams's literary master-pieces finds something but not a great deal here. A number of scholars have gone the limit in trying to view the *History* as a direct precursor of *The Education* in the expression of scientific philosophy, and in the process have made some very fertile suggestions about Adams's intellectual development, but in fairness to the *History* itself we must acknowledge, as George Hochfield, Peter Shaw, and Richard C. Vitzthum have pointed out,[7] that its philosophical basis is moral rather than mechanistic, and that elements of "scientific" explanation in its pages are minor compared to more traditional modes of historical explanation.

There is no question that a kind of pseudoscientific force determinism was in his mind when he wrote the *History*, however, and in his correspondence with his friends, free to give rein to speculations which were unsupportable in the traditional discipline of history, he could indulge this inclination: of Jefferson, Madison, and Monroe, whom he had treated in his biography of Gallatin, he confided in 1883,

> I am at times almost sorry that I ever undertook to write their history, for they appear like mere grasshoppers kicking and gesticulating on the middle of the Mississippi River. . . . They were carried along on a stream which floated them, after a fashion, without much regard to themselves. . . .
>
> My own conclusion is that history is simply social development along the lines of weakest resistance, and that in most cases the line of weakest resistance is found as unconsciously by society as by water.[8]

In the *History* itself scholars have found various elements of metaphor, intimation, and theme which grow out of Adams's scientific interests at the time, and which are relatable (variously, I would submit) to the quest that much later his protagonist in *The Education* centers upon, the quest for a dynamic theory of history. In *Henry Adams: Scientific Historian* William Jordy follows the traces in the *History* of a scientific dynamic, finding them in frequent metaphors of power or force, in the moderate shift in emphasis away from the efficacy of individual characters and toward the larger evolution of institutions, and in the grand unifying themes of rising nationalism and democracy. J. C. Levenson too sees the larger design of the *History* primarily in terms of historical generalizations like nationalism and claims that "although he let the word "physics" appear only once in the body of the text, social formulae framed in the vocabulary of science were already a part of his thinking equipment."[9] Ernest Samuels in *Henry Adams: The Middle Years* sees force dynamics as playing a far greater role in the *History*, maintaining that "the science of it is obviously the indispensable 'myth' of the whole literary structure"; he explains that "myth" thusly:

Adams was not explicit about the nature of the great undercurrent forces in American life, nor did he attempt to evaluate their components. . . . The very difficulty of scientific measurement continually threw him back upon a *mystique* of force, a hypostatized something that mysteriously united all phenomena, physical and psychic, into a cosmic machine. Such was the American trend toward nationalism, "the silent undercurrent which tended to grow in strength precisely as it encountered most resistance from events."

Samuels accounts for the deterministic philosophy that lay behind Adams's use of this "myth" as follows:

It is apparent from all the scientific allusions that pervade the *History* that he believed that there was one scientific hypothesis by which the data of history could be successfully organized, the evolutionary hypothesis of Herbert Spencer.[10]

At the opposite extreme of opinion, Vitzthum, although recognizing Adams's frequent use of metaphors from science, such as those "which oppose inertia or static mass to activity, motion and efficiency," insists that they

are no more prevalent in the *History* as a whole than those taken from other areas of human experience—for example the many figures based on breaking waves or blowing winds, on military combat, on biblical or classical mythology, or on the drama and especially on Shakespeare. Adams seems to show no special preference for scientific imagery. Like all the other kinds in the *History*, it serves a largely illustrative, rather than thematic, function.[11]

There is no question of the existence of the metaphors and thought patterns of a scientific determinism in the *History*; whatever the scholars' disagreements about their significance in that work, clearly they show, for our purposes, Adams learning to view the universe as a system of impersonal, deterministic forces.

As time passed Adams became increasingly fascinated with this cosmic level of speculation and its application to contemporary society and history. Its metaphors, in the period between the *History* and *Mont-Saint-Michel and Chartres*, recur frequently in his correspondence, especially to his younger brother Brooks: "To come home, merely to watch the blind forces at work, without even a pretence, on any side, of intelligent direction, or relation to a system, or a consciousness of an ultimate end, is the more trying because I see that the mess would be worse if the forces were intelligent."[12] In 1897, commenting on the course of civilization since the great depression of 1893, he states, stressing the metaphors of mechanics and the sense of blind determinism: "As far as I can see, the various forces are now fairly well defined. The disruption of '93 has definitely rearranged society, and we need not fret about new disturbances because we cannot any longer either increase or decrease the forces."[13] Looking back on his father's difficulties as Ambassador to Britain during the Civil War, a subject to which he returned in similar terms in *The Education*, he writes: "That we saved our skins in London was God's mercy, and the work of blind forces that no one understood or measured."[14] At times in the mid-nineties Adams shows an intimation of a more ambitious theory, resembling Spencerianism or some kind of allegorical application of the science of mechanics, but it remains for the time being only an intimation:

> My conclusion . . . is . . . that our so-called civilization has shown its movement, even at the centre, arrested. It has failed to concentrate further. Its next effort may succeed, but it is more likely to be one of disintegration, with Russia for the eccentric on one side and America on the other.[15]

Any thought of societal mechanism inevitably suggested to Adams coercive movement in some undesirable direction: "I have of late tended to see in it the compulsion which is to suppress still more the individual and to make society still more centralized and automatic."[16]

By the mid-1890s, then, force categories were in the front of Adams's mind. As yet he had only developed them in his correspondence, and even there only as a partly playful, partly serious kind of extended metaphor, but all the ingredients for a full-fledged theory were there: the metaphoric extension of the language of physics to social, historical, and even personal phenomena, the deterministic causal framework, and even a kind of teleological pessimism, a vision of the end and purpose of all the universe's travail. Had Adams trusted these categories and Stallo's anathema "the old metaphysical spirit" sufficiently, it would have been easy for him to articulate a system as much like Spencer's in scope and naiveté as it would be unlike it in tone. But Adams was not to take the step into absolutism; he was rather to dangle in ambiguity and irresolution, escaping the determinism inherent in his preconceptions only through doubt and irony. It was an unusual choice, given the age in which he lived, a pioneering example of how style could sustain one when ideas failed. His experience with this dilemma of metaphysical surety may well have been a determining factor in guiding him away from a career in the realms of Truth and toward one in the realm of art.*

* I find Vern Wagner's concept of "suspension," in *The Suspension of Henry Adams* (Wayne State Univ. Press, 1969), an interesting category for looking at Adams, and my conception (independently arrived at, by the way) is in some ways similar to his. In studying the interrelationships of Adams's ideas and his literary style, Wagner sees Adams as suspended in a state of inconclusion, using indeterminacy as the basis of a humorous literary style. It is an intriguing

In the mid-1890s, however, his main intellectual concern was still the field of history. The writing of history, as Adams then saw it, seemed destined to become scientific, and he used his position as president of the American Historical Association to try to alert his fellow historians to this tendency and to its vast and potentially dire social consequences. The occasion was the Association's 1894 meetings and the medium was *The Tendency of History*, a written address given *in absentia*. The approach he took was hard and uncompromising: "That the effort to make history a science may fail is possible, and perhaps probable; but that it should cease, unless for reasons that would cause all science to cease, is not within the range of experience." [17] Adams envisioned the same kind of "scientific history" that Fiske strove to produce, saying that already it was the dream of four out of five historians to "successfully apply Darwin's method to the facts of human history," and to "reduce all history under a law as clear as the laws which govern the material world." [18] Adams had no particular law to recommend—indeed except in an occasional chance phrase like the one in which he foresaw that the next fifty years would "*raise history to the rank of a science*" (my italics) he even expressed no value judgments whatever about the whole tendency.

Even without advocating scientific history it was possible to slip into its patterns, though, as Adams did in projecting the kind of social response the scientific historian might anticipate. "The world is made up of a few immense forces, each with an organization that corresponds with its strength," he asserted, specifying the church, the state, property, and labor as forces conceivably hostile to scientific history because they would undoubtedly be affected by it. In the very terms of his analysis, in the implicit paradigm of moving mechanical forces, Adams is adopting, however intentionally, the language and presuppositions of the scientific historian. Scientific history itself even becomes a kind of force in this representation, going against and affecting forces of undoubtedly greater strength. Still Adams withheld giving explicit credence to scientific history and its universe of force.

That Adams was not even clear about science's method and the nature of its theory is indicated in several ways as he attempted in *The Tendency* to foresee its application to history. Like the scientists of the early nineteenth century but unlike many of his own day he sees the relationship of cause and effect as absolutely necessitous, a matter (as it was for Helmholtz) of simple deterministic enforcement. The course of history, then, must be strictly determined and

---

perception. Unlike Wagner, however, I do not perceive this state as consistent in Adams's thinking, nor as a position he was advocating. Nor do I see Adams as a basically humorous writer (in any traditional sense of those words) because of it. In my view, Adams's "suspension" was often genuine vacillation which he struggled against rather than recommended, seeing his own ideas as perhaps the best contemporarily available but nonetheless ultimately absurd.

(putting aside for a while the philosophical and emotional implications of that idea) the historian in possession of the formula for this determinism had the opportunity—the responsibility, even—to project the future:

> Any science assumes a necessary sequence of cause and effect, a force resulting in motion that cannot be other than what it is. Any science of history must be absolute, like other sciences, and must fix with mathematical certainty the path which human society has got to follow.[19]

The possibility of extending scientific history into prophecy fascinated Adams throughout the rest of his life. Based though it was on a naive determinism, he had, as we shall see, a number of goes at it in subsequent years.

In addition to Adams's obsolete conception of the nature of scientific causality he had another odd and contradictory conception, less easy to understand. Observing that "a change has come over the tendency of liberal thought since the middle of the century" in its shift from Darwinian optimism to *fin de siècle* gloom, he claimed that whereas if the science of history had been established in Darwin's time it would have been optimistic, now, in keeping with what he perceives as the changed intellectual tone, it would have to be pessimistic.[20] Throughout his career Adams had an extraordinary sensitivity to the *tone* of scientific theories, although it is surprising to find such a statement in *The Tendency*, implying as it does that scientific theory is not nearly so definitive and absolute as the rest of the essay assumes that it is, that despite science's absolute determinism and predictive certainty its theories were based upon shifting human temperaments as well as upon the nature of the physical world. In some of Adams's thinking, then, science and emotion seemed to have a mutual influence.

It is not difficult to understand the feeling of Adams and other historians of the nineties that their discipline was in a state of crisis and needed to find a new direction if it were to survive as a viable and relevant enterprise. The omniscient point of view traditionally characteristic of history writing was becoming untenable given the crumbling of the absolute systems of belief by which historical phenomena had traditionally been understood and judged. Science seemed to offer a new and possibly more reliable system of absolutes, and one which, since it was in itself a dominant factor in the rapid change of society, might well prove to be change's best interpreter.

The dream of scientific history was, however, a pipe dream. Science had no way of attaining the kind of omniscience and the kind of permanence the nineteenth-century historians believed in and envied; and even if it had, there was no possibility of using the laws of physical nature to epitomize human affairs except by means of metaphor. Spencer and Fiske had already done that to the limit and well beyond, but had not in the process established a science of history—historical knowledge was still dependent upon the individual historian.

Although "scientific history" was to prove to be a dead end, it fascinated Henry Adams for the rest of his life. He never gave himself over to it unequivocally, however: he never found the universal formula, often hedged the scientific generalizations in his writing with irony and ambiguity, and never became the Herbert Spencer of the history profession. Still, whatever his doubts and premonitions, he had the whole dream spread out before him when his younger brother Brooks wrote *The Law of Civilization and Decay* (1895); it affected Henry deeply. He could feel more than a brother's pride in this work, since he had discussed its thesis with Brooks many times,[21] had made suggestions of a historical nature for a second edition[22] and had promoted the work by praising it in the highest possible terms to everyone to whom he wrote or spoke about it:

> I think it is astonishing. Indeed it is the first time that serious history has
> ever been written. He has done for it what only the greatest men do: he has
> created a startling generalization which reduces all history to a scientific
> formula which is yet so simple and obvious that one cannot believe it to be
> new. My admiration for it is much too great to be told. I have sought all
> my life those truths which this mighty infant, the seer unblessed, has struck
> with the agony and bloody sweat of genius. I stand in awe of him.[23]

The Law had two primary characteristics especially interesting to Henry, vast scope and a parascientific thesis. Encompassing history from ancient Rome to modern Europe, it discounts the importance of human thought and emphasizes such factors as the instincts of fear and greed, and the patterns of mercantilism, trade routes, and the like. As he explains in his preface to the second edition, Brooks believes that those factors behave according to a larger dynamic which is "based upon the accepted scientific principle that the law of force and energy is of universal application in nature," and in its largest terms is characterized by "oscillations between barbarism and civilization, or, what amounts to the same thing, in its movement from a condition of physical dispersion to one of concentration." Given these (somewhat Spencerian) assumptions and these translations of historical fact into metaphors from mechanics, the "Law" itself is statable in terms as clear as schoolbook science: "Probably the velocity of the social movement of any community is proportionate to its energy and mass, and its centralization is proportionate to its velocity; therefore, as human movement is accelerated, societies centralize."[24]

There is a certain kind of catchy appeal to generalizations of this sort, although the fact that such concepts as "the energy of a society" or the "velocity of social movement" are not only unquantifiable but even undefinable ought to mark the use of science here as purely metaphorical, despite Brooks's insistence on the universal application of the laws of "force and energy." Henry accepts his brother's metaphors, telling him that "your economical law of History is, or ought to be, an Energetic Law of History. Concentration is Energy, whether political or industrial." [25]

Henry Adams expressed himself in terms such as these for the rest of his life, and he tended to go back and forth across the border between literal and metaphorical uses of scientific language, often even within the same exposition. After the publication of Brooks's *Law* Henry did considerable probing to discover his own law, trying out a number of scientific theories on the phenomena of history and world affairs. In a letter to Cecil Spring Rice, for example, he uses both the kinetic theory of gasses and the Newtonian theory of gravitation in discussing the German situation:

> By bumping against all its neighbors, and being bumped in turn it gets and gives at last a common motion, which is, and of necessity must be, a vortex or cycle. . . . [If I could ascertain two elements,] the industrial and the capitalistic . . . I think I could fix approximately the elements of the human orbit, which is necessarily limited by the same conditions of mass, etc. which limit the orbit of the planet itself. [26]

The underlying assumption of such a statement is, of course, a universe of force. In a letter to John Hay in 1900 he states: "But, after all, politics is a matter of the conflict of forces. Forces are chiefly mathematics. What's the mathematical formula for the world now?" [27] There is no precise answer to that somewhat fanciful question in the discussion of world conditions that follows, only a feint in the direction of viewing Japan, Russia, and England as quantities, but the tendency in his thinking to move from parascientific translation of details to another great law is both clear and almost automatic.

In the year 1900 and shortly afterward, Adams immersed himself even more completely in the new science. Ernest Samuels feels that an important new phase in Adams's thought began when he saw clearly that science and technology themselves were forces profoundly affecting the course of civilization. [28] The Paris exposition of 1900 certainly impressed him deeply, especially its exhibition of a dynamo, of which Adams was moved to write to John Hay that it was sheer power, godlike but not a god, inexplicable and unfathomable.

> You are free to deride my sentimentality if you like, but I assure you that I,—a monk of St. Dominic, absorbed in the Beatitudes of the Virgin Mother—go down to the Champ de Mars and sit by the hour over the great dynamos, watching them run so noiselessly and as smoothly as the

planets, and asking them—with infinite courtesy—where in Hell they are going. They are marvelous. The Gods are not in it.[29]

In 1901, according to Samuels, he even put aside his work on a draft of *Mont-Saint-Michel and Chartres* in order to study more science.[30] At this stage his thought was becoming more science-centered, more apocalyptic, its frame of reference becoming both more universal and more personal. He wrote to Brooks in 1902:

> I apprehend for the next hundred years an ultimate, colossal, cosmic collapse; but not on any of our old lines. My belief is that science is to wreck us, and that we are like monkeys monkeying with a loaded shell; we don't in the least know or care where our practically infinite energies come from or will bring us to. . . . It is mathematically certain to me that another thirty years of energy-development at the rate of the last century, must reach an *impasse*.
>
> This is, however, a line of ideas wholly new, and very repugnant to our contemporaries. You will regard it with mild contempt. I owe it to my having always had a weakness for science mixed with metaphysics. I am a dilution of Lord Kelvin and St. Thomas Aquinas.[31]

IT WAS with this complex spirit upon him that Adams completed and published (privately) *Mont-Saint-Michel and Chartres* in 1904. He had long been a devoted student of the Middle Ages and had taught medieval history at Harvard, and his understanding of that distant age was both comprehensive and deeply particular. He focused his book on the eleventh-, twelfth-, and thirteenth-century cathedrals of northern France, and the whole texture of medieval life and culture of which they were an integral part. But although the subject is scholarly and medieval, his approach is literary and thoroughly modern. Modern civilization is, in fact, a kind of implicit subject of the book, never quite directly discussed, but always present in the background—in the general categories, in the figures of speech, in the point of view—providing a set of counter-themes and a whole comparative frame of reference. And beyond that, Adams's reaction against a modern universe described and dominated by deterministic science seems to have dictated, by a process of antithesis, the fundamental positive values he found in medieval life. Sensing meaninglessness and multiplicity in his own age, he found that the Middle Ages had Truth and Unity; seeing the causal explanations in his own age relied ultimately on the nonhuman mechanics of force, he found in the Middle Ages such causal agents as piety, love, and belief in quasi-human ideals; feeling that human understanding in his own day was imprisoned in the muddled confines of scientific rationalism, he found that in the Middle Ages a man's intuition, emotionality, esthetic appreciation, and reason could all be acceptable approaches to understanding, sometimes in a kind of ideal integration. Thus Adams selectively reconstructed the past, largely out of ideal elements he felt were absent in modern life, and then yearned for it elegiacally as a departed time when life was whole and meaningful. As myth, *Chartres* records another loss of paradise, lamenting it from a fallen and degenerate state, in a valueless universe of force.

The point of view from which Adams presents *Chartres* gives him much of the interpretive freedom he needs by putting the whole work in a framework that is more literary than historical. As we read the book we are not put under the illusion that we are witnessing history itself from some kind of pseudo-omniscient vantage as we are with conventional history writing, but that we are, in the terms Adams establishes in his preface, hypothetical nieces being guided through the cathedrals of France by an extremely knowledgeable and esthetically sensitive uncle. Playing the uncle to nieces was one of Adams's favorite roles in social life, and his literary use of it in *Chartres* put his deep and sometimes daring insights beyond the cavils of the Historical Association. Regardless of the extent to which he really felt that the study of history was to be scientific in the future, his two greatest works, *Chartres* and *The Education*, examining the deepest meanings of medieval and modern times respectively, renounce detached objectivity and absolute authority in the very terms of their idiosyncratic approaches. The problem of relativity of perspective was to become both the great agony and the great opportunity of twentieth-century literature—all of the great works since 1900 have had to come to terms with it—and just as his friend Henry James had been exploring and charting the possibilities of limited point of view in fiction, Adams himself experimented with limited point of view in nonfictional forms. The gambit freed him from the burden of absolutism and enabled him to apply his creative imagination to complex subjects in literary forms that were self-created and to some extent unprecedented.

The uncle of *Chartres* guided his nieces through three stages of medieval style: the eleventh century, characterized by Romanesque architecture, Mont-Saint-Michel and the Song of Roland; the twelfth century, characterized by mixed or transitional architecture, Chartres Cathedral and the almost universal worship of the Virgin; and the thirteenth century, characterized by Gothic architecture, Beauvais Cathedral and the philosophy of St. Thomas Aquinas. He stressed the fundamental unity within each period—both its unanimity on ultimate objectives and its harmony of expressive modes—and the unity of the whole of medieval times. Whether or not the universe was actually a unity was a vital question to him, perhaps the most vital question of all, and although he could not find an absolutely certain answer he did the next best thing (although it is a rather poor substitute after all) in studying an age which was unified because it believed in cosmic unity. As he points out, "Europe was a unity then, in thought, will, and object. Christianity was the unit."[32] Christianity had different modes in different times and places, though, and in Normandy in the eleventh century the mode was masculine, militant, heroic—a matter of uncomplicated allegiance like that of vassals to a lord—and its dominant symbol was St. Michael: "the Archangel stands for Church and State, and both militant" (1). This kind of unity can be seen in Mont-Saint-Michel although that edifice was built and rebuilt over a long period of time by different abbés and architects. What unifies the structure, our expositor-uncle asserts, is

> the instinct of the Archangel's presence which has animated his architecture. The masculine, military energy of Saint Michael lives still in every stone. The genius that realized this warlike emotion has stamped his power everywhere, on every centimetre of his work, in every ray of light; on the mass of every shadow; wherever the eye falls; still more strongly on all that the eye divines, and in the shadows that are felt like the lights. (40)

And what unifies the cathedral unifies the age as well, infusing into the Crusades and into the literature of the time that same spirit which animates Romanesque architecture:

> With Mont-Saint-Michel, the "Chanson de Roland" is almost one. The "Chanson" is in poetry what the Mount is in architecture. . . . The poem and the church are akin; they go together, and explain each other. Their common trait is their military character, peculiar to the eleventh century. The round arch is masculine. The "Chanson" is so masculine that . . . the only Christian woman so much as mentioned was Alda, . . . the betrothed of Roland. (12, 22-23)

In his insistence on the theme of unity Adams creates a new and highly specialized style in which the hypothetical uncle speaks. Attempting to demonstrate or suggest a unity of pattern or motif throughout disparate aspects of medieval civilization, he accumulates associative correspondences and builds his paragraphs around these associations. At times the correspondences are more figurative than literal, and at times a strained metaphor is all that makes them correspond at all, but when the technique works it tends to validate stylistically the very thematic points under discussion at the time. A typical instance occurs in this discussion, inferring a correspondence of the Mount itself, the organization of the church and the organization of the state:

> Perched on the extreme point of this abrupt rock, the Church Militant with

its aspirant Archangel stands high above the world, and seems to threaten heaven itself. The idea is the stronger and more restless because the Church of Saint Michel is surrounded and protected by the world and the society over which it rises, as Duke William rested on his barons and their men. Neither the Saint nor the Duke was troubled by doubts about his mission. Church and State, Soul and Body, God and Man are all one at Mont-Saint-Michel, and the business of all is to fight, each in his own way, or to stand guard for each other. (8)

When our hypothetical uncle changes the scene to Chartres he shows the unity of the Middle Ages in a new kind of integration, polarized around the figure of the Virgin. By comparison, the age of St. Michael expressed fewer and simpler impulses, a totally masculine and therefore harsher, grander but less beautiful character. The uncle seems far more interested in Chartres Cathedral and the age of its creation and flourishing: he identifies emotionally within this age to a far greater degree, and he dwells more minutely on the details of the cathedral itself and the culture of the time. Indeed his concentration on the details of the cathedral (its construction, statuary, lighting, and glass), on the motifs of the literature of the day and on the role and personality of the Virgin herself goes well beyond any function in contributing to the book's meaning and myth. There is no doubt that Adams means to create in us with this emphasis a sense of what the Middle Ages were really like, but the amount of emotion and care he lavishes on this objective suggests that he is projecting into this period of history a utopian vision of a lost golden age.

He begins with the cathedral. As the monumental product of the limited social and economic energies of its day he finds it awesome; as a work of art—presided over by the character of the Virgin herself, who oversaw the building of her cathedral, the uncle insists, in the same way St. Michael oversaw the building of his—the uncle finds it more awesome still. The Virgin embodied mankind's highest ideal of femininity, created out of man's deepest needs. Thus there was a satisfying completeness about the age that worshipped her. Since that time, the uncle feels, man has strayed away from this and every other source of his inner wholeness: "The scientific mind is atrophied, and suffers under inherited cerebral weakness, when it comes in contact with the eternal woman—Astarte, Isis, Demeter, Aphrodite, and the last and greatest deity of all, the Virgin" (198).

The exact nature of the femininity the Virgin brought into medieval religion and life was determined not only by human need but by existing patterns in the social organization, in literature, and in the personalities of actual queens and noblewomen of the time. The social role of woman was both simple and very comprehensive to the uncle: "The superiority of the woman was not a fancy but a fact. Man's business was to fight or hunt or feast or make love. . . . The woman ruled the household and the workshop; cared for the economy; supplied the intelligence, and dictated the taste" (199). Thus when an artist sought to celebrate an ideal of femininity like the Virgin of Chartres, he could go to the highest examples of femininity of his time for standards of taste:

> Since Mary differed from living queens only in infinitely greater majesty and refinement, the artist could admit only what pleased the actual taste of the great ladies who dictated taste at the Courts of France and England, which surrounded the little Court of the Counts of Chartres. (100)

Such contemporary patterns gave to the architects of the cathedrals, the tellers of tales, and the reverent antiquarian uncle something simple and all-important: "While the Virgin was miraculously using the power of spiritual love to elevate and purify the people, Eleanor [queen of Louis VII] and her daughters were using the power of earthly love to discipline and refine the courts" (213). They and the poets who wrote for them created the tradition of courtly love, which, as the uncle saw it, gave a new depth to religion and a new pattern to worship.

> If one has to make an exception, perhaps the passion of love was more serious than that of religion, and gave to religion the deepest emotion, and the most complicated one, which society knew. (218-219)

This new feminine influence gave to the art of the cathedral beauty, light, color, and imagery like that of the madonna or the prodigal son, signifying tenderness, forgiveness, and love. But most important, as the uncle sees it, man could now find compassion, individual favor, and relief from his own fallibility in a religion where previously he could only find abstract justice.

> God was Justice, Order, Unity, Perfection; . . . the Mother alone was human, imperfect, and could love; she alone was Favour, Duality, Diversity. . . . If the Trinity was in its essence Unity, the Mother alone could represent whatever was not Unity; whatever was irregular, exceptional, outlawed; and this was the whole human race. The saints alone were safe, after they were sainted. Everyone else was criminal, and men differed so little in degree of sin that, in Mary's eyes, all were subjects for her pity and her help. (263)

Trapped in legalism much the same way as the twentieth-century uncle-expositor felt himself trapped in mechanism, the people of the twelfth century humanized their religion in a way in which the uncle undoubtedly wished he could humanize his philosophy.

> Mary concentrated in herself [he insists] the whole rebellion of man against
> fate; the whole protest against divine law; the whole contempt for human
> law as its outcome; the whole unutterable fury of human nature beating
> itself against the walls of its prison house, and suddenly seized by a hope
> that in the Virgin man had found a door of escape. (276)

That the hypothetical uncle sees Christianity before the period of Virgin-wor-
ship as a monolithic, impersonal, and deterministic creed is one of his most
significant historical "interpretations" in terms of his own twentieth-century
predicament. That the universe could ever be a simple deterministic unity was
unthinkable for him. He decries this tendency of medieval thought in terms
which, significantly, are borrowed from modern physics: "If a Unity exists, in
which and toward which all energies centre, it must explain and include Dual-
ity, Diversity, Infinity—Sex!" (261). His rejection of the monolithic unity of
deterministic science in his own century is clearly implied.

The fault lay in a propensity to rely too exclusively on human rationality.
The uncle acknowledges the great achievements of medieval scholastic philosophy in explaining and unifying the universe, but demonstrates too the collective and unsystematized wisdom of the people of the twelfth century in
relying on intuition, art, and mysticism as well. Scholastic rationalism was to
become an edifice almost as magnificent as a cathedral, but in it, Adams finally
implies, were the seeds of the scientific rationalism that was to give modern
man the inescapable universe of force.

The uncle sees in the career of Abelard the expression of the scholasticism
of the twelfth century. Attempting "the conquest of heaven by force of pure
reason" (287) Abelard is presented as the key to understanding both twelfth-
century reason and much that followed. But in the long chapter which the
uncle devotes to this matter we are told that pure reason foundered on the
philosophical problem of universals and particulars, which is unresolved even
to this day: if one is a "realist" and maintains that universals are real, one
ends up in pantheism; and if one is a "nominalist" and maintains that they are
only nominally real, one ends in materialism. Either choice is a dead end.
Purely rationalistic philosophy leads one ultimately to an unresolvable dilemma.

The precise antithesis of rationalism, pure mysticism, representing an emotional, intuitive means of realizing unity, is also viewed by the uncle as ultimately unsatisfactory. The mystic's solution to the problems of meaning and
unity were not very widely applicable ("a few gifted natures could absorb
themselves in the absolute, but the rest lived for the day" [347]), and even for
those for whom it was applicable, its end product was not a meaningful unity
but rather the absence of all distinctions, a kind of mindlessness such as St.

Francis showed when he expressed his love for "'our sister death'" in the same tone as his love for sister moon or stars.

In the view of the uncle, both emotionless reason and reason-less emotion are ultimately too limiting, as were their twelfth-century avatars, scholasticism and mysticism. Mankind's greatest hope lay in an ideal integration, a precarious balance of reason and emotion as fine as the balance of Romanesque and Gothic architecture in Chartres Cathedral, an artistic and human triumph which grew out of the essentially transitional quality of the twelfth century:

> The sum is an emotion—clear and strong as love and much clearer than logic—whose charm lies in its unstable balance. The Transition is the equilibrium between the love of God—which is faith—and the logic of God— which is reason; between the round arch and the pointed. One may not be sure which pleases most, but one need not be harsh toward people who think that the moment of balance is exquisite. The last and highest moment is seen at Chartres, where, in 1200, the charm depends on the constant doubt whether emotion or science is uppermost. (321-322)

Thus the uncle sees in Chartres Cathedral how human inner integration and a viable understanding of cosmic unity can, indeed must, come at one and the same time. Along with all of the other things which the uncle says or implies are lacking in modern society, this psychic integration is undoubtedly the most important. That the twentieth century has this lack is more clearly and ingeniously implied as the uncle leads his nieces into the thirteenth century and makes them feel the similarity of its triumphant scholasticism to modern scientific rationalism.

For the twelfth century it was the worship of the Virgin that gave the cathedral and the lives centered around it the emotional meaning that made for completeness. To churchmen, however, rampant Mariolatry at best made the Church and the society excessively feministic, and at worst, under the influence of the Virgin's indiscriminate compassion, undermined civil order and divine justice and tended toward anarchy. When the uncle viewed the churchmen's attitude, he could not but be aware of the terrific price they were ready to pay and ready to exact from all future generations in order to put not only religious philosophy but human life itself on a more circumscribable, rationalistic basis: "The Church itself never liked to be dragged too far under feminine influence, although the moment it discarded feminine influence it lost nearly everything of any value to it or to the world, except its philosophy" (275). If modern man lived in a fallen state, the fall came here, with thirteenth-century man seduced by a dream of the absoluteness of his own reason.

Not that the uncle saw reason itself or rationalistic philosophy as evil the way that St. Francis did. It was not the triumph of reason so much as the overthrow of the balance which he lamented. He still felt the importance of philosophy to our understanding of things, and that its finest examples could almost rival the great cathedrals as expressions of finite man's attempt to comprehend infinity as unity: "These great theologians were also architects who undertook to build a Church Intellectual, corresponding bit by bit to the Church Administrative, both expressing—and expressed by—the Church Architectural" (349).

The greatest of these theologians was Saint Thomas Aquinas, and the uncle devotes the final chapter of *Chartres* to describing the achievement of his philosophy rather than describing any particular Gothic cathedral. He persists, however, in using metaphors and analogies from cathedral architecture in discussing the philosophy. He speaks of the doctrine of free will as the flèche of Aquinas's church, of the doctrine of the trinity as a tower, and of the doctrine of God's relationship to his created universe as the vaulting of the nave, and these metaphors enable him to assert the unity of human aspiration at the same time that, in his pose as summer tourist, he escapes the controversy and criticism that would undoubtedly have come to him had he presented this chapter as a straightforward explication of Thomist philosophy.

The uncle admires Saint Thomas's philosophy not only for its durability and its unity (it "sheltered God and man, mind and matter, the universe and the atom, the one and the multiple, within the walls of an harmonious home" [350]), but for the answers it offered to the abiding and perhaps unanswerable questions of philosophy. Aquinas was able to avoid both pantheism and materialism by means of his theory of the relationship of God and his creation: "God emanated time, force, matter, mind, as He might emanate gravitation, not as a part of His substance, but as an energy of His will, and maintains them in their activity by the same act, not by a new one" (358); and he was able to account for free will in man, without violating the tenet of God's uniform control of the universe, by regarding man as capable of reflex action from the energy that God, as the Prime Motor, supplied to all the universe (much in the way that a conductor of electricity functions in relation to a dynamo).

The uncle's comparison of medieval scholasticism and modern science is not accidental in this and in numerous other contexts. He regards modern science as a parallel endeavor, similar in approach and concepts, as well as a direct outgrowth of Aquinas's Church Intellectual and its total commitment to reason. Once the influence of the Virgin was excluded from man's attempt to grasp and express unity, this was the route speculation had to take; the only substantial difference between the world views of the thirteenth and the twentieth centuries was that the latter's was less sure and less satisfying.

Science hesitates, more visibly than the Church ever did, to decide once for all whether unity or diversity is ultimate law; whether order or chaos is the governing rule of the universe, if universe there is; whether anything, except phenomena, exists. . . . Science has become too complex to affirm the existence of universal truths, but it strives for nothing else, and disputes the problem, within its own limits, almost as earnestly as in the twelfth century, when the whole field of human and superhuman activity was shut between the barriers of substance, universals and particulars. Little has changed except the vocabulary and the method. (291-292)

The increasing complexity of the universe has resulted in the increasing complexity (and lack of self-confidence) of human rationality, and this to the point where the modern scientist might admit to Saint Thomas, "To your old ideas of form we have added what we call force, and we are rather further than ever from reducing the complex to unity" (353). Henry Adams's own frustration with modern science resounds behind the carpings of the hypothetical uncle. Adams's persona speaks for him in demanding absolute truth and cosmic unity in an age in which, as he at times can see, such items are irrelevant anachronisms. Things were much simpler in the Middle Ages when even pure rationality could come so much closer to fulfilling a man's need for unity. Modern man has the same basic needs, but less effective means of meeting them.

As it is presented in *Chartres*, the human condition fundamentally altered little throughout recorded history. The correspondences the uncle identifies, for instance, between the human needs found in one age and those in another, or between one age's expression of unity and that of another, imply that there is very little that is new under the sun:

Whether anything ultimate exists—whether substance is more than a complex of elements—whether the "thing in itself" is a reality or a name—is a question that Faraday and Clerk-Maxwell [sic] seem to answer as Bernard did, while Haeckel answers it as [Bishop] Gilbert did. . . . The absolute substance behind the attributes seems to be pure Spinoza. (320-321)

Terminology changes, so that what one age called "form" another called "force," and modes of expression changed, so that one age built cathedrals and another built dynamos, but other than a shift in the direction of complexity (a shift which unfortunately exposed to man the radical limitations of his reason, as embodied in modern science) nothing is significantly new in the human situation.

One age at least, as the uncle shows, was able to make sense and unity out of its universe by means of reason, and the remains of that age, Beauvais

Cathedral and the philosophy of Saint Thomas Aquinas, are magnificent monuments not only to man's yearning for meaning but to his ingenuity and art as well. And prior to that age was one even greater, in which not only man's intelligence, ingenuity, and art were involved in his acts of understanding and creation, but his emotions and intuition as well. The cathedral that men built for the Virgin of Chartres is for the uncle the pinnacle-expression of a unified age.

It was one of the great tragedies of history that the Virgin now looked down "from a deserted heaven, into an empty church, on a dead faith" (197). Now that human reason could be seen to be so obviously fallible and inconclusive, and human intuition seemed stultified or totally inoperative, one could only look back with longing on an age in which action and understanding were motivated by an ideal of divine femininity (courtly, personally close, forgiving) rather than by the chance acceleration of mechanical forces. Mythically, then, *Mont-Saint-Michel and Chartres* is like a postlapsarian view of Eden; although its subject is paradise, its concern is the fallen state.

Adams's awareness of his limited twentieth-century viewpoint and his use of the hypothetical uncle persona give the book much of its integrity as historiography and much of its value as literature. However strong and sincere was his temperamental inclination toward "scientific history," in this work his creative imagination took him well beyond what could be achieved by subsuming the course of history under some paramechanical law. That was Brooks's much-admired approach, and it is greatly to Henry's credit that he went his own highly individualistic way. Oddly enough, his approach is far closer to that of the new nonabsolutistic science of his day than was that of anyone's "scientific history," for there is nothing either absolutistic or reductionistic about *Chartres*. The observer's standpoint is limited and fallible, and historical phenomena have a wealth of interrelated causal factors, not the least important of which is human emotionality. The book's basic insight and individualistic style mark it as one of the most original books in American literature. The originality of its structure will be discussed later (pp. 128-129), after some relevant ideas from *The Education* have been considered.

THE CLIMACTIC work of Henry Adams's literary career was *The Education of Henry Adams* (1907). Like *Chartres* it is a work of great virtuosity and originality; but here the twentieth century is confronted directly in all its incomprehensibility and ill-boding determinism. Despite the attempt of the literary executor of *The Education*, Henry Cabot Lodge, to honor his friend by shifting the interest of the book to the man himself with a subtitle

"An Autobiography," the book's center remains the education and not the man educated: as Adams says in his preface, "Since his [Rousseau's] time, and largely thanks to him, the Ego has steadily tended to efface itself, and, for purposes of model, to become a manikin on which the toilet of education is to be draped in order to show the fit or misfit of the clothes. The object of study is the garment, not the figure."[33] The real problem the book addresses, then, is discovering the nature of the modern world and coming to terms with it under the handicap of an eighteenth-century education, or indeed of any education.

Again in this book, as in *Chartres*, the central question is one of unity: "From cradle to grave this problem of running order through chaos, direction through space, discipline through freedom, unity through multiplicity, has always been, and must always be, the task of education, as it is the moral of religion, philosophy, science, art, politics, and economy" (12). The problem is that the visions of unity and value prevailing in the past are no longer applicable in the terrifying multiplicity of the scientistic, industrialized, radically changing world of modern man. This is the lesson Adams drives home in a narrative based on his own intellectual coming-of-age from his boyhood in the 1840s to his decrepitude in 1905.

In this book Adams is again able to attain artistic freedom through his use of an unusual narrative point of view. There are really three Henry Adamses to consider in *The Education*: there is a relatively incompetent, traditionally oriented, slow-to-learn protagonist who is persistently being corrected and instructed by reality; then there is the verbose, worldly, and somewhat sardonic narrator, extremely given to irony, paradox, and negativistic hyperbole, who narrates the protagonist's struggles at some distance and in the third person; finally there is the author himself, like the narrator but not identifiable with him, who, with a strange mixture of audacity and self-effacement (although he compared his artistic labors here to those of Rousseau and St. Augustine, he was extremely reticent about publication and radically restricted circulation of the work), ambiguously allowed his creation out into the world. There is no universal, final version of Truth, then, even about himself. He avoided the mock-omniscient perspective of both conventional and scientific history, just as he evaded the conventions of the autobiography, finding considerable artistic freedom in the altering and mixing of genres.

As part of the book's steady insistence on the theme of unity and multiplicity, the diversity of the protagonist's experience—in law, politics, journalism, history, science, art, economics, philosophy, and private life—is specifically represented, as are the groping attempts of both the protagonist to discover unifying patterns moment-by-moment and of the narrator to find or hypothesize them retrospectively. And since the modern world which the protagonist's education unsuited him to comprehend was dominated by science, it is not surprising that a number of the crucial unifying patterns are based on scientific law and expressed in scientific language. In writing the story of a twentieth-century education along these lines, Adams was keenly aware that his work was an experiment in literary form. His letters repeatedly referred to it as such. For example, he stressed to Edith Morton Eustis this nature of both *Chartres* and *The Education*: "The two volumes have not been done in order to teach others, but to educate myself in the possibilities of literary form. The arrangement, the construction, the composition, the art of climax are our only serious study."[34] He ranked his experiment in literary form with some of the most notable autobiographical works in the Western world; he senses the failure of all of them although he feels his own failure most strongly. As he wrote to William James, "Of them all, I think St. Augustine alone has an idea of literary form—a notion of writing a story with an end and object, not for the sake of the object, but for the form, like a romance. I have worked ten years to satisfy myself that the thing cannot be done today."[35] As we shall see, this concern for form is in many ways related to the vision of the universe of force of which the book traces the development.

The pattern of the emerging world-view of the book and the rhetoric of its experimentation with literary form emerge gradually, but they are deeply implicit in the wealth of autobiographical details even from the beginning. The scientific world of the twentieth century colors every nuance of the narrator's tone although, in the part of the book dealing with his childhood and early manhood, protagonist Adams could have no inkling of what his seemingly stable world would become. The contrast in perspectives makes for irony, which is the dominant tone throughout. The boy born into the distinguished, learned, and wealthy Adams family was "heavily handicapped" (3); Boston, the self-presumed mecca of wisdom, piety, and culture, was nothing more than "troglodytic" (3); and in all essentials of education, the boy who was offered all the advantages of this environment "stood nearer the year 1 than . . . the year 1900" (53).

The eighteenth-century principles with which the boy was imbued by nineteenth-century Boston were to be the greatest obstacles to his understanding his own times and his acting efficaciously in them. As stated by the narrator their shortcomings are obvious:

> Viewed from Mount Vernon Street, the problem of life was as simple as it was classic. Politics offered no difficulties, for there the moral law was a sure guide. Social perfection was also sure, because human nature worked for Good, and three instruments were all she asked—Suffrage, Common Schools, and the Press. On these points doubt was forbidden. Education was divine and man needed only a correct knowledge of facts to reach perfection. (33)

Religion was a reassuring kind of doctrineless ameliorism, and society, in the interest of decorum, succeeded in ignoring sex as a principle or a social force ("from women the boy got the domestic virtues and nothing else" [40]). For one with such a background, education had to begin with disillusionment.

Reality continually jarred the boy, and the sureties of his early education were chipped away with every new experience. His first trip to Washington exposed him to the moral contradiction of the state of Virginia: a slave state, an immoral state, but yet beautiful in its scenery and distinguished in its political tradition; his first real exposure to the inner workings of politics confronted him with another violation of principle: his political ideal, Charles Sumner, became a United States Senator through collusion with the pro-slavery Massachusetts Democrats; a trip to Europe after college (Harvard College he rated as a "negative force" [60] in his education, since it weakened his earlier principles but supplied him with no new ones) exposed him to new strains: the paradox of the English social system with both aristocracy and poverty-stricken industrial classes, the meaningless regimentation in the German Gymnasium in which he taught for a time, and the great vitality and anarchy of Rome, all of which were incomprehensible in terms of his earlier acquired principles. Even a meeting with Garibaldi pointed to no moral for him except the extreme complexity that underlies an extremely simple personality.

In 1860, at the age of twenty-two the protagonist Henry Adams returned to the United States to become private secretary for his father, then Congressman from Massachusetts. The position of private secretary gave him a peculiar vantage point from which to view the machinations of statecraft on the eve of the Civil War. This proved to be another drastic stage in his education, as he began to divine that human events were out of human control: what happened had little to do with men's intentions and nothing to do with their principles.

> He dropped back on Quincy like a lump of lead; he rebounded like a football, tossed into space by an unknown energy which played with all his generation as a cat plays with mice. The simile is none too strong. Not one man in America wanted the Civil War, or expected or intended it. A small minority wanted secession. The vast majority wanted to go on with their occupations in peace. Not one, however clever or learned, guessed what happened. Possibly a few Southern loyalists might dream it as an impossible chance; but none planned it. (98)

The "unknown energy" is vague and frighteningly deterministic, but it is clearly no mere nonce figure of speech; retrospectively, there was no doubt that "Henry was a helpless victim, and, like all the rest [e.g., Lincoln, Seward, Sumner], he could only wait for he knew not what, to send him he knew not where" (109).

When the "unknown energy" split the nation and thrust it into war, it sent Adams's father to England as ambassador and gave the young private secretary a new but no less baffling field in which to continue his investigations into the causes of human events. When the British, who should have been strongly opposed to slavery on principle, moved in the direction of recognizing the Confederacy, it was another setback for the Bostonian view that moral law was a sure guide to politics; the private secretary could understand this move only in terms of power—that the British, regardless of principle, desired the lessening of America's influence in the world which came with the division of the nation. And in an episode in which the British were discovered to be supplying the Confederacy with armored ships and were balked in the effort by the forceful intervention of Minister Adams, the private secretary could find no thread of consistent ideals or intentions in the actions and reactions of the various British statesmen involved in the affair, despite his avowal that "its practical value as education turned on his correctness of judgment in measuring the men and their forces" (173). In time he could decide only that it was a lesson in British eccentricity, "in the sheer chaos of human nature" (153): "All the world had been at cross-purposes, had misunderstood themselves and the situation, had followed wrong paths, drawn wrong conclusions, had known none of the facts" (161–162). "The English mind," he claimed, "was one-sided, eccentric, systematically unsystematic, and logically illogical" (180). Such eccentricity could be a force in human affairs, the secretary could see, but "the sum of these experiences in 1863 left the conviction that eccentricity was weakness" (193).

In terms of his education the protagonist had discovered that forces rather than principles underlay human affairs, and he had learned that human eccentricity could be a force. Once aware of this he saw eccentricity and its chaotic results everywhere in British society. In terms of social life in London, he decided that "Society had no unity; one wandered about in it like a maggot in cheese" (197); in the world of art, to which he had been introduced in London, he found similar human chaos as he discovered that the critical establishment in London not only could not agree on the authenticity of a drawing he had purchased, presuming it to be a Raphael, but they could not even deliver a unanimous judgment as to its artistic merit. And at the same time that the private secretary was learning the nature of eccentricity in its various forms, he felt his own personal life drifting into dilettantism and purposeless fragmentation. In his life as in his world-view at this stage there was eccentric force but there was no Unity.

Society's answer to the problem of unity in the latter 1860s was Evolution, and the protagonist Henry Adams, searching for the solution to his own problems, "became a Comteist, within the limits of evolution" (225), and rashly offered to Sir Charles Lyell to help spread the fame of his new (1866) edition of *The Principles of Geology* in America by writing an essay on it for the American journals. The narrator's sense of irony is very strong at this point because, given the perspective he has gained throughout the rest of *The Education*, he sees and cannot help but project the futility of trying to subsume cosmic unity under a single unverified scientific law. The practice was common and the young protagonist could only follow the thinkers of his times, but subsequent experience would show him how naively fallible they all were:

> He was a Darwinist before the letter; a predestined follower of the tide; but he was hardly trained to follow Darwin's evidences. Fragmentary the British mind might be, but in those days it was doing a great deal of work in a very un-English way, building up so many and such vast theories on such narrow foundations as to shock the conservative, and delight the frivolous. The atomic theory; the correlation and conservation of energy; the mechanical theory of the universe; the kinetic theory of gases, and Darwin's Law of Natural Selection, were examples of what a young man had to take on trust. Neither he nor anyone else knew enough to verify them. (224)

And most fallible of all was the whole philosophy of Evolution set forth by Lyell and interpreted to Americans by, among other disciples, the young Henry Adams.

> Natural Selection led back to Natural Evolution, and at last to Natural Uniformity. This was a vast stride. Unbroken Evolution under uniform conditions pleased every one—except curates and bishops; it was the very best substitute for religion; a safe, conservative, practical, thoroughly Common-Law deity. . . . The idea was only too seductive in its perfection; it had the charm of art. (225-226)

As the young man grappled with evolutionary theory to try to make it his own way of attaining unity, he was increasingly worried by the seeming lapse in Natural Uniformity represented by the glacial epoch and by the seeming lack of Natural Evolution represented by certain species, like the Pteraspis which showed no noticeable change whatever since the Silurian Age. Adams remained an evolutionist for a while, but it took an arbitrary decision on his part to remain one in the face of such problems. Underneath it all he could see only power evolving.

> Ponder it over as he might, Adams could see nothing in the theory of Sir Charles but pure inference, precisely like the inference of Paley, that if one found a watch, one inferred a maker. He could detect no more evolution

in life since the *Pteraspis* than he could detect it in architecture since the Abbey. All he could prove was change. Coal-power alone asserted evolution—of power—and only by violence could be forced to assert selection of type. (230-231)

Increasingly, as the protagonist's baffling career develops, his intimations of a universe of force grow stronger and his general speculations tend to be figured in the language and theory-patterns of physics. Other more conventional categories drop away: the national debacle of the Gold Conspiracy and the whole Grant administration showed him not only that "the moral law had expired—like the constitution" (280), but that "the progress of evolution from President Washington to President Grant, was alone evidence enough to upset Darwin" (266). Climactically, his personal life provided him with the incident that confronted the protagonist with the impersonal universe of force which had been implicit in the narrator's view of his life from the very outset. Observing the slow, tortured death of his sister by lockjaw destroyed all the categories of his understanding and left him with only a nightmare vision of force:

> For the first time, the stage-scenery of the senses collapsed; the human mind felt itself stripped naked, vibrating in a void of shapeless energies, with resistless mass, colliding, crushing, wasting, and destroying what these same energies had created and labored from eternity to perfect. Society became fantastic, a vision of pantomime with a mechanical motion; and its so-called thought merged in the mere sense of life, and pleasure in the sense. (288)

Having seen through the "illusions of Nature" Adams needed an extended vacation in the Alps to restore, however unconvincingly, his faith in the stability of those illusions:

> For the first time in his life, Mont Blanc for a moment looked to him what it was—a chaos of anarchic and purposeless forces—and he needed days of repose to see it clothe itself again with the illusions of his senses, the white purity of its snows, the splendor of its light, and the infinity of its heavenly peace. (289)

For the narrator, forces are both real and ultimate; other interpretations of experience are illusory. At this stage the protagonist sees this too, although he cannot as yet go farther than to envision it as a nightmare. When he subsequently began to teach history at Harvard University, then, he brought with him out of the chaos of his life and the world the bleak recognition that "in essence incoherent and immoral, history either had to be taught as such—or falsified" (301).

A twenty-year period, from 1872 through 1892, is dropped out of the narrative of the life of Henry Adams in *The Education*, an omission which, besides keeping the length of the book under reasonable control, reemphasizes the author's determination to focus on the education rather than on the man educated. In the life of Henry Adams the author, the omitted years contained monumental events such as his marriage and the suicide of his wife and the writing of *The History of the United States*, but in the book the interim is empty except for some reflective allusions to the protagonist's increasing disillusionment and sadness. And there is subsequently a more marked preoccupation with the language and categories of force-mechanics.

After the twenty-year break the narrator sees force everywhere, but now the habit has grown rational, relatively constructive, and no longer like nightmare in tone. Of the depression and panic of 1893 he says, "Blindly some very powerful energy was at work, doing something that nobody wanted done. . . . Evidently the force was one; its operation was mechanical; its effect must be proportional to its power; but no one knew what it meant, and most people dismissed it as an emotion—a panic—that meant nothing" (338). The submission of the country to the gold standard and its implications of a society "capitalistic, centralizing, and mechanical" was "a submission long foreseen by the mere law of mass" (344). And (significantly for an understanding of the whole book) the narrator discusses education itself in the same terms: "Education should try to lessen the obstacles, diminish the friction, invigorate the energy, and should train minds to react, not at haphazard, but by choice, on the lines of force that attract their world" (314). The imagery of force and magnetism here is more than a mere metaphor to the narrator, as we shall see; also, it is already apparent from his concept of the mind as something that reacts both "by choice" and "on the lines of force" that the problem of the status of ethics in a deterministic universe is as real to him as it is to his protagonist.

In the mid-1890s the protagonist, still searching for unity, or at least for a system by which to understand his world, begins to try his hand at some statistical curve-plotting meant to bring the present, recent past, and near future into some kind of quantitative relationship. Studying the developmental stages, at various time intervals, of steamship power and tonnage or of coal production yields him nothing substantial as yet, other than a sense like that of his brother Brooks of the dizzying acceleration and uncertain direction of mankind's progress, but this study of quantitative relationships seems to promise more than did the fixed, idealistic concepts of the eighteenth century or the theories of qualitative progress of the nineteenth. At the same time he was also trying to figure the human element into the equation. He had earlier learned that man acted according to interest rather than ideals; further reflection showed him that the study of culture ought possibly to be a study of human dynamics if it were to educate one to useful realities: "The object of education, therefore [he concludes], was changed. For many years it had lost itself in studying what the world had ceased to care for; if it were to begin again, it must try to find out what the mass of mankind did care for, and why" (352-353).

The study of human dynamics was fascinating to the protagonist, and the more he pondered the sources of power in various ages (as "what the mass of mankind did care for"), and began to divine what he felt was the curve of the development of history, the closer he felt to some all-encompassing law. Interestingly enough, in this he closely resembled the enthusiastic scientific historians Adams referred to (with, possibly, some slight traces of disdain) in *The Tendency of History*, each one feeling that the definitive law of history was almost within his conceptual grasp. In pursuing his quarry, protagonist Adams decided that if one were plotting a curve one would need fixed points through which to plot it, and for the great curve of human history he chose the twelfth and the twentieth centuries, a pair of widely separated periods about which he had special knowledge and strong feelings. He dedicated himself to the attempt to "align" the two ages, to "bring them into a common relation" not only for the sake of historical knowledge but also for the purpose of making a "triangulation" that would reveal the course of the future. So great was his absorption in this problem that when his very close friend, John Hay, was named secretary of state, and when Hay's China policy proved a triumph, it provided only a minor subplot to the story of this period in his life.

The alignment of these two periods in terms of force dynamics led Adams to his most provocative and characteristic symbolism, that of the Virgin and the dynamo. The protagonist discovered the dynamo as a symbol of infinite, anarchical force at the Great Exposition of 1900 in Paris, under the tutelage of the eminent American scientist Samuel Pierpont Langley:

> To him [Langley], the dynamo itself was but an ingenious channel for conveying somewhere the heat latent in a few tons of coal hidden in a dirty engine-house carefully kept out of sight; but to Adams the dynamo became a symbol of infinity. As he grew accustomed to the great gallery of machines, he began to feel the forty-foot dynamos as a moral force, much as the early Christians felt the Cross. The planet itself seemed less impressive, in its old-fashioned, deliberate, annual or daily revolution, than this huge wheel, revolving within arm's-length at some vertiginous speed, and barely murmuring—scarcely humming an audible warning to stand a hair's-breadth further for respect of power—while it would not wake the baby lying close against its frame. Before the end, one began to pray to it; inherited instinct taught the natural expression of man before silent and infinite

force. Among the thousand symbols of ultimate energy, the dynamo was not so human as some, but it was the most expressive.

... For Adams's objects its value lay chiefly in its occult mechanism. (380-381)

The dynamo converted force, transformed it from one form into another, and did it, Adams thought, "occultly," and in such magnitude as could be considered by old standards of power infinite. Sheer power was the dynamo's only meaning, but it was a profound one, awesome to man's imagination, and one which pointed the way to the future.

The Virgin became the symbol for the protagonist, not of a catholic religion, but of the force of her sex. As a symbol of Woman, inheritor of the function of Venus, of Diana of the Ephesians, and of every other female deity mankind had worshipped: "She was goddess because of her force; she was the animated dynamo; she was reproduction—the greatest and most mysterious of all energies" (384). Considering human actions and energies as essentially the same as the energies produced by a dynamo, Adams concluded that "symbol or energy, the Virgin had acted as the greatest force the Western world ever felt, and had drawn man's activities to herself more strongly than any other power, natural or supernatural, had ever done" (388-389).

Both as protagonist and as narrator Henry Adams is aware that such an analysis of human events presupposes a different sort of axis for history than any that had been used hitherto. In the Adams terminology, it was a question of "sequence." "Historians undertake to arrange sequences," the narrator points out, "—called stories, or histories—assuming in silence a relation of cause and effect" (382). He describes the protagonist's search for a viable "sequence" in these terms: "Satisfied that the sequence of men led to nothing, and that the sequence of their society could lead no further, while the mere sequence of time was artificial, and the sequence of thought was chaos, he turned at last to the sequence of force" (382).

That human history is best described in terms of the sequence of force was a staggering discovery for the protagonist, and one from which the narrator himself had not even quite recovered. He is to some extent aware that he risks semantic subjectivism:

Clearly if he was bound to reduce all these forces to a common value, this common value could have no measure but that of their attraction on his own mind. He must treat them as they had been felt; as convertible, reversible, interchangeable attractions on thought. He made up his mind to venture it; he would risk translating rays into faith. (383)

The determination of their value is seen by both protagonist and narrator as a subjective and relative matter, although the characterization of "them" as "forces" in the first place is not. Author Adams seems to be assuming (as he often did in his marginalia: see below, pp. 134-135) that forces are absolute, although even his narrator and protagonist here understand the hypothetical nature of assigning them values and tracing their curves. Force-sequences remain, in *The Education*, less than absolutely real but more than hypothetically posited.

For both the narrator and the author Henry Adams the sequence of force cannot remain an organizing idea for history without also becoming an architectural principle for history-writing. Adams's persistent concern with form has already been documented in previous pages, but we can see in *The Education* itself the narrator relating the ideas of purpose and "force," of structure and "sequence" in reference to the kind of literary composition attempted in this book and its predecessor:

> The pen works for itself, and acts like a hand, modelling the plastic material over and over again to the form that suits it best. The form is never arbitrary, but is a sort of growth like crystallization, as any artist knows too well; for often the pencil or pen runs into side-paths and shapelessness, loses its relations, stops or is bogged. Then it has to return on its trail, and recover, if it can, *its line of force*. The result of a year's work depends more on what is struck out than on what is left in; on *the sequence of the main lines of thought*, than on their play or variety. (389; my italics)

This very obvious, conscious concern for literary form and "sequence" has a great deal to do with Adams's artistic purposes in both *Chartres* and *The Education*, and it sheds interesting light on the structures and other of the most ingenious stylistic elements of both books. Additionally it stands as an example of the deepest sort of influence of science and scientific ideas on literature. The general subject of structure and "sequence" is well worth pursuing here so that its revelations can bear on the discussion of the conclusion of *The Education*.

In a reference to the writing of *Chartres*, the narrator of *The Education*, discussing the great force of the Virgin, states, "The historian's business was to follow the track of the energy; to find where it came from and where it went to; its complex source and shifting channels; its values, equivalents, conversions. . . . The pursuit turned out to be long and tortuous, leading at last into the vast forests of scholastic science" (389). Thus Adams encourages us to view his whole approach in *Chartres*—his tracing of the human emotion aroused by the Virgin and expressed through the architecture and glass of the cathedrals, the ballads, the social relations, the philosophy and so forth—as we would view a scientist tracing the conversion of energy in a locomotive from coal to heat to steam to motion. The human response drawn by the Virgin is the implied and mysterious quantity, like energy itself identifiable only through a correlation of its various sequential manifestations. This interpretation of the structure of *Chartres* has, of course, deeply mechanistic implications (the universe of force seems to be more fundamental than the universe of faith if the former is more inclusive and provides the paradigm for the latter), and it is a radical way of looking at a book that is often appreciated for its close approximation to Christian reverence. It is certainly not indispensable to an appreciation of the originality and effectiveness of the book to perceive the analogy between its structure and the scientific theory of the "shifting channels" of force, but it is significant that Adams chose to look back on that structure in this way. Even with respect to form, it would seem, *Chartres* can be regarded as a far more "modern" and original book than it at first appears.*

In *The Education*, structure is even more specifically and integrally "scientific," as we can see from the vantage point of Adams's concept of the sequence of force. Unlike *Chartres*'s, the approach in *The Education* is not analogous to following a given force through a number of significant conversions, but analogous to following an atom which not only is acted upon by a great many particular forces, but which also shares many of the same states of being as those passed through by the forces themselves. The narrator specifically points to the particle-in-a-shifting-field-of-forces theme: "One had been from the first, dragged hither and thither like a French poodle on a string, following always the strongest pull, between one form of unity or centralization and another" (226). At its most explicit, phrased in terms of the Dynamic Theory, this theme states that "the sum of force attracts; the feeble atom or molecule called man is attracted; he suffers education or growth; he is the sum of the forces that attract him; his body and his thought are alike their product" (474). Thus the protagonist, the human particle, is presented as wandering through his life trying to understand and to act with effectiveness and economy in a universe of specific developing and deterministic forces, many of the most important of which are places, persons, events, or ideas designated

---

* John J. Conder was the first to publish an extensive interpretation of *Chartres* and *The Education* based on what Adams says about the works as experiments in literary form and as efforts to trace sequences of force. In his book, *A Formula of His Own: Henry Adams's Literary Experiment* (Univ. of Chicago Press, 1970), Conder views Adams's use of subjectively based equivalences—between cathedral architecture, philosophical rationalism, and force in *Chartres*, and between personal experiences, social movements, and force in *The Education*—as esthetic means to achieve a single didactic purpose, manifest even in Adams's late essays "A Letter to American Teachers of History" and "The Rule of Phase Applied to History," to focus modern man's attention on the theme of determinism and free will and show him that he must deal with supersensuous forces "in the age of supersensuous chaos" (151). Although I do not find Adams quite so single-mindedly didactic, Conder's thesis seems to me extremely fertile and his ideas about the structure of *Chartres* and *The Education* appropriate indeed.

by the chapter titles. For example, there are "Quincy (1838–48)," "Boston (1848–54)," "Harvard College (1854–58)," "Darwinism (1867–68)," "President Grant (1869)," "Chicago (1893)," "The Dynamo and the Virgin (1900)," "The Grammar of Science (1903)."

Furthermore, if we look at the inner organization of the narrator's representation of these larger forces, we frequently find within chapters (and even within paragraphs or sentences) sudden associational jumps from one topic to another very different one, a strategy (or quirk) which suggests that the unity of the specific structural unit is not basically topical but rather has something to do with some attitude, purpose, or perception of the narrator, who is being represented as thinking along nontopical lines. In keeping with both Adams's avowed interest in literary form and the "education" his narrator has supposedly undergone, the lines along which the narrator is thinking while he constructs his disquisition are often relatable to sequences of force, the correspondences between seemingly disparate things often being correspondences of states or conditions or effects of force. For example, in Chapter XXVI ("Twilight"), discussing the increasing incomprehensibility of both American politics and the science of geology, the narrator points the way to the elusive unity by tentatively concluding that "politics and geology pointed alike to the larger synthesis of rapidly increasing complexity" (402). Or earlier, when it seemed that there was no unity or direction in the forces in the protagonist's life, he concludes that "for the moment, politics had ceased to disturb social relations. All parties were mixed up and jumbled together in a sort of tidal slack-water. The Government resembled Adams himself in the matter of education. All that had gone before was useless, and some of it was worse" (254).

At times whole chapters are organized around particular phases of force. Chapter XIX ("Chaos") groups together the essentially meaningless and chaotic events in the protagonist's life in the year 1870, such as the unexpected death of his sister, his resultant discovery of the chaos underlying seemingly meaningful experience, the suspicious refusal of the journals to print his article on the gold conspiracy of 1869, and the beginning of war in Europe which "the public seemed to look on . . . as a branch of decorative art" (290). Chapter XXX ("Vis Inertiae") yokes the disparate topics of Russia's retarded development as a nation and the uncertain and seemingly purposeless role of women in contemporary society; the two topics are unified by the fact that the narrator sees them as examples of inertial force, "race inertia," and "sex inertia," which at the time were quiescent and generally ignored but were subsequently liable to become highly significant determinants of human history. Similar too is the treatment as "new forces" in Chapter XXXII ("Vis Nova") of the coming Russo-Japanese War and the new orders of industrial power symbolized for the protagonist by the St. Louis Exposition. Other chapters too partake of this form of organization: Chapter XII ("Eccentricity"), capitalizing on the fact that "eccentricity" is a term of both character analysis and of mechanics, groups together as eccentric forces the characteristic unpredictability of the English mind, the political effect of British support of the Confederacy, and the protagonist's strangely peripheral role in Society and life; and Chapter XXVII ("Teufelsdröckh"), operating according to a kind of dialectical theory of contradictory forces, finally and sardonically leaves the protagonist a member of the two-man party of Conservative Christian Anarchists. Conder's book points up several such force-correspondences and effectively demonstrates how Adams's representation of American society, English society and himself is characterized by the force-theme of increasing fragmentation, degradation, and "the failure of sequence in human affairs."[36] Stylistically and structurally, therefore, force-theory has a great deal to do with the nature of *The Education*.

The theory of qualitatively different stages in the development of force is of course Spencerian, but although Adams read Spencer and made passing reference to him in *The Education* he adopted neither the exact terms of Spencer's evolution nor its overall outcome. There are occasional glimpses of Spencerian evolutionary theory, to be sure; for example, America opted for "the whole mechanical consolidation of force" when it went over to the gold standard (345); and in 1901 "the National Government and the national unity had overcome every resistance, and the Darwinian evolutionists were triumphant over all the curates; yet the greater the unity and the momentum, the worse became the complexity and the friction" (398). Yet there is no dramatic avowal of a Spencerian cosmos, or indeed of any cosmos. Spencer's system was, of course, optimistic and amelioristic, and would therefore be basically out of tenor with Adams's perceptions about the nature of his world. And as the protagonist was later to come to realize—in the discovery that closed the last gap between his own hopeful questing and the narrator's disillusioned irony—any such conceptualization of the universe is a kind of subjective dream.

Meanwhile the protagonist finds the idea of forces and the sequence of force extremely seductive, and he tends to see everything in these terms:

> Adams never knew why, knowing nothing of Faraday, he began to mimic Faraday's trick of seeing lines of force all about him, where he had always seen lines of will. Perhaps the effect of knowing no mathematics is to leave the mind to imagine figures—images—phantoms; one's mind is a watery mirror at best; but, once conceived, the image became rapidly simple, and the lines of force presented themselves as lines of attraction. . . . By this path, the mind stepped into the mechanical theory of the universe before knowing it, and entered a distinct new phase of education. (426-427)

Mystified and shaken by this new direction of his thought, the protagonist mused over the lines of force of a magnet, searched avidly for the key to the unity of thought in the Middle Ages, and began to reorient his whole view of history ("modern politics is, at bottom, a struggle not of men but of forces" [421]). The result of all this reorganization of perspective was not a theory but a project; as the narrator explains it,

> Any schoolboy could see that man as a force must be measured by motion, from a fixed point. Psychology helped here by suggesting a unit—the point of history when man held the highest idea of himself as a unit in a unified universe. Eight or ten years of study had led Adams to think he might use the century 1150–1250, expressed in Amiens Cathedral and the works of Thomas Aquinas, as the unit from which he might measure motion down to his own time, without assuming anything as true or untrue, except relation. The movement might be studied at once in philosophy and mechanics. Setting himself to the task, he began a volume which he mentally knew as "Mont-Saint-Michel and Chartres: a Study of Thirteenth-Century Unity." From that point he proposed to fix a position for himself, which he could label: "The Education of Henry Adams: a Study of Twentieth-Century Multiplicity." With the help of these two points of relation, he hoped to project his lines forward and backward indefinitely, subject to correction from any one who should know better. (434-435)

Tracing such a relationship, given Adams's terms of analysis, could not but reveal that force evolved in the direction of greater complexity, incomprehensibility, and disintegration.

But before the protagonist could set up an evolutionary theory, science had another shock for him which affected the whole endeavor. Henry Adams the protagonist had begun in the early 1900s to have intimations about the limitations of human thought, but these in no way prepared him for the epistemological disaster of his encounter with *The Grammar of Science* of Karl Pearson. He had understood the disunity of modern thought relative to the unity of thought in the thirteenth century, and realized even that unity itself now needed to be based on something other than thought; he also had realized that, viewed psychologically, organized thought was not particularly characteristic of the mind ("His normal thought was dispersion, sleep, dream, inconsequence; the simultaneous action of different thought-centres without central control" [434]). But these realizations faded into inconsequence beside the radical Positivism of *The Grammar of Science*.

Henry Adams's whole response to modern science and its theory of knowledge crystallized in his response to Karl Pearson. That human mentality could get no closer to ultimate reality and unity than Pearson and Mach and Poincaré and Stallo said it could seemed to the author, narrator, and protagonist of *The Education* the final and ultimate absurdity of the human condition. By and large Adams accepted the authority of these new epistemologists (especially since they had been recommended to him by Langley, upon whom he relied as his personal guide to the new science), but he could never reconcile himself to what they said. The description of what the protagonist learned from Pearson has deep undertones of authorial resentment:

> He told his scholars that they must put up with a fraction of the universe, and a very small fraction at that—the circle reached by the senses, where sequence could be taken for granted—much as the deep-sea fish takes for granted the circle of light which he generates. "Order and reason, beauty and benevolence, are characteristics and conceptions which we find wholly associated with the mind of man." The assertion, as a broad truth, left one's mind in some doubt of its bearing, for order and beauty seemed to be associated also in the mind of a crystal, if one's senses were to be admitted as judge; but the historian had no interest in the universal truth of Pearson's or Kelvin's or Newton's laws; he sought only their relative drift or direction, and Pearson went on to say that these conceptions must stop: "Into the chaos beyond sense-impressions we cannot scientifically project them." We cannot even infer them: "In the chaos behind sensations, in the 'beyond' of sense-impressions, we cannot infer necessity, order or routine, for these are concepts formed by the mind of man on this side of sense-impressions"; but we must infer chaos: "Briefly chaos is all that science can logically assert of the supersensuous." The kinetic theory of gas is an assertion of ultimate chaos. In plain words, Chaos was the law of nature; Order was the dream of man. (450-451)

The narrator's attitude toward Pearson in this passage is typical; it everywhere bristles with hostility and sarcasm. The heavy charge of negative emotion running through the book is now somewhat differently directed: no longer aimed at narrowly old-fashioned preconceptions, rank hypocrisy or clearly fallible new theories, it is here directed at the very ideas that must be accepted if one is to be unsparingly educated.

Although the education of the protagonist goes on, the author, it seems, could accept a universe of force but not a supersensuous chaos. The continuity of the history of thought has been broken, Truth has become merely "a medium of exchange," and the kind of absolute unity that the protagonist had made the principal object of his life's quest is now plainly inconceivable in any sense whatever, for humanity was to live without any hope of certitude or order in the post-Pearsonian universe:

> The Child born in 1900 would, then, be born into a new world which

would not be a unity but a multiple. Adams tried to imagine it, and an education that would fit it. He found himself in a land where no one had ever penetrated before; where order was an accidental relation obnoxious to nature; artificial compulsion imposed on motion; against which every free energy of the universe revolted; and which, being merely occasional, resolved itself back into anarchy at last. (457-458)*

These gloomy conclusions about the universe and the tendency of modern thought were accompanied by an increasing tendency on the part of the narrator to view the protagonist's role in life as that of a withdrawn historian. Numerous times the narrator insists that as "historian" he has no stake in these ideas as such or in their effect on human thought, but he only means to chart the course of their influence quantitatively, as forces in human affairs. His detachment was bitter, however, and he found it humanly impossible to maintain a consistent, quantitatively oriented objectivity in viewing the course of things.

All that [the] historian won was a vehement wish to escape. He saw his education complete, and he was sorry he ever began it. As a matter of taste, he greatly preferred his eighteenth-century education when God was a father and nature a mother, and all was for the best in a scientific universe. He repudiated all share in the world as it was to be, and yet he could not detect the point where his responsibility began or ended. (458)

Behind author Adams's admitted hostility toward the new scientific epistemology (and the kind of future he thought it promised), there is a real question as to the degree to which he understood it. Of course the structural pattern of *The Education* is such that each of the sections moves from stability to shock and disorientation and concludes in confusion and failure. This cyclic structure combined with the hyperbolic prose constitutes the stylistic mode of the book, but the encounter with *The Grammar of Science* is more than just another repetition in a fixed and by this time somewhat tiresome pattern, for evidence both within and without *The Education* shows that critical epistemology was indeed an area in which Henry Adams's education failed. Adams's annotations in his copy of *The Grammar* clearly indicate his continuing determination to view phenomena in terms of conventional naive realism. When Pearson, for example, attacks the naive view of physical causality by saying that in a causal relation there is no enforcement but only a "routine of experi-

---

* John Carlos Rowe takes a very different conceptual route from mine in his *Henry Adams and Henry James* (Cornell Univ. Press, 1976), but he too identifies an absurdist tendency in this aspect of Adams's thought: "The notion that reason can discover only its own reflection in its dealings with a blind universe of force seems central to both Adams's thought and later literature concerned with an absurd reality" (240).

ence," Adams querulously asks "what is gained by the change in words?" which shows that he understood the new attitude toward causality as merely a semantic shuffle.[37] Similarly, on the important matter of the meaning of the term *force*, Pearson's idea (basically that "force is . . . an arbitrary conceptual measure of motion without any perceptual equivalent" [257]) is utterly incomprehensible to Adams, for when Pearson claims that "this definition of force is perfectly intelligible," Adams argues him into obscurity by saying, "How so? Force is a measure of 'how.' Next it becomes a measure of motion. Apparently it is a measure of relation. Ultimately it measures only itself."[38] It was not only Pearson who failed to educate Adams about the status in reality of the concept of force (even in spite of *The Grammar*'s inclusion of a devastating criticism of Spencer's various indiscriminate uses of the term): Stallo too insisted, in a passage in *Concepts and Theories of Physics* which Adams underlined, that force itself had no independent reality and the use of the term should be abolished;[39] Oliver Lodge's statement, in *Modern Views of Electricity*, that "lines of force" have no more and no less existence than have "rays of light," elicited Adams's retort in the margin, "but he says they 'pull.' Is that not existence?"[40] Even Lucien Poincaré's summation, in *The Evolution of Modern Physics*, of the legitimate role of the new physics in society, Adams rejected with a credo of his own, "Feeble conclusion! Physics are force, and force is the object of nature."[41] The concerted assault of all his scientific mentors was thus not enough to teach Adams a consistent and legitimate use of the concept of force. In his revisions of the 1907 edition of *The Education* he felt enough uncertainty to interpose the concept of mind-force into several of his existing uses of the term, thereby increasing its figurativeness, but he allowed to stand such basic and final pronouncements by his narrator as the following:

> Science has proved that forces, sensible and occult, physical and metaphysical, simple and complex, surround, traverse, vibrate, rotate, repel, attract without stop; that man's senses are conscious of few, and only in a partial degree; but that, from the beginning of organic existence his consciousness has been induced, expanded, trained in the lines of his sensitiveness; and that the rise of his faculties from a lower power to a higher, or from a narrower to a wider field, may be due to the function of assimilating and storing outside force or forces. (487)

Despite Adams's study of the new scientific epistemology and despite his disbelief in traditional absolutes, then, a concept of force as being actual and absolute seems to have been unavoidable for him.

The disparate and often ambiguous materials of the first three quarters of *The Education* hardly seem such as could be amalgamated in a unified and didactic conclusion, yet this is exactly what narrator Adams attempts to supply in the final quarter with his Dynamic Theory of History. Predictably, it is a puzzling construct. In many ways it does what it should in its literary context—it brings many of the themes to culmination; it makes explicit the idea behind the structure and style of the narration up to that point; and it fulfills the book's form in the way which is standard in autobiographies, "educations" and *Bildungsromanen*, by showing the protagonist arriving at the point of highest perspective, arriving, that is, at the point of awareness from which the narrator delivers the narration. But the Dynamic Theory of History is not presented as the framework of truth, but as another of author Adams's intellectual playthings. The rhetoric of indeterminacy pervades the book right to its very heart.

> One sought no absolute truth. One sought only a spool on which to wind the thread of history without breaking it. Among indefinite possible orbits, one sought the orbit which would best satisfy the observed movements of the runaway star Groombridge, 1838, commonly called Henry Adams. . . .
>
> Therefore, . . . he sat down as though he were again a boy at school to shape after his own needs the values of a Dynamic Theory of History. (473)

The shape of the completed Dynamic Theory is the pattern of the universe of force: "A Dynamic theory, like most theories, begins by begging the question: it defines Progress and the development and economy of Forces. Further, it defines force as anything that does, or helps to do work. Man is a force; so is the sun; so is a mathematical point, though without dimensions or known existence" (474). Force is the basic unit of this analysis, and although unabashedly metaphorical in its definition, it is nonetheless to be conceived of as inescapably necessitous. Man does not control forces, insists the narrator; he is controlled and educated by them. The Dynamic Theory simply views human history as a force system, the irresistible movement of which is toward increasingly greater acceleration and multiplicity.

The narrator runs through the history of Western civilization (the approach Brooks used in *The Law of Civilization and Decay*), applying this formula to some of its crucial developments and turning points. He shows, for example, that the strongest early force in man's domain was the divine, the whole universal infinity of force envisioned by man as a unity and studied in the "science" of religion. With the coming of Christianity and its symbol of the cross, the Theory states, attractive force attained a new plateau of consolidation and magnitude, well beyond the levels reached by primitive and even Roman societies. But there were forces other than religion abroad too, the diverse forces of nature against which human forces were always engaged, and man-created forces such as gunpowder which made any equilibrium in history only a temporary hiatus in the ineluctable course of change. With Francis Bacon, according to the Theory, the direction of thought-force changed: man attended to the various forces of nature, and unity was "left to shift for itself" (484). As force increased in acceleration and diversification under these conditions, man's position became increasingly critical: "As Nature developed her hidden energies, they tended to become destructive. Thought itself became tortured, suffering reluctantly, impatiently, painfully, the coercion of new method" (486). The "stupendous acceleration" of force in the nineteenth century and "the appearance of the new class of supersensuous forces" (such as radium) necessarily resulted in man's bewildered alienation and threatened ultimate disaster. "This, then, or something like this, would be a dynamic formula of history," the narrator claims (478). His formula, it should be noted, begins with a postulate but ends with a mood.

Its discovery has also brought the protagonist to the standpoint of the narrator; but because "any law of movement must include, to make it a convenience, some mechanical formula of acceleration" (487), the Law of Acceleration becomes the next and last object of the protagonist's quest and the narrator's explanation. With it the education is completed. Again there is an element of casual arbitrariness about its postulates but an ironclad necessity about the progress it describes. "The ratio of increase in the volume of coal-power may serve as dynamometer" (490), although other measures such as the increase in horsepower capacity, in heat intensity or in the size and range of navy guns would serve as well, the narrator claims. What is absolutely sure is increasing acceleration, and whatever the rate—the doubling of the quantity every ten years is the coal-power rate he decides "seemed carefully conservative"—"the force evolved seemed more like an explosion than gravitation, and followed closely the [precipitous] curve of steam" (491). For the rate of change in the human mind, in thought-force, the narrator suggests "the formula of squares to serve for a law of mind. . . . As the human meteoroid approached the sun or centre of attractive force, the attraction of one century squared itself to give the measure of attraction in the next" (492). So many minds are trying to understand and utilize force in so many ways in the twentieth century, the narrator feels, that "if any analogy whatever existed between the human mind, on one side, and the laws of motion, on the other, the mind had already entered a field of attraction so violent that it must immediately pass beyond, into a new equilibrium, like the comet of Newton, to suffer dissipation altogether" (496). Already the narrator could see signs of the apocalypse:

They chased force into hiding-places where Nature herself had never known it to be, making analyses that contradicted being, and syntheses that endangered the elements. . . . Every day Nature violently revolted, causing so-called accidents with enormous destruction of property and life, while plainly laughing at man, who helplessly groaned and shrieked and shuddered, but never for a single instant could stop. The railways alone approached the carnage of war; automobiles and fire-arms ravaged society, until an earthquake became almost a nervous relaxation. (494-495)

If such progress were "prolonged one generation longer," sheer survival "would require a new social mind" (498).

The whole vision is, finally, irrationally hyperbolic, tinged with paranoia. The very unscientific feeling, as old as the fears of man, that nature is taking vengeance for man's unwarranted prying is a strangely contradictory terminal point for a dynamic theory of history. There seems to be, finally, too small and too dangerous an emotion prompting this funneling-down of reality into the mold of an apocalyptic determinism—a kind of despair which is very satisfied to feed on itself. As the protagonist of *The Education* confronts the modern scene armed with his dynamic formula, he sees everywhere signs of a power-hungry world-gone-mad; arriving in New York from Paris in 1905, he observes, again in the mode of a force-nightmare, that

> the outline of the city became frantic in its effort to explain something that defied meaning. Power seemed to have outgrown its servitude and to have asserted its freedom. The cylinder had exploded, and thrown great masses of stone and steam against the sky. The city had the air and movement of hysteria, and the citizens were crying, in every accent of anger and alarm, that the new forces must at any cost be brought under control. (499)

Even granting that there was much in the situations of New York and the world in 1905 to confirm such a hyperbolic vision, its very surreal figurativeness indicates that it takes its quality more from inner than outer weather, more from the fulfillment of some intuition or the completion of some emotion than from the observation of actual conditions. This was the fundamental limitation of Adams's Dynamic Theory: it was too likely to become a solipsistically self-validating apocalypse, justifying the very attitudes of hurt and bitter aloofness out of which it sprang. It could be a real danger to sanity.

The Dynamic Theory shares with Spencer's Synthetic Philosophy the assumptions that everything designatable, even metaphorically, as forces will behave like mechanical force, and that the entire universe can be described in terms of a moving system of forces. The resemblance stops there, however. Adams had thrown off Spencerian optimism with the idea of simple and uniform evolutionary progress, and what remained was only the starkly impersonal determinism of a force system that related to no human ideas of value or order. Adams did not like the way the world was going, and he found absurdly unacceptable the most reliable and modern ways of representing and understanding it. His own method, consequently—again unlike Spencer's—is cagey and complex. The Dynamic Theory and the process of its formulation are confoundingly metaphorical: the protagonist's career serves as a metaphor for the course of Western civilization, but finally the course of Western civilization serves as a metaphor for the narrator's mind. There is no simple way to take it.

The book ends in a baffling diversity of tones. Running counter to the Dynamic Theory's end-of-the-world vision of accelerating force and human futility is a last-page obituary tribute to John Hay in which Adams praises his distinguished friend's accomplishments in statecraft and represents him as a tragic hero cut down by death at the height of his fame and achievement.* I find no traces of irony here, only conventional, sincere and heartfelt eulogy, which, in the high value it puts on real human achievement, holds the universe of force in abeyance. But then in the book's last paragraph the focus shifts back to the world and the tone back to irony as the narrator hypothetically envisions the return to earth of the three great friends, Adams, King, and Hay in their centenary year, 1938, and suggests, in an irony calculated to chill future generations, that perhaps "for the first time since man began his education among the carnivores, they would find a world that sensitive and timid natures could regard without a shudder" (505).

Actually there is no effect in the book that is unmitigated, no generalization about man or the universe which isn't at one time or another contradicted, implicitly or explicitly. Adams thought of the book as written to a didactic purpose, and the terms of his own analysis are significant:

> When I read St. Augustine's *Confessions*, or Rousseau's, I feel certain that their faults, as literary artists, are worse than mine. We have all three undertaken to do what cannot be successfully done—mix narrative and didactic purpose and style. The charm of the effort is not in winning the game but in playing it. We all enjoy the failure. St. Augustine's narrative subsides at last into the dry sands of metaphysical theology. Rousseau's narrative fails wholly in didactic result; it subsides into still less artistic egoism. And I found that a narrative style was so incompatible with a didactic or scientific style, that I had to write a long supplementary chapter to explain in scientific terms what I could not put into narration without ruining the narrative. The game was singularly simple in that sense, but never played out successfully by any artist however great.[42]

Looking back, Adams apparently felt that the Dynamic Theory was what he

---

* Peter Shaw too has cited this passage as mitigating the book's theme of personal and human failure with "a belief that the exceptional man could beneficently influence history," in "The Success of Henry Adams," *YR*, LIX (Autumn 1969), 78.

was driving at in *The Education*, and (as we have already seen from internal evidence) that the Theory provided a shaping principle for its themes and style. But not only is there a richness and vitality in the book far beyond and counter to the potentials inherent in a mechanical theory of the universe, but also the theory itself is given frankly ambivalent, even antagonistic treatment at times by the narrator. If the book finally instructs in anything, it is not in metaphysical dogma but in the impossibility of metaphysics and the radical limitations of human understanding. Its resemblance in this respect to Augustine's *Confessions* is more like a parody than an imitation; Adams's scientific metaphysics gave him nothing like the surety Augustine got from his Christianity.

Despite the incoherences there is no question that Adams produced a better book by contending with his philosophy of forces than he could have by straightforwardly advocating it. As a factor generally in the narrator's mind and generally abrasive, force theory gives the book's particular details and events a subtler and more powerful effect. That the multifarious details of modern life should suggest a cosmic pattern, and that that pattern should turn out to be this particular one, is, in view of all man's traditions and expectations, highly dramatic; that the narrator should accept this pattern grudgingly, tentatively, and inconsistently both compounds the drama and attests to his insight, candor, and ultimately unyielding idealism.

The explanation of the theory itself is flat, regardless of Adams's attempt to enliven it by putting it in the narrative framework of his protagonist's coming-to-awareness. It strikes us as narrow, more simplistic than simple, more like the product of obsession than of far-ranging reflection. I doubt that Adams would have wanted this to be so (he would much rather have been another Augustine), but the Dynamic Theory was the best he could come up with, philosophically and scientifically, at the time, and he had to take it for what it was with all its limitations.

Such is the nature of literary art that the success of the work is not dependent on the universal acceptability of the philosophy. Poor ideas can, and often do, inform good literature. In *The Education* it is the literary mode, not the philosophical content, which gives the book its power. We witness a sensitive and somewhat pessimistic mind encountering the whole moiling, indigestible brew of turn-of-the-century politics, ideas, art, social life and science; insisting on a metaphysics of order in a postmetaphysical age; viewing in an emotionally unregenerate state the whole intellectual regeneration modern men must undergo; and it is this complex of thoughts and feelings, events and persons that gives us the deepest meanings we get from the book. The style and structure too, keyed as they are to the phases of the force-universe and to the themes of personal failure and human absurdity, establish by means of literary craft a tacit but apprehendable context of meaning for every detail of the narrative. A conventional philosopher of that time, like Spencer or Fiske, would necessarily (because of the traditional modes in which he thought and wrote) have to objectify this whole network of thoughts and experiences, make a rationalized abstract of it and present this intellectualized model of reality with a good deal of impersonal certainty. Taking the Dynamic Theory of History in itself we can see that this is what Adams the protagonist of *The Education* tried to do, and the results are predictably unsatisfactory. But Adams the author had the genius to present this theory in a full context of observed and felt experience, and in a freely ingenious literary mode, and he produced thereby a work which would be enduringly valid whatever the fate of his concept of the universe of force.

HENRY ADAMS wrote *The Education* in his late sixties, and with its private printing in 1907 his writing career reached its high point. Afterwards the ebb was rapid; what writing he did went along old channels, with no new rush of inspiration. He worked fitfully at revising *Chartres* and *The Education* for publication (the changes he made were virtually inconsequential; his revising of them acted more to delay their publication than to have any other effect); he contributed to *The Letters of John Hay and Extracts from His Diary*,[43] and wrote *The Life of George Cabot Lodge*,[44] both relatively undistinguished efforts on behalf of deceased personal friends; and he wrote two essays, *The Rule of Phase Applied to History* and *A Letter to American Teachers of History*.[45] These latter essays are essentially two more struggles with scientific history, but without the redeeming artistic framework, without the explicit complexity of narrative personae of *Chartres* and *The Education*. Adams presents these theoretical constructs—hypothetical though universal—directly, with a straightforward though somewhat tentative advocacy, and the essays are by far the less interesting for it. They are valued by many Adams scholars for the light they shed on Adams's intentions and the development of his thought, although some, like Vern Wagner, view them as satirical in intent, but no attempt is made to regard them as either great thought or great literature.

The two essays share with *The Education* the motif of modern man predicting the future of civilization or extrapolating it from a basis in scientific thought, and they share with the 1894 essay *The Tendency of History*, the intention of shocking historians and educators into a new orientation toward their endeavor. As Adams put it candidly in a letter, "What I have wanted for the last twenty years, was to force some sign of activity into . . . history, which seems to me dead as the dodos. In my despair of galvanizing it into life by any literary process, it occurred to me that some little knowledge of physico-chemical processes might show me a means of acting on it from outside." [46] In *The Rule of Phase Applied to History*, he produced what he referred to as "a supplementary chapter, too didactic to make part of a narrative" of *The Education.* "My object," he continues, "was to suggest a reform of the whole University system, grouping all knowledge as a historical stream, to be treated by historical methods, and drawing a line between the University and technology." [47]

The attempt to unify all knowledge, to show the temporal development of civilization, and to find some one scientific or metascientific principle underlying that development still testify to the very deep impression on Adams made by Comte, Spencer, and brother Brooks. Living, however, under the influence of Stallo, Pearson, and Mach, he realized that he could make no claims about the definitiveness or truth of his theories. And to increase his incertitude to a point near agony, there was his realization that he was almost totally incapable of understanding the most advanced theories of modern science. "I do not know enough mathematics" is his constant lament, and such admissions as "I want Kelvin's writings, and I know I can't read a page of them. Is it not exasperating to see what one wants, and feel one's incapacity to seize it?" [48] In other contexts these feelings could precipitate a hyperbolic humility which, in a way, was not far from the truth: "I am incapable of comprehending the simplest, as the most complex reasoning. Therefore I don't reason; I try only to plaster other people's standard text books together, so as to see where we are." [49] Philosophical theorizing demands confidence if it demands anything, but Adams played the role of an unconfident metaphysician by spreading disclaimers in every direction ("treat the theory not according to its truth but according to its convenience" he in effect tells the audience of *The Rule*, [50] and to his brother Brooks he says "the paper is a mere intellectual plaything") [51] and by humbly seeking scientific help with the manuscript.

The Rule itself fully warranted all of Adams's hesitancy. The scientific help he got was from Professor Henry A. Bumstead of Yale, who read a first draft and offered numerous tactfully worded suggestions. Adams badly needed the lessons in scientific method and terminology Bumstead gave him, for indeed his grasp of modern science does seem to have been as weak as he claimed it was. He needed to be told such things as that the terms "movement," "velocity," and "acceleration" are not roughly synonymous, that potential energy is not concealed kinetic energy; that some connections Adams calls "logical" are really analogical; that light is not polarized by a magnet; that entropy is not merely deadness; that "lines of force" are not a physical reality; that Adams applied what he called "the law of inverse squares" incorrectly, and that he even neglected to figure it inversely; and finally that scientific thought did not manifest some discontinuous "change of phase" since Newton.[52] But even shortening and extensive revision failed to improve *The Rule* appreciably.

Its fundamental shortcomings are obvious from a simple summary of its theory. Willard Gibbs's Rule of Phase ought, Adams thinks, to be as useful in societal as in chemical phenomena: if we take Gibbs's definition of "phase" ("an equilibrium"), Stoney's theory of the hierarchy of phases (solid, fluid, vapor, electricity, ether, space, and pure mathematics), and Comte's theory of the successive stages through which civilizations pass (although he basically saw only three: the theological, the metaphysical, and the Positive), we ought to be able to arrive at a physically based, mathematizable account of the human past and future. All that was then needed was a translation of historical phases into their analogous physical phases ("when did the solid age end and the fluid begin?" "Was society now a fluid or a gas?"), and the assigning of arbitrary (for the time being) numerical values to them according to the length of their time span. Since "nature . . . loves the logarithm, and perpetually recurs to her inverse square,"[53] a process of squaring time-intervals can be used; a trial run both indicates that the Religious Phase of man's history lasted for 90,000 years, and projects a future which would "bring Thought to the limit of its possibilities in 1921."[54] The finished essay is clearly a product of the vaguely understood science, the facile analogizing, and the apocalyptic yearning that went into it. It seems to have drawn (much to Adams's chagrin) almost no response from those to whom he sent it, and with good reason. Even Bumstead had to admit, after he could be a bit more appreciative toward the later essay, *A Letter*, that "I could not altogether avoid the feeling that there was something arbitrary and artificial in the analogies you drew."[55]

The argument in *A Letter to American Teachers of History* is based on the Second Law of Thermodynamics, a theory that fills, better than any other Adams had hitherto tried, his need for a scientific keystone for his doom-metaphysics. It did not seem to bother him that instead of the universe accelerating itself to its death in an explosion of etherealization that it now promised to degrade itself into a dead ocean of entropy. What mattered was that the end be reputably scientific and that it be soon. Again there are the familiar motifs of the unification of knowledge around a scientific generalization and the restructuring of university education with scientific history at its core. Again there is the deep ambiguity about how Adams means his ideas to be taken. To his friend Raphael Pumpelly he wrote, "Of course, the *Letter* is intended as a historical study of the scientific grounds of Socialism, Collectivism, and Humanitarianism and Democracy and all the rest";[56] while to Brooks he said, "It is a jibe at my dear historical association,—a joke, which nobody will know enough to understand."[57] As with his earlier scientific-historical theories he seems to want to push it as far as his audience is willing to accept it, but also to be ready to relinquish it totally. Adams sent foregone disclaimers only to his brother Brooks, who, ironically enough, totally disregarded them and after his brother's death published the two late essays in *The Degradation of the Democratic Dogma* as entirely serious theory.

With his somewhat belated discovery of the Second Law of Thermodynamics, Adams had found a theory which could include all phenomena (even mental phenomena) without analogizing. If the universe is a closed system in which there is a finite quantity of energy which increasingly dissipates irrecoverably (mainly through heat loss), then indeed the universe is totally foredoomed, mind and matter. The sun will cool, temperatures and energy levels will equalize throughout the universe, and consciousness, life, and movement will cease forever.

"I take the sun much to heart," lamented Darwin, confronted by the Second Law,[58] but Adams in *A Letter* became an ardent and thoroughgoing Degradationist, gathering an extremely various collection of evidences of the universe's decline and presenting it with macabre relish. He took the Second Law to mean that all aspects of the universe were in a simultaneous decline; virtually any disastrous or even unfortunate happening supported his general theory. Adams seems to have done a great deal more research for this demonstration than for any of his works since *Chartres*—his quotations from scientific and pseudoscientific sources are extensive and his supporting details are numerous. Not only does he find the sun cooling, but the earth is losing temperature; vital energy is falling off since the great growth-peaks of the plant kingdom in the carboniferous and of the animal kingdom in the miocene eras; man too in many ways is inferior to his supposed animal ancestors, weaker in his senses and his physical vitality, strong only in intellectuality, which probably is only an enfeebled function of the will anyway; society too is weakening, as evidenced by a falling birth rate and rising rates of suicide, disease, and insanity; and modern culture is demonstrably inferior to that of classical times. Degradation is a cosmic tide, everywhere manifest. *A Letter* is Adams's last full-scale attack on evolutionary theory and the optimistic outlooks of Comte, Darwin, Spencer, and most of his contemporaries; it is his last ambitious attempt to spin, out of his own deep disillusionment and frustration, a web of theory that would support and justify those feelings within him.

In the bleak mood that permeated his correspondence in the year 1910, Adams looked back on the major phase of his career as a series of bungled attempts at what he now thought he had wanted most to do. "The only book I ever wrote that was worth writing was the first volume of the Series—the *Mont-Saint-Michel*," he said. "The volume began the demonstration of the law which this *Letter* announces, and the *Education* illustrates."[59] The world moved on, oblivious of the law of its degradation, and as it did, Adams's senile rage at socialists, Jews, optimists, and modern times mellowed into a renewed interest in medieval times. He spent his last years largely in a phase beyond scientific apocalypse, translating the texts and listening to the music of the Middle Ages.

THUS HENRY ADAMS, in attempting to structure his vision of chaos and degeneration, went from one scientific theory to another, seeking at least a satisfying metaphor where he could not have absolute truth, "prod[ding]" (as Robert Hume puts it) "the universe ironically into various successive shapes, trying to decide which one displeased him least." [60] His insight was channeled, by his temperament, by his world and by the implications of the force-categories basic to his thinking, into an apocalyptic determinism at the nether extreme from metaphysical optimism and even simple human hope. There would be no more false complacency about the cosmos, no more man-flattering metaphysics if he could help it, no more crashing disillusionment by that route. And if scientific epistemologists insisted that all ideas were fabrications, all order a dream, he was willing to let the matter stand right there and promulgate a deterministic metaphysics in an indeterminate, ironic mode. In all likelihood, he must have felt, it was what the whole absurd show deserved.

It is not at all as a man of ideas that Adams will be remembered. Not only was his thinking unoriginal, but at times he even showed himself unable to comprehend the ideas he was borrowing. Yet our cultural tradition puts more stock in him by far than in the great Synthetic Philosophers of his time. There is wisdom in this particular "judgment of time," as indeed there generally is. Not concerned to build and defend a particular intellectual system, an extension of his ego, he remained always highly sensitive to ideas of both his own time and of past ages, reacting with both intelligence and deep feeling, as a citizen of the world who was intensely concerned about its makeup and import. His ideas were not uniquely his own but his vision was, and, as an artist, he learned to use his personal vision as both a point of approach and as a subject in his best works, rather than affecting a naive pseudoobjective view of the universal Knowable as had the Synthetic Philosophers. Thus there is a larger structure—of emotion and personality and quest—in which the obsolescence-prone ideas exist.

The concept of the universe of force haunted Adams and exasperated him, but he overcame it in his art. It formed his conception of the world, but he knew that it did, and could fix it in a perspective that diminished its import and hedged it with irony and uncertainty. He could even control it by using it as an arbitrary pattern for the structure and style of his works. So little is a great artist at the mercy of a seemingly ineluctable world-view.

5. FRANK NORRIS: NAIVE OMNISCIENCE AND THE UNIVERSE OF FORCE

I've got an idea that's as big as all out-doors.

Frank Norris to Harry M. Wright, April 5, 1899

Frank Norris stands in sharp contrast to Henry Adams as a thinker and a writer. Although his short life was contemporaneous with Adams's mature years and both men clearly show the influence of universe-of-force concepts, Norris's intellectual style was different, as was his whole approach to the writer's craft. Whereas Adams sought out the best thinkers of his day and questioned, challenged, and tested their ideas in various approaches and modes, Norris picked up what was at hand, absorbing ideas from second- and third-rate thinkers and from the popular milieu, and held these conceptions so uncritically that their shallownesses and contradictions became his own. Adams was skeptical, ironic, and intellectually complex, where Norris was wholeheartedly enthusiastic about his ideas, absolutistic, and intellectually naive.

Such intellectual naiveté was no rare commodity among American writers of the turn of the century. Not only Norris but Jack London, Theodore Dreiser, and a number of lesser "realists" were gripped by general ideas which they, in their avid innocence, found eye-opening and revolutionary, but which now seem merely to tinge their works with traces of the quaint and dated. Their philosophizing and explaining is generally embarrassing. Intellectual embarrassment is not necessarily fatal to the spell of fiction, however. Although we can learn little or nothing from their conscious attempts to teach, we can still be moved, and quite legitimately, by the depth and power of these writers' symbolic representations of human experience, for they are novelists after all, and the essence of what novelists do stands in a strange, sometimes remote relationship to their general ideas about life. A philosopher, in a sense, takes the human context of his ideas for granted, focusing on the conceptual backgrounds, interconnections, and implications of ideas, regardless of who thinks these ideas and what they mean in his life. A novelist like Norris, on the other hand, tends more or less to take the ideas as absolute givens and focus

*his creative attention on the individual lives in which the ideas play a role.
Henry Adams seemed to be aware of this disparity of foci when in his introduction to* The Education *he urged the philosopher's perspective—the predisposition that the general ideas and not the individual experience, the suit of
clothes and not the mannikin should get his reader's attention—although the
individuality of the experiences and of the narrative voice make that book a
uniquely rich combination of treatise and novel (and even vindicate the editor's misunderstanding in subtitling it* An Autobiography*). Norris seems to
have had no such awareness, but his works are clearly those of a novelist in
this sense. His philosophical ideas are absolutes which generate or explain
individual realities; for Norris, the mannikin is far more interesting than the
clothes.*

*But even giving him that license as a novelist, we are embarrassed to see his
predilection for cheap, mass-marketed readymades. Saxon supremacy, redblooded primitivism, evolutionary optimism, idealized sexism, Nordau on degeneration, Lombroso on criminal mentality—it's a naive and flashy wardrobe
and a serious handicap for any fictional mannikins, however intensely conceived.*

*Norris's work contrasts with Adams's too in his approach to literary form.
Whereas Adams in both* Chartres *and* The Education *essentially creates literary approaches and forms that embody the individuality of his particular insights, Norris generally accepts well-established, conventional forms and tries
to modify and intensify them and integrate them into his own particular vision. Norris wanted, perhaps more than anything else, to be the Novelist, and
he cast himself as such (even calling himself "the boy Zola" in college), and
he never quite got beyond the influence of his early idols. There is a sense in
which he didn't outlive his apprenticeship. His works too often seem imitative
and not entirely within his artistic control, and his fictional modes tend to
come from models chosen from a rather narrow and idiosyncratic compass of
reading. His subjects, themes, and techniques seem heavily dependent on the
prior work of Emile Zola, of William Dean Howells, and, perhaps, of Edgar
Allan Poe. Paradoxically, Norris's most original vein seems to be a mixture of
these seemingly incompatible modes, a kind of amalgam of naturalism, goth-
icism, and the novel of manners.*

*Illustrative of Norris's whole approach to philosophical ideas and literary
form is his handling of the problem of narrative point of view. Again a comparison with Adams is instructive, because whereas Adams's basic skepticism,
his sense of the fallibility of human knowledge, and his literary inventiveness
led him to employ a literary point of view that was probing, tentative, and
self-aware, Norris's unreflective, derivative, and basically absolutistic approach to ideas and form led him to naive omniscience. His narrators, like*

those of most literary realists, know everything and have access everywhere, although they tend to focus intently on a single character or group of characters. Their knowledge, although not often generalized or didactic, is final, absolute, whether it be knowledge that a square head is a sign of degeneracy, that a strong woman needs mastering by a strong man, or that the laws of the universe ultimately work for the good. Norris's narrators in effect act on the assumption that human experience is explainable by reference to an absolute, unified, and true body of knowledge, and they set forth their explanations with all the confidence and naiveté of a Helmholtz or a Spencer constructing an absolute model of the real universe. Thus Norris gambles a great deal of reader credibility on the quality of that body of knowledge.

Fundamental to his broadest grasp of universal causality and human fate was, as we shall see, an optimistic Americanized version of the universe of force. Its origins in his thinking have been clearly established—as a student at the University of California he had been taught by one of its leading proponents, Joseph LeConte. It went hand in hand with the naive omniscience of Norris's narrators (as indeed it had with the naive absolutism of Spencer and his followers, including Professor LeConte), and it could, when he cared to call upon it, supply for his narratives an awesome cosmic background, a scientifically accredited set of causal explanations and a deep and abiding sense of either menace or reassurance, depending on what was called for by the fictional occasion. The universe of force could seemingly answer the big questions and still leave a novelist free to be a novelist.

The appearance of the universe of force in his works is intermittent. In Vandover and the Brute and McTeague there are occasional explanations of human fate in terms of larger forces, and in several of Norris's works there are no references to the universe of force at all. But in his magnum opus, the incomplete trilogy of the Wheat, the universe of force is central to the trilogy's structure and essential to the themes, imagery, and philosophical resolution of its first volume, The Octopus. In considering Frank Norris, then, we see the universe of force in the hands of a novelist, who uses it in creating a purely fictional, essentially esthetic construct, drawing on its potential, in both his strength and his weakness, in the fabrication of what he hopes will be the deathless embodiment of his individual vision.

FRANK NORRIS (1870–1902) cast himself as a radical novelist of his day, generally standing against the gentility and ideality of popular American fiction. He wrote several melodramatic novels of serious intent, several adventure potboilers and finally launched into a highly ambitious trilogy, "The Epic of the Wheat," two volumes of which had been completed when he died suddenly at the age of thirty-two. He had studied art in London and Paris, subsequently attended the University of California (1890–1894), Harvard University (1895–1896, where he studied creative writing), and had capped his education in the manner that was becoming standard for American novelists of the age of Realism, by working as a journalist (with a tour of duty as a reporter in South Africa and later in the Spanish-American War and a two-year position on the staff of *The Wave* of San Francisco). He seems to have wanted to become a novelist from the beginning, certainly from the time of relinquishing his art career. "I entered college with the view of preparing myself for the profession of a writer of fiction,"[1] he declared while at Berkeley, and indeed beginning writing then in earnest, he put together much of a novel, *Vandover and the Brute* while at Harvard, and, settling in San Francisco, stepped fully into the role of novelist with the publication of *Moran of the Lady Letty* in 1898 and *McTeague* in 1899.

His stated ideas about prose fiction provide a good introduction to his whole approach as a novelist and a thinker, as well as showing his relationship to several important currents in the literary stream of his day. His concept of fiction was closely related to emotional response and was seemingly built backwards from the idea of reader effect. His mentor and model Novelist was French realist Emile Zola; anticonventional, deeply involved in the big questions of his time, dramatic and psychological, Zola's works were extremely moving to Norris, and Norris's novelistic theory was fundamentally his version of what Zola's novels did.

Norris's theories appeared principally in reviews and articles for newspapers and periodicals (*The Wave*, *The Chicago American*, *World's Work*, *The Boston Evening Transcript*), and at the base of his thinking was his conception of the wide public he was addressing and the pallid sentimental fiction which was popular with them. From the standpoint of a radical Zolaist writing for a popular audience he came on as revolutionary and uncompromising, announcing that the novel needed to develop a whole new relationship to life, stressing Truth rather than entertainment as its object, and focusing on realities instead of on the shallow and hypocritical stuff of so much current and previous fiction.

At the same time, Norris saw the "Realism" of such writers as William Dean Howells as an incomplete remedy, since, in its focus on the average, the everyday, the inconsequential, it stopped at the description of surfaces and never got "through the clothes and tissues and wrappings of flesh down deep into the red, living heart of things." What was needed was "Romanticism," a type of fiction that "takes cognizance of variations from the type of normal life," that studied the deep and the dramatic and the different, and to which "belongs the wide world for range, and the unplumbed depths of the human heart, and the mystery of sex, and the problems of life, and the black, unsearched penetralia of the soul of man."[2] Ideally, Norris urged, the best literary form was "Naturalism," which combined Realism's accuracy and Romanticism's Truth; its best examples were the novels of Émile Zola.[3] Norris's orientation toward fiction, then, was toward the depiction of both the dramatic, bizarre variations that reveal deep truths beneath human experience, and the accurately documented surfaces—of characters, of environments, of mores—that recreate the recognizable world. The former motive led him to melodrama, the latter to documentary realism and the novel of manners.

The results in his novels of this disparate mix are curious—even more curious than the reality-system we are given by Zola, and less coherent. As we move, say, in *McTeague* from the copious mundane details of everyday life on Polk Street to the climactic savagery of McTeague and a melodramatic denouement in Death Valley, or perhaps in *The Octopus* from the ordinary, even ritualized details of farming and socializing to the "Romanticism" of such images as that of a Cyclopean locomotive destroying innocent sheep, that of an ascetic shepherd's telepathy and the symbolic reincarnation of his long-dead sweetheart, that of a disastrous shootout and that of a widowed mother's pathetic starvation, it is evident that there are extremely wide parameters of possibility in the world of Norris's fiction. Fate or forces act radically on the normal and ordinary, transforming it into something monstrous or extreme. Out of the dilettante Vandover comes the wolf-brute; out of the everyday comes the apocalyptic. An exception is *The Pit*, where the formula seems to be reversed, with the resulting loss of power over the reader's imagination which is a common theme of Norris criticism.

It is tempting to use Jungian categories to interpret the phenomenon of Frank Norris's fiction.[4] Norris's visions seem to occur in places familiar to our foreconscious minds, but their stuff is the stuff of our dreams. Norris's story motifs—the primitivism, the superiority-inferiority, the masculinity-femininity, the against-odds struggle—evoke elemental responses in ways that could be readily explained in terms of the operation of subconscious archetypes of universal human experience. It is not as a craftsman or as a thinker that Norris gets his following, I would submit, but as this peculiar sort of melodramatist of realism. Despite the artistic failings of his fiction—the shallowness of his thinking, the many overdrawn effects, the crude characterizations, the uneven prose skill, the narrative incoherence, and the unremitting technical conventionality—a great many readers are fascinated by Norris's vision, affected, I think, by the way the melodrama can suddenly loom out of the prosaic surface and if afforded a willing suspension of disbelief, affect the reader's deepest feelings and fears.

Given his propensity for bizarre melodrama it seems ironic that Norris strove so after rational explanation in his fiction. Naive omniscience was inherent in his very role as Novelist, and seldom did a motif rise out of his storyteller's subconscious without acquiring a protective covering of scientific or pseudoscientific theory. Norris had an absolutist's sense of causality, and his concept of force helped him fill the explanatory gap between universal determinism and specific human events. In his theory of literature he tended to identify the broadest collective determinants of human affairs as "force," and to assert that the finest class of novel was that which "proves something, draws conclusions from a whole congeries of forces, social tendencies, race impulses, devotes itself not to a study of men but of man."[5]

His critical prose gets less precise as it gets more theoretical, often cultivating impressiveness at the expense of clarity, but we can in general discover from it that he most valued the novel which reached that level of universal determinism on which the "elemental forces" operated.

> It must tell something, must narrate vigorous incidents and must show something, must penetrate deep into the motives and character of typemen, men who are composite pictures of a multitude of men. It must do this because of the nature of the subject, for it deals with elemental forces, motives that stir whole nations. These cannot be handled as abstractions in fiction. Fiction can find expression only in the concrete. The elemental forces, then, contribute to the novel with a purpose to provide it with vigorous action. In the novel, force can be expressed in no other way. The social tendencies must be expressed by means of analysis of the characters of the men and women who compose that society, and the two must be combined and manipulated to evolve the purpose—to find the value of x.[6]

What the abstractions, the "elemental forces" might be is left rather vague here ("motives that stir whole nations"? "social tendencies"?), but Norris obviously felt that their causal primacy should be felt through the depiction of the novel's particulars.

Norris seems to have derived both novelistic inspiration and philosophic explanation from a conception of a deterministic universe—the "value of x" stable in terms of "elemental forces." Not in any sense an original thinker, Norris got his grand conceptions close at hand, largely where one might expect, from his idol Zola and from the ubiquitous American evolutionism.

From Zola he seems to have gotten his whole approach to fiction: his sense of subject, scope, structure, and even (to some extent) of theme and tone are directly relatable to the novels of Zola we know he read. And in terms of the philosophical framework with which we are concerned, such novels as *L'Assommoir*, *Germinal*, *La Terre*, and *La Bête Humaine* presented Norris with a deterministic view of man and his experience wherein the forces (although rarely so termed) of heredity, instinct, society, economics, milieu, and so forth formed an explanatory framework upon which the whole fabric of human experience could be displayed. In the original planning for his multi-volume chronicle *Les Rougon-Macquart*, Zola reminded himself, "Choose, above all, a philosophical tendency, not in order to exhibit it, but so that it may link my books together. The best would perhaps be materialism, that is to say the belief in forces about which I need never be explicit."[7] He was fascinated with the mechanics of pre-Mendelian heredity, as he showed in reminding himself of his difference from Balzac: "My work will be less social than scientific. . . . Instead of having principles (royalty, Catholicism), I shall have laws (heredity, innateness)."[8] Zola's whole sense of natural law causality was both materialistic and absolute. When in *Les Rougon-Macquart* he traces several generations of personal and social misfortunes to the brain lesion of an ancestress, he is merely asserting again, as he does in so many other ways, his basic unifying principle that human events follow necessitously from physical causes. The forces, whether specified or not, are the forces such as are studied in physics, biology, and psychology; and they, Zola tried to say in his fiction, determine it all. Behind him lay a whole tradition of Continental scientism, materialism, and determinism such as is exemplified in Taine, Marx, and Büchner and which Norris absorbed, not intellectually and abstractly, but indirectly through the powerful images of Zola's fiction.

More direct, perhaps, was Norris's rapprochement with Americanized evolutionism. He had an active mind although a relatively untrained one, and attuned as he was to the dramatic rather than the logical aspects of ideas, he was bound to have encountered impressionably and near-at-hand the great controversy still raging over evolution in the 1890s. The versions of evolution most popular in his culture were of course the theistic, progress-oriented ones discussed in Chapter 3 above, and it is to these that Norris's few philosophical enthusiasms can be traced. The work of tracing has been done (and done thoroughly) by Donald Pizer,[9] who persuasively builds an approach to Norris out of a study of the relationship between the themes of his works and the ideas of Joseph LeConte, Norris's science professor at the University of California. LeConte (see pp. 80–82, above), who saw the agency of God in the operation of the Spencerian forces and was an ardent advocate of the compatibility of religion and science was, as Pizer has shown, a revered and dynamic figure whose class Norris attended five times a week during his junior year. Although Norris made no known or retrievable references to LeConte, the deep streak of theistic evolutionism is apparent in his writings, and it seems reasonable to assume with Pizer that a strong influence in fact existed. Certainly LeConte's concept of force as "the universal energy of nature," its action on matter being identifiable with the action of God on Nature, is relatable to the theme of transcendent optimism at the end of *The Octopus*; and similarly his idea of the hierarchy of forces emerging in the course of evolution—physical force succeeded by vital force succeeded by spiritual force—might well be seen as the conceptual basis of Norris's studies of the personal degeneration, the retrograde evolution, of the protagonists of "Lauth," *Vandover and the Brute* and *McTeague*. LeConte's is an optimist's universe, where the ultimate fulfillment of the benevolent will of God is guaranteed by the natural operation of "resident forces"; in Norris's novels the tone is far less sunny and the reassurance far more dearly bought, but this popular American conception of evolution otherwise seems to have both reinforced the novelist's sense of the universe as a deterministic mechanism and to some extent offered an optimistic palliative to the anxiety induced by that vision.

Norris was attracted by a number of other philosophical notions more or less compatible with his cosmic determinism. They tended to be popularly expounded, opposed to conventional Christianity and democracy, naturalistic rather than theistic or humanistic in their ethical orientation, and inherently melodramatic. Most prominent among them were the ideas associated with his pseudoanthropological primitivism: "The founder of the red-blooded school in America," one of his biographers, Ernest Marchand calls him.[10] In this vein, Norris viewed experience in terms of primal urges and instincts which were only partially covered over by civilization. In some story-contexts he presented this covering as a kind of mask or illusion which concealed the shocking reality underneath, in others as a genuinely moral restraint on potential savagery, and in still others as a perverted artificial inhibition of a natural drive. Basic instinct could be seen as either a source of good and strength (as in "Dying Fires" and *The Octopus*), as an expression of atavism and evolutionary retrogression (as in *McTeague* and "A Case for Lombroso"), or as some kind of liberating but awesome and potentially dangerous mixture (as in *A Man's Woman* and "A Reversion to Type").

Norris's primitivism involved not merely motifs of reversion and animal instinctualism but motifs of primal sex roles as well. In this sexist idealization, the Man's world was the world of striving and achievement, of dominance and conquest and sexual aggression, and the Woman's world was one of morality, of appreciation of the esthetic aspects of life, and of sexual passivity. The discovery of these fundamentally proper roles is a theme in such works as *Moran of the Lady Letty*, *The Octopus*, and *The Pit*.

Sociopolitically Norris's primitivism found expression in a kind of evolutionary racism, a belief in the natural superiority and worldwide manifest destiny of the white Anglo-Saxon race which appears in *Moran*, *The Octopus*, and elsewhere. Just as Orientals are naturally treacherous and Mediterraneans are naturally bloodthirsty, the Saxon is the upholder of civilization, morality, and progress. It is clear from its sexist and racist aspects that Norris's primitivism is characterized by its simplifications, stereotypes, and caricatures—of men, of women, of races, of human nature—the "ideas" as such being worthless at best. Norris's use of such shallow and pernicious stereotypes is in no wise justifiable in terms of the melodramatic effects he can achieve by using such narrative shortcuts.

"Norris accepted determinism only in so far as it appealed to his dramatic sense," Franklin Walker notes, and other scholars tend to agree on the lack of deterministic consistency.[11] Instinctual, natural, and environmental forces, in other words, tend to be invoked by Norris in particular contexts and for particular rhetorical purposes, guided by his "dramatic sense." In fact, despite all his aggressive naturalism, there is a wide streak of conventional moralism in Norris's writings. His fiction shows an overriding sense of personal and poetic justice, from the wages-of-sin motif of *Vandover and the Brute* to the grain's retribution on S. Behrman in *The Octopus* or the comeuppance of Dave Scannel, the wicked financier in *The Pit*. However, this is another aspect of Norris's fiction that is not pervasive and consistent, other than in his tendency to round off his plots with acts of justice. The moralism seems, like the pseudoscientific determinism or the primitivism, to be a stop that he pulls when he feels its novelistic appropriateness. The determinant seems not to be that Norris believes that the universe has this or that basic nature, but that certain dramatic situations are best produced or enhanced by the presence of certain philosophical assumptions. The critical status and consistency of these assumptions are probably matters about which such a novelist would feel less anxiety than impatience.

The question of consistency of belief, or coherence of vision, is nevertheless one with which a thoughtful reader cannot help but concern himself, and one which comes up constantly in Norris criticism. For example, Charles Child Walcutt points out that Norris was unable to "think through to any fundamental conclusions about the relations between naturalism (i.e., materialistic monism) and the conventional universe of free will and moral responsibility," and Richard Chase sees "a tension between Norris the liberal humanist and ardent democrat and Norris the protofascist, complete with a racist view of Anglo-Saxon supremacy, a myth of the superman, and a portentous nihilism." Ernest Marchand has cited the conflict between his basic moralism and the views sometimes expressed in his works that men are "mere nothings," presenting Norris as in revolt against estheticism and "the genteel reticences" in such a way that "perhaps inevitably he slipped over into the frank apotheosis of force." William Dillingham sees the narrative perspective in such books as *Vandover and the Brute* as wavering "from censure to objectivity" and Donald

Pizer has commented on Norris's contradictory tendencies to give himself over to both "cultural primitivism and mechanical progress." [12]

Several critics have seen development in Norris's ideas, rather than mere inconsistency. Marchand claims that "Norris groped his way from the notion of the primordial struggle for existence to the concept of a common social enterprise in which individual self-assertion must yield to the general good"; and Pizer cites the theme of "widening social allegiance" in Norris's later books and his growth into a more complex vision of the relationship of free will and determinism, and attempts as well to discover a basic coherence in Norris's thought in theological evolutionism, claiming that "for the most part his world view embodies a traditional paradox [of free will and determinism] which he attempts to 'reword' within the [evolutionary] formulas of belief of his time." [13] Finally, however, explanations based on Norris's dramatic sense seem to me the most comprehensively acceptable.

The narrative point of view of naive omniscience is of course the vehicle for the metaphysical and moral diversity contained in Norris's works. It is comprehensive and amorphous enough as a standpoint so that the dramatic and emotional values in his materials can be maximized in storylike fashion and the omniscience stretched to cover any resulting disparities of attitude, focus, or theme. The narrator can account for, judge, resolve, complicate, or enrich any particular point by drawing on his store of universal knowledge.

BUT HOW, specifically, do Norris's ideas operate in his works and what part does the universe of force play? Granted that the philosophical guises and attitudes the omniscient narrator could assume in his works were various and sometimes even incompatible, that of spokesman for the universe of force seems to have come to hand, early or late in his career, when Norris wanted a cosmic perspective, an ultimate level of causal explanation. Then he recalled his LeContian teaching and the forces that moved through all things. The universe of force appears in his early works as a background metaphysical assumption and as an occasional thematic explanation, in his middle works rarely at all, but in his late projected trilogy as an important metaphysical statement and (he hoped) a unifying structural principle.

Norris wrote the story "Lauth" at the time he was attending LeConte's classes.[14] It is sheer apprentice work, all bogus historical melodrama, pop evolution, and overwriting, but it shows quite clearly how Norris could conceive of and use the concept of force. The title character—the focus of the omniscient narrator in the first part of the story—is a student in medieval France, caught up suddenly in a desperate civil skirmish. When Lauth's first crossbow

shot finds a victim, the narrator describes him undergoing a reaction typical
of Norris's heroes and of pop primitivism in the redblooded nineties:

> At the sight of blood shed by his own hands all the animal savagery latent
> in every human being woke within him—no more merciful scruples now.
> *He could kill.* In the twinkling of an eye the pale, highly cultivated scholar,
> whose life had been passed in the study of science and abstruse questions
> of philosophy, sank back to the level of his savage Celtic ancestors.[15]

Lauth's bloodlust frenzy expends itself, he himself is seriously wounded, and
he dies, contemplating his death with disbelief and nonacceptance.

The narrator's focus then shifts to Lauth's professor of medicine and chemistry and close friend, Jacquemart de Chavannes, who broods about death
over Lauth's body like a bereaved but godless Professor LeConte. Life is a
force, he (anachronistically) decides, but "what becomes of this life, this force?
Science will tell you that, like matter, force is inexhaustible; where then does
it go after quitting its earthly tenement? . . . *It must go somewhere*, for life
was a force and force was inexhaustible" (131). He sets no stock in either soul
or afterlife but, reasoning in the manner of a monistic (and decidedly amateur)
force conservationist, he decides that "the force called life . . . *must . . . exist
in death itself*" (132), and that his theory can be proved by the resuscitation
of Lauth. Despite the objections of his more conventionally godly colleague
Anselm, Chavannes sets to work with potion, sheep's blood, and lung-bellows:
"I do not pretend to induce life of any kind by my own exertions. I merely
arouse and assist those forces that are now held bound and inert" (136).

But the outcome of all man's materialistic scientific ingenuity is that Lauth
lives again, for a while, but he lives grotesquely and incompletely, crying one
time out of his stupor, "*This is not I*; where am *I*? For God's sake, tell me
where *I* am" (143); and he quickly slips backward on the evolutionary ladder,
going from "a dull, brutish torpor" to a stage of "wagging its shaggy head
. . . and venting unnatural mutterings," to mere "scuttling," and finally a stage in
which "a horrible, shapeless mass lay upon the floor. . . . It lived, lived not as do
the animals or the trees, but as the protozoa, the jellyfish, and those strange
lowest forms of existence wherein the line between vegetable and animal cannot be drawn" (145). After it dies, finally and forever, the last word is given to
Anselm, who proposes that human life is comprised of the trinity of body,
soul, and life. When the soul of Lauth left at his first death, the only life possible in his body was a subhuman life; because of man's place on the scale of
creation, then, "the *soul* of man is the chiefest energy of his existence" (147).

"Lauth" is an immature parable, but it is typical of a great deal of Norris's
subsequent and (usually) better work. Thematically, it shows his interests in
redblooded primitivism and in a type of human degeneration which is linked

to retrograde evolution. It shows him highly sensitive to popular conceptions of evolution, of the scientist, and of the relationship of science and religion. Its message is highly moralistic and highly conventional (the solutions are not nearly so pat in his better work). Its mode is melodrama, and it has some of the characteristic Norris word skill in its Poe-like descriptions of the disgusting ("he fell in a fit upon the floor, foaming and wallowing" [143]; "the unbroken silence of the shaggy yellow lips was even more revolting than its former inhuman noises" [145]).

In this work Norris presents force as being the underlying causal motive of the universe, and he clearly has the idea that forces correlate (the force of life is *in* the force of death and needs to be transferred back out) and the idea that force is conserved (although the statement that force is "inexhaustible" sounds like a college student's notebook translation of "indestructible"). The universe-of-force explanations are given by Chavannes in the story, although the narrator seems to abide by them too, since they are attested by the initial success of Chavannes's experiment. And with Anselm's final explanation, adding to the force-conservation paradigm the idea that spirit is the element essential to man's position on the scale of creation, the narrator is clearly in LeConte's camp.

The relationship of the atavism of the first part of the story to the evolutionary retrogression in the second half is not at all clear, other than that both come unbidden and both involve melodramatic departures from civilized norms. Donald Pizer makes the plausible suggestion that, in keeping with his LeContian evolutionism, Norris means us to see from the two parts of the story that man is an animal but not all animal,[16] but the lack of any clear connection other than the mere appearance of both motifs in the same story, and the tonal and thematic differences between the treatments of Lauth, liberated from civilization, temporarily running to blood-frenzy, and Chavannes "scientifically" creating a soulless monstrosity which physically regresses back through the course of evolution on its way to inertness, suggests that however potentially unifiable are its philosophical materials, the story is not, in fact, artistically unified. Naive omniscience can include it all, but the atavism and the devolution seem like separate narrative frameworks.

Fascinated with the subject of human degeneration conceived of as evolutionary regression, Norris built two early novels, *Vandover and the Brute* and *McTeague*, on versions of it. The causes of degeneration are located by the narrator in the biological nature and the social milieu of the characters, and there is consequently infrequent reference to a larger force-universe in these books. When the affluent and sensitive gentleman-student Vandover declines into a bestial and broken creature, it is because of his animal human nature and his weakness of character, his idling, wasting, debauching, and guilt, because of social circumstances such as the double sexual standard, the affluence that prepared him so poorly to be self-supporting, and the exploitive materialism of his friend Charlie Geary, and because (as Donald Pizer has shown Norris implying) Vandover was suffering from the symptoms of a syphilitic brain infection. In *McTeague*, when the coarse but good-natured unlicensed dentist becomes a brutish drunkard, an instinct-ridden atavist who murders his wife and his former best friend, it is because of his animal nature and his unfortunate hereditary makeup (as the square-headed son of a drunkard), because his wife was a compulsive miser about her lottery prize and his friend was bitterly envious that he had let McTeague marry his former best girl, and because social circumstances barred McTeague from the education he needed to get a dentist's license and continue practicing. The immediate causality in these novels is handled without reference to the universe of force.

In both *Vandover* and *McTeague* there is, however, often a clear sense of determinism, of resistless force behind and beneath these explicit levels of biological and social causation, and it occasionally comes through in a philosophical passage. The universe of force provides at times a harsh and merciless background for Vandover's fall. At one point, well into his decline, after a moment when "he felt as though he was losing his hold upon his reason" he looks out his window over the city at night:

> All the lesser staccato noises of the day had long since died to silence; there only remained that prolonged and sullen diapason, coming from all quarters at once. It was like the breathing of some infinitely great monster, alive and palpitating, the sistole and diastole of some gigantic heart. The whole existence of the great slumbering city passed upward there before him through the still night air in one long wave of sound.
>
> It was Life, the murmur of the great, mysterious force that spun the wheels of Nature and that sent it onward like some enormous engine, resistless, relentless; an engine that sped straight forward, driving before it the infinite herd of humanity, driving it on at breathless speed through all eternity, driving it no one knew whither, crushing out inexorably all those who lagged behind the herd and who fell from exhaustion, grinding them to dust beneath its myriad iron wheels, riding over them, still driving on the herd that yet remained, driving it recklessly blindly on and on toward some far-distant goal, some vague unknown end, some mysterious fearful bourne forever hidden in thick darkness.[17]

And later when, heartsick, he lets out an instinctive (but "unerring") cry in the night "Oh, help me! Why don't you *help* me?"

There was no answer, nothing but the deaf silence, the blind darkness. But in a moment he felt that the very silence, the very lack of answer, was answer in itself; there was nothing for him. Even that vast mysterious power to which he had cried could not help him now, *could* not help him, could not stay the inexorable law of nature, could not reverse that vast terrible engine with its myriad spinning wheels that was riding him down relentlessly, grinding him into the dust. (214)

Not infrequently in Norris's fiction there is some indefiniteness about whether a given perception belongs to a character or to the narrator—let it not be overlooked that such a confusion in moments of stress can sometimes work to the writer's advantage in augmenting the reader's sense of identification with a protagonist's disordered state—and here the representation of the universe's basic force, symbolized as locomotive, exists in this uncertain area. The first passage seems to be a more objective perception than Vandover would be capable of as he "ran, almost reeled, to the open window, . . . rolling his eyes wildly," and seems more the view of the narrator than of the character at that point, although the second passage twelve pages later repeats the same metaphor in nearly the same language, pretty certainly under the designation "he felt." The whole force-universe idea, with its attendant image of a locomotive running down helpless creatures (a curious anticipation of a memorable scene in *The Octopus*—several memorable scenes, in fact) may have been Vandover's delusion, but the narrator seconds it. There is authority in this representation of Vandover as a Darwinian misfit crushed by Spencerian force, despite the contrary aspects of moralism and Christian dualism which dominate the novel.

There is thus a kind of amorphous fluidity about Norris's naive omniscience here which enables him in writing the novel to flow back and forth between subjective and objective representations of his character, between cosmic paranoia and scientific detachment, and even between Darwinian determinism and Christian moralism. Each projection of the narrator holds sway for its full emotional value while it is being presented, giving the novel great immediacy and impact, but in concert these contrary visions are ultimately more distracting than provocative. The universe of force and, indeed, determinism itself are used tellingly but intermittently in this novel, as Norris's quest for melodrama and for explanation carries him beyond even the broad philosophical inclusiveness of Professor LeConte.

In *McTeague* the protagonist Mac is depicted near the end of the novel as a fugitive from justice after the murder of Trina, free of the (to him) intricate and at times baffling human milieu of San Francisco, brutalized and primitive, relating comfortably to the elemental forces of the earth, to "a tremendous, immeasurable Life [which] pushed steadily heavenward without a sound, without a motion," to the gigantic cañons, "silent, huge, and suggestive of colossal primeval forces held in reserve." Living for a while a kind of throwback existence as a miner,

> he passed his nights thus in the midst of the play of crude and simple forces—the powerful attacks of the Burly drills; the great exertions of bared bent backs overlaid with muscle; the brusque, resistless expansion of dynamite; and the silent, vast, Titanic force, mysterious and slow, that cracked the timbers supporting the roof of the tunnel, and that gradually flattened the lagging till it was thin as paper.
>
> The life pleased the dentist beyond words. The still, colossal mountains took him back again like a returning prodigal, and vaguely, without knowing why, he yielded to their influence—their immensity, their enormous power, crude and blind, reflecting themselves in his own nature, huge, strong, brutal in its simplicity.

And as in *Vandover* elemental Life-force is symbolized by ominous night-sounds:

> In the daytime they were silent; but at night they seemed to stir and rouse themselves. Occasionally the stamp-mill stopped, its thunder ceasing abruptly. Then one could hear the noises that the mountains made in their living. From the cañon, from the crowding crests, from the whole immense landscape, there rose a steady and prolonged sound, coming from all sides at once. It was the incessant and muffled roar which disengages itself from all vast bodies, from oceans, from cities, from forests, from sleeping armies, and which is like the breathing of an infinitely great monster, alive, palpitating.[18]

The connection between primitive instinct and primeval force is more interestingly made in an earlier passage which establishes the vast extent of the novel's determinism. This passage, through which Richard Chase has said "we feel blowing . . . the cold ideology of the era of Herbert Spencer,"[19] occurs just after Mac and Trina have kissed and felt one another's attraction, as the narrator attempts to offer an explanation and prognosis of this somewhat unlikely romance:

> McTeague has awakened the Woman, and whether she would or no, she was his now irrevocably; struggle against it as she would, she belonged to him, body and soul, for life or for death. She had not sought it, she had not desired it. The spell was laid upon her. Was it a blessing? Was it a curse? It was all one; she was his, indissolubly, for evil or for good.
>
> And he? The very act of submission that bound the woman to him for-

ever had made her seem less desirable in his eyes. Their undoing had already begun. Yet neither of them was to blame. From the first they had not sought each other. Chance had brought them face to face, and mysterious instincts as ungovernable as the winds of heaven were at work knitting their lives together. Neither of them had asked that this thing should be— that their destinies, their very souls, should be the sport of chance. If they could have known, they would have shunned the fearful risk. But they were allowed no voice in the matter. Why should it all be? (77–78)

Thus "chance" and "mysterious instincts" make up the ultimate formula for this human relationship; it often seems that while human motives and impulses are generally explained by Norris's narrator in terms of biology, human fate is referrable to the universe of force.

Yet even this is not a consistent conception in *McTeague*. Human fate might be explained by an omniscient narrator in terms of elemental forces, but the course of happenings in the novel seems to be directed by a rather conventional-minded novelist. Charles Child Walcutt has accurately pointed out that the plot of *McTeague* moves by means of coincidences, foreshortenings, and unlikelihoods, and he appropriately concludes that except for the absence of free will, "the structure consists . . . of very much the sort of plot that might be found in any novel of adventure or intrigue."[20] There is little sense of force-determinism in this structure.

The universe of force operates only incidentally, then, in *Vandover* and *McTeague*, and when in *Moran of the Lady Letty* (1898), *Blix* (1899), and *A Man's Woman* (1900) he tried the genres of the adventure novel and the popular romance, preaching straightforward redblooded masculinity and femininity, Norris found himself even less in need of cosmic and mechanistic explanations of phenomena. The universe of force was always at least potentially a part of his thinking, however, because in the next and final stage, the most important in his career, the concept is an integral and essential part of both his grandest inspiration and its articulation in narrative.

HIS ARTISTIC imagination had virtually reached a dead end in its explorations of the adventure-romance, idealized sexism, and "naturalistic" melodramas of degeneration, when in 1899 he got the idea that would redirect his career, rededicate his art, and revise his place in American literature. "I've got an idea that's as big as all out-doors," he wrote his friend Harry M. Wright,

. . . It involves a very long, very serious and perhaps a very terrible novel. It will be all about the San Joaquin wheat raisers and the Southern Pacific, and I guess we'll call it The Octopus.—catch on? I mean to study the whole question as faithfully as I can and then write a hair lifting story. There's the chance for the big, Epic, dramatic thing in this, and I mean to do it thoroughly.—get at it from every point of view, the social, agricultural, and political. Just say the last word on the R.R. question in California.[21]

But there was even more than this to his grand design, since, as he wrote to William Dean Howells,

My Idea is to write three novels around the one subject of Wheat. First, a story of California (the producer), second, a story of Chicago (the distributor), third, a story of Europe (the consumer) and in each to keep to the idea of this huge, Niagara of wheat rolling from West to East. . . .

The idea is so big that it frightens me at times but I have about made up my mind to have a try at it.[22]

He conceived of the Wheat as force and force as the key to the structure of his trilogy. In a unifying chain of correlations he could see the fruit of the California earth becoming a potent paper commodity on the Chicago grain exchange, and, ultimately, the hope and the force of life for starving European peasants. The Wheat could be seen as behaving like a force, moving autonomously, impersonally, and irresistibly, regardless of the desires and efforts of men and regardless even of powerful institutions.

The conception had great dramatic awe and rightness for Norris, offering opportunities for an enormous range of affective story materials, and at the same time integration within a framework that was in keeping with what Norris knew as the best scientific philosophy of the day, the school of Le-Conte, Fiske, and Herbert Spencer. Force-thinking had the potential to generate themes of considerable drama and scope for a novelist, and, tied in as it was to all-inclusive and ultimate concepts of natural causality, it could provide its own philosophic omniscience, complete with an explanatory framework for virtually the most diverse collection of phenomena the novelist could want to include in a single vision.

Producing a monumental work like this is the sort of thing Zola would have done, too—in fact it was to a surprising extent what Zola *had* done in novels like *La Terre*, *Germinal*, and *La Bête Humaine*. The series of titanic novels linked together by a deterministic theme, the depiction of people caught up by the movement of great forces, and even some of the specific character types and imagery of railroads, of the mother earth, of almost ritualistic mob scenes, all similar in Norris's work to what had been done by Zola,[23] reveal that in launching into his new Idea, Norris was returning to the original source of his inspiration as a novelist.

The vast scope of this project was certain to put extraordinary pressure on Norris's resources as a novelist, especially pressure to account for and to unify the great number of different kinds of events he meant to include as part of the Epic of the Wheat. His enthusiasm for all sorts of affective story materials led him into some pathways not chartable on the map of wheat-force or any force. The chance of doing "the big, Epic, dramatic thing" was to Norris worth risking incoherence for, whether or not he was even fully conscious of the gamble. The idea was magnificently ambitious, but Norris's technical powers, especially his powers of restraint, were not strong enough for him to realize it fully and coherently.

The Octopus shows the strain clearly, in the sheer proliferation of stories and approaches. The subject of the narrative is a prolonged conflict between a group of California wheat growers and the railroad, encompassing the effects of the struggle on the personal fates of a number of participants. It is generally recognized that Norris got some of his basic story ideas for *The Octopus* from the Mussel Slough Affair, in which the conflict between California wheat farmers and the Southern Pacific Railroad had in fact resulted in violence and death. In the novel the battle between the wheat growers and the railroad constitutes the central plot line, defining the stages of rising action, climax, and denouement, as the growers protest the railroad's ruinous rates for shipping their grain, organize in their opposition, attempt to suborn the state Railroad Commission and, losing that gambit and threatened with eviction from their land, attempt a climactic, violent stand, by which a number of them are killed, the rest subsequently being defeated, evicted, and demoralized. A number of the individuals who participate in this general action, then, are stories in themselves, like Magnus Derrick, the highly principled leader of the growers' association who, once persuaded to engage in bribery and subornation, finds himself blackmailed, dishonored in his own eyes, and publicly disgraced; and like Buck Annixter who, deeply torn between his love for a pretty milkmaid and his own innate and crotchety bachelorhood, discovers in an epiphany the humanizing effect of love, and marries the girl, only to be killed in the showdown at the drainage ditch. S. Behrman, the contemptible representative of the railroad, consistently ingenious in his schemes to defraud and pauperize honest people, is in the end, in his time of triumph, slowly buried by the wheat cascading into the hold of a grain ship. James Dyke, faithful railroad engineer for over ten years, unjustly and summarily fired, is gratuitously ruined again by a railroad rate rise when he tries to become a hop farmer; he turns to train robbery and is finally caught and imprisoned, leaving his mother and little daughter defenseless in the world. Such plots are, of course, the standard fare of fiction of the period, offering adventure and romance, tragedy and sentimentality, suspense, social criticism, moralism, and even, in the Annixter story, a little awkward humor. Norris's willingness to strive for strong effects with very conventional, even trite means is particularly evident in a scene near the end of the novel in which he counterpoints, by means of alternating passages, the pathetic starvation of Mrs. Hooven (widow of one of the slain farmers now homeless with her little daughter on the streets of San Francisco), and an especially opulent dinner party given by a vice-president of the railroad. Norris's employment of a great many materials and approaches—some original and some thunderingly conventional—in his desire to write a sweeping, stunning, "hair lifting" tale gave the novel a kind of epic vastness, but it also undermined narrative coherence, tone and narrator credibility, and introduced a diverse array of crosscurrent motifs such as those of fate, force, and free will, of mysticism and materialism, of indifferent Nature and natural love, and of poetic justice, cosmic determinism, and social protest.

It is all conveyed to us by a naively omniscient narrator. He is a storyteller with strong poetic and metaphysical bents, a flair for the dramatic, and a great deal of sensitivity to injustice. He seems highly aware of the momentousness of his narration, at times even giving the illusion of epic recitation—for example, although usually the characters speak and think in their own words, when they meditate about metaphysical significances they tend to use a special set of verbal formulas characteristic in their poeticality of the narrator's own stylized recitation. The narrator introduces the reader to the conflict of the wheat farmers and the railroad by following the arrival of a newcomer, the young poet Presley, but he does not limit himself, as it seems he might have, to Presley's perceptions. Thus he both has a point of reference and he hasn't. He uses Presley's comprehension but is not limited to it. He himself is the one with the full understanding and the final explanations toward which the characters—including Presley—grope. In shifting perspectives freely and diversely, the narrator tends to immerse himself wholly in each new situation, sanctioning its particular implications and meanings as absolute. Yet as the source of all the novel's various meanings, the source of all its wisdom and explanations, immediate and ultimate, he seems sometimes to be inclined in several different directions at the same time, taking a variety of positions not entirely unifiable, even within the parameters of omniscience. As narrator he expects too much of his own power to include, to dramatize, to explain and to unify. And it is this omniscient narrator who teaches us to view the situation in terms of forces.

The imagery and the philosophizing of the novel are the narrator's means of establishing the concept of the universe of force; they enrich the plot with flashes of significance and (of course) dramatic effect, while moving the narrative toward the final transcendent unity which seems intended to integrate and justify the manifold human miseries that have largely made up the substance of the plot. In these aspects Norris earns some credit for originality.

The novel's visualization of the railroad is one of its more spectacular and unconventional features (except for some precedence in Zola), and force imagery is one of the keys to its depiction. The railroad is clearly a force to the narrator, and it is perceived as such by those characters who do any thinking on the subject, although, depending on their subjective involvements, they tend to see it metaphorically as not only force but monster or octopus too: irresistible and autonomous to be sure, but also sinister if they feel threatened by it. This strain of symbolism is apparent as a locomotive is seen by both Presley and the wife of rancher Magnus Derrick as "a terror of steam and steel . . . with its single eye, Cyclopean, red, shooting from horizon to horizon."[24] When Presley comes upon a herd of sheep massacred on the tracks by a speeding locomotive, he imagines, as the narrator pulls all his mythic and metaphoric stops,

> the symbol of a vast power, huge, terrible, flinging the echo of its thunder over all the reaches of the valley, leaving blood and destruction in its path, the leviathan, with tentacles of steel clutching into the soil, the soulless Force, the ironhearted Power, the monster, the Colossus, the Octopus. (36)

As it was with the protagonist of *The Education of Henry Adams* when he was faced with the death of his sister, an event he took to be a direct encounter with the unmitigated forces of nature, Presley too reels in a kind of nightmarish vision of force-gone-wild. The locomotive is, of course, symbolic of the railroad company itself, and this representation coincides with other more direct characterizations of the railroad as both an octopus and an uncontrollable force.

At other times, however, the narrator, answering to other types of narrative requirements, projects a different view, although still in the conceptual pattern of the universe of force. Urging Presley towards a less paranoid, more philosophical vision, the railroad's president, Shelgrim (himself specifically regarded by the other characters "a product of circumstances, and inevitable result of conditions, characteristic, typical, symbolic of ungovernable forces" [72]) explains to him after the tragic climax, "I can *not* control it. It is a force born out of certain conditions and I—no man—can stop or control it" (396). And then when the frontstage antagonist, the railroad's local agent Behrman asks Presley at the end, "What could you have gained by killing me?" (430), the idealist-poet acquiesces to this view of the railroad as a force obeying only its own laws and thus sanctions Shelgrim's implied metaphysic of the inevitability and the indifference of force.

There is a pattern to the novel's projections of force, although it is one which is neither entirely consistent nor consistently operative. The universe of force underlies the novel's structure, and the narrator's concept of wheat-force, developing sporadically but insistently out of the wheat imagery and the philosophizing about the wheat, gives the novel its philosophical unity.*

In keeping with Norris's conception of the trilogy, the narrator of *The Octopus* uses the wheat, in conjunction with phenomena of nature and economics, as the fundamental entity in a vast metaphorical correlation/conservation system in the novel. It is ubiquitous and it is frequently depicted in relation to its equivalent in land, labor, wealth, or nourishment. Watching a ticker tape for the fluctuations in the price of grain in the world's markets, the growers could feel that "the ranch became merely the part of an enormous whole, a unit in the vast agglomeration of wheat land the whole world round, feeling the effects of causes thousands of miles distant" (38). And even Behrman, as he watches the "river of grain" which he has extorted from the farmers pour out of the grain chute into the sacks, recognizes that the labor and heartache of the raising is at this point transformed into food to pour into the mouths of the hungry (424). Of course Norris had not needed a concept of force conservation in the back of his mind to view the grain economy as a system of correlations; indeed, the idea of conservation itself may have originally been based in part upon an economic analogy. But the facts that wheat was viewed as a force and that the system of nature and economics of which it was a part was characterized by correlations such as these, would, in the early 1900s, set resonating a fundamental conception of the universe of force, with all its metaphysical and attitudinal corollaries.

The wheat force, embodying the elemental forces of nature and economics, figures crucially in three of the novel's important themes, and in so doing it supplies the ideational foundation of the novel's development toward philosophical resolution and narrative closure. Out of the concept and imagery of wheat force come the theme of nature as a force- and chance-based system of natural selection, a framing theme of the education of Presley in the ways of the universe of force, and a theme of reconciliation of human ideals and cosmic indifference.

Magnus Derrick's wife is the character who first senses the presence of natural force and divines its Darwinian implications, although she is at the time characterized as alienated, Victorian, and shy. Looking out over an immense field of wheat,

---

* Much credit should go to Donald Pizer for identifying a philosophical unity in *The Octopus* which derived from the ideas of Spencer, Fiske, and LeConte. See especially *The Novels of Frank Norris*, Chapters 1 and 4. I am somewhat less convinced of the artistic unity of the novel than he seems to be, but I admire and share his approach.

the one-time writing-teacher of a young ladies' seminary, with her pretty deer-like eyes and delicate fingers, shrank from it. She did not want to look at so much wheat. There was something vaguely indecent in the sight, this food of the people, this elemental force, this basic energy, weltering here under the sun in all the unconscious nakedness of a sprawling, primordial Titan. (42)

And when it seems to her that her husband is increasingly vulnerable to the forces of wheat, economics, and nature, she extends this basically prudish reaction, and her innate "shrinking from the harshness of the world" (124) materializes in a more horrifying vision:

> She recognized the colossal indifference of nature, not hostile, even kindly and friendly, so long as the human ant-swarm was submissive, working with it, hurrying along at its side in the mysterious march of the centuries. Let, however, the insect rebel, strive to make head against the power of this nature, and at once it became relentless, a gigantic engine, a vast power, huge, terrible; a leviathan with a heart of steel, knowing no compunction, no forgiveness, no tolerance; crushing out the human atom with soundless calm, the agony of destruction sending never a jar, never the faintest tremor through all the prodigious mechanism of wheels and cogs. (124)

She is right, of course. Her gentility, disorientation and shrinking from reality notwithstanding, she accurately foresees what will happen to her husband and his allies, and, in terms of natural law, why it will happen. The function of these passages of reflection is not, as it might at first seem, the characterization of a disoriented character, but accurate foreshadowing and the establishment of a true philosophical perspective.

Presley, although not characterizable by disoriented gentility, also sees natural force precisely this way; after the tragic climax, in a surge of anguish and disillusionment, he realizes:

> Nature was, then, a gigantic engine, a vast Cyclopean power, huge, terrible, a leviathan with a heart of steel, knowing no compunction, no forgiveness, no tolerance; crushing out the human atom standing in its way with nirvanic calm, the agony of destruction sending never a jar, never the faintest tremor through all that prodigious mechanism of wheels and cogs. (396)

In this perceptive set, which sets forth the vision of two separate individuals in a manner that is absolutistic in its near identity in both, the message is simple: indifferent or hostile forces crush whoever or whatever stands in the way. The flagrant locomotive imagery is of course no chance allusion. The symbolism of the novel, beginning at the point where the locomotive slaughtered the sheep who strayed into its path and including the rabbit drive scene (in which masses of innocent and somewhat anthropomorphized rabbits are cornered and slaughtered for a kind of folk-celebration barbeque), has all along been systematically establishing this theme up and down the Darwinian ladder. The forces of nature operate a chance or circumstantial system of natural selection. It was, you will recall, Vandover's perception too—a nature-machine crushing those who falter in its path—and here it operates impartially on rabbits or sheep, ranchers, or villains.

The example of the villainous S. Behrman makes the point in a simple physical sense as well as symbolically. He allows himself a moment of foolish hubris, strutting the deck of the grainship regarding himself "the Master of the Wheat" (423) which is cascading into its hold. The wheat itself knows no master, however, but, as the narrator tells us, it is a natural force simply in and of itself:

> No human agency seemed to be back of the movement of the wheat. Rather, the grain seemed impelled with a force of its own, a resistless, huge force, eager, vivid, impatient for the sea.

Behrman literally feels its grim and dangerous impersonality when "he put his hand once into the rushing tide, and the contact rasped the flesh of his fingers and like an undertow drew his hand after it in its impetuous dash." He gets in its way when "his foot caught in a coil of rope, and he fell headforemost into the hold" (441). With increasing panic he battles for his life against the now specifically hostile wheat pouring on him "incessantly, inexorably" (443), and when he loses the battle, when finally "it covered the face," "in the hold of the *Swanhilda* there was no movement but the widening ripples that spread flowing from the ever-breaking, ever-reforming cone; no sound, but the rushing of the Wheat that continued to plunge incessantly from the iron chute in a prolonged roar, persistent, steady, inevitable" (444). Thus the wheat literally acts out its force-role, which Mrs. Derrick and Presley had divined, "with nirvanic calm" "crushing out the human atom standing in its way." The fact that in this case the "human atom" was a creature of unmitigated selfishness and socioeconomic sadism merely serves to prove that the novel's universe is not, as it sometimes seems, simply malevolent; indeed this episode is a melodramatic example of poetic justice as well as an evidence of the overall impartiality of natural selection by natural forces.

This natural selection is variously apprehended by the characters in the course of the narrative, their reactions ranging from a subjectively based paranoia to a resigned philosophical detachment, and although each of their perceptions is given full credence at its moment by the narrator, there is a gradual, approximate overall movement toward the more objective viewpoint. The novel moves beyond shock and disillusionment and toward resigned acceptance of the indifferent forces of nature, and the framing theme of Presley's education-in-life is its most coherent embodiment. As he proceeds through the stages of disengaged esthete, idealistic reformer, disillusioned pessimist, and, finally, stoical evolutionary optimist, Presley's understanding of the indifference of the natural forces is crucial. Crucial, that is, but, like the philosophical progress of the book not clearly and coherently developed. When near the story's end Presley talks with the railroad's president about what it all meant, in a scene which is one of the novel's explanatory climaxes, when he hears from Shelgrim that the railroad runs itself, that it is an uncontrollable, unstoppable force the way the wheat is an uncontrollable, unstoppable force, both ruled by the law of supply and demand, he wonders then, in an epiphany of force, "Was no one, then, to blame for the horror at the irrigation ditch? Forces, conditions, laws of supply and demand—were these then the enemies, after all? Not enemies; there was no malevolence in Nature. Colossal indifference only, a vast trend toward appointed goals" (396). Presley's realization then runs into the passage quoted earlier, beginning "Nature was, then, a gigantic engine . . . " and depicting the forces of nature as a rampaging locomotive with "nirvanic calm." There is nothing new in this realization at this point, however, to us or to Presley, except the question of "blame for the horror" (and the use of lower case for "nirvanic"). Presley had, well before the irrigation ditch massacre, perceived the wheat as

> a mighty force, the strength of nations, the life of the world. . . . Indifferent, gigantic, resistless, it moved in its appointed grooves. Men, Lilliputians, gnats in the sunshine, buzzed impudently in their tiny battles, were born, lived through their little day, died, and were forgotten; while the Wheat, wrapped in Nirvanic calm, grew steadily under the night, alone with the stars and with God. (307)

Presley, then, earlier knew most of what he seemed to be discovering in his epiphany. Additionally, the indifference of the wheat-force has been perceived by other characters in the novel as well, by characters as different in knowledge and character as Mrs. Derrick and S. Behrman, by everyone, in fact, who has stepped back and taken the long-range view of it. As in *McTeague*, references to human fate are occasions for reference to a universe of indifferent force, but in *The Octopus* the narrator employs a variety of characters, all meditating in his voice, to project this theme for him. And the fact that Norris, pursuing what he conceives to be some epic narrative effect, has his narrator express Presley's realization in many of the same words as Mrs. Derrick's much earlier semiparanoid nature-locomotive meditation only serves to increase the confusion of this moment of "discovery." If the novel offered any other philosophical frame of reference, we would have to feel that the author was being ironic about Presley's discovery and even about his naive narrator's presentation of it. But Norris seems to have no sense of the possibility of the fallibility of a narrator.

On the explicit philosophical level, then, the novel seems to be rolling toward some predetermined conclusion, some ultimate explanation which has been in the narrator's mind all along and of which the characters—almost any of the characters, interchangeably—have caught fitful glimpses in the course of their travail. The reader sees only Presley take the final step in this inquiry, however, as the theme of his education culminates in the novel's grand philosophical reconciliation of man and natural force. Having recognized that life is governed by an accidental system of natural selection determined by forces which are alien and indifferent to man, and still needing a viable attitude to take toward such incomprehensibly tragic events as had occurred, he begins to have intimations of transcendental optimism. Near the end of the novel Presley looks out over the immense sweep of harvested San Joaquin land,

> and as Presley looked there came to him strong and true the sense and the significance of all the enigma of growth. He seemed for one instant to touch the explanation of existence. Men were nothings, mere animalcules, mere ephemerides that fluttered and fell and were forgotten between dawn and dusk. Vanamee had said there was no death. But for one second Presley could go one step further. Men were naught, death was naught, life was naught; FORCE only existed—FORCE that brought men into the world, FORCE that crowded them out of it to make way for the succeeding generation, FORCE that made the wheat grow, FORCE that garnered it from the soil to give place to the succeeding crop.
>
> It was the mystery of creation, the stupendous miracle of recreation; the vast rhythm of the seasons, measured, alternative, the sun and the stars keeping time as the eternal symphony of reproduction swung in its tremendous cadences like the colossal pendulum of an almighty machine—primordial energy flung out from the hand of the Lord God himself, immortal, calm, infinitely strong. (436)

In order to reach a firm and final affirmation Presley must follow the prophetic teaching of Vanamee. This character—a shepherd, an ascetic, a mystic—wanders somewhat incongruously through this otherwise naturalistic novel and provides, finally, the key element of its philosophical reconciliation. When first introduced into the novel he is a brooding, hermit-like character who has an unassuaged grief of sixteen years' standing and the mysterious power to summon people psychically at a distance. The great tragedy of his life was the loss of his Angéle, his incomparably pure sweetheart who died in childbirth after being raped, shockingly and inexplicably, by an unknown assailant. Sixteen years later Vanamee still stalks the earth, love-lorn and world-denying, devoting his life to grieving for her and, as the plot thickens, to trying to summon her from the beyond. His efforts finally succeed, at least symbolically: he summons her look-alike daughter who, unbeknown, lives nearby, and who at the moment of truth breathlessly takes her mother's place in Vanamee's arms. And it is on this sample of gilded-age fictional decadence that Norris builds most immediately and explicitly the philosophical resolution of his novel.

The climactic scene is orchestrated thusly: just before Angéle II appears, Vanamee counsels Presley,

> "there is only life, and the suppression of life, that we, foolishly, say is death. . . . Life never departs. Life simply *is*. . . . The grain we think is dead *resumes again*; but how? Not as one grain but as twenty. So all life. Death is only real for all the detritus of the world, for all the sorrow, for all the injustice, for all the grief. Presley, the good never dies. . . ."

To Presley's traumatic disillusionment over the drainage ditch massacre Vanamee says,

> "Look at it all from the vast height of humanity—'the greatest good to the greatest numbers.' What remains? . . . Evil is short-lived. Never judge of the whole round of life by the mere segment you can see. The whole is, in the end, perfect." (437)

And as if to set a seal on what he teaches, Angéle II emerges out of the sun-flooded field of ripened wheat and runs to his arms. The narrator, in a determined effort to carry the symbolism of the novel out to an even more explicit point, asserts "Angéle was realized in the Wheat" (439). Here the seemingly indifferent wheat-force is represented as ultimately beneficent, the source, finally, not only of cosmic reassurance but of human values and romantic fulfillment as well.

The understanding that Presley finally achieves, viewing his whole experience in the light of both Shelgrim's and Vanamee's teachings, is articulated in the long meditation with which the novel ends. With it his education is complete, and man is reconciled to the universe of force. Unqualified, and without the slightest indication in the final three paragraphs that it is Presley who is doing the thinking, this meditation stands, all uplift and organ music, as a double-voiced peroration, the last word of both Presley and the narrator.

> Men—motes in the sunshine—perished, were shot down in the very noon of life, hearts were broken, little children started in life lamentably handi-

capped; young girls were brought to a life of shame; old women died in the heart of life for lack of food. In that little, isolated group of human insects, misery, death, and anguish spun like a wheel of fire.

But the WHEAT *remained.* Untouched, unassailable, undefiled, that mighty world-force, that nourisher of nations, wrapped in Nirvanic calm, indifferent to the human swarm, gigantic, resistless, moved onward in its appointed grooves. Through the welter of blood at the irrigating ditch, through the sham charity and shallow philanthropy of famine relief committees, the great harvest of Los Muertos rolled like a flood from the Sierras to the Himalayas to feed thousands of starving scarecrows on the barren plains of India.

Falseness dies: injustice and oppression in the end of everything fade and vanish away. Greed, cruelty, selfishness, and inhumanity are short-lived; the individual suffers, but the race goes on. Annixter dies, but in a far-distant corner of the world a thousand lives are saved. The larger view always and through all shams, all wickednesses, discovers the Truth that will, in the end, prevail, and all things, surely, inevitably, resistlessly work together for good. (448)

This optimistic version of the universe of force has been assumed by the narrator all along and he has revealed it when the occasion seemed to call for it. Earlier, in the scene where the wheat again begins to sprout after Annixter has sat in the field all night coming to the realization that he loves Hilma, the narrator observes that

once more the force of the world was revivified . . . and the morning abruptly blazed into glory upon the spectacle of a man whose heart leaped exuberant with the love of a woman, and an exulting earth gleaming transcendent with the radiant magnificence of an inviolable pledge. (253)

The central symbol of the wheat has itself an inherent beneficent teleology, its purpose being the sustenance and increase of life. And, stretching the same pattern to its limit, even a locomotive that slaughters sheep on its way somewhere has some constructive end toward which it moves. On the level of economic force, too, the same teleological pattern prevails, as Presley's friend, the manufacturer Cedarquist points out by saying at one point that "the farmer and the manufacturer [are] both in the same grist between the two millstones of the lethargy of the Public and the aggression of the Trust" (209), and at a later point acknowledging that "We'll carry our wheat into Asia yet. The Anglo-Saxon started from there at the beginning of everything and it's manifest destiny that he must circle the globe and fetch up where he began his march" (445).

Insofar as *The Octopus* has a philosophical backbone, it is the philosophy of the long run, of the general tendency or the statistical average—what Vanamee and Presley call "the larger view," "the full round of the circle whose segment only he beheld," a faith in "the greatest good to the greatest numbers" (448). The forces—the wheat, nature itself, economics, and even to some extent the railroad—will impersonally destroy or maim any who get in their way, and to those victims the forces will seem hostile. But those forces are governed by laws—the law of supply and demand, economically; the cycle of renewal and fruition, biologically—and those laws are basically good. The universe thus tends toward fulfillment, betterment, growth, although locally and in the short run it may not seem as though it does. Evil becomes a kind of accident that occurs on the way to a higher good.

The omniscient narrator, in the position of knowing everything and needing to account for everything has armed himself with a variant of American Spencerianism, and has used that simple, comprehensive, and upward-looking paradigm to structure his epic narrative, to give it depth, philosophical resolution, and closure. If, with his diverse cast of characters, each differently involved with the wheat-force, Norris had decided to show each character perceiving it personally and individually, the novel could have been, like *Moby-Dick*, an examination of the multiplicity of "truth" and a challenge to naive absolutism. Instead, by stressing the unanimity of philosophical reactions, he has given us the statement of a rather shallow faith. It is untested and unchallenged in the narrative (although it is at times ignored). In his anxiousness to establish his Spencerian model, the narrator uses every philosophical passage in the novel, no matter which character's mind and experience the passage develops out of, to point to it, even to the extent of making different characters think in the same words or of showing the interpreter-character Presley aware at one point of ideas that he later discovers. This is Norris using his narrative omniscience naively.

His choice of unifying paradigms was appropriate in terms of its currency and inclusiveness, but because of the way in which it was built into *The Octopus*, its limitations became the novel's. Optimistic evolutionism, Spencerianism, but expressed in terms of human travail and the teleology of the wheat instead of the interaction of abstract forces evolving toward coherent heterogeneity, it is a conception which John Fiske or Joseph LeConte could assent to, granting them a clearer assurance of the guidance of a personal God.

Along with its know-it-all absolutism, American Spencerianism's great failing was its duplicity in dealing with the crucial social issues of its day. Although citing human betterment and social integration as ideals not only essential to man but sanctioned by the whole teleological course of evolution as well, American Spencerianism generally stood against reform and social justice movements, trusting the course of natural evolution to produce social change, and celebrating individualistic capitalism as an end product of cosmic progress. The concept of evolving forces tends to make all human effort seem presumptuous and irrelevant, and it is extremely difficult in viewing *The Octopus* to see how a novel could be resolved by that concept when it began with such an egregious social abuse as the railroad's exploitation of the wheat farmers. Indeed, a good deal of the criticism levelled at the novel concerns the way in which its cosmic perspective tends to vitiate its social themes.[25] Norris seems to feel the social injustice keenly—there is conviction in the vividness of his portrayal of it, and that conviction is likely what was behind his avowed intention to "just say the last word on the R.R. question in California"—but he seems to believe the Spencerianism too, and the two perspectives are irreconcilable, especially in the hands of an undiscriminating, naively omniscient narrator.

It is characteristic of cosmic force-philosophy, of course, that it tends to transcend human problems rather than confront them. As we think back over the novel, reviewing the specific situations in which we readers had been encouraged to feel emotional involvement—the loyal and independent James Dyke imprisoned, the noble Magnus Derrick crushed and demoralized, Hilma Tree widowed, Minna Hooven forced into prostitution, and her mother starving pathetically on the streets—it does not seem reassuring or even relevant for us to be told that in the long run forces work for the greatest good of the greatest number. Cosmic reassurances won't answer here and negate our feelings of pathos and sympathy, of simple humanity and social outrage. Belief in a benevolent universe of force is appropriate only, perhaps, to Presley, Vanamee, or the capitalists, Shelgrim and Cedarquist, to people to whom the forces have brought fulfillment and happiness or who suffer only vicariously and are finally free to go off and observe life in other arenas. The narrator seriously risks his credibility in announcing the ultimate benevolence of the forces in a voice that seems to be his own; when the last notes of pathos and social protest have blended into the final chord of evolutionary optimism he seems too simplistic, too fuzzy-minded and even too inadvertently callous for his assumed role of all-comprehending authority.

The position we must finally come to, however, is that Spencerianism does not totally dominate and determine *The Octopus*. Norris's scheme was too ambitious, his range of human sympathies and his zest for literary effects were too diverse, finally, to admit of unification through any absolutistic philosophy. The universe of force concludes the book and provides its unifying inspiration and much of its explanation, but it fits over the diverse fictional materials intermittently, an uneven and distorting map. Force explanations are not operative throughout. When railroad president Shelgrim humanely raises the salary of an accountant in his office because the man is turning to alcoholism in his despair, and at the same time the railroad, acting through Behrman, is destroying Dyke twice, the message seems to be that human intentions, not forces, are the determining factors in men's fates and that evil is the result of nastiness on the middle level of management. Likewise the whole situation of Magnus Derrick is developed in conventionally moralistic terms, his character being based on moral integrity and his downfall precipitated by his own moral compromise and by Behrman's evil skulduggery; the case of Dreiser's Frank Cowperwood, developed rather strictly according to force categories is far different, as shall be seen in Chapter 7.

It is possible to see the diversity of *The Octopus* as a novelistic, rather than a real-life, existential diversity, however. At times it is almost as if Norris sees in terms of story-materials, with events and character types introduced into the novel complete with their own implicit moral judgments, attitudes, fictional themes, and likely plot-outcomes. In trying, then, to produce the epic "as big as all outdoors" and to "get at it from every point of view" and "say the last word," Norris seems, with an extremely plastic, undiscriminating narrative point of view, to be pushed toward following out each story line in its own terms, so that we get clear traces of all the different modes of fiction he admired—the epic, the melodrama, the local-color western, the sentimental novel of manners, the social protest novel, the *Kunstlerroman*, the story of romantic mysticism, and of course the fate- and science-haunted naturalistic novel—each with the gravitational pull of its own thematic and attitudinal field. The scheme was simply too ambitious, as Norris was basically too derivative a novelist to invent the literary form and the philosophical vision that would integrate it all. The result was an impressive, problematical, fictile novel, a colossal, hairlifting failure, for which each reader can essentially have his own interpretation.

The critical history of *The Octopus* is clearly understandable if this is the case.[26] The novel can be (and has been) construed to be a social-protest novel with some false notes of Social Darwinism, a study of man's relation to nature with some spurious social criticism, a naturalistic novel with some gratuitous mysticism, a romantic novel with a distracting hankering after documentation and determinism, or, variously, an illustration of the theme of love, the theme of primitivism, the theme of emotion opposed to rationality, and so forth. They are all likely and worthwhile ways to look at the novel, but each of them needs to assume that certain elements are inessential, distracting or downright deplorable; which particular elements are seen as irrelevant depends on which elements are seen as central. It is difficult to get much beyond the position Charles Child Walcutt stated a good many years ago: "The wheat books, magnificently conceived, fail structurally because they contain conflicting and contradicting sets of ideas all of which Norris was apparently trying to prove through the action of his story." [27]

The idea of the universe of force, as well as supplying a transcendent synthesis (which actually conflicts with some of the story materials it was intended to integrate), gives *The Octopus* enhanced dramatic imagery and a sense of higher stakes in the action, a sense that what we are witnessing is only a small part of a much larger—even a universal or cosmic—drama. It gives a resolution for the theme of Presley's education; knowledge of force fills out his conception of the world as it had for the protagonists of Herbert Spencer's *Autobiography* and *The Education of Henry Adams* previously, and as it would subsequently in Jack London's *Martin Eden* and Theodore Dreiser's autobiography. The universe of force also gives *The Octopus* a conventional sense of closure, as the narrator tries to suggest (however fallibly) that there is a framework of natural explanation which accounts for the most extreme human misfortune and still affirms earthly beneficence. It falls short of integrating the novel as it was presumably meant to do, and it proved not to be, finally, a standpoint from which deep human and social concerns would effectively be presented, but its very ambitious employment is clearly a sign of Norris the Novelist striving for originality and creative currency in his work.

THE SECOND novel in the Epic of the Wheat trilogy, *The Pit*, was the last Norris was able to complete before his untimely death. It depicts the wheat-force in its intermediate stage, as a monetary factor competitively manipulated by financiers for their own advantage, although the force of the growing crop in the California earth and the need among populations of hungry consumers is also clearly felt. In scope and tenor this novel is quite different from *The Octopus*; it focuses more narrowly, on the attempt of a single man, financier Curtis Jadwin, to corner the wheat market, and it delves deeply into the personal and domestic effects of his actions, rather than the social or metaphysical issues they pose. Again the narration is delivered in a mode of naive omniscience, and again the narrator is quasi-attached to the perceptions of a newcomer on the scene, this time Laura Dearborn (later Jadwin), whose initiation into the depths and complexities of the situation parallels the reader's.

The narrative requirements, to some extent unlike those of *The Octopus*, involve a rather different use of philosophical perspective and a different relationship to the universe of force. The very heart of the difference can be seen at the end of the novel in a meditation primarily in the mind of Laura Jadwin, whose husband has narrowly missed total financial ruin and psychic disintegration in his failure to sustain a corner on the wheat market:

> She repeated to herself his words, again and again:
>
> "The wheat cornered itself. I simply stood between two sets of circumstances. The wheat cornered me, not I the wheat."
>
> And all those millions and millions of bushels of Wheat were gone now. The Wheat that had killed Cressler, that had ingulfed Jadwin's fortune and all but unseated reason itself; the Wheat that had intervened like a great torrent to drag her husband from her side and drown him in the roaring vortices of the Pit, had passed on, resistless, along its ordered and predetermined courses from West to East, like a vast Titanic flood, had passed, leaving Death and Ruin in its wake, but bearing Life and Prosperity to the crowded cities and centres of Europe.
>
> For a moment, vague, dark perplexities assailed her, questionings as to the elemental forces, the forces of demand and supply that ruled the world. This huge resistless Nourisher of the Nations—why was it that it could not reach the People, could not fulfill its destiny, unmarred by all this suffering, unattended by all this misery?
>
> She did not know.[28]

Again as in *The Octopus* the concluding themes are those of an irresistible force, of its indifference to the desires or welfare of individual humans, of its moving according to the great law of supply and demand, and of its bringing, finally, the greatest good to the greatest number. The difference between this philosophical conclusion and that of *The Octopus* is a matter of attitude and emphasis. The stress here is not on the reassuring thought of force's ultimate benevolence but on the question of force's justice—the issue of theodicy, naturalistically posed. *The Pit* then concludes imagistically with Laura's perception of the Board of Trade building where her husband's obsession and agony have been acted out, a perception previously entertained in nearly the same words by Jadwin himself at one point and by the narrator at another, all of whom have seen, by this shifting omniscience, "the pile of the Board of Trade building, black, monolithic, crouching on its foundations like a monstrous sphinx with blind eyes, silent, grave—crouching there without a sound, without sign of life, under the night and the drifting veil of rain" (421). The tone is menacing and mysterious, and the message is one of the inhuman indifference of the forces that determine men's lives.

It is important to relate the difference between the closing statements of the two novels, not so much to some inferred change in Norris's philosophical outlook, as to the very different narrative contexts for which they supply the closure. Conventionally, novelistic closure involves a return to the broadest thematic level of a particular narrative for a resolution of doubts or uncertainties, or at least a general summary of the most general themes—a final assertion of a link between the particular events of a narrative and some general or universal significance. And although the most general themes of *The Octopus* and *The Pit* are the same, their narrative contexts are not, and this difference is what determines that the philosophical closure of the first will bring forth reassurance and that of the other will leave us with a sense of menacing indifference. In *The Pit*, total catastrophe has been averted; the worst has not come to pass. The wheat-force has broken Jadwin's fortune, but it has only *nearly* broken his marriage and his physical and psychological health, and, most crucially, it has broken his obsession with commodity market gambling. Jadwin is left, poorer but wiser, with a rational, moderate life and a reinstated marriage. Force has hurt him only in his least estimable aspects, those of the daring and powerful manipulator. As readers of the novel we do not need philosophical reassurance the way we needed it to cope with the multiple tragedies in *The Octopus*; here we are already reassured by the denouement. What Norris rightly judges we need from the philosophical closure of his story of the chastened overreacher is some suggestion of the mysteriousness, the inexorability and the indifference of the avenging forces of nature. Thus the concept of the universe of force proved quite useful to Norris twice but in different ways, its principal aspect in each of the two novels probably dependent more on esthetic, novelistic exigencies than on purely philosophic concerns.

The universe of force figures in several other specific ways in *The Pit*. The novel's scope being narrower than that of *The Octopus*, the narrator has less need of philosophical concepts which unify and explain, but he does use universe-of-force concepts directly to help him establish the dramatic setting and the plot-resolution, and indirectly to aid in the characterization, in addition to their thematic functions in yielding statements about social, natural, or metaphysical matters.

The dramatic setting is established by the omniscient narrator in terms of force through the use, again, of a number of observations made by various characters—by any, in fact, who happen to be doing any viewing or thinking; again the narrator's vision has the unanimous assent of his characters. Laura Dearborn, newly arrived from Barrington, Massachusetts, responds to the vastness and energy of Chicago (in an echo of Dreiser's *Sister Carrie*) in terms of romantic awe and force-fear:

> The Great Grey City, brooking no rival, imposed its dominion upon a reach of country larger than many a kingdom of the Old World. . . . The assault of veins of anthracite [was] moved by her central power. Her force

turned the wheels of harvester and seeder a thousand miles distant in Iowa and Kansas. Her force spun the screws and propellers of innumerable squadrons of lake steamers. . . .

It was Empire, the resistless subjugation of all this central world of the lakes and the prairies. Here, midmost in the land, beat the Heart of the Nation, whence inevitably must come its immeasurable power, its infinite, infinite, inexhaustible vitality. . . .

"There is something terrible about it," she murmured, half to herself, "something insensate. In a way it doesn't seem human. It's like a great tidal wave. It's all very well for the individual just so long as he can keep afloat, but once fallen, how horribly quick it would crush him, annihilate him, how horribly quick, and with such horrible indifference! I suppose it's civilisation in the making, the thing that isn't meant to be seen, as though it were too elemental, too—primordial; like the first verses of Genesis." (62–63)

And Jadwin too, not yet her husband or even her suitor, and not yet dreaming of trying to corner the wheat,

had long since conceived of the notion of some great, some resistless force within the Board of Trade Building that held the tide of the streets within its grip, alternately drawing it in and throwing it forth. . . . It was as if the Wheat, Nourisher of the Nations, as it rolled gigantic and majestic in a vast flood from West to East, here, like a Niagara, finding its flow impeded, burst suddenly into the appalling fury of the Maëlstrom, into the chaotic spasm of a world-force, a primeval energy, blood-brother of the earthquake and the glacier, raging and wrathful that its power should be braved by some pinch of human spawn that dared raise barriers across its courses. (79, 80)

These passages are, of course, expressive of the narrator's own picturesque view of primordial wheat-force; they are an important part of the setting for Jadwin's dramatic and almost crazed endeavor to control the entire market; and they are, indeed, plot-foreshadowing.

When the climax comes, then, its agent is the force of the wheat which naturally and mercilessly overthrows Jadwin's attempts to control it. The corner on the market which he had achieved had given him enormous wealth and control: singlehandedly he could set the price, bring prosperity to the growers and starvation to the consumers of the wheat; he could ruin his adversaries, act as a moral force himself, punishing the unscrupulous and saving their victims; he could extort for himself whatever price the market could bear. But even at the moment of his triumph the forces are contriving his downfall: the farmers under the lure of prosperity have planted wheat on every available acre, and the earth is bringing forth a harvest of such proportions that no man's wealth and energy will be able to control it. Nature's force is intimated to Jadwin in a vast indefinite sound (very much like the sound of the great forces heard in the night by Vandover and McTeague), which comes out of the hurly-burly of the floor of the exchange:

> Out of that hideous turmoil, he imagined, there issued a strange unwonted note; as it were, the first rasp and grind of a new avalanche just beginning to stir, a diapason more profound than any he had yet known, a hollow distant bourdon as of the slipping and sliding of some almighty and chaotic power.
> It was the Wheat, the Wheat! (373)

To maintain his hold he finds himself fighting "the very Earth itself" (347, 374).

> Why the Wheat had grown itself; demand and supply, these were the two great laws the Wheat obeyed. Almost blasphemous in his effrontery, he had tampered with these laws, and had roused a Titan. He had laid his puny human grasp upon Creation and the very earth herself, the great mother, feeling the touch of the cobweb that the human insect had spun, had stirred at last in her sleep and sent her omnipotence moving through the grooves of the world, to find and crush the disturber of her appointed courses. (374)

There is no stopping this resistless natural force, "coming in, coming on like a tidal wave, bursting through, dashing barriers aside, rolling like a measureless, almighty river, from the farms of Iowa and the ranches of California, on to the East—to the bakeshops and hungry mouths of Europe" (388). Thus, for his effrontery, Jadwin is ruined. From the beginning it had been foreshadowed that anyone who tampered with the forces would be crushed; Jadwin dared and he paid the price. Force in this novel thus plays a retributive rather than a purely circumstantial role. And the universe of force has given the narrator a lavishly poetic and dramatic way of representing the plot resolution of this novel.

It has also presented him with a new sort of opportunity for characterization, although he avails himself of it far less explicitly and extensively than did his colleague Theodore Dreiser a decade later in his financier trilogy. Dreiser was to discover that he could represent his characters and their interactions in the business milieu in terms of forces of relative strengths and various directions, his tycoon-protagonist being a man of considerable inner force which could be impeded only by opposition by a force or combination of forces of greater strength (see Chapter 7 for a full discussion of this approach of Dreiser's). Norris's narrator comes close to representing Jadwin and his colleagues of the pit as individual forces in a force-field: both the narrator and Laura characterize Jadwin as a man who is "'strong'" (11, 72) in this milieu in which, to Laura, the tycoons and manipulators "seemed, in a sense, more terrible than the city itself—men for whom all this crash of conflict and commerce had no terrors. Those who could subdue it to their purposes, must they not be themselves more terrible, more pitiless, more brutal?" (63). A man of force even in his courtship, "Jadwin was aggressive, assertive, and his addresses had all the persistence and vehemence of veritable attack" (113). Much affected by his force, Laura gives in to it, and Jadwin's grain exchange enemies learn to their dismay that his force is superior to theirs, but the natural force of the wheat is of a different magnitude altogether, and it overwhelms him.

Norris develops an interesting new theme in his depiction of Jadwin's single-minded struggle to master the wheat market, that of the depersonalization, the dehumanization of the man obsessed with pitting his force against the forces of other men and of circumstances. The closer Jadwin comes to acting as a force in a field of forces the farther he strays from his sentience, his morality, his humanity. Henry Adams had had this insight too, seeing modern man as denying at his peril the great inertial force of the female sex by involving himself so thoroughly in the pursuit and exercise of mechanical forces. For both writers it seems that force-obsessed man removes himself from a truer center of his being, woman, and falls victim to forces that he cannot control; this situation, which Adams sees in complex intellectual irony against the backdrop of man's whole history and cultural development, Norris projects as a nightmarish melodrama:

> Jadwin was in the thick of the confusion by now. And the avalanche, the undiked Ocean of the Wheat, leaping to the lash of the hurricane, struck him fairly in the face.
>
> He heard it now, he heard nothing else. The Wheat had broken from his control. For months, he had, by the might of his single arm, held it back; but now it rose like the upbuilding of a colossal billow. It towered, towered, hung poised for an instant, and then, with a thunder as the grind and crash of chaotic worlds, broke upon him, burst through the Pit and raced past him, on and on to the eastward and to the hungry nations.
>
> And then, under the stress and violence of the hour, something snapped in his brain. The murk behind his eyes had been suddenly pierced by a white flash. The strange qualms and tiny nervous paroxysms of the last few months all at once culminated in some indefinite, indefinable crisis, and the wheels and cogs of all activities save one lapsed away and ceased.

Only one function of the complicated machine persisted; but it moved with a rapidity of vibration that seemed to be tearing the tissues of being to shreds, while its rhythm beat out the old and terrible cadence:

"Wheat—wheat—wheat, wheat—wheat—wheat."

Blind and insensate, Jadwin strove against the torrent of the Wheat. (392)

Such vivid degeneration had always been Norris's descriptive speciality, and here, linking it, by means of the concept of force, to the crucial sociopsychological problem of mechanistic dehumanization, Norris brought a new area of insight into his art. Moreover, his moral perceptions were involved in this insight in a more integral and unified way than they were in his thinking on the similar theme of redblooded primitivism, about which his own attitudes were ambivalent and in some respects divorced from his moral perception.

Like *The Octopus*, *The Pit* has centers of interest, themes, and means of depiction unrelated to the universe of force. The domestic drama of Laura Jadwin's marriage, a story line far tamer than the all-out melodrama of the pit, frequently upstages that more spectacular plot, bringing its standards of relevance and value to the fore; and Jadwin's moral deterioration is at one point interrupted while he deals out poetic justice to the crooked manipulator Dave Scannell and his pathetic victim, old Hargus, the deterioration being resumed and intensified a few pages later, after the poignant satisfaction of that moment of retribution has faded.

As the omniscient narrator again deals out diverse and manifold story materials, a certain amount of intellectual and attitudinal self-contradiction is introduced, and this is evident both in the novel's intermittent determinism and in its ambivalent focus on social issues, both areas being, as we have seen, specially problematical ones for the proponents of the universe of force. The narrator at one point introduces quite unambiguously the idea that the grain exchange is indeed part of the moral universe, affected by the free and intentional actions of individual men and itself clearly an instrument of social justice. The idea is presented by Charlie Cressler, several times used in the novel as a spokesman for moral responsibility:

"It's like this: If we send the price of wheat down too far, the farmer suffers, the fellow who raises it; if we send it up too far, the poor man in Europe suffers, the fellow who eats it. . . . The only way to do so that neither the American farmer nor the European peasant suffers, is to keep wheat at an average, legitimate value. The moment you inflate or depress that, somebody suffers right away. And that is just what these gamblers are doing all the time, booming it up or booming it down. Think of it, this food of hundreds and hundreds of thousands of people just at the mercy of a few men down there on the Board of Trade." (129)

This set of effects is recognized by the narrator and other characters too in the course of the novel; it is not a misinformed or warped perspective, although it is in many other contexts a neglected perspective. As Jadwin (our protagonist, the husband of Laura and the supporter of Sunday Schools) is battling off a concerted conspiracy (led by the appropriately named Crookes) by precipitously raising the price of the grain, the narrator seems to encourage our allegiance to our hero rather than our awareness of the ethics of economics. At other times, contrastingly, a pure determinism seems to prevail, and forces—as Spencer would have pointed out—act as Forces, according to their own laws, drawing Jadwin willy-nilly ever deeper into speculation (his imagination, will, and desire controlled by "wheat—wheat—wheat, wheat—wheat—wheat") and inundating him, all in the same gradual but mighty surge. This, of course, is the insight with which the novel closes—in the thoughts of Laura Jadwin, to be sure, but typical of Norris's style of narration and therefore not in any way qualified, enlarged, or overridden.

There may indeed ultimately be inherent in this novel a complex insight about free will and force, survival-struggle and ethical responsibility; there certainly are a variety of earnest and sometimes provocative points made. The various insights about these matters seem to occur in separate contexts, however. At no point is there a moment of complex and comprehensive insight, even in the narrative and philosophical closure. The novel's gross insight seems to be arrived at miscellaneously—accidentally, we might even suspect—gathered up by the narrator in pieces along with the various affective story materials he collects, some of which combine crucially and revealingly, and some of which do not.

IN SUM, then, Norris's standpoint of naive omniscience did not enable him as novelist to explore, understand, and control his ideas fully enough, either philosophically or esthetically. No perspective ever quite prevails in his work or ever wholly integrates his vision. The universe-of-force paradigm was quite congenial to this peculiarly plastic, absolutistic point of view, but even it informs his works only intermittently. Its particular advantages resided in the possibilities it offered for both unconventional and vastly integrative insight, but its absolutistic, mechanically deterministic base and blandly universal (Americanized) optimism proved to be detrimental limiting and determining factors in the art of fiction. Norris the novelist could not remain within the universe of force, nor should he have.

6. JACK LONDON: RADICAL INDIVIDUALISM AND SOCIAL JUSTICE IN THE UNIVERSE OF FORCE

What then, we ask, is likely to be the effect of this revolution on morality? Some effect it can hardly fail to have. Evolution is force, the struggle for existence is force, natural selection is force. . . . But what will become of the brotherhood of man and the very idea of humanity?

Goldwin Smith, "The Prospects of a Moral Interregnum," *Atlantic Monthly*, 1879

In this chapter we see another American novelist of the turn of the century deeply influenced but not entirely dominated by the idea of the universe of force. Jack London (1876–1916) was self-educated, and his avid reading of Spencer's First Principles *was the key moment in his intellectual development. He became the most explicitly and thoroughly Spencerian of any of the American authors; in his important novels* The Sea Wolf *and* Martin Eden *he used the concept of a force-universe as if he were playing a trump. Another melodramatist with a strong taste for images of primordial struggle and primitive strength, London was somewhat more oriented toward philosophical and social ideas than was Frank Norris. The basic paradigm of the-novelist-as-intellectual was the same in both men, though: both had a strong yearning to understand the deepest meanings of life and to represent experience's surfaces and essences candidly and truthfully, but both were unable to find any but second-rate ideas or to get entirely free of some of the most limiting of the stock conventions of the fiction of their day. The point of view of naive omniscience was one of these conventions too, a typical recourse of literary realists anxious to explain life in their works. Still London (like Norris) was a compelling maker of images and stories, and through his fictional imagination was able at times to transcend the shallow or shopworn substance of his ideas.*

London tried to take his universe of force straight; it was a harsh and impersonal vision to him, and one which overthrew the genteel and blandly benevolent conceptions that were so widely popular in America and that were belied by his rich firsthand experience in deprivation, injustice, and brutality. He saw the universe as force, impersonal and irresistible in both its natural *and social aspects, and the poor individual was up against it, in spite of all his hopes and dreams and desires. Thus the primary virtues were strength and clearsighted candor, individualistic virtues justifiable in terms of both their short-run survival value and their innate nobility, for in the long run there was no hope at all. Culture was claptrap and morality was sham. Yet (and this is where his thought begins to be interesting and his works more complicated), running in many ways counter to the gospels of instinct, individualism, and inevitability, London had an empathy with the unfortunate and a sensitivity to social injustice so direct and powerful that it carried him beyond Norris's sort of evolutionary optimism and beyond Spencer's philanthropic ameliorism into the idea that the institutions of society, however evolutionary in origin, were unjust and ought to be changed by political action. To Spencer's individualism and determinism, London added a socialism which was partly heartfelt improvisation and partly second- or third-hand Marx. Thus his best works of fiction, although their intellectual materials are unpromising, become inquiries into the complex problems of the individual in nature and in society, explorations, in fact, of London's own disparities of vision. Whatever (self-contradictory) assuredness London demonstrated as a thinker, as an artist he showed in his best works an intuitive awareness that there was more to life than any single paradigm could express.*

IN COMPARISON to Henry Adams and Frank Norris, Jack London seems like a literary Horatio Alger, a poor roustabout who became a famous and relatively wealthy author on the strength of raw talent and sheer determination. Caught in his early life between his own appetite for experience and the grinding economic necessities of the social class he was born to, he lived the life of a kind of proletarian adventurer, having been (among other things) a deckhand, a coal stoker, a Klondiker, a wage-slave in a laundry, a hobo, a waterfront brawler, a drunk, and a convict. His first education came from the streets and waterfronts, the sea and the wilderness, and perhaps the clearest thing it taught him was that he did not want to be poor. In 1899 he set himself the incredible task of becoming a writer and thinker; he brought to that endeavor a range of experience unusual even for an American author, a strong feeling that the bourgeois optimism conventionally used to rationalize experience was pure cant, and a personal capacity for self-dedication and self-discipline which was nothing short of phenomenal. He plunged into a self-directed program of serious reading and writing and maintained it through a long period of hardship and discouragement until it paid off. He studied philosophy, physics, sociology, biology, history, political science, and poetry, and he tried writing essays, stories, sketches, travel pieces, journalistic reports, poems, fillers, and even humorous anecdotes. He thought very seriously and sincerely, but he wrote anything that might sell. In his period of apprenticeship he was hungry, and he had no leisure to develop esthetic detachment or a voice of his own.

But success came, and to some extent on his own terms. His very genuine fascination for motifs of personal capability, strength, courage, survival-in-the-face-of-odds—the whole myth of frontiersmanship, in fact, laced with the Darwinian dream of elemental survival—found a ready market in Teddy Roosevelt's America. London first put himself before the bookreading public in 1900 with *The Son of the Wolf*, and with *The Call of the Wild* in 1903 his fame was made. He continued to write prolifically (he *always* wrote prolifically, from his early attempts in 1899 until his death in 1916), and with the publication of all of his manuscripts virtually assured, he poured out book after book. Most of them were adventure stories, many of them set in primitive environments, but there were other types of works too—political novels, romantic novels, autobiographical narratives, journalism, social and political treatises and miscellany—not all of them crowd pleasers. And money and fame were now his, in large quantity.

His main assets as a writer were his experience, his candor, and his determination; his main liability was lack of sufficient concern for the quality of what he wrote. He wrote a great deal—a thousand words a day, regularly, rain or shine, on sea or land, the total output of his seventeen years as an author running to some fifty-five books, counting posthumous collections—and whereas some of this writing is serious, vivid, and probing, much of it is careless, self-indulgent, and imitative. He wrote quickly, with little or no revision, and with one eye on the market. Not only did he use a number of conventional and trite narrative shortcuts, stock characterizations and such, but he borrowed and even possibly stole ideas from fellow authors. Sinclair Lewis in his apprentice days was hired by London to supply story ideas, some of which were duly written up and sold, and several times in his career London had to defend himself publicly (and sometimes not very convincingly) from the charge of plagiarism of other authors' published works. Because of his approach to his craft his work is extremely uneven, his deepest and keenest insight often obscured in the haste and the triteness of the telling. Significantly, when he talked about his writing he was preoccupied with the quantitative rather than the qualitative aspects of his craft. How many words a day he was able to write, how many copies his books sold, how much money they made for him—these were his main concerns; rarely did he discuss quality, rarely differentiate between his works on that basis.

His intellectual education was sporadic but intense. He was genuinely interested in ideas, especially metaphysical and sociopolitical ideas, and he gave himself wholly to what appealed to him. The ideas had to be big, dramatic, and radically nonconventional, and if they were, the subtler elements of validity and truth could go by the boards for all he cared. He was a better thinker than Norris or Dreiser (he, at least, seems to have understood Spencer), but still he was derivative, uncritical, and too easily impressed. He was most influenced by Spencer and the German force-philosopher who prided himself on being a strict materialistic monist, Ernst Haeckel. Darwin was another strong influence, as were Marx, Nietzsche, and sociologist Benjamin Kidd, with minor influences by Max Nordau, John W. Draper, and Brooks Adams. It is a strange list, with little consistency in quality or kind; but as Charles Child Walcutt has said of it, "this medley of conflicting and contradictory ideas represents an 'advanced' mind of about 1900."[1] The "advanced" ideas London latched onto in 1899 he essentially held through the rest of his life. Significantly absent as influences are any representatives of conventional Christian, genteel Victorian, or optimistic evolutionary thought. His intermittent academic education had left him with no partiality for ideality.

Joan London's biography of her father casts considerable doubt on her father's first-hand acquaintance with some of the thinkers who it is generally assumed influenced him, asserting that it was mainly in conversations with his friend Frank Strawn-Hamilton that he got his ideas. But even wanting to say this, she acknowledges the depth of his encounter with Spencer; of Darwin, Spencer, Nietzsche, and Marx she says, "He read very little of any of them, and studied none. Darwin and Spencer were gobbled in one exciting reading, although he later returned to Spencer and read him more carefully."[2]

The appeal that Spencer's system had for him is relatable not to its optimism, as is so often the case, but to its comprehensiveness and its ostensibly firm basis in scientific physical fact. It seemed to London both universal and unassailable. "I am trying to assimilate Spencer's philosophy just now, so that there is a chance that I may yet attain to happiness,"[3] he wrote in 1900, only partly joking, to his future second wife, Charmian, and in a piece of advice to aspiring writers which he published in 1899, he had revealed his own Spencerian viewpoint in urging on them the necessity of a Spencerian sort of philosophy to their art: "If your knowledge is sparse or unsystematized, how can your words be broad and logical? And without the strong central thread of a working philosophy, how can you make order of chaos?" he asked, and he went on to prod them to study "history, biology, evolution, ethics."[4] That the quintessential questions all had Spencerian answers is evident in an extended exhortation London used in 1900 upon Cloudesley Johns, a friend with whom he carried on an earnest philosophical correspondence at the turn of the century and for some years afterwards:

To be well fitted for the tragedy of existence (intellectual existence), one must have a working philosophy, a synthesis of things. Have you a synthesis of things? . . . What significance do the following generalities have for you:—Matter is indestructible; motion is continuous; Force is persistent; the relations among forces are persistent; the transformation of forces is the equivalence of forces; etc., etc.? . . . Have you ever thought that all life, all the universe of which you may in any way have knowledge of, bows to a law of continuous redistribution of matter? Have you read or thought that there is a dynamic principle, true of the metamorphosis of the universe, of the metamorphoses of the details of the universe, which will express these ever-changing relations? Nobody can tell you what this dynamic principle is, or why; but you may learn *how* it works. Do you know what this principle is? If you do, have you studied it, ay, carefully and painstakingly? And if you have not done these things, which have naught to do with creeds, or dogmas, with politics or economics, with race prejudices or passions; but which are the principles upon which they all work, to which they all answer because of law; if you have not, then can you say that you have a firm foundation for your philosophy of life?[5]

London continually referred to Spencerian ideas in this way, as making up the "foundation" or "fundamentals" or "central thread" of a man's philosophy. Spencer's theory of cosmic Evolution and Dissolution is rapturously invoked in one published essay as "the wildest vision the scientific vision has ever achieved."[6] London even studied Spencer's essay on literary style in trying to become a writer, and in later years he recommended it to other aspiring writers, although it has little real connection with either Spencer's philosophy or London's style.

London's worship of Spencer, far-reaching though it was, was not complete and unquestioning, however. In two fairly important ways London dissented from Spencer, and therein lies some of the individuality as well as some of the inconsistency of his thought. Tempting though it inherently was to accept all Spencer in a single piece, London was sufficiently dissatisfied with his agnosticism and with much of his social philosophy to oppose him in those areas. His feelings on the former issue led him to Haeckel and those on the latter led him to Marx.

Spencer's agnosticism, worked up into the carefully elaborated epistemology of the Unknowable seemed like pussyfooting to London, who wanted his materialism straight. As can be seen in the above-quoted letter to Johns, London pushed materialistic Spencerianism, devoid of the agnostic framework. And Fiske's accomodation of Spencer and Christianity seemed to London a complete blind alley. As he had written to Johns two weeks earlier in 1900,

Spencer was not openly, that is, didactically favorable to a material basis for thought, mind, soul, etc., but John Fiske has done many queer gymnastics in order to reconcile Spencer, whose work he worships, to his own beliefs in immortality and God. But he doesn't succeed very well. He jumps on Haeckel, with both feet, but in my modest opinion, Haeckel's position is as yet unassailable,[7]

and in another letter,

What's this chemical ferment called life all about? Small wonder that small men down the ages have conjured gods in answer. A little god is a snug little possession and explains it all. But how about you and me, who have no god?

I have at last discovered what I am. I am a materialistic monist, and there's dam little satisfaction in it.[8]

And in 1914 he is still in that camp:

I have always inclined toward Haeckel's position. In fact, "incline" is too weak a word. I am a hopeless materialist. . . . I join with Haeckel in being what, in lieu of any other phrase, I am compelled to call "a positive scientific thinker."[9]

Karl Marx was a materialistic monist too, but one with a social vision far different from the *laissez-faire* individualism of Spencer and Haeckel, and it was a vision far closer to the feelings and perceptions that Jack London brought away from his early experiences. He seems to have read very little of Marx, and to have gotten most of his social theory as his daughter claimed, at second or third hand, but he was no less fervent for that, looking back upon his conversion to revolutionary socialism as a kind of dawning: "I joined the groups of working-class and intellectual revolutionists, and for the first time came into intellectual living."[10] He remained, in his own way, an active and outspoken socialist until almost the end of his career.[11]

Still, Darwin and the Social Darwinists spoke strongly to him too, as did Nietzsche in his powerful iconoclasm, assuring that the ghost of competitive individualism would never quite be laid to rest. The doctrine of biological evolution had been "flatly accepted" in its description of "the survival of the fittest," he asserted in his essay "Wanted: A New Law of Development," and he went on to add that "it is in the struggle of the species and against all other hostile forces in the environment, that this law operates; also in the struggle between individuals of the same species."[12] The human qualities called forth in such struggles were awesome to London, although of course antithetical to humanitarian socialism.

Ultimately there is no reconciling Spencer, Marx, Darwin, and Nietzsche in a single vision of man in society, and London struggled with these perspectives throughout his life, recapitulating in his own mind and art the philosophical travail of his times. He shows some signs of being aware of the disparities; his interest in the sociologist Benjamin Kidd helped him to see it intellectually. Kidd was himself a Social Darwinist and a second-rate sociologist, but he clearly enough saw a serious disparity between natural and political evolution. In his book, *Social Evolution*, along with a good deal of sententiousness on the subject of racial superiority in the struggle for survival, he points out that whereas according to Darwin's paradigm human evolutionary progress depends on free and aggressive intraspecific competition, mankind's political evolution seems to be in the direction of humanitarian socialism. London discussed this situation in the same terms in the 1902 essay "Wanted: a New Law of Development," expressing the hope that some new evolutionary social insight would soon be arrived at, because according to current understanding the socialistic future, while being more humane, would also retard evolutionary progress. That, of course, was exactly the problem with these concepts, but London never quite saw it as a conceptual problem, nor did he (or anyone else) ever discover the New Law of Development.

The particular "synthesis of things" that London produced out of these disparate influences, the "philosophy of life" that underlay his art, began in the universe of force, variously envisioned. Rather than seeing value or purpose underlying the universe, London saw "LAW, inexorable, blind, unreasoning law, which has no knowledge of good or ill, right or wrong; which has no preference, grants no favors."[13] The law of the universe was cyclical, materialistic, and totally deterministic, as the wise old character in *The Scarlet Plague* proclaims in an Ecclesiastes-like lament:

> Just as the old civilization passed, so will the new. It may take fifty thousand years to build, but it will pass. All things pass. Only remain cosmic force and matter, ever in flux, ever acting and reacting and realizing the eternal types—the priest, the soldier, and the king.[14]

Spencer's laws of evolution and dissolution hold sway, as matter and matter's offshoots consolidate in more definite, coherent, and heterogeneous patterns as the universe is on the evolutionary swing. London's universe operates like Spencer's Knowable.

Life, for London as for Spencer, is a matter of response and adjustment on the part of an organism to external pressures, and so is, in an important way, determined by the universe-machine. As London put it,

> All evolution, all change, is from without, in; not from within, out. The fundamental characteristic of all life is IRRITABILITY. In the [sic] other words, capacity for feeling pressures from without. Life itself is an equilib-

rium, between what is within and what is without. . . . If all forces which impinged upon organism [sic] were constant, you would have a constant organism. There would be no change. And there would be no development. The economic pressure from without, forces the change, forces the idea, causes the idea.[15]

He thought of the "pressures from without" as operating primarily in nature and society, two differentiated but fundamentally similar force-spheres. In *A Daughter of the Snows*, for example, London endows Jacob Welse, the older-generation Klondike hero with this very Spencerian wisdom:

Accustomed to do battle with natural forces, he was attracted by the com-mercial battle with social forces. . . . In the mellow of time, he got a proper focus on things and unified the phenomena of society precisely as he had already unified the phenomena of nature. . . . The same principles under-laid both; the same truths were manifest of both.[16]

What is the response of a man of spirit to the adversities and limitations heaped on him by the determining forces? This is the subject on which Lon-don's imagination was most keenly poetic, because what he felt a man strove for in the cosmic and futile struggle was not just pragmatic survival but a romantic kind of mastery which affirmed his worth in spite of the universe. Why did London want to bear both the expense of designing and building a yacht and the hardship and risk of sailing it around the world? I quote at length from his explanation in *The Cruise of the Snark*, not only for his ideas on the subject of the individual's response to the forces of nature but for the poetry of his vision as well:

Here am I, a little animal called a man—a bit of vitalized matter, one hundred and sixty-five pounds of meat and blood, nerve, sinew, bones, and brain,—all of it soft and tender, susceptible to hurt, fallible, and frail. I strike a light backhanded blow on the nose of an obstreperous horse, and a bone in my hand is broken. I put my head under the water for five min-utes, and I am drowned. I fall twenty feet through the air, and I am smashed. . . . A splinter of lead from a rifle enters my head, and I am wrapped around in the eternal blackness.

Fallible and frail, a bit of pulsating, jelly-like life—it is all I am. About me are the great natural forces—colossal menaces, Titans of destruction, unsentimental monsters that have less concern for me than I have for the grain of sand I crush under my foot. . . . They are unconscious, unmerciful, and unmoral. They are the cyclones and tornadoes, lightning flashes and cloud-bursts, tide-rips and tidal waves, undertows and water-spouts, great whirls and sucks and eddies, earthquakes and volcanoes, surfs that thunder on rock-ribbed coasts and seas that leap aboard the largest crafts that float, crushing humans to pulp or licking them off into the sea and to death— and these insensate monsters do no know that tiny sensitive creature, all nerves and weaknesses, whom men call Jack London, and who himself thinks he is all right and quite a superior being.

In the maze and chaos of the conflict of these vast and draughty Titans, it is for me to thread my precarious way. The bit of life that is I will exult over them. The bit of life that is I, in so far as it succeeds in baffling them or in bitting them to its service, will imagine that it is godlike. It is good to ride the tempest and feel godlike. I dare to assert that for a finite speck of pulsating jelly to feel godlike is a far more glorious feeling than for a god to feel godlike.[17]

When the conflict between the forces and the human atom is conceived of as the struggle of man against nature, it was comparatively easy to take an unambiguous attitude toward it (at least in that preecologically minded age) and to depict it in a dramatic and exhilarating way in either nonfiction or fiction. London made the depiction of this conflict his stock in trade (in more than one sense), as in the Klondike tales, for example, where the rigors of cold and snow, raging river, savage wolf packs, and the deadly expanses of "white silence" are forces which determine men's lives and test their mettle. The fittest survive, and Darwinian or even Nietzschean individualism is not out of place, although human cooperation is also a value London sets a great deal of store by in these fictional environs.

When the forces man had to face were social forces, however, the determinism was not so clear-cut, and the individual's response could not be so "godlike." Instead of "draughty titans" there were the slow-grinding millstones of poverty and despair, formidable like the snows, the villains and the wolf-packs, but far more difficult to confront and conquer. If a man were to stand up and assert himself like a two-fisted Darwinist of the slums, he could only attack either the intangible and virtually invulnerable conditions or other men as accessible and vulnerable as himself; the first would be futile and the second brutish. London knew the situation well, both experientially and theoretically, and he wrestled with it often in his works.

When he took an abstractly philosophical approach, he pictured man as the helpless victim of the universe of force. Socialism was man's only hope, but

the cardinal tenet of Socialism is that forbidding doctrine, the materialistic conception of history. Men are not the masters of their souls. They are the puppets of great, blind forces. The lives they live and the deaths they die are compulsory. All social codes are but the reflexes of existing economic conditions, plus certain survivals of past economic conditions. The insti-

tutions men build they are compelled to build. Economic laws determine
at any given time what these institutions shall be, how long they shall operate, and by what they shall be replaced.[18]

Thinking along the same lines while writing a glowing review of Norris's *The
Octopus*, he made a point of quoting very admiringly the speech railroad
president Shelgrim gives to Presley in explaining that the forces control the
men and not the men the forces.[19]

London conceived of socioeconomic forces as behaving according to the
Spencerian paradigm, developing in the direction of increased integration, coherence, and definition:

> From man's drawing the world closer and closer together [by such means
> as the railroad, the telegraph, etc.] his own affairs and institutions have
> consolidated. Concentration may typify the chief movement of the age—
> concentration, classification, order; the reduction of friction between the
> parts of the social organism.[20]

Unlike Spencer, who saw social concentration as progress in the direction of
altruistic individualism, London saw it as culminating in socialism. The dynamic of the Spencerian force-system does indeed seem to incline it in that
direction despite Spencer's efforts to direct it toward an outcome which was
for him more palatable. Henry Adams of course had thought of the concentration of force as leading to socialism although he bitterly deplored that prospect. London pictured it as the millenium:

> All [people and institutions] are organizing for pleasure, profit, policy, or
> intellectual pursuit. They have come to know the strength of numbers,
> solidly phalanxed and driving onward with singleness of purpose. These
> purposes may be various and many, but one and all, ever discovering new
> mutual interests and objects, obeying a law which is beyond them, these
> petty aggregations draw closer together, forming greater aggregations and
> congeries of aggregations. And these, in turn, vaguely merging each into
> each, present glimmering adumbrations of the coming human solidarity
> which shall be man's crowning glory.[21]

Given this general view of things, there was indeed a viable stance an individual could take toward the intangible determining forces: he could become
a socialist and try to help bring about "the coming human solidarity." That,
of course, is what Jack London himself did. He joined the socialist party and
contributed both money and time, speaking and writing in the cause of revolution.* One of the infrequent unambiguously heroic characters in London's

---

* He claimed that his political activities cost him thousands of dollars in royalties because his
books were systematically boycotted, and this was probably so.

fiction, Ernest Everhard in *The Iron Heel*, is an idealized projection of such an individual response to the deterministic social forces.

Beneath his philosophical approach London vividly sensed the meaning of poverty. He had been there himself during his own early hard times and then later as a kind of experiment in empathy and social consciousness when he lived among the destitute in the East End slums of London gathering material for *The People of the Abyss* (1903). This foray into personal eyewitness journalism is still a work of considerable directness and power; the book employs no grand metaphors for social determinism and deduces no cosmic theories, but it gives an unmistakable sense of the individual and social costs of people's hopeless struggle with the cycle of poor wages, high rent, crowded and unsanitary living conditions, malnutrition, illness, and despair. The determinism is as obvious as the fetid air, and Spencer's sanguine view of the highly and humanely evolved industrial state seems in comparison tragically shortsighted. "In the East End fifty-five percent of the children die before five years of age," London tersely states.[22] His response to the East End spectacle was unintellectual, moral, and very personal; walking with two hopelessly destitute and out-of-work East End men, he notices them stopping occasionally to pick up from the sidewalk and eat little bits of organic debris. He describes their conversation and his feelings thusly:

> Naturally, their guts a-reek with pavement offal, they talked of bloody revolution. They talked as anarchists, fanatics, and madmen would talk. And who shall blame them? In spite of my three good meals that day, and the snug bed I could occupy if I wished, and my social philosophy, and my evolutionary belief in the slow development and metamorphosis of things—in spite of all this, I say, I felt impelled to talk rot with them or hold my tongue.[23]

London characteristically gave or loaned money prodigally to anyone who was down and out, he wrote a number of angry books and essays, and he looked toward revolution. If people were caught in the machinery of inevitability, you did all you could to help them.

If it were oneself who was caught, or a protagonist, the situation seemed to call for a supreme effort of individualism, however. Whatever London's philosophical doubts about the freedom of the will—"man is not a free agent, and free will is a fallacy exploded by science long ago. . . . Matter and the motion of matter make up the sum total of existence"[24]—he and most of his protagonists acted like what they willed and what they did mattered very much indeed. London himself not only used his own bootstrap self-improvement to escape the cycle of poverty, drift, and vulnerability of his early life, but he continued his campaign of self-assertion to become a wealthy and influential man with a yacht to captain, a ranch to oversee, and an Oriental houseboy to be served by. He sought and enjoyed the prerogatives of the individually powerful—magnanimously, to be sure, but nonetheless oriented toward a "crowning glory" which was antithetical to "the coming human solidarity." He lived in the central moral contradiction of his society. The imperatives of individualism and social justice were as unavoidable as they were incompatible.

In his avowedly autobiographical writings he treats the belief in the Nietzschean type of aggressive egoism as an immature idea of his youth: "I was very young and callow, did not know much of anything, and though I had never heard of a school called "Individualism," I sang the paean of the strong with all my heart." [25] As we are about to see, in his fiction he had more subtle and searching ways of dealing with the problem of individualism than by simply viewing it as a callow idea superceded by its more mature antithesis. Many of his major works focus on this problem—*The Sea Wolf*, *Martin Eden*, *The Kempton-Wace Letters*, and *Burning Daylight*—usually by way of a major character who is an outspoken and charismatic individualist. Charisma and fate are at odds in these works, however, and fate is London's instrument of morality. In four different ways, London says that in the context of an indifferent, mechanistic universe, unbridled individualism exercised in an interpersonal or social realm leads ultimately to conflict, isolation, and death. London did his work well in these novels, developing his individualists with such sinister attractiveness that he spent the rest of his life explaining to a public who were only too receptive to visions of heroic individualism that these books were really anti-individualistic. As he insisted in a letter to a critic in 1912, "I believe in a culture far beyond present-day culture. I do not believe in war. I am not an individualist. *Sea Wolf*, *Martin Eden*, *Burning Daylight* were written as indictments of individualism. Martin Eden died because he was an individualist." [26] Even later he revealed to a friend that his single greatest disappointment with his critical audience came because while "lots of people read *The Sea Wolf*, no one discovered that it was an attack upon the super-man philosophy." [27] The degree to which we are taken along with Wolf Larsen's or Burning Daylight's individualism corresponds to the depth and seriousness with which London is engaging the problem in these books. The individual's act of aggressively overcoming nature is glorious, but the individual's act of aggressively overcoming man is the closest thing to sin the materialistic monist knows.

A GOOD MANY of London's writings have little or nothing to do with the universe of force or indeed with any of his philosophical ideas. The stories he ground out for magazine publication were generally made out of stock elements of popular adventure or romance fiction, and their level of insight is limited to what is typical of these genres. The same is true of some of his novels. In his works of journalistic nonfiction, works such as *People of the Abyss, The Road, The Cruise of the Snark*, and *John Barleycorn*, his sense of conventional genre is far less operative, and they are genuinely interesting for their direct and personal veracity, although the metaphysical ideas that preoccupy him in his essays and correspondence remain far in the background. His cosmic concerns are more substantially involved in a number of his novels which have so far proved more or less durable, and it is to them that we now turn.

Several works manifest the universe of force importantly but only subliminally, more as an intimation of cosmic determinism than as an acknowledged explanation of phenomena. There are the Alaskan wilderness stories, for example, most notably *The Call of the Wild* and *White Fang*. London conceived of these two books as (among other things) Spencerian parables, although no explicitly Spencerian explanations were used in them. *White Fang*, written as a companion piece to the extraordinarily popular *Call*, he admitted conceiving of as "beginning at the very opposite end—evolution instead of devolution; civilization instead of decivilization."[28] Both books have dog heroes, but whereas in the latter the dog changes from tame to feral (as he is stolen from his owner in California, shipped to Alaska, and eventually runs wild when his new owner is killed), in the former a wild wolf-dog gradually learns to survive and thrive in captivity. The actions upon which these books rather exclusively focus were thus illustrations, London felt, of First Principles although the First Principles themselves are never stated.

Their presence is clearly felt in the descriptions of nature, though. In *White Fang*, in describing the effects of the "White Silence"—the vast and still winter desolation—on life in the persons of two doomed men (minor characters) trekking across it, the narrator observes that: "It crushed them into the remotest recesses of their own minds, pressing out of them, like juices from the grape, all the false ardors and exaltations and undue self-values of the human soul, until they perceived themselves finite and small, specks and motes, moving with weak cunning and little wisdom amidst the play and interplay of the great blind elements and forces."[29] The natural environment is thus an agent and symbol of the universe of force. As London scholar Earle Labor has appropriately pointed out, the White Silence has a close relationship to the "awesome naturalistic genie" of Haeckel and Darwin.[30]

The governing element of these adventure books is adventure, however, and London's narrators, like Norris's, sometimes shift conceptions of the physical universe for effect. At times there is a tendency to anthropomorphize nature as, for example, in *White Fang* when the narrator asserts that there is a "hint of laughter" in nature observing man's futile struggle, or that "the wild aims always to destroy movement" (3, 4).

From a third-person dog's-eye-view, the world is just as materialistically deterministic as Haeckel conceived it. Both dogs are made strong and lean by the rigors of the North, weak and docile by starvation, mean by mistreatment, and loyally affectionate by intelligent kindness. And to make the determinism complete, even the human beings (all limited to minor roles by the books' perspective) are formed and deformed by the Forces: for instance, it is said of the escaped convict overcome by White Fang in the finale of that novel that "he had been ill-made in the making. He had not been born right, and he had not been helped any by the moulding he had received at the hands of society" (315). The old "LAW, inexorable, blind, unreasoning law" holds near-absolute sway in the books, and its metaphoric counterpart is the inescapable icy bleakness that surrounds the action and causes much of it.

The determinism of these two dog books might be expected to be more radical than anything a wide popular audience would accept, but both novels can actually be read as optimistic books in which the deterministic factors do more to add to the excitement than to interfere with the sentimental response. The anthropomorphizing and heroizing of the dog are actually more prominent in these novels than is the naturalism, which really only supplies the circumstances in which the dog can show his noble soul. The dogs are so very human and noble, and the narrative rhetoric is so obviously aimed at producing emotional effects in the reader, that both novels seem quaint and sentimental now, and neither their wind-in-the-fur sense of adventure nor their potential as evolutionary melodrama can quite save them from that.

London's fiction was deeper and more maturely engaging when he wrote about human beings who were able to understand the universe of force and react to this philosophic knowledge. Generally, in his Klondike tales and a great deal of his other fiction as well, only the narrator is aware of the universe as a deterministic mechanism (if indeed anybody is); the characters in these works remain oblivious of their predicament, and, unlike the way such situations generate powerful central ironies in Stephen Crane's fiction, their obliviousness often matters relatively little. No wonder that Henry Steele Commager could assert that London's scientific philosophy was a kind of decorative superfluity.[31] But in a number of major works, including *The Sea Wolf* and *Martin Eden*, in focusing on what it means to a character to know the terrible truth about the universe, London attains considerably more depth in his fiction.

This treatment of the awareness of his characters was first evident in *The Kempton-Wace Letters*, a strange sort of book which he produced in 1903 in collaboration with an intense intellectual friend, Anna Strunsky. The book is a wide-ranging debate, in the form of a fictional exchange of letters, centering on the topic of love but extending out into many other questions about ultimate values in life. The correspondents are prototypical opponents in turn-of-the-century America: Herbert Wace is a young man and a "new" man. He is an American (a Californian, at that), an economics instructor working on his doctorate in social sciences, a candid "realist" who identifies with the new, scientific approach to reality. Dane Kempton is one generation his senior and a representative of conservative tradition. He is an Englishman, a poet and man of letters, a sentimental idealist who identifies with traditional religion and humanism. Both points of view are argued articulately and with persuasive inner consistency, Anna Strunsky composing Kempton's letters and London composing Wace's.

Kempton's love for Wace's dead mother and his extensive role in the young man's upbringing bind them together and make their interchange basically sympathetic, but there can be no doubt about their separation on many fundamental issues. Their disagreement is precipitated by Wace's announcement that he plans to marry a beautiful and talented young woman whom he does not love. He claims it is a rational, practical, no-nonsense decision on both their parts. Kempton is shocked that Wace would think of marrying without love, and he replies with fatherly admonitions about the scientific faddishness that is luring Wace away from the deepest traditional human wisdom. London invokes the universe of force and his own background in materialistic monism in developing Wace's self-justification. Wace looks at the phenomenon of love in the whole context of Spencerian evolution. Beginning with Spencer's definition of the essential nature of life "to adjust the inner relations with the outer relations," he goes on to show the foundation of love in unicellular "things sexless and loveless"[32] and its origin in the impelling necessities of "Nutrition and Reproduction" (64). Stressing the determinism and rationalism of his view, Wace says,

> As Ernst Haeckel, that brave old hero of Jena, explains—"The irresistible passion that draws Edward to the sympathetic Otilla, or Paris to Helen, and leaps all bounds of reason and morality, is the same *powerful, unconscious*, attractive force which impels the living spermatozoon to force an entrance into the ovum in the fertilization of the egg of the animal or plant—the same impetuous movement which unites two atoms of hydrogen to one atom of oxygen for the formation of a molecule of water."
>
> But with the advent of intellectual man, there is no longer need for obeying blind and irresistible compulsion. . . . As he controls and directs the great natural forces . . . so will he control and direct the operation of the reproductive force so that life will not only be perpetuated but developed and made higher and finer. (153–154)

While Wace argues thus that what mankind most needs is an understanding of the deterministic forces and a rational use of them for the improvement of his lot, Kempton counters that this is metaphysical reductionism ("there are forces stronger than force, shadows more real than reality" [28]) and an emotionless, calculating, and egotistical approach. The universe and life, he argues, should properly inspire wonder and joy. Wace early (though slantedly) defined their perspectives: "Life itself appealed to you, while to me appealed the mechanics of life. . . . Yours was a world of ideas and fancies, mine a world of things and facts" (17).

Each point of view has its full inning, and no decision, synthesis, or compromise is arrived at. On these facts rests the (considerable) integrity of this book. London puts all of his own modern scientific philosophy into Herbert Wace's letters, and a good measure of vehemence as well, and by comparison Strunsky/Kempton's seem at times like archaic sentimentality, although there are occasional flashes of clear perception and humane wisdom. But for all Wace's intellectual superiority (his knowledge is broader, more specific, scientific, of a different and more usable order), what he stands for does not ultimately prevail in the book, since his fiancée Hester, coming to understand his true feelings toward her, regretfully submerges her love for him and breaks off the engagement. Herbert Wace ends up with all science, candor, and practicality on his side, operating according to London's own favorite ideas, but hopelessly alone, isolated from the human companionship (and even the reproduction of the species) which would have been his for the loving. His dreams were unselfish, good, and faithful to Spencerianism, but Hester's sober refusal to submit herself to the dream, although she loves the dreamer, constitutes a moderate but unmistakable reproach to Herbert Wace's whole orientation.

If London was sincere in this book (rather than pandering to a market), and if he did exercise control over its outcome (rather than turning its direction over to his collaborator)—both of which conditions have to be regarded with some skepticism in view of authorial habits he manifests elsewhere—he can be credited here with a candid and interesting job of dialectical self-analysis. At any rate, *The Kempton-Wace Letters* clearly suggests some of the personal and interpersonal costs of both radical individualism and the "new knowledge" that London himself espoused.

HIS NEXT working of these motifs was a year later, 1904, in *The Sea Wolf*. Here the philosophical debate was far more extreme—more a kind of combat, actually—and it was developed in a context of high melodrama. The universe of force has as its spokesman Wolf Larsen, the "Wolf" of the title, and as a radical Nietzschean individualist he gives materialistic monism the harshest, most challenging, most self-alienating expression it receives in any of

London's books. The Wolf is the melodramatic antagonist, and the object of much of his antagonism, of all of his philosophical antagonism, in fact, is characterized in such a way as to increase the melodrama. Humphrey Van Weyden, protagonist and first-person center of consciousness, is a delicate and cerebral young upper-class *belletrist*, not unlike the sensitive rationalist who is confronted with moral monstrosities in some of Poe's fiction. Van Weyden is placed in the unlikely position of cabin boy on Larsen's outbound sealing schooner *The Ghost*; he is delivered into the hands of the Wolf by the first of four (yes, four) fortuitous sea accidents which bring about the book's events. The plot, it must be admitted, is naively contrived and operatic, more a means of getting from one emotional and philosophical climax to the next than a representation of real-life causality. Its logic is the logic of romance, melodrama, and nightmare; its guiding purpose is an unabashed striving for effect.

The ferryboat upon which Van Weyden had been crossing San Francisco Bay collides in the fog with a steamer, and our protagonist is pulled out of the bay and into the world of *The Ghost* where Captain Wolf Larsen, its absolute ruler, chooses to entertain a whim to fill out his shorthanded crew and initiate this sensitive and effete gentleman into the realities of life rather than accept a reward for returning him to San Francisco. Van Weyden is renamed "Hump" by Larsen and assigned against his will the lowest position on the ship, where he must endure not only the physical hardships and indignities, not only the malice and brutality that pervade the ship from Captain down to cook, but also a concerted assault on his metaphysical and ethical beliefs from Larsen who, once Hump shows his intellectual propensities, is bent on teaching him the inevitability of materialistic "individualism." The novel's philosophical combat thus begins in gross happenstance and sheer inequality.

To Hump's idealism and avowed belief in immortality, Wolf replies,

> "I believe that life is a mess. . . . It is like yeast, a ferment, a thing that moves and may move for a minute, an hour, a year, or a hundred years, but that in the end will cease to move. The big eat the little that they may continue to move, the strong eat the weak that they may retain their strength. The lucky eat the most and move the longest, that is all." [33]

To Hump's belief in the value of life, Wolf says:

> "Why, if there is anything in supply and demand, life is the cheapest thing in the world. . . . Of cheap things it is the cheapest. Everywhere it goes begging. Nature spills it out with a lavish hand. Where there is room for one life, she sows a thousand lives, and it's life eats life till the strongest and most piggish life is left." (60–61)

> "[Thus] might is right, and that's all there is to it. Weakness is wrong.

Which is a very poor way of saying that it is good for oneself to be strong, and evil for oneself to be weak—or better yet, it is pleasurable to be strong, because of the profits; painful to be weak, because of the penalties." (70–71)

And when Hump naively asks him if he then doesn't believe in altruism, he immediately identifies the Spencerian allusion and while Hump marvels at Wolf's acquaintanceship with "the great philosopher's teachings," Wolf takes the stand of a hard-line individualist:

"It's just so much slush and sentiment, and you must see it yourself, at least for one who does not believe in eternal life. With immortality before me, altruism would be a paying business proposition. I might elevate my soul to all kinds of altitudes. But with nothing eternal before me but death, given for a brief spell this yeasty crawling and squirming which is called life, why, it would be immoral for me to perform any act that was a sacrifice. Any sacrifice that makes me lose one crawl or squirm is . . . a wicked thing." (72)

Hump, recoiling, categorizes Wolf as "an individualist, a materialist, and, logically, a hedonist" (73), and Wolf simply concurs, ignoring the implicit moral reproach in Hump's terms.

Interestingly enough, Wolf Larsen is to some extent described and measured by his Spencerianism. He candidly admits that,

"I understood quite a good deal of 'First Principles,' but his 'Biology' took the wind out of my sails, and his 'Psychology' left me butting around in the doldrums for many a day. I honestly could not understand what he was driving at. I put it down to mental deficiency on my part, but since then I have decided that it was for want of preparation. I had no proper basis. Only Spencer and myself know how hard I hammered. But I did get something out of his 'Data of Ethics.' That's where I ran across 'altruism,' and I remember now how it was used."

And Hump puts Larsen's Spencerianism in perspective:

I wondered what this man could have got from such a work. Spencer I remembered enough to know that altruism was imperative to his ideal of highest conduct. Wolf Larsen, evidently, had sifted the great philosopher's teachings, rejecting and selecting according to his needs and desires. (71–72)

Elsewhere Van Weyden judges him in these terms: "He betrayed the inaccuracies of the self-read man, and, it must be granted, the sureness and directness of the primitive mind" (73–74).

But such a condescending view of Larsen is not allowed to stand, and that is one of the most interesting aspects of this novel. Larsen, the "self-read" man, is as much a challenge to Spencerianism as it had been a measure of him. Hump's complacency falters at times, and both his and the reader's reactions tend to be widely ambivalent toward Wolf's radical individualism. On the surface it seems negativistic, egotistic, and amoral, although in the context of the novel it catches us on a deeper level with its power, its candor, and its accuracy in explaining life aboard *The Ghost*. London could develop it with conviction; he had been there too. Of his own earlier period of psychological and philosophical turmoil he said in a letter to a friend, "About this time I was not in a very happy state. You will remember yourself, the black moods that used to come upon me at that time, and the black philosophy that I worked out at that time and afterwards put into Wolf Larsen's mouth." [34] Juxtaposed in *The Sea Wolf* to Van Weyden's pale idealism, the "black philosophy" has no significant rivals; given London's dramatic purposes in the novel, and without Anna Strunsky to articulate the conventional alternative to materialistic monism, what was a debate in *The Kempton-Wace Letters* turns into a one-sided exhibition of an anticonventionality which both repels and engages.

And the Wolf's character is out of the same cloth. He reeks of power: although not unusually large he is always described with adjectives such as "strong," "massive," "square," "virile," and "vigorous," and he always acts with "decision" and "firmness." He can at times be brutally repulsive, administering beatings to everyone almost for the pleasure of doing it, and contemptuously probing people's psyches "with the cruel hand of a vivisectionist" (67). His actions are frequently described in animal terms, such as his "springing at" someone or "snarling" a reply. But paradoxically, he is often deeply sympathetic or admirable: Van Weyden notes the "total lack of viciousness . . . in his face," the "primal melancholy from which he suffered" (87), and is extremely responsive to a kind of primitive nobility with which Larsen is endowed. "All powers seemed his, all potentialities," says Van Weyden, and Larsen himself quotes, as expressive of his own inner feelings, Satan's lines in *Paradise Lost* ending, "better to reign in hell than serve in heaven" (221).

Larsen's fascination for Van Weyden is strong and his influence is deep. Although Hump tries to show a pat sense of control, he is really deeply shaken by the man and his ideas. "Wolf Larsen stormed the last strongholds of my faith with a vigor that received respect, while not accorded conviction" (74), he can observe at one point, while at another realizing that "my innocence of the realities of life had been complete indeed. I laughed bitterly to myself, and seemed to find in Wolf Larsen's forbidding philosophy a more adequate explanation of life than I found in my own" (126). While he vacillates philosophically, he is getting stronger, more courageous, and more self-reliant. The harsh tutelage is obviously doing him good, and Hump fears that materialistic individualism is being experientially confirmed and his moral nature is being undermined. He even begins to act like the Wolf: after backing down the bluff of the cowardly and domineering cook for whom he was forced to work, Hump admits, "the Cockney became more humble and slavish to me than even to Wolf Larsen. . . . I carried the dirk in a sheath at my hip, sailor-fashion, and maintained toward Thomas Mugridge a constant attitude which was composed of equal parts of domineering, insult, and contempt" (83).

This conflict, inner and outer, represents a revealing kind of dilemma for the reader, but it is averted rather than crucially faced or resolved in the novel as a second shipwreck-coincidence puts Maud Brewster aboard *The Ghost*. Maud is a beautiful, young, unmarried poetess whom Humphrey had once extravagantly praised in a review as "the American Mrs. Meynell." Of course, he admiring her poetry, and she admiring his sensitive insight into her poetry, they are made for each other; the magnitude of this coincidence off the coast of Japan probably measures the strength of the necessity London felt to get a sweetly appropriate mate-woman into the story for Humphrey and to save him from going the way of the Wolf.

London may have intended to intensify the drama with this plot-stroke, but much of the novel's thematic tension is simply overriden as the roles of all the principal characters are redefined along the lines of conventional melodrama. Not only is Maud herself a stock heroine, but she brings with her all the claptrap of romantic adventure (the drama of chastity preserved, of the narrow escape from danger, of the shyly delayed but oh-so-welcome declaration of love, and so forth), which forces Hump and the Wolf into the stock roles of romantic hero and villain. London's plot-contrivance enables Hump to get off of the ship and out of the Wolf's influence, and to prove that he has attained independent manhood as well; but with Maud doing no more than bearing up amazingly for such a fragile woman throughout the rigors of a lifeboat-escape in a heavy storm, and Wolf doing no more than stagily snarling and fulminating, pursuing, and finally dying, fortuitously though somewhat pathetically of a brain tumor, the artistic gains were hardly worth the losses. It is no accident that this novel was made into a Hollywood movie no less than seven times.

A qualified kind of determinism obtains in the novel; London frequently invokes or implies strong environmental forces to explain why the characters are the way they are, although he represents a few of them as able to break the causal chain and act with a qualified sort of freedom. Thomas Mugridge is not free; he was made the contemptible coward he is by the life he had to live in the slums of London and among brutal seamen. Maud has been formed by the milieu in which she has spent her life, where ideals, abstractions, and altruism prevail, but she is still capable of acts of physical courage and endurance. Humphrey, showing the same kind of environmentally caused gentility early in the story, begins to give way to a new set of shaping forces on *The Ghost*, only to have his idealism rekindled by the presence of Maud; he makes a stand against Larsen, freely, one presumes, and with all the idealism of his first education and all the physical strength and self-reliance of his second. Larsen himself has come to be no more than a ruthless sealing captain because, as he explains to Hump, invoking the parable of the mustard seed fallen upon barren ground, "My father and mother . . . were poor people and unlettered. They came of generations of poor unlettered people—peasants of the sea who sowed their sons on the waves as has been their custom since time began. There is no more to tell" (89). Yet there is also his near-miraculous self-education, his uncaused individual determination to learn the truth about existence; it did not make him a famous novelist, but it did demonstrate the existence and at least partial efficacy of his individual will.

When his individual will leads him to aggression against his fellow human beings, the result is alienating, self-corroding. Even before Hump arrives on *The Ghost*, Larsen stands alone against all the rest; any sign of his weakness in this Darwinian jungle of his own making would surely lead to his death. And after the hero and heroine escape, abetted and reassured by mutual self-sacrifice, Wolf is left to a lonely and vindictive search for them, and to the onset of his blindness and debility. The illness is an extremely arbitrary touch on London's part, but symbolically appropriate for the "black" state of total alienation which Wolf's own aggressive individualism has brought upon him. "Godlike" he has been indeed, standing against the "draughty titans" in this universe of force, but whatever admiration his Nietzschean stance has elicited has been mixed with repugnance toward his interpersonal actions and pity for his final blind and helpless isolation. Such is Jack London's complex vision of radical individualism in the universe of force in *The Sea Wolf*.

WHEN JACK LONDON wrote a novel closer to his own experience than any he had previously written—showing how a mind much like his own had been formed and how a success much like his own had been achieved—his cosmic theories, his Spencerianism, and materialistic monism, played a greater part than in his other fiction. *Martin Eden* (1909) is both more dramatic than *The Kempton-Wace Letters* and less melodramatic than *The Sea Wolf*, while it presents a version of the whole sailor-to-sage period of London's own life which is only slightly, though crucially, fictionalized. It is a *Bildungsroman* in which the protagonist progresses from lower-class illiteracy to mastery of the Knowable and ultimately to despairing world-weariness, with a concomitant gain in wealth and social stature and a concomitant loss of faith in the middle-class girl who had inspired his rise. It is a Spencerian novel of a self-made man, and at the same time a socialistic statement about the shallowness of the bourgeoisie, the insincerity of their motivations and the commerciality of their thought and art. It is also another of London's tragedies of radical individualism, especially interesting in that Martin Eden succeeds in asserting himself against the determining factors of upbringing and social structure—and he succeeds without Wolf Larsen's kind of intraspecific aggression—but his success is without triumph, and the end of this self-made individualist too is alienation and death.

Martin Eden is presented in the first pages of the novel as a twenty-year-old sailor and knockabout, who, having rescued Arthur Morse, the son of a well-to-do middle-class family, from some drunken hoodlums in a ferryboat brawl, is being introduced into the Morse family. It is a stock situation of popular fiction of the day, but carefully and interestingly developed by London. The opening chapters are keynoted by contrast: the preciously and expensively decorated Morse home as against the burliness and ungainly vitality of the young sailor; the Morses' polite manners and their "correct" speech as against Martin's self-uncertainty and linguistic barbarism; their social ease as against his traumatically tense awkwardness. He exudes force and crudeness, they culture and refinement; the third-person point-of-view (with access to all thoughts but with special interest in Martin's) puts this across.

Principally it is Arthur's sister Ruth who makes the strongest impression on the impressionable sailor's mind. As he sees her, "she was a pale, ethereal creature, with wide, spiritual blue eyes and a wealth of golden hair."[35] She is twenty-three, a student at the University of California, and to Martin a paragon of culture and learning as well as of beauty. Almost immediately he wants to devote himself to her and to make himself worthy to be part of her life. On her part, belatedly maidenly and inexperienced with men, she feels a great social and cultural superiority, mixed with a strange new sort of fascination for his strength and vitality. She secretly desires to put her hands on his strong sunburned neck and draw strength from contact with him.

Their relationship develops, Pygmalion-like. She encourages him to read and guides his course of study, she corrects his grammar and teaches him middle-class ideals of culture and success; he follows her directions avidly, glorying in her attention and striving in every way to become the kind of man she wants him to be. His idealizing worship of her strengthens as he makes progress in manners, speech, dress, and learning, and her supposedly detached involvement intensifies into something that begins to give her prestige-conscious family feelings of alarm.

The lovers' one early difference is on the subject of work, she disapproving of his lack of a secure middle-class career, and he knowing both the futility of physical labor and the pettiness of a business career. His dream is to succeed totally in Ruth's terms, to accept her cultural education wholly seriously and become a writer. But as he begins to devote himself tirelessly to this goal (he, who a short time ago was virtually illiterate!), she feels deep misgivings and tries to urge him to take a regular job.

At this point he discovers Spencer. After hearing Spencerianism advocated by a soapbox orator, he gets *First Principles* from the library and changes his life:

> So the great discovery began. . . . This night, after algebra and physics, and an attempt at a sonnet, he got into bed and opened "First Principles." Morning found him still reading. It was impossible for him to sleep. Nor did he write that day. He lay on the bed till his body grew tired, when he tried the hard floor, reading on his back, the book held in the air above him, or changing from side to side. He slept that night, and did his writing next morning, and then the book tempted him and he fell, reading all afternoon, oblivious to everything and oblivious to the fact that that was the afternoon Ruth gave to him. (107)

Martin is fascinated by the concept of universal laws *First Principles* gives:

> Here was the man Spencer, organizing all knowledge for him, reducing everything to unity, elaborating ultimate realities. . . . There was no caprice, no chance. All was law. It was in obedience to law that the bird flew, and it was in obedience to the same law that fermenting slime had writhed and squirmed and put out legs and wings and become a bird. (108)

He waxes rhapsodic at this concept of the interrelatedness of things, a reaction curiously like that of some of the first force conservationists:

> In the meat on the platter he saw the shining sun and traced its energy back through all its transformations to its source a hundred million miles away, or traced its energy ahead to the moving muscles in his arms that enabled him to cut the meat, and to the brain wherewith he willed the muscles to move to cut the meat, until, with inward gaze, he saw the same sun shining in his brain. (108)

He greedily absorbs the philosophy which not only inspires his imagination but which answers all questions: "What, in a way, most profoundly impressed Martin, was the correlation of knowledge—of all knowledge" (109).

While it unifies, correlates, and inspires, Spencerian philosophy also answers the needs of the scientific, post-Darwinian times. The pale idealism of Ruth's traditional humanistic culture has nowhere near the toughness or explanatory power of the scientific, fact-centered Spencerianism. Thus Spencer, as well as taking away some of Martin's time to be with Ruth, also gives Martin's philosophic thought a distinct edge over hers in relevance and comprehensiveness. From the moment of his reading Spencer, Martin begins to gain the ascendancy over Ruth in their relationship. Although his idealized image of her fades more slowly, he soon ceases to be at all influenced by her education and her advice about how to live his life.

Not only does Martin Eden become a Spencerian—learning his craft of writing from Spencer's *Philosophy of Style*, finding Spencer's *Autobiography* "as replete for him with romance as any thrilling novel" (278), and forming his ideas in Spencerian terms ("thanks to the school of scientific philosophers he favored, he knew the biological significance of love" [193])—but the narrator too uses Spencerian diction ("she was drawn by some force outside of herself and stronger than gravitation, strong as destiny" [178]) and even refers to Spencerian principles in explanation of some of the elements of the story:

> The same pressures and caresses, unaccompanied by speech, that were efficacious with the girls of the working class, were equally efficacious with the girls above the working class. They were all of the same flesh, after all, sisters under their skins; and he might have known as much himself had he remembered his Spencer. (182)

This is a revelation Spencer would no doubt be surprised to see himself credited with, and it is but one example of the narrator going beyond even Martin Eden in applying Spencer. There is no satire here, no wider perspective than the Spencerianism Jack London himself had been so extremely impressed by at a comparable period in his own life. The philosophical base of this novel is another of the freaks of American culture, as Jack London, radical novelist, in 1909 uses Spencerianism—so often used in previous decades as a comfortably accommodating philosophy of the capitalistic upper classes—as a starkly anti-bourgeois soapbox radicalism.

Perhaps the highest moment of Martin's Spencerian triumph occurs when he puts down one of Ruth's most venerated English professors by asserting (he, the self-educated ex-sailor) that Professor Caldwell's thinking tended to "leave out the biological factor, the very stuff out of which has been spun the fabric of all the arts, the warp and woof of all human actions and achievements" (241). The professor sadly admits the charge and allows that he had been criticized but once before in those terms—by Joseph LeConte.

For all his superiority Martin long remains unsuccessful as a writer, and it is this fact, combined with strong pressure from the Morse family, which finally separates Ruth and Martin. She doesn't really understand either his work or his ambitions, and he refuses to play her bourgeois game of ducking into some secure little corner of life, so they break off their relationship, which in more tranquil times had become an engagement.

Martin had been a fighter since childhood, first physical (a notable brawler and amateur boxer), then intellectual, and he was proud of his strength and contemptuous of weakness. This outlook, reinforced by pseudobiological theory about the fit and the unfit and crystallized for him by Nietzsche, led ultimately to a philosophy of "individualism." He detests socialism in any form and rejects vehemently even the few restraints put by government on individualism in business. This characteristic of Martin Eden was later to become the main point in London's repudiation of him when, to his chagrin, much of his audience and even many critics insisted on discussing Martin as if he were Jack London, a mirror-trick of theirs which either made London a Nietzschean or Eden a socialist, or both. London insisted that Eden was "a temperamental, and, later on, an intellectual Individualist . . . a proper Individualist of the extreme Nietzschean type," who failed in "being unaware of the collective human need." [36]

The novel tends to bear out London in his interpretation of this point, although not very clearly or convincingly. Eden's friend and mentor, Brissenden, is a socialist who oppose Eden's "individualism" and espouses socialism because it is a superior and inevitable alternative to "the present rotten and irrational system," and because "you must be handcuffed to life somehow" (327). London also shows Eden helping weak people of his acquaintance and admitting to himself in doing so, "Martin Eden . . . you're not a brute, and you're a damn poor Nietzscheman" (364).

But readers who tried to see London as Eden and as Nietzscheman were not merely maliciously misreading him. London's public persona had all kinds of radical possibilities for the public mind, and in this case readers were abetted in the Nietzschean misreading by a flaw in the novel's technique. At root it is a problem of point-of-view, of determining where the narrator stands in relation to the character, because by the time the reader gets to the part of the novel that deals with the Individualism he has already been through a good many episodes that would be self-justification for a narrator who was also the protagonist, and (especially) he has witnessed the convergence of the world-views of the protagonist and the narrator on the grounds of Spencerianism. Martin Eden has seemed to be maturing into the narrator until the last one-fourth or so of the novel; at that point it is not easy for a reader to pick up the indications that London means to widen the distance between character and narrator.

Another problem with Eden's Individualism is that his contempt for the masses of the unfit is unconvincingly depicted. He only talks like Nietzsche; he feels and acts like London in every particular instance. Wolf Larsen was a far better exemplar of Individualism. London merely seems determined, in the last fourth of this novel, to break the ties by which Martin Eden is "handcuffed to life," and abstract Nietzscheanism is one of the means he tries (not very successfully) to use.

Other of Martin's ties to life are more convincingly disestablished. His love for Ruth died when she failed to live up to his image of her; he felt betrayed by her and her bourgeois world, although in exaggerating her ideality he had been more betrayed by his own imagination. His attachment to the world of everyday experience is poisoned by his hatred of the bourgeois principles by which it runs. His work, his writing, albeit a satisfactory outlet for his energies is ignored or misunderstood or reviled by friends and editors alike; his brilliant friend Brissenden dies, never allowing his own great poems to pass over an editor's desk.

Thus when Martin's writing suddenly achieves fame and prosperity for him, nothing essential is changed by the success; success *can* change nothing, because it is based on no more than accident and fad. The works that succeed for him are the same works that had earlier failed; their intrinsic value is unchanged, and, in fact, still unappreciated. And Martin himself is similarly served: formerly looked down upon and rejected by the bourgeoisie, he is now lionized. He is highly resentful because, give or take a few thousand dollars, he is the same Martin Eden as before, with the same "*work performed*" (the refrain runs through his mind again and again). There is never any possibility of his success or his fair-weather friends "handcuffing him to life." The praise and appreciation he gets can, in fact, only serve to intensify his world-weariness in leading him to cynical conclusions about mankind and his society.

Ruth's final and futile attempt to revive Martin's love perhaps alienates him more than anything else that he experiences. Compromising her reputation by coming to his rooms alone at night (but with her brother waiting outside in a doorway to escort her there and back), and now willing to dare anything for Martin's love (although now that he has a secure future, her mother approves of him as a match for her daughter), she finds only a cold welcome. To Martin her action is the ultimate bourgeois insincerity.

Finally, alone and totally disillusioned (a lower-class ex-girlfriend tells him he's "sick in his mind") Martin performs a few very appropriate charitable acts with his burgeoning wealth (including handing a thousand dollars to a down-and-outer at whose flat Martin had once attended a free-ranging discussion of Spencer and Haeckel), and then breaks all ties with life by slipping overboard out of the porthole of a steamer and swimming down to a depth from which not even his unsubduable involuntary will to live could save him.

Martin Eden is another casualty of radical individualism, but with a philosophical difference that makes this novel cut deeper than *The Sea Wolf* had. It is not so much an egotistical and aggressive individualism that dooms Martin Eden as a go-it-alone program of self-development and inquiry into the nature of things. What he finds is a set of basic truths which society—petty, self-justifying, hypocritical—survives by ignoring; he is thus alienated from it not through personal brutality but through being true to what he knows. "Good" society is symbolized by Ruth Morse instead of Maud Brewster, and caught between a universe of force and such a society of complacent self-delusion, Martin Eden suffers isolation, disillusionment, and death.

The novel is largely successful despite its many faults, and I would rank it as London's best, although there is no unanimous critical agreement on this ranking. It is undeniably clumsy as "inner drama" (London never seems to know what to do with the outside environment while a character is thinking), and there is too much philosophical rant in it which seems naive and rote-learned. London undoubtedly meant to depict the hero's search for truth and his arrival at a very advanced, factual, and superior set of insights through Spencer. Today, however, we are more likely to feel we are watching an unsophisticated protagonist trying somewhat ineptly to come to terms with ideas and coming to rest finally in an impressive but decidedly second-rate synthesis. The book works fairly well from this aspect, although the narrator needs more distance from the character's ideas. Even unimpressed by the novel's semi-Spencerian individualism we can respond to its intellectual urgency and its candid and immediate representation of a genuine point of crisis in American thought and experience. Every synthetic philosophy is, late or soon, vulnerable to obsolescence, and the supposedly timeless work of art that is explicitly reliant on a philosophy is sure to have serious problems of interpretation and acceptance eventually. *Martin Eden* is interesting despite these problems and even despite the awkwardness, the rant, and the excessive amount of self-justification in the author's depiction of his hero, and it is so, I feel, because it does engage London's experience directly, in its own terms, and without the short-circuiting intrusion of stock fictional elements which is so often apparent in his work. The logic of narrative was usually a very pat and conventional thing for London, and the mixture in *Martin Eden* with the logic of truth-seeking helped him go more deeply into what he knew and could represent.

TWO MORE works of London deserve mention in the context of his approach to the universe of force in his works. *Burning Daylight* (1910) is the story of an individualist-hero who in the end reforms and does find happiness. Daylight is a character who has prodigious energy and ability, but who throughout much of the novel attempts to avoid all entanglements; he enjoys comradeship but he withdraws from anything closer. He is also a heroic battler who overcomes the adverse forces, first of the natural world in the Klondike, then in the world of finance in the United States. He is strong and aggressive but moral in both milieus; the world of finance is so pictured that the men he must oppose and overcome are unscrupulously bent on destroying him; his actions are thus defensive and even constructive rather than predatory. In the end, however, he finds the world of finance dragging down his spirit at the same time that he falls in love with a worthy young woman who wants to live simply and close to nature. He abandons his career as financier, marries her, retires to a California ranch much like London's own, and thus finds happiness.

London thinks of each milieu, Alaska, American high finance, and Sonoma Mountain, as a kind of force-economy. A pair of starving men on a trail through the Alaskan wilderness shoot and eat a squirrel, and the narrator reflects, in a passage that sounds like *Martin Eden* or one of the early force-conservationists,

> Such is the chemistry of life, that this small creature, this trifle of meat that moved, by being eaten, transmitted to the meat of the men the same power to move. No longer did the squirrel run up spruce trees, leap from branch to branch, or cling chattering to giddy perches. Instead the same energy that had done these things flowed into the wasted muscles and reeling wills of the men, making them move,—nay moving them.[37]

And when the hero forsakes high finance for farming and domesticity he finds corresponding patterns of challenge and reward; the two endeavors are but disparate regions of the same force economy:

> Daylight, who had played the game in its biggest and most fantastic aspects, found that here, on the slopes of Sonoma Mountain, it was still the same old game. Man had still work to perform, forces to combat, obstacles to overcome. . . . He found no less zest in calculating in squabs than formerly when he had calculated in millions. . . . The domestic cat that had gone wild and preyed on his pigeons he found, by comparative standard, to be of no less paramount menace than a Charles Klinker in the field of finance, trying to raid him for several millions. (340–341)

The patterns are the same everywhere, the novel asserts, and a man is best off choosing a milieu which brings him the greatest and most permanent personal advantages, like love and closeness to nature. There is no challenge of radical individualism in this book, and its hero finds that he can be happily "handcuffed to life" even in a force-universe.

The Iron Heel (1907) is an apocalyptic political anti-utopia which still has some appeal for devotees of that genre or for doctrinaire socialists. It forecasts seven centuries of the political future of the modern world in which the socialist ferment of the early twentieth century was crushed by the oligarchy (the "Iron Heel"), which ruled absolutely for three hundred years, after which it was overthrown and replaced by a millenial socialism. The perspective of the book is a modified "looking backward" arrangement wherein an editor in the period of enlightened socialism is presenting and commenting on the diary of the wife of a great socialist leader of the period of the oligarchy's rise to power. This socialist leader, Ernest Everhard (!) is the novel's idealized hero; strong, masterful, far-sighted, and invincible in argument, it is not surprising, knowing London, that he would also be a materialistic monist with a vision of society's future made of Spencerianism slightly laced with Marx. "Not only is it inevitable that you small capitalists shall pass away," he says in one of a number of straw-man debates which make up a large part of the substance of the novel, "but it is inevitable that the large capitalists, and the trusts also, shall pass away. It flows on and on, and from little combination to large combination, and from large combination to colossal combination, and it flows on to socialism, which is the most colossal combination of all."[38] He is also a determinist: "No man in the industrial machine is a free-will agent except the large capitalist, and he isn't, if you'll pardon the Irishism" (67). And armed with Spencer and Haeckel he devastates ecclesiastical metaphysicians with such "sledge-hammer attacks" as the following: "As Spencer says, the data of any particular science are partially unified knowledge. Philosophy unifies the knowledge that is contributed by all the sciences" (11). Interestingly enough, London wanted this hero too associated with Nietzsche, although he was a socialist and humanitarian. His wife calls him "a superman, a blond beast such as Nietzsche has described," although the latter-age commentator glosses Nietzsche for his readers as "the mad philosopher of the nineteenth century . . . who caught wild glimpses of truth, but who, before he was done, reasoned himself around the great circle of human thought and off into madness" (6). Thus London gives sentimental allegiance to Nietzsche at the same time he wholly repudiates his ideas in this socialistic framework.

The Iron Heel is not a very effective novel. It is made out of too much one-sided debate and too much summary of huge class-power shifts, and not enough that is as gripping or immediate as the scene of the destruction of the Chicago commune with which the book ends. Throughout most of the book the sense of injustice and frustration is too generalized, Ernest Everhard, the hard-boiled socialist, is too one-sidedly heroic, and his ideas (always borne out by subsequent events in the book) are too often not as deep or amazing as London obviously thought they were. Relying on Spencerianism to characterize an intellectually superior protagonist and to represent the evolution (especially the future evolution) of society was not the most effective way to produce a lasting work of literature.

NOW THAT the Spencerian brand of scientific philosophy has passed out of relevance, how is its influence on London to be evaluated? Obviously, in accepting Spencer's and Haeckel's generalizations as universal and eternal truths, London tied his work down to something that would decay; his books are outmoded precisely to the extent that Spencerianism is essential to the truth they represent—*Martin Eden* somewhat, *The Iron Heel* considerably, and his broadly theoretical essays totally. It is tempting to deplore the influence of scientific philosophy and to attempt to wish it away entirely, as does Arthur Calder-Marshall in his lucid and useful introduction to *The Bodley Head Jack London*: "With love, security and a deeper education, he might have become a figure of the stature of the great masters. He had the largeness and vitality. But he was cramped by the 'scientific' materialism he accepted as gospel from 'the books.'" Calder-Marshall calls him "the deliverer bound in the chains of materialistic monism."[39]

But before we blame London's principal shortcomings on a faulty philosophy, we ought to have a very clear idea of the nature of its influence on him in the context of the other resources, imaginative and intellectual, available to him. Especially, we must take into account his lack of technical originality and his relatively limited and conventional concept of what fiction was. The great number of instances in his work of formulized plots, awkwardly contrived causality, trite characterization and conventional, carelessly handled point-of-view are in no way attributable to materialistic monism. Calder-Marshall himself discusses the typical example of London's treatment, in the story "The Scorn of Woman," of a strip-tease dancer London had actually encountered in the Klondike;[40] in comparing the woman London records having met, with the fictional character he made her into, Calder-Marshall shows that London romanticized his materials markedly, warping reality in the direction of the conventions and niceties of popular fiction. The principal influence which stifled his vision was not the influence of scientific philosophy so much as that of conventional, mass-market fiction.

Finally, perhaps when it is a creative writer we are considering, an individual's philosophy should be evaluated not so much with respect to its "truth," its consistency, or its adequacy for all people in all times, as to its instrumentality in abetting or hindering him in his ability to see a great deal in human experience and to represent it in his art. It is not that the quality of a writer's philosophical conclusions is somehow detachable from the value of his work, because this is not so, but more that, since the writer deals in concrete representations of experience, a philosophy's function in opening or closing areas of experience to him affects the value of his work at a more fundamental level.[41] From this approach, London's involvement with universe-of-force concepts looks somewhat different. Although to a later age those concepts appear quite unpromisingly restrictive, to London in his own time they were in fact both liberating and suggestive. There was no long future for them philosophically, but they enabled him as novelist to go beyond the categories of stock adventure and romance fiction into the realm of ideas, to find for himself a cogent basis for a radical rejection of conventionality and to feel the tensions and guilts involved in such a rejection. He thus gained a clear perspective on the characteristic antagonism of his day between old and new modes of thought and behavior. And London's commitment to the universe-of-force concepts was directly necessary to his representation of the struggle for understanding in several of his characters, and of the problem of how to lead one's life once one was in possession of the deterministic truth about the human predicament. As his characters faced the truth and confronted their society with it, then, the contradictions inherent in his age's favorite concepts of personal and social morality, of radical individualism and social justice, were revealed.

Force-philosophy was obsolete before London appropriated it, but it gave him both the impulse and the terminology to turn his fiction inward, and it infected his moral vision with doubt, complexity, and tension, making it more mature and revealing by far than it would have been, say, if Wolf Larsen and Martin Eden had never opened the *First Principles*.

7. THEODORE DREISER: AT HOME IN THE UNIVERSE OF FORCE

IF FORCE TRANSMUTES

If force transmutes, and clouds are dewy air
   Touched by the cooling breath of upmost sky;
If trees are but the earthly form of heat,
   And flowers prisoned sun-rays passing by:
Then are your eyes some dream of distant days,
   Some scene translated from Arcadian Time;
Their flash the meter of Hellenic lays,
   Their depths the deepest blue of some Hesperian clime.

If force transmutes, and all the emerald grass
   But represents the change of air and rain;
If sedges waving by the glassy stream
   Their presence owe to some protean chain:
Then are your lips, your cheeks, your splendid hair,
   The after-glow of sunny days of yore;
Then does their bloom the richness of that time,
   When earth basked fulsome in the glad forenoon, restore.

If force transmutes, and naught through ages dies,
   And all the forms that now about me wave
But represent the large, diviner wish
   That each its way to the ideal shall pave
If all is gain: then is your beauty rare,
   The essence of the fairest days of time;
Your lips, your cheeks, your hair, your voice, your eyes
The acme of such change—your right to Paradise.

Theodore Dreiser, Demorest's, 1899

The works of Theodore Dreiser, unlike those of Adams, Norris, and London, are expressive of a value system that is basically and generally in keeping with the universe of force. This is not to say that they are not expressive of a variety of other philosophical orientations as well, or that they represent the universe of force as a friendly and fulfilling habitat for man, but that the view of the causes, consequences, and significance of man's actions as represented in Dreiser's fiction is fundamentally compatible with his view of the universe as a mechanistic, deterministic welter of forces. Dreiser projects his universe of force with none of the intellectual irony, the bitter tones of absurdity and rejection that Henry Adams had, and he seldom gave the sense, as Frank Norris and Jack London did, that in describing the universe of force he was repeating a well-learned but imperfectly assimilated lesson. Of the four writers, Dreiser most fully internalized the universe of force; he was at home there if he was at home anywhere.

It had first come upon him with the impact of a religious conversion; it in effect liberated him both intellectually and emotionally. His father's strict fundamentalist Catholicism and his society's idealistic moralism had both seemed to him untrue to life, hypocritical and callous in hounding people for the consequences of their natural instincts. The ideas of free will and moral responsibility he could only see as ironies, given the world as it really was, and his discovery of mechanistic force systems in the works of a number of scientific and pseudoscientific writers gave him a model of the human universe he could accept as both more realistic and more humane than the one he saw as prevalent in America. Like Norris and London, he lived in a little intellectual world, and the universe of force was an enormous new thing in it.

He was thunderstruck when he discovered Spencer's First Principles *shortly before he began writing novels; he misunderstood Spencer to be saying that the universe was simply a blind and purposeless mechanism, and he assented without a reservation or a qualm. Thereafter he was attracted to any theory, scientific or mystic—even the simplistic, the ill-supported, and the obscurantistic—that represented man as determined by outer and inner forces. In studying his education we are introduced to a new wave in the Americanization of the universe of force, followers and heirs of Fiske, Haeckel, LeConte, and Cope who took the concept a step further in popularization and diversification. Dreiser labored hugely to build these concepts into a definitive philosophical system. A poorly educated man who thought with his feelings, he was doomed as a philosopher before he began, but the "system" of thought he produced is in its own way as elaborate and bizarre as any we have thus far considered; even in its obscurity and incoherence it is a fitting end-point for the development of the universe of force.*

As a novelist Dreiser was the sort of realist who felt an extraordinary need to get things explained: to represent his characters' motives and actions as cogently and as comprehensibly as possible, to offer in many instances scientifically based explanations of their operant determinisms, and even to correct popular misconceptions about the causes and significance of human endeavor. His works are primarily based in his experience, but the impulses towards paradigmatic representation and didactic explanation are never far beneath the surface. Dreiser's narrators, like Norris's, are able to get all of their various responsibilities met only by operating in a pliant mode of naive omniscience.

Such being the nature of narrative for him, Dreiser invoked the universe of force in a number of his books to supply the patterns, significances, and lessons of experience. As we shall see, he found that social and interpersonal causality could be cast in terms of forces, as could personal motivations and actions. In extreme form in the Cowperwood trilogy, human motivation, interaction, and fate could virtually be diagrammed as a complex system of vectors. And as the narrator stepped back from the immediate concerns of a novel and viewed the whole human drama panoramically, what he saw was a picturesque welter of impersonal forces which could supply an awesome cosmic framework for his narrative.

There is cold comfort in such a force universe. Even while freeing us of the guilts and hypocrisies of a free-will system it graphically confronts us with our individual and specific limitations. In its terms we are driven and determined by forces, both inner and outer, which are beyond our will and often alien to our desires. In his books Dreiser anatomized and dramatized these human limitations repeatedly, artistically ritualizing an act of rebellion and compassion. He was more at home in the universe of force than in any more ordinary conceptual realm, but even there he felt the bitter anguish of an anomalous human predicament. That emotion, transmuted in his works into the peculiar tragic irony of the universe of force is one of the more interesting elements of the art of Theodore Dreiser.

THE TWO basic facts about Dreiser's intellectual life are that he hungered after experience and explanation, and that he was consistently and deeply in rebellion against both his father's guilt-ridden fundamentalism and the norms and sanctions, the inhibitions and hypocrisies of the whole community of Christian respectability. Omniverousness and rebelliousness are, in fact, about the only elements of consistency in his life and works. Many of his diverse enthusiasms are legendary: he was strongly attracted by sex and showgirls, Communism, millionaires, mechanistic science, ouija boards, Freudianism, and mysticism; he relished newspaper work, cities, travel, orators, flappers, and money; scientific, liberated, sentimental, polygamous, superstitious, shockingly candid, he was sweetly generous yet stubbornly egotistical (even vindictive), crusadingly antiphilistine yet highly sensitive to clothes, money, and reputation; he wrote serious fiction, philosophical essays, travel books, success-story interviews, fashion features, and "On the Banks of the Wabash." He lived the life of a liberated, newly intellectual, universal midwestern American man-of-his-times.

He envisioned himself in the vanguard of thought, in the role of opposing traditional ideas—especially those traditional ideas about religion, morals, or social conventions by which he had been made to feel so oppressed in his youth and early manhood—but his tenuous understanding of tradition and his lack of real critical perspective diminished his philosophizing to the status of self-assertion, self-justification, outcry. His education was intense but random. As he records in the *Dawn* volume of his autobiography, he had performed so well in school that his teacher, Miss Mildred Fielding, had sponsored him for a year at the University of Indiana, and urged him, "Read Spencer. Read a life of Socrates. Read Marcus Aurelius and Emerson." [1] He continued the habit of wide-ranging reading and philosophical pondering throughout his lifetime, but his sense of historical culture remained insubstantial, and he got a more compelling education on the streets of Chicago, identifying emotionally with the up-to-the-minute life around him and intellectually with an indiscriminate gaggle of interpreters of that life: scientists, pseudoscientists, popularizers, sensationalizers, philosophers, and spiritualists. At times it indeed seems as if Dreiser lacked even (in the words of Larzer Ziff) "a sense of the common assumptions of American life," [2] and revived again (in the words of F. O. Matthiessen) "the frequent American need to begin all over again from scratch." [3]

Philosophizing was very real to him throughout his career. His first nonreportorial publications were entitled "Reflections" and signed "The Prophet," and among his early publications are many philosophical discussions and exhortations; during his artistic maturity he wrote and published a set of philosophical reflections, collecting them in 1902 in *Hey-Rub-a-Dub-Dub!*; in his latter years he diverted a considerable amount of his creative time and energy away from his fiction for researching and writing his gargantuan philosophical fragment, variously titled "The Formula Called Man" and "Notes on Life," never publishable during his lifetime, and only recently abridged, arranged, and edited by Dreiser scholars and published by a scholarly press. [4] Despite criticisms from people whose opinions he otherwise valued (his friend and supporter H. L. Mencken had written him that "*Hey-Rub-a-Dub-Dub* largely appeals, I believe, to the defectively educated"); [5] Dreiser persevered in his philosophizing as though he were on the brink of some great discovery: "*Hey, Rub* contains the sub-stone of a new and better philosophy, something on which can be reared a sounder approach to life than is now voiced. Some one is going to come along who will get it and make it very clear," [6] he wrote a friend in 1921, and in 1935 he wrote to Simon Flexner, director of the Rockefeller Institute, that "something creatively astounding seems to be waiting for proper biological, chemical and physical attention." [7] He never quite discovered the key, however, and there is no avoiding the conclusion that the expository product of his striving, searching, and dogmatizing is shallow and inconsiderable stuff. Its tenor is set by the commonplace agnosticism he announces as if it were a new revelation, by the Sunday-supplement science with which he demolishes what he conceived of as ordinary men's norms and ideals, by the callow mysticism he hankers after, undercutting both agnosticism and scientific rationalism.

It would be unfair and beside the point to dwell on Dreiser's incompetence as a philosopher, however, because it is as a novelist that he is interesting to us, and, as we have already seen, people are not necessarily ineffective novelists because they have faulty or out-of-date or poorly developed philosophical conceptions. And then too, Dreiser's cerebration, as a number of critics have noted, was really closer to feeling than to thinking—he arrived at an attitudinal sense of things rather than a consistent rational paradigm of the universe. As Robert Penn Warren has pointed out, he was a thinker "who automatically absorbed ideas into the bloodstream of his passionate being. He was not concerned with consistency within a logical frame, with the rules of the game; he was concerned with how an idea 'felt.'"[8] Thus Dreiser's intellectual consistency was emotional, and, as I shall suggest in analyzing his works, situational, rather than rationally consistent.

His philosophical quest was basically metaphysical. In a pattern which by now has become quite familiar in our examination of literary men, when he looked to science or scientific philosophy he was looking for answers to ultimate questions, for a kind of substitute for the religion in which he no longer believed. And although his ideas changed frequently with altering circumstances and new influences, the object of his quest stayed the same. Specifically, his thinking both began and ended in a sense of awe at what he perceived as the harshness and beauty of a universe made up of determining forces indifferent to man and inscrutable; his inveterate philosophizing was an attempt to account for, or at least take an attitude toward that very unsettling perception. It is certainly reasonable to suggest, as several critics have, that Dreiser's habitual philosophical orientation was an advantage to him as a novelist. Vernon Parrington makes the point about him that "the larger view of life gives detachment"[9] and Irving Howe states that "As a philosopher, Dreiser can often be tiresome; yet his very lust for metaphysics, his stubborn insistence upon learning 'what it's all about' helped to deepen the emotional resources from which he drew as a novelist."[10] The philosophy itself might be deplorable, but its effect on the novelist as novelist is certainly another question.

The universe of force was a part of Dreiser's thinking from the very beginning of his career as a writer. As Dreiser traced his own intellectual development in his autobiography, the important and character-forming stages were the rejection of the conceptual scheme of Christianity and the liberating, mind-bending discovery of the awesome new scientific philosophy of the likes of Spencer, Huxley, and Tyndall.

After an early life characterized (by himself) as one of curiosity, questioning, and increasing discomfort with conventional concepts and mores, he came across the new philosophy through Herbert Spencer, and it seems to have struck him with shock and disillusionment, but at the same time to have opened a whole set of new possibilities. His later remembrances of the event differ somewhat in particulars, such as where and at what time his conversion took place,* but they all agree on the import of his discovery of Spencer and the universe of force. The account in *A Book About Myself* is the best-known and most revealing:

> At this time I had the fortune to discover Huxley and Tyndall and Herbert Spencer, whose introductory volume to his *Synthetic Philosophy (First Principles)* quite blew me, intellectually, to bits. Hitherto, until I had read Huxley, I had some lingering filaments of Catholicism trailing about me, faith in the existence of Christ, the soundness of his moral and sociological deductions, the brotherhood of man. But on reading *Science and Hebrew Tradition* and *Science and Christian Tradition*, and finding both the Old and New Testaments to be not compendiums of revealed truth but mere records of religious experiences, and very erroneous ones at that, and then taking up *First Principles* and discovering that all I deemed substantial— man's place in nature, his importance in the universe, this too, too solid earth, man's very identity save as an infinitesimal speck of energy or a "suspended equation" drawn or blown here and there by larger forces in which he moved quite unconsciously as an atom—all questioned and dissolved into other and less understandable things, I was completely thrown down in my conceptions or nonconceptions of life.
>
> Up to this time there had been in me a blazing and unchecked desire to get on and the feeling that in doing so we did get somewhere; now in its place was the definite conviction that spiritually one got nowhere, that there was no hereafter, that one lived and had his being because one had to, and that it was of no importance. Of one's ideals, struggles, deprivations, sorrows and joys, it could only be said that they were chemical compulsions, something which for some inexplicable but unimportant reason responded to and resulted from the hope of pleasure and the fear of pain. Man was a mechanism, undevised and uncreated, and a badly and carelessly driven one at that.[11]

---

* He seems to have told Frank Harris in an interview in 1919 both that he was introduced to the ideas of Spencer by a Dane with whom he worked in a Chicago hardware store before his newspaper career began, and that he first read Spencer in New York after quitting *The World*. In *Dawn* (1931) he mentions learning about Spencer from a roommate at the University of Indiana. In *A Book About Myself* (1922) he places his discovery of Spencer in Pittsburgh after his first trip to New York but before he worked on *The World*. A letter to Mencken on May 13, 1916, similarly puts the discovery in Pittsburgh in 1894.

Not only did Dreiser see Spencerianism as liberating him from the last vestiges of Christianity, but he saw it as giving him a whole new view of the world and man's place in it as "an infinitesimal speck of energy . . . blown here and there by larger forces," or, in another account, "a chemical atom in a whirl of unknown forces."[12] This absolute and picturesque determinism is not, of course, particularly accurate Spencerianism, but it is the image Dreiser derived from the description of the evolution of force in *First Principles*. In a similar way, as we shall see, he transformed Spencer's idea of the Unknowable into a kind of mysterious but purposeful and existent unconceivable. Like other writers we have examined in the philosophical context of the universe of force, Dreiser received Spencer's ineffectively defined and delimited concepts only in his own peculiar way, sensitive to their poetic and dramatic overtones but oblivious of the rationalistic essence and optimistic tone of Spencer's system.

Although born of Dreiser's own intellectual shortcomings and emotional proclivities, his discovery of pessimistic "Spencerianism" left him stunned: "I fear that I cannot make you feel how these things came upon me in the course of a few weeks' reading and left me numb, my gravest fears as to the unsolvable disorder and brutality of life eternally verified. I felt as low and helpless at times as a beggar of the streets."[13] And he remained true, in his fashion, throughout a long career and numerous attachments to other diverse and mutually incompatible ideas, to the insight vouchsafed him in this experience.

Dreiser's earliest public references to his Spencerianism came in 1896 and 1897 in *Ev'ry Month*, a magazine he edited (and largely wrote) for a music publishing company owned by his songwriting brother Paul and several partners. He had had a good deal of newspaper experience in Chicago, Pittsburgh, and New York by that time, had undergone his conversion to pessimistic Spencerianism, and was here trying to present its message in a popular, upward-looking way in his regular column, "Reflections," by "The Prophet." *Sister Carrie* was three or four years in the offing. In an 1896 piece, in an issue decorated with pictures of Clara Barton, actress Bertha Galland, and Boudereau's romantic painting "The Shepherdess," he considered the ideas of the helplessness, in the face of great natural forces, of man,

> the necessary, but worthless dust of changing conditions, and that all the fourteen hundred million beings who swarm the earth after the manner of contentious vermin, are but one form which the heat of the sun takes in its protean journey towards dissipation. . . . He does not seem to be considered in the great economy of nature, and any moment may see him completely destroyed, in order that some element or force may complete its mission unimpeded.

Yet for this popular audience he mitigated his pessimism by pointing out that, "forces may sway inconsiderate of him now, but in time they will bend to his will," and (in a teleological mood) that "force is but force, and if not regulated for a purpose, why need it bloom as a rose yonder, drift as a cloud there, flow as a brook through the grassy meadows, or walk as a human in all the charm and radiance of manhood?"[14] From the very beginning, then, Dreiser could, at least in certain exigencies, see a mysterious and beautiful purpose behind the insensate and indifferent forces of nature.

On one occasion he offered to the readers of *Ev'ry Month* a recommendation of Spencer which was fulsome and rhapsodic, a feature-writer's *tour de force*, an (over-) extended metaphor describing the philosopher as if he were a great military conqueror:

> His is the generalship of the mind—the great captaincy of learning and literature, the field-marshalship of the forces of reason. As Napoleon studied the military map of Europe, so Spencer studied the intellectual map of the world. . . . From point of knowledge to point of knowledge he victoriously proceeded, here annexing this domain of truth, there laying waste that fortress of untruth. . . . Everything submitted to him; each province of knowledge took its subordinate place in his empire of the mind; everything fell into his order and scheme, and he has now proceeded to rule in peace.
>
> Our minds belong to the universe which Spencer has united; our thoughts upon its meaning are subject to the laws which he has laid down.[15]

Furthermore, Dreiser concludes, as with Cyrus uniting Persia, Spencer's conquest was completed before news of it was carried to all of the domains. The piece is tedious and overblown, but significant for the fact that Dreiser chose Spencer as his Cyrus of philosophy.

His momentous exposure to Spencer was only the beginning of Dreiser's avid lifelong interest in metaphysical thought that was based in science or pseudoscience. He was always yearning after absolutes and mysteries so there was little chance that he would ever understand the true import of the science of his day, but the theories and systems he did connect with fed his imagination and confirmed his general view of things. His principal mentors were the intellectual heirs of Fiske, LeConte, and Cope—amateur philosophers and popularizers of naturalistic systems, largely—although in their work the abiding optimism of popular nineteenth-century thought had darkened into the grimmer tone of early twentieth-century determinism. Dreiser had no intellectual discrimination whatever between types of scientific thinkers—crackpots and ouija boards gave him ideas as satisfying as those of genuine scientists; his discrimination was all emotional. To attract him, a scientific idea had to be deterministic, dramatic, and handy.

One of Dreiser's earliest exposures to contemporary science and scientific philosophy came by way of his readings in Appleton's handy International Scientific Library, the series edited by Edward Livingston Youmans (see pp. 90–91, above). Ellen Moers has pointed out that he used John Lubbock's *Ants, Bees and Wasps* of that series to get details for his story "The Shining Slave Makers,"[16] and there is ample evidence in his correspondence that he read works of Darwin, Huxley, and Tyndall in that series in the 1890s. He frequently recommended Joseph Tyndall's *Heat as a Mode of Motion* to his friends and readers, although it seems unlikely that he really read the book and understood it. Tyndall, of course, was a distinguished contributor to the correlation-and-conservation-of-force movement (see pp. 26, 57, above) and so would have been congenial in a general way to Dreiser's Spencerianism, but *Heat as a Mode of Motion* is a relatively technical work, experimentally oriented, assuming a fair amount of knowledge on the part of its readers of thermodynamic theory and the work of other scientists, and offering extremely little metaphysical reference. It therefore seems more likely that Dreiser learned of the import of Tyndall's book in some second-hand philosophical context than that he read it himself. In reading works by Darwin and Huxley he was, of course, absorbing evolutionary ideas and learning to take a scientific, naturalistic view of man's nature and place in the universe, unlearning Christian teaching, and finding confirmation of his "Spencerian" metaphysics.

Just before the turn of the century, during the time when he was working on *Sister Carrie*, Dreiser became acquainted with, and deeply influenced by, an offbeat psychologist named Elmer Gates (of the Elmer Gates Laboratory of Psychology and Psychurgy, and author of *The Relations and Development of the Mind and Brain*). Dreiser read Gates's works, fell under the influence of his jargon, and attempted to promote Gates's ideas. Gates was interested in human volition, especially its elemental mechanical and chemical aspects, and it was from Gates that Dreiser got the theory of katastates and anastates which in *Sister Carrie* somewhat speciously accounts for Hurstwood's decline and Carrie's rise in terms of hypothetical chemicals, poisonous or helpful, respectively, engendered in the blood by bad emotions or good ones.[17]

Another relatively early influence was Carl Snyder, whose book, *The World Machine: The First Phase, the Cosmic Mechanism* Dreiser read shortly after its publication in 1907, and whom Dreiser met some years later.[18] Snyder was a journalistic, semirhapsodic popularizer of scientific philosophy, more interested in his own machine metaphor than in empirical science *per se*. In following out his history of man's conceptions of the universe, Snyder saw as the crucial moment in building toward the enlightened present that point when man "came definitely to conceive the whole scheme of world formation as a mechanical process, following simple and well-understood laws; likewise that the incessant destruction of worlds is the result of a larger but still purely mechanical process." [19] This, of course, sounds like the philosophical paradigm of the mid-nineteenth-century scientists, and their end product, Herbert Spencer. Snyder's view not only had the kind of mechanistic cosmos that appealed to Dreiser, but it engendered the kind of wistful pessimism Dreiser often felt when speculating on the transcience of human things. Said Snyder from his cosmic perspective, "So far as we can now perceive, human civilization is but a flutter of consciousness amid the wide cycle of life that sweeps through from lichen and bacterium to saurian monster and back again. And the cycle of life is but an evanescent moment in the history of the globe." [20] The tone here is, of course, familiar to those who know the typical endings of Dreiser's novels, with their drawing back to a cosmic viewpoint from which all human striving is vain and transitory.

Around 1915 Dresier seems to have undertaken an extensive program of reading in science and scientific philosophy which culminated in his book of philosophical essays, *Hey-Rub-a-Dub-Dub!* (1920). In 1915, after the writing of *The Titan* and *The "Genius"* and before *An American Tragedy*, he applied for a study room at the New York Public Library to read up on physics and chemistry,[21] and he avidly studied various forms of mechanistic psychology. In the course of this inquiry Dreiser discovered the work of Jacques Loeb, whose ideas augmented and gave additional scientific sanction to conceptions of the mechanistic bases of life he had already drawn from Spencer, Gates, and Snyder. A distinguished biophysiologist and member of the Rockefeller Institute for Medical Research, Loeb affected Dreiser both with his writings, such as *Comparative Physiology of the Brain and Comparative Psychology* (1900) and *The Mechanistic Conception of Life* (1912), and, later, in personal acquaintanceship. Loeb's overall mechanistic bent appealed to Dreiser—he defined the purpose of his book *The Mechanistic Conception of Life* as "an attempt to analyze life from a purely physico-chemical viewpoint" [22]—but his specific scientific contributions that were of great interest to the novelist were in the experimental study of tropisms:

> The scientific solution of the problem of will seemed then to consist in finding the forces which determine the movements of animals, and in discovering the laws according to which these forces act.[23]

And in human terms,

> Our wishes and hopes, disappointments and sufferings have their source in instincts which are comparable to the light instinct of the heliotropic animals. The need of and the struggle for food, the sexual instinct with its poetry and its chain of consequences, the maternal instincts with the fe-

licity and the suffering caused by them, the instinct of workmanship, and some other instincts are the roots from which our inner life develops. For some of these instincts the chemical basis is at least sufficiently indicated to arouse the hope that their analysis, from the mechanistic point of view, is only a question of time.[24]

Loeb's approach follows from the nineteenth-century theories of force conservation and evolution, and metaphysically it is characterized by the same kind of absolute trust in scientific rationality and the same kind of faith that human values and human progress are inherent in the mechanistic process of the universe that were maintained by Helmholtz and Spencer:

> If our existence is based on the play of blind forces and only a matter of chance; if we ourselves are only chemical mechanisms—how can there be an ethics for us? The answer is, that our instincts are the root of our ethics and that the instincts are just as hereditary as the form of our body.[25]

Such a belief is, of course, close to the foundation of Dreiser's naturalism, although, as we shall see, its implications and its tonal quality are considerably different for the novelist from what they were for the philosopher-scientist.

Dreiser omnivorously sought out mechanistic psychology, and he applied himself to the works of every scientist or pseudoscientist he could learn of who took that approach. George W. Crile was a professor of surgery at Western Reserve University, whose work, *Man, an Adaptive Mechanism* (1916), Dreiser also read in working on the *Hey-Rub-a-Dub-Dub!* essays. Not only do Crile's ideas foreshadow many of Dreiser's, but some of his rhetoric sounds Dreiserian as well. He was a thoroughgoing universe-of-force biologist/psychologist who began with the thesis that "man is essentially an energy-transforming mechanism obeying the laws of physics, as do other mechanisms,"[26] and Crile developed from that point a complex conception of man's mechanistic electrochemical evolutionary adaptations. "Matter circulates eternally," he premised, and stressed, as did Loeb, that man's responses were basically as tropistic as those of plants and animals. In emphasizing the idea of the laws of evolutionary adaptation, he confirmed Dreiser's own free adaptation of Spencer's idea of equilibrium in articulating his own vision of that principle:

> It is the omnipresent working of this universal law of equilibrium, compromise, or "adaptation," which is at the bottom of that appearance of homogeneity and peace which leads the casual observer to believe that nature is the result of design. The peace he sees, however, is but the relative peace of the center of a mighty whirlpool, or the grim, trenchant peace of the battlefield deserted after carnage; and the harmony is but the harmony of gigan-

tic wheels driving round in perfect rhythm, but, as they drive, grinding like the "mills of the gods, exceeding small and most exceeding fine."[27]

In other forays into mechanistic psychology in the late teens and early twenties, Dreiser introduced himself to behaviorism through John B. Watson's *Psychology from the Standpoint of a Behaviorist* (1919), and to Freudianism through both H. W. Frink's *Morbid Fears and Compulsions* (1918), and a personal friendship with the eminent Freudian A. A. Brill. There is some traceable impact of these conceptions in Dreiser's work of the mid-twenties and after, but his basic ideas about human nature and psychology seem to be those mechanistic ones derived from Gates, Loeb, and Crile, with Spencer in the background.

Undoubtedly the oddest purveyor of scientific or pseudoscientific ideas to Dreiser was Charles Fort. Fort, in whose veracity Dreiser seems to have had unbounded confidence, was a dedicated eccentric who lived reclusively and spent his time gathering notes from newspapers, books, and magazines about metascientific oddities, and writing strange pseudoscriptural manuscripts which preached an essentially phantasmagorical view of the universe, complete with rains of frogs or cannon balls, mysterious hieroglyphics, shapes in the sky, extraterrestrial visitations and the like, all of which showed that "our whole quasi-existence is an intermediate stage between positiveness and negativeness or realness and unrealness."[28] Fort's tone is difficult to decipher. There is wit and irony in his presentation as well as craziness, and he is clearly taking the position that science and rationality are too narrow and prosaic to comprehend reality, and demonstrating that idea satirically; his *The Book of the Damned* (1919) is devoted to uncovering strange phenomena that have been "damned" to oblivion by orthodox, exclusionist science. At the same time he seems to be sincerely urging fantastic theory:

> I began with a notion of some one other world, from which objects and substances have fallen to this earth; which had, or which, to less degree has a tutelary interest in this earth; which is now attempting to communicate with this earth. . . .
> I think we're property.
> I should say we belong to something:
> That once upon a time, this earth was No-man's Land, that other worlds explored and colonized here, and fought among themselves for possession, but that now it's owned by something.[29]

Dreiser seems to have taken Fort very seriously, and he not only hounded his own publisher, Horace Liveright, until he published *The Book of the Damned*, but he also repeatedly urged his friends to read Fort's work, despite receiving snappish replies from Mencken and H. G. Wells.[30] For all Fort's fogginess and irrationalism he had a distinctly Spencerian orientation, viewing existence as an intermediate stage in which all things move toward "positiveness," by which he meant "harmony, equilibrium, order, regularity, stability, consistency, unity, realness, system, government, organization, liberty, independence, soul, self, personality, entity, individuality, truth, beauty, justice, perfection, definiteness."[31] Fort's cosmic process operates, in other words, like a thesaurus-gorged force evolution, a kind of (probably unconscious) parody of Spencer's *First Principles*, but Dreiser seems to have been principally affected by Fort's ideas that existence is only an intermediate stage between unreality and reality, and that human beings might be merely the pawns of external, extraterrestrial powers that manipulate them for their own purposes.

In the mid-1930s, with all of his novels published but *The Bulwark* and *The Stoic*, Dreiser went through another spurt of reading and investigation in the areas of science and scientific philosophy in working on his titanic "Notes on Life," a project he intended to result in a definitive philosophical statement that would publish as a book. The only outcome was an enormous, shapeless manuscript which after his death wound up in the University of Pennsylvania Dreiser collection; only recently (1974) has it been abridged, shaped and edited by Marguerite Tjader and John J. McAleer and published by the University of Alabama Press. The philosophical concerns of Dreiser's later career were essentially the same as those of his earlier years; when he sought data and ideas he began by looking to his old authorities, like Loeb and Crile, and (again) his central interests were to discover the mechanical, chemical, and electrical bases of all phenomena and to prove that man's life was insignificant and determined by inner and outer forces beyond his control. He corresponded with such people as Crile, with Calvin Bridges (a geneticist at California Institute of Technology), with Robert Millikan (Nobel physicist), and with Simon Flexner (director of the Rockefeller Institute), and he read books and articles ranging from *The Reader's Digest* to Amy Rowland's *The Phenomena of Life* (1936) to Thomas H. Morgan's "The Relation of Genetics to Physiology and Medicine."[32] But his concern was always to fill in and bolster the ideas he had formed earlier, to arrive at a unified and scientific mechanistic theory of life. Dreiser's research of this period added little in the way of new ideas to his repertoire and it of course could have no effect on his major works, all of which had already been written. He tended to interpret scientific phenomena a little differently then, however, finding in them the intimations of universal purpose and design that were, as we shall see, a major enthusiasm of his later years.

During the peak of Dreiser's 1930s' absorption with scientific philosophy, he became interested in Howard Scott's Technocracy movement. Sociopolitical in its theories and aims, Technocracy viewed energy as the crucial quantity in society much the same way that Henry Adams often did, although the proponents of Technocracy differed markedly from Adams in reasoning that society consequently ought to be guided and managed by technicians. Dreiser espoused Technocracy in the thirties, and it became part of his social thinking, along with the previously acquired Social Darwinism, Naturalism, and Marxism.

Again, it is important in tracing Dreiser's scientific education to keep in mind that his intellectual enthusiasms were many, various, indiscriminate, and sometimes contradictory. At any moment he could mix his undying allegiance to Spencer or Loeb with a strong dose of Emerson, Marx, or Mary Baker Eddy. He was an utterly uncritical enthusiast of ideas who never really outgrew the superstitions of his childhood, who was always in awe, both of religious mysteries and of the latest thing in science.

THE SET of beliefs which he finally arrived at is both curious and symptomatic of the age. Dreiser, in his novelist-sage mantle, left a great many credos—in his philosophic writings (*Hey-Rub-a-Dub-Dub!* and "Notes on Life"), in his autobiography (*Dawn* and *A Book About Myself*), in his journalism (the "Reflections" of The Prophet, *A Traveller at Forty*, *Dreiser Looks at Russia*, and other miscellaneous pieces), and in his letters and several interviews; additionally, his vague philosophical system has been examined in a number of good critical books (to which a reader may turn for a broader understanding of his thought).[33] Essentially, Dreiser is customarily and correctly viewed as a naturalistic thinker with strong religious inclinations which became more definite and pronounced late in his career.

The characteristic function of the universe-of-force component in his thought can be seen in a number of its interrelated aspects from a single quotation from a metaphysical essay called "Equation Inevitable" in *Hey-Rub-a-Dub-Dub!*:

> Man, or at least a part of him, a fragment of the chemical whole of which he is part of an expression, wishes and writes laws to confirm . . . [moral ideas], but in spite of all so-called spiritual instruction, an ordered scheme of spiritual rewards and punishments, he is still not chemically able to accommodate himself to these things—not all of him, at least. Nature, his sheer, rank human nature, which sinks deep below into mechanistic, chemical and physical laws and substances, will not let him. Instead he resorts to subtlety, craft—a very unspiritual but plainly natural or chemical

thing. The fact is that the power of certain individuals to do is only limited by the power of certain other individuals to resist, and their natures and tendencies are by no means the same. Yet this squares with the first or pyknotic law of energy, as laid down by Vogt. The self-integrating force of one individual is limited by the self-integrating force of all other individuals; which is, if it is anything, Newton's law worked out in human affairs. There is a rough law of balance indicated by this opposition and strain, but nothing more.[34]

The first point to notice is of course the substitution of a naturalistic for an idealistic or religious basis for metaphysics and ethics, complete with the imprecise and indiscriminate evocation of scientific authority. (Newton is of course Newton, but he has a number of "laws" and none of them looks exactly like Dreiser's paradigm of social life. Vogt, according to Donald Pizer, is a theorist generally unknown in the English-speaking world, whose theory Dreiser found in Haeckel's *The Riddle of the Universe*.[35] Dreiser repeatedly insists that nature goes her own callous way, despite human dreams and ideals; he even suggests that the dreaming itself is merely a function of nature: "Nothing flourishes . . . so well as vain theory. Energetic thought is all but taboo. False dreams and false hopes are invariably encouraged by apparently some chemical or mechanical condition in the so-called brain of man himself."[36] There is a strong sense of human inconsequence that comes with this view, a sense of the universe's indifference to man's irrelevant aspirations and choices, a sense even (noticing the resemblance to Fort's idea) that man is merely a tool or a plaything of some mysterious higher power.

The second point to notice about Dreiser's statement and his philosophic views at mid-career is that he saw the basis of reality as some sort of force system; as he said, "mechanistic, chemical and physical laws" are at the bottom of all things, and those laws, he often implies, operate at least roughly according to Spencer's paradigm, " . . . life in every form has tended to evolve from the simple to the complex."[37] When he considered man's morals and his fate from the aspects of force and evolution, Dreiser was very pessimistic, but when he considered the universal spectacle in and of itself he could be as optimistic and appreciative as Loeb, Helmholtz, or any enthusiast; the fact that it was a Spencerian universe of force could be a great reassurance:

The freshness of the world's original forces is one of the wonders which binds me in perpetual fascination. . . . The great currents of original power which make the world, are fresh and forever renewing themselves. . . . A never-resting stream . . . the force and persistency of the winds . . . . The earth upon which I stand, strange chemic dust. . . .

That is but one of the wonders of life: their persistence.[38]

And although what humanity strives for is generally evolutionary stagnation, "yet from somewhere, fortunately, out of the demiurge there blows ever and anon a new breath, quite as though humanity were an instrument through which a force were calling for freshness and change."[39]

Dreiser repeatedly and consistently insists that human motivation is part of the universal force network, and although he sometimes allows that man has certain nonmechanical reflective and introspective capacities, he often takes an entirely reductionist viewpoint, as if Loeb's tropisms accounted for thought as well as motivation:

> Man responds quite mechanically, and only so, to all such stimuli as he is prepared, or rather constructed, to receive—no more and no less. . . . This constitutes the sum and substance of his free will and intelligence—responding to these various stimuli which are neither more nor less than the call bells of chemical, or perhaps better yet, electrophysical states which require certain other electrophysical or chemical atoms to keep them in the forms in which they chance to be.[40]

In this context the depth and mysteries of human thought and feeling become no more than mechanical phenomena whose laws had not as yet been clearly formulated. Dreiser's most notable fumbling attempt to explain feelings in terms of the simple forces was his explanation of sexual attraction and love in terms of "chemisms."[41] Of course to "explain" the compelling attraction two people feel for each other (like the attraction between Jennie Gerhardt and Lester Kane) by referring to the action of nonempirical "chemisms" inside them is to achieve no realer level of explanation than to refer to the inveiglements of Aphrodite or the blind-shot arrows of Cupid. Dreiser certainly thought the difference was more than semantic, but actually it is only a choice of mythologies, classic or "scientific." His wholehearted allegiance was on the side of the "scientific," and that is all his invocation of "chemisms" really means. He even felt the action of chemisms in himself: his biographer, W. A. Swanberg, reports a conversation Dreiser had with his friend, Hy Kraft: "'It's not my fault,' Dreiser told Kraft, 'you walk into a room, see a woman and something happens. It's chemical. What are you going to do about it?'"[42] Similarly in his autobiographical volume *Dawn* he refers his sisters' sexual vagaries to "the nature-made chemisms and impulses that evoke and condition our deeds."[43] Sexual morality becomes, of course, a kind of *laissez-faire* matter with no particular personal responsibility attached to it since it is a matter of mechanistic determining forces, and Dreiser seemed thoroughly satisfied with this explanation in his experience as well as in his writing.

There is the unstated assumption by Dreiser of a kind of psychology of vectors, in which a person's actions and character are determined by the relative force of the various impulses, needs, and stimuli which assault him. The individual, whose drives are formed by this conflicting welter, is then, on a different plane, himself a vector whose personality has, or is, a given degree of force:

> In the last analysis personality appears to be a sense of power resting on a feeling of capability or wisdom and usefulness, and hence a right to be. . . . That which places one human being over another and sets differences between man and man is not alone intellect or knowledge . . . but these plus, other things being equal, the vital energy to apply them or the hypnotic power of attracting attention to them—in other words, personality.[44]

In his autobiographical writings one of the most characteristic ways Dreiser has of identifying people who impressed him is to speak of their "force" or their "forcefulness," using the word, I would maintain, in a more-than-figurative sense. Personal force seems to be inevitably linked to egoistic self-assertion in Dreiser's mind, judging both from individual instances in the autobiographical writings and from generalizations he at times makes about man's "instinct toward individuality."[45]

His vision of man's social existence is, then, atomistic, mechanistic, and rooted in conflict at a level even more basic than the customary "survival of the fittest" principles of Social Darwinism, in the same way that the laws of chemistry and physics are prior to the laws of biology.

> Man, as a representation of chemical and physical impulses coming from somewhere, has an innate desire for power for extreme movement for himself; but so have all other mechanical or physical representations of that impulse. And it is but the balancing pressure of his fellows which keeps him in position at or near a median line.[46]

Thus men are vectors in the social force-field, and they have every sanction of nature so to behave.

Although the individual is liberated, in Dreiser's system, from the restraints of conventional morality, his situation is lonely and precarious. The forces of nature and society conduce only to the survival of the mass, not of the individual. If the individual is to survive, he must conform to those forces, however stifling to his own "instinct toward individuality"; if he is to prevail, however ephemerally, he must do so through conflict and struggle, since he can fulfill his own will only in the face of an indifferent nature and at the expense of social stability and the "instinct toward individuality" of all his fellow men. It is the same problem of individualism and social justice that Jack London wrestled with so interestingly and inconclusively. Dreiser, less the moralist and more the mechanist, has a ready explanation; but although the issue is explained, it is far from comfortably resolved for him.

He saw it all as a matter of natural forces. The forceful individual is every bit as much a threat to society as social force is to the individual, yet this is the way of nature and of evolutionary progress. The crucial example in Dreiser's nonfiction, as in the fiction, is the industrial tycoon, who appropriates to himself as much social force (underlings, money, and women) as he can in the pure interest of self-gratification. Journalist Dreiser had been brought up on America's ambivalent attitude toward its millionaires, both in the writings of the social critics, reformers, and muckrakers who saw the Rockefellers, Carnegies, and Goulds as exploiters of the common man and perverters of our democratic institutions, and in the writings of those journalists who deeply admired these men for their ability, money, and power. Dreiser himself had, on different occasions, written on both sides of this issue. When he was in his most philosophical mood, however, as when he wrote the essay "The American Financier" in *Hey-Rub-a-Dub-Dub!*, he saw such men as amoral and inevitable, unfair and unscrupulous yet benefiting humanity in the long run, working, paradoxically, both with the flow of force to produce progress, and against it to advance themselves. A potentially tragic figure, the financier is

> the coldest, the most selfish, and the most useful of all living phenomena. Plainly it is a highly specialized machine for the accomplishment of some end which Nature has in view. Often humorless, shark-like, avid, yet among the greatest constructive forces imaginable. . . . They, too, are but minute factors in the total machinery, little able to forefend against disaster or the ultimate nothingness that swallows them.[47]

On the other side of the social controversy, the social reformer, although less interesting to Dreiser the novelist, likewise was a medium of expression for natural force: "He merely represents an inevitable tendency in nature to maintain a balance or equation between one type of mood and another, only one of which can be dominant for a time and of which he becomes the passing representative." In other words, when things are brought to a certain pass, Christ or the reformer "cannot help coming."[48] Social morality, then, is simply a matter of force-dynamics.

Thus, for Dreiser, what substitutes for a moral law of society is just that idea of "balance" or "equation" that he mentions so frequently. In Pizer's view, "this idea of equation was immensely useful to Dreiser as a way of giving shape to many of his underlying beliefs and feelings,"[49] and indeed, Dreiser does seem to have thought a great deal, although none too clearly, about this principle, and he dedicated to it the whole of the long essay, "Equation Inevitable" in *Hey-Rub-a-Dub-Dub!*. The idea resembles Crile's "universal law of equilibrium," and Dreiser claims to have found the idea in Spencer, although, as with most ideas he adopted, he modified it beyond recognition. His idea of the "equation inevitable" has two distinct aspects to it, although he never recognized them as such. First, in the framework of naturalistic ethics, he saw nature as having an inbuilt tendency to maintain a balance of forces, an idea which may be a clumsy approximation of Spencer's concept of equilibrium:

> All we can say is that Nature has supplied us with certain forces or chemic tendencies and responses, and has also provided (rather roughly in certain instances) the checks and balances which govern the same. . . . Roughly, equation is always holding in one or many forms—dependent equations, which consist of many, many equations or balances, joined in some still greater one or synthesis—and apparently always will.[50]

In this aspect life seemed to Dreiser dependent on a static balance—"the slightest disturbance of the existing equations which produce life as we see it, as Loeb and Crile and others have shown, ends in monstrosities or confusion, and life as we know it ceases"[51]— and man's ethical imperative, naturalistically based, of course, was relatively clear:

> "Murder," say . . . scientific seekers after truth, or at least their facts point to this, "is a disturbing and disrupting process. It destroys the equation best expressed in 'Live and let live.' It affects individual peace. If you do so unto others, they will do so unto you. Chemically and physically, according to the law of reaction or equation, they cannot very well avoid it. Therefore do not murder."[52]

In its other aspect, in the framework of cosmic contemplation, Dreiser tended to see his equation theory as a kind of axiom that every force had its own particular contrariety and therefore no change or progress was even metaphysically possible:

> Heat is balanced by cold in the universe; light by no light; matter by force; tenderness by savagery; lust by asceticism; love by hate; and so on *ad infinitum*. Nothing is fixed. All tendencies are permitted, apparently. Only a balance is maintained.[53]

In this aspect the universe is a stalemate, and man has no ethical imperative because all forces automatically have their own counterforces. Thus the logic-defying "equation inevitable" is another of Dreiser's woolly philosophical monstrosities.

Although in certain frames of mind Dreiser was pontifical about the universe of force—the scientific philosopher explaining the true nature of reality to a lay audience—in other frames of mind he was uncertain and muddled, an agnostic for whom science was nonsense and all meaning seemed to be slipping away. "Life is to me too much a welter and play of inscrutable forces to permit, in my case at least, any significant comment," [54] he would say in that mood, or perhaps even in a tone of impotent frustration inveigh against what seemed to be the blind and purposeless forces that created man to be ignorant:

> What a condemnation, this, of that seeming sentence below or above Man, this creative if blind energy that so condemns Man to this—this complete ignorance which he may not escape. The almost devilish indifference to the fate or state of creatures so erected, if not by its knowledge and will at least out of its indestructible energy.[55]

Science, in the slipping moment, was no help at all, a fact which he confronted with a rare ironic relish, like Henry Adams discovering an absurdity: man, we have been told, is

> a diversified arrangement of molecules or atoms or electrons, protons, quantums (I am using the current scientific lingo for these amazing mysteries). . . . But all finally and inexorably, as the physicists see it, electrical— so that someone has already said that God is electricity. In other words, to go back to the sentient Greeks, He is Jove with his bolts!
>   But what then is electricity? Atoms
>   And what are atoms? Electricity
>   Wonderful!

Faced with the crumbling of all of the various absolutistic categories, with the failure (like Adams's) to discover essences in science, with what for him was the ultimate incomprehensibility of man and the universe, philosopher Dreiser sometimes even turned to the idea that all existence is merely an illusion: "I find life to be . . . a complete illusion or mirage which changes and so escapes or eludes one at every point."[56] Thus the question of human knowledge was for Dreiser throughout most of his career a dilemma, either horn of which pointed straight to pessimism. Man was either unknowing, or he was insignificant (or, quite possibly he was both). "In short," he wrote to Michael Gold, who had criticized him for being confused and futilitarian, "my pessimism springs not from pity for the minute individual attempting to cope with so huge and difficult a thing as life but also from the obvious futility of man as anything but a pleasure seeking fly."[57]

But whether the universe seemed deterministic or futile or illusory, it still often seemed zestful to Dreiser; the whole welter of motive and accident, success and failure, knowledge and incomprehensibility, "taken as a whole is scintillant, brisk, interesting, forceful."[58] And again, "Great forces are at work, strong ones, and our own little lives are but a shadow of something that wills activity and enjoys it, that wills beauty and is beauty."[59] One of Dreiser's most characteristic responses to the universe of force, then, was esthetic, the response of a fascinated spectator, despite the considerable anguish about human life he manifests on other occasions. In his cosmically esthetic mood even death and suffering were part of "the true color or zest" of life.[60] And his ideas seemed to follow his moods, rather than otherwise.

It would be an overstatement to say that in his late years Dreiser came to religion, but there is no doubt that many of his philosophical statements in the 1940s came closer to articulating conventional theistic beliefs than any of his earlier pronouncements. His addition of God to the universe of force was done in the customary way, reminiscent of John Fiske and the other American Spencerians who theologized the Unknowable: "My scientific, as well as my philosophic studies, compel me to feel that there can be but one primary creative force, or soul, the discoverable physical as well as chemical laws of which appear to be obeyed by all matter and energy—or matter-energy."[61] The universe still operates in a mechanistic, scientifically describable manner, according to this view, but the manifest forces are directed by a primary force, and that primary force has purpose. The key to this reassuring view was Dreiser's "discovery" of cosmic design in a moment when, after examining crystals under the microscope at Woods' Hole laboratory one July day in 1928, he discovered in some yellow wildflowers the same beautiful design he had been examining under the microscope; many years later he interpreted the experience: "Suddenly it was plain to me that there must be a divine, creative intelligence behind all this—Not just a blind force, but a great Artist, who made all these things with such love and care."[62] Dreiser's primary force or "Creator" was a god typically revered by scientists awed by the variety, the intricacy and the order of the universe as revealed by scientific inquiry, a god that the force conservationists enthused over and the American Spencerians found refuge in, but it contained elements of the Emersonian Oversoul as well. It culminated Dreiser's lifelong habit of using scientific ideas metaphorically in an essentially metaphysical if not religious quest.

> Studying this matter of genius in design and beauty, as well as the wisdom of contrast and interest in this so carefully engineered and regulated universe—this amazing process called living—I am moved not only to awe but to reverence for the Creator of the same concerning whom—his or its presence in all things from worm to star to thought—I meditate constantly.[63]

Dreiser's late cosmic religiousness seems to have had little if any effect on his sense of human nature, of determinism, of social justice, and his other philosophical ideas, and he doesn't even seem to have gotten his Creator concept together with his often-stated idea that man is merely a tool of indifferent cosmic forces. The Creator discovered through the design seems to have been a kind of isolated cosmic consolation emerging for him in the 1940s at the far end of his typical meditation on the beauty of the universe's inscrutable welter.*

Dreiser's thought had always been patterned thus. A certain mood or a certain initial topic would lead his thought inevitably to its particular Dreiserian conclusion. Beginning for example, with a perception of a struggling individual or of failure, he tended to conclude that our lives were determined by indifferent forces; the situation of a strong man succeeding always suggested Social Darwinism to him, although success itself always evoked the ephemeral and illusory quality of life. There was a streak of egotistical contentiousness in this patterning too: when he addressed or talked about conventional moralists he urged scientific determinism, but when addressing or discussing scientists he rediscovered the unexplainability and seeming spirituality of things. In this way much of his philosophizing seems to have filled needs other than intellectual for him, since the approaches and conclusions of his thought generally put him in a superior and inconoclastic role and had some particularly dramatic, poetic, or ironic character.

Certainly the logical consistency of his various conclusions wasn't one of his central concerns, nor was their scientific validity. Not a philosopher, Dreiser was a creative artist involved with ideas. Reactive, dramatic, egotistical, he involved himself with ideas only on his own terms. However, the universe of force appealed to Dreiser, the man of his times, basically and in a variety of ways. Force was force, and it was generally primary, no matter what the particular context of his thought.

IN WRITING his fiction, Dreiser (as is generally recognized) drew first and most fully on his own personal experience rather than on any intellectual system of abstractions; in the words of Larzer Ziff, "Dreiser did not allow belief to control experience."[64] Realism for him meant truth to his experien-

---

* Pizer, however, offers the interesting thesis that Dreiser's later efforts toward social reform can be viewed as consistent with his force-philosophy in that once he had "moved to a faith that these forces are part of a divine, though still mechanistic, plan, . . . the need to achieve a greater balance between such opposing forces as strength and weakness or wealth and poverty is sanctioned not only by the mechanism of equation but by the underlying spirit of love—that is, of force as creative energy or God—in all life." *Uncollected Prose*, 26.

tial, felt knowledge of things, and out of that primary knowledge grew his affinity for certain fictional motifs, characters, and patterns. Yet the generalizations, although secondary, were essential to him as a writer of realistic fiction, since it also seems to have been an inherent and unquestioned element of his realism that everything—characters, motives, events, social and cosmic meanings—be explained as fully as it was humanly possible to explain them. Of course, one could never hope to attain absolute explanation, as Dreiser would almost grudgingly admit when speaking of the art of fiction—"I know by now that life may not be put down in its entirety even though we had at our command the sum of the arts and the resourcefulness of the master of artifice himself"[65]—but he seems to have felt that it was the business of the writer to try. In explaining or accounting for the phenomena of human experience, Dreiser, again the realist, had little faith in the symbolic and nondiscursive aspects of his art and relied heavily instead on the seemingly literal scientific and pseudoscientific generalizations in which his age had such unbounded faith. It was in this manner that Dreiser relied on the universe-of-force concepts in his work, and the strain that his implicit literary theory put on him as a thinker and on his works (especially his early works) as artistic wholes was considerable.

And since Dreiser was, as we have seen, a thinker who had fixed but sometimes incompatible conceptual responses to different philosophical situations, his works at times could easily veer toward fragmentation of approach, despite their conventionally coherent plot-lines. Richard Poirer perceptively identifies this phenomenon of incoherence in *Sister Carrie*: "What is perplexing is that he [Dreiser] creates no plastic coherence among the lurid varieties of self-characterization that emerge from his language. His relationship to the reader and to his material is fragmented."[66] Philosophically, at least, this problem is precipitated in large part by Dreiser's groping and nonce-situational attempts to get everything explained.

By now no one should need further cautioning that Dreiser is not coherent, but another condition exists that needs to be taken into consideration in examining the scientific-philosophical content of his works, and that is the matter of his various collaborators. With the exception of *Sister Carrie* all of his novels were worked on by hands other than his own, as he had the habit of sending his manuscripts to others—colleagues, editors, and even girlfriends—who would make revisions as well as offer suggestions about them. The extent to which his various friends affected particular books we do not know, but we do know that he relied on the judgments of several of them quite extensively—the extreme shortening and editing of *An American Tragedy* by Louise Campbell and Sally Kusell being a clear example.[67] It is unlikely that any of them added any philosophical material, but they well might have reduced or coordinated it. Thus when Dreiser gets less randomly and sweepingly explanatory, as in *An American Tragedy*, it is difficult to know to whom to give the credit.

Dreiser's works manifest universe-of-force orientation and concepts in various ways and degrees. First, his play *Laughing Gas* from the collection *Plays of the Natural and the Supernatural*, although only a literary curiosity, is the purest, most explicit expression of Dreiser's conception of the relationship between man and the universe of force. In his literary criticism he identifies such an awareness of cosmic relationship as an essential characteristic of profound literary works: "Each [of these works] suggests in its way . . . that unescapable and yet somehow pitiable finiteness in the midst of infinity which, think as we will, contrives to touch and move the understanding."[68] *Laughing Gas* explores that relationship both explicitly and symbolically in a form unusual for Dreiser, an expressionistic closet drama. Dreiser attempted a few such ponderous flights of fancy in *Plays of the Natural and the Supernatural*, and in *Laughing Gas* he had, according to his biographer W. A. Swanberg, the added inspiration of a personal experience with laughing gas, used as an anaesthetic in a minor surgical operation.

The action of the play is an operation to remove a neck tumor, performed on J. J. Vatabeel, an eminent physician; the substance of the play is his hallucinations while under the anaesthetic, counterpointed with the operating room emergency that occurs when the surgical procedure turns out to be far more serious than had been anticipated and the oxygen supply runs out. After a minimum of preliminaries, Vatabeel is administered the anaesthetic and begins his journey through the force cosmos; first "The Rhythm of the Universe" speaks: "Om! Om! Om! Om! . . . "[69] Then Vatabeel, "*Functioning through the spirit only*," is "*conscious of tremendous speed, tremendous space, and figures gathered around him in the gloom*" (89). As the operation proceeds Vatabeel has a flicker of fear of dying, but as "*the arc of his flight bisects the first of a series of astral planes*," Force speaks:

> Alcephoran (*A power of physics without form or substance, generating and superimposing ideas without let or hindrance* . . .): Deep, deep and involute are the ways and the substance of things. Oh, endless reaches! Oh, endless order! Oh, endless disorder! Death without life! Life without death! A sinking! A rising! An endless sinking! And an endless rising!
> The Rhythm of the Universe: Om! Om! Om! Om! Om! Om! (90)

As on the conscious level the crisis develops and more oxygen is urgently sent for, Alcephoran and The Rhythm are joined by Demyaphon, the chemical force of the laughing gas, which speaks climactically the universal truth to man: the depths of the universe are beyond any human knowing—"you are a mere machine run by forces which you cannot understand" (103)—and the forces of the universe send man around the same set of experiences again and again—"the same difficulty, the same operation, ages and worlds apart" (105). Vatabeel makes the enormous and arbitrary effort necessary to continue life, and he narrowly comes through, but aware now of the insignificance of man in the vast sea of determining forces, the endlessness and meaninglessness of life in the universe, he comes through the final, the laughing stages of the anaesthetic laughing cynically and sardonically:

> Oh, ho! ho! Oh, ha! ha! ha!
> I see it all now! Oh, what a joke! Oh, what a trick!
> Over and over! And I can't help myself! . . .
> And the very laughing compulsory! vibratory! a universal scheme of laughing! Oh, ho! ho! ho! . . . I have the answer! I see the trick. The folly of medicine! The folly of life! . . . What fools and tools we are! What pawns! What numbskulls! . . . (His face has a sickly flatness, the while he glares with half-glazed eyes, and shakes his head.) (115–116)

The Dreiserian irony is that although he survives, he survives disillusioned.

The play reads today like an unconscious self-parody, but its ideas, of course, were the ones Dreiser was most serious about. Perhaps for this reason he wrote to Mencken (incredibly) that *Laughing Gas* was "supremely the best—personally I think the best thing I ever did." [70] At any rate, he made the epiphany of this atypical little piece the discovery of the universe-of-force concepts he himself felt so stimulated and threatened by.

In Dreiser's fiction the works most thoroughly and consistently involved with the universe of force are the novels in the Cowperwood trilogy, *The Financier* (1912) and *The Titan* (1914) especially, and *The Stoic* (1947) to a somewhat lesser extent. Based on the actual career of financier Charles Tyson Yerkes, the trilogy presents the story of the achievement and travail of this new American myth-figure, the tycoon, in the setting of a universe of force and a world of stark Darwinism. Frank Cowperwood's character and actions are perfectly suitable, given a universe where "the large, placid movements of nature outside of man's little organisms would indicate that she is not greatly concerned," [71] a universe whose creator seemingly rewards deception and ruthlessness rather than truthfulness and justice (as Dreiser points out in the zoological parable, "Concerning Mycteroperca Bonaci," at the end of *The Financier*).

As *The Financier* opens, the boy Frank Cowperwood is characterized as being clear-eyed and strong ("there was real strength in that sturdy young body" [25]), and he soon shows mid-nineteenth-century Philadelphia his force and precociousness by buying seven cases of Castile soap at auction and reselling them at a profit to the family grocer. Soon thereafter he goes quickly from success to success, first in apprentice jobs in the grain and commission business, and later in brokerage and banking. Meanwhile he ponders the question "How is life organized?" His first philosophical imaginings are focused when he witnesses a lobster gradually overcome and devour a squid in a fish store display. In this passage (one of Dreiser's most famous) the boy discovers, in a kind of Darwinian epiphany, that life lived on life, "men lived on men" (14). Later, as his astuteness, single-mindedness, and amorality greatly widen the range of his successes, and he ponders the difference between the strong men he admires and whose vision he shares, and the poor and inadequately endowed, he decides that "again, it was so very evident, in so many ways, that force was the answer—great mental and physical force" (243). Realizing that conventional morality is only a sham, Dreiser's tycoon forms an ethical philosophy in keeping with the ideas of personal force, Social Darwinism, and cosmic indifference: "'I satisfy myself,' was his motto; and it might well have been emblazoned upon any coat of arms which he could have contrived to set forth his claim to intellectual and social nobility" (244).

One of the principal ways in which he seeks satisfaction is sexually. Throughout the trilogy, Cowperwood's career is twofold—commercial and amorous—and in both realms he is audacious, unscrupulous, and generally successful, despite the considerable complications and dangers involved. Dreiser uses a great deal of universe-of-force terminology to explain the causes and effects of love in Cowperwood's life.[72] Frank Cowperwood's "force" is invariably what first interests a woman in him, and his perception of "force" in her is what assures that a reciprocal relationship is beginning. In *The Financier* for example, when Cowperwood meets Aileen, the young daughter of his powerful ally in the financial world, Edward Malia Butler, we are told of her that

> talent of a raw, crude order was certainly present—a native force which had been somewhat polished, as granite may be, by the feelings, opinions and conventions of current society, but which still showed through in an elemental and yet attractive way. . . . No other woman or girl whom he (Cowperwood) had known had ever possessed so much innate force as this one possessed, none so much vitality and vivacity. (158–159)

Of course Dreiser has a great many other ways to describe her charms, but *force* is the word he repeatedly uses to designate her vitality and sex appeal. And it appears that a mechanical erotic magnetism is operative as Cowperwood's force draws her:

> The color mounted to her cheeks and up to her temples. Mr. Cowperwood

was the kind of man to know. He was so intensely forceful. His own quiet intensity matched her restless force. He was the one man whose force did seem equal to hers. (211)

The flavor of his spirit was what attracted and compelled, like the glow of a flame to a moth. . . . When he touched her hand at parting, it was as though she had received an electric shock, and she recalled that it was very difficult for her to look him straight in the eye. Something akin to a destructive force seemed to issue from them at times. (246–247)

From the time she had first seen him . . . until now, there had been a strong pull from him to her. She was drawn as some planets are drawn by the sun. (251)

In explaining Aileen's attraction for Cowperwood, Dreiser, in his 1927 revision of the novel, still every bit the mechanistic psychologist, theorized, "For by now he was intensely drawn to her, as he could feel—something chemic and hence dynamic was uppermost in him now and clamoring for expression."[73] The explanations of erotic attraction in terms of forces and force-correlations are repeated throughout the trilogy as are Cowperwood's erotic encounters. In *The Titan*, then, married to Aileen, Cowperwood meets Rita Sohlberg:

She was essentially dynamic and passionate. Cowperwood was beginning to stand out in her mind as the force that he was.[74]

The very chemistry of life seems to play into the hands of a situation of this kind. Once Cowperwood was thinking vividly, forcefully, of her, Rita began to think in a like manner of him. (*Titan*, 119)

Later he meets Stephanie Platow, and their affair begins once "her interest in Cowperwood, his force and ability, was intense" (*Titan*, 231). Even the more spiritual Berenice Fleming, for whom he long yearns with a pure esthetic and paternalistic fervor (for him she is "youth, individuality, energy"), has her interest aroused when "she gathered quite accurately the totality of Cowperwood's age, force, grace, wealth, and worldly ability" (*Titan*, 354). And even the suitor she rejects when she goes to Cowperwood at the end of *The Titan* declares, "I love you with all the honor and force in me" (*Titan*, 456–457). The effect of the persistent use of this strange pseudoscientific terminology in describing this sequence of fickle passions is to make them seem both supra-volitional and in accord with the laws of nature.

Another of the ways in which the trilogy presents us with a model of life as a force-vector system is in its depictions of the vectors of individual passion and will in conflict with the "forces" of conventional, moralistic society. Human behavior is at times presented by Dreiser's all-knowing and somewhat pedantic narrator as if it were a verbalized problem in physical dynamics: when Aileen Butler is considering a liaison with the already-married Cowperwood in *The Financier*, we are told that

> It is a question what would have happened if antagonistic forces could have been introduced just at this time. Emotions and liaisons of this character can, of course, occasionally be broken up and destroyed. The characters of the individuals can be modified or changed to a certain extent, but the force must be quite sufficient. Fear is a great deterrent—fear of material loss where there is no spiritual dread—but wealth and position so often tend to destroy this dread. (*Fin.*, 252)

Stated this way behavior can be expressed formulaically: if the force of character (squared) plus the erotic attraction plus the material wealth is greater than the material insecurity plus the "spiritual dread" (if any) plus any other antagonistic forces, the affair is bound to be consummated, as this particular one indeed is. The crucial factor in Dreiser's equation was always the personal force, however:

> Dogma may bind some minds; fear, others. But there are always those in whom the chemistry and physics in life are large, and in whom neither dogma nor fear is operative. Society lifts its hands in horror; but from age to age the Helens, the Messalinas, the Du Barrys, the Pompadours, the Maintenons, and the Nell Gwyns flourish and point a subtler basis of relationship than we have yet been able to square with our lives. (*Fin.*, 261)

And Dreiser frequently enough reminds us that with the likes of Cowperwood, Aileen, and Berenice we are dealing with people in whom "the chemistry and physics in life are large." Thus, in simplified terms, the trilogy presents us with an elemental conflict: human will and desire against convention and circumstances. The outcome is determined by the relative strength as forces of the various factors.

In depicting financial competition as a social phenomenon Dreiser's vector analysis is naturally quite prevalent. Some men are social forces (notably Cowperwood and all the men at the top of the economic ladder), and others are not. The forceful men—amoral, thoroughly self-possessed, daring, and blunt—are recognizable by their cool and calculating style, by their unemotional attitude toward business and political affairs, by the clear hard looks in their eyes. And they are thoroughly unself-indulgent; other, lesser people want money for the comforts it will buy them, "whereas the financier wants it for what it will control—for what it will represent in the way of dignity, force, power" (*Fin.*, 350). Lesser people exist for the financier only to be aligned by his force-field: the little men in business and politics to be manipulated or suborned, like Stener the city treasurer in *The Financier*; the women to be used sexually or socially, like the first Mrs. Cowperwood and Aileen Butler; and even the artists to be employed to enhance the great man's dignity and force, like the architect in *The Financier* and the painters in *The Titan*. And of course the masses of people who use the natural gas, ride the street-railways, vote in elections that the financiers are struggling to control are insignificant, unthinking creatures fit only to be led or misled as the men of power choose. The vision is as undemocratic as it is amoral.

Given this system of values in the trilogy, high drama occurs only when there is opposition between men of force. When in *The Financier* Cowperwood rises to financial prominence in Philadelphia, opens his own banking house, and begins to gain control in such areas as the street-railway system, the established men of power see him first as a bright, audacious, somewhat helpful man, but later, as his adventures threaten their interests and even their control of the local financial scene, they recognize him as the Darwinian threat that he is and take every action they can to thwart him. Then their personal encounters with him are icily cordial, steely-eyed, fraught with natural antagonism and wariness. Depicting this high-stakes coolness seems to have been one of Dreiser's main interests in writing the trilogy; the basic situation recurs in *The Titan* as Cowperwood invades the Chicago financial world to take control of natural gas and assault the street-railway systems, and in *The Stoic* as he moves his operations to London to consolidate and control the subway system. In each case, it should be noted, Dreiser the literary realist carefully details the means and machinations of these conflicts, generally from the inside of both sides of the situation. Dreiser's social paradigm in these books is an atomistic, Darwinistic force-vector system, but that system is certainly presented concretely and particularly, rather than abstractly or formulaically.

The social vector system is a highly complex one. The personal financial and political forces interact with erotic forces, social forces, and even the forces of chance to produce the final fate-vector. In each of the three novels Cowperwood is thwarted by some combination of these forces. The specific situation in *The Financier* is the most cataclysmic. Cowperwood's early financial alliance with Edward Butler introduces him to Butler's daughter Aileen. The powerful and mutual erotic force between Cowperwood and Aileen sets them at odds with conventional society and, when one anonymous member of that conventional society informs Aileen's father and Cowperwood's wife of the illicit alliance, their forces too are turned against the tycoon. In his financial deals too he experiences a reverse: just as the financial powers of Philadelphia are girding against him, the Great Chicago Fire destroys a number of important businesses and the bottom drops out of the market. This unpredictable force of chance occurs just when Cowperwood, in conspiracy with the city treasurer, had been deeply engaged in illicitly investing the city's money. He is caught short and he finds nothing but hostility from the financial elite, who are spurred on by the revengeful Butler and are anxious for Cowperwood to fail so they can pick up his holdings. The financial forces even turn into political forces working to overcome Cowperwood, as the reform of the city treasurer's office and the freeing the city from the influence of unscrupulous operators like Cowperwood become a crusade, first among cynical politicans and then in the population at large. Even the reformer (as Dreiser later pointed out in his essay "The Reformer" in *Hey-Rub-a-Dub-Dub!*) comes on the scene as a kind of reactive force. As a result, Cowperwood fails, not because he broke moral laws or overreached himself, but because the forces—erotic, social, circumstantial, financial, and political—happened to interrelate and combine in opposition to his will, and they were together too strong for him. In *The Financier* he recoups his fortune, after his failure and a term in jail, in lightning-fast manipulation during the market crash of 1873, and he heads for Chicago with Aileen. In *The Titan* he rises to colossal heights in Chicago finance only to be thwarted again by a combination of social, moralistic, financial, and political forces. In *The Stoic* he enters upon a similar course in London only to have it interrupted by his death.

Finally the best way to account for this ebb and flow of forces that is Cowperwood's career is in terms of the "equation inevitable," which the narrator offers retrospectively at the end of *The Titan*:

> At the ultimate remove, God or the life force, if anything, is an equation, and at its nearest expression for man—the contract social—it is that also. Its method of expression appears to be that of generating the individual, in all his glittering variety and scope, and through him progressing to the mass with its problems. In the end a balance is invariably struck wherein the mass subdues the individual or the individual the mass—for the time being. For, behold, the sea is ever dancing or raging. (*Titan*, 550–551)

Thus Dreiser in the context of this trilogy seems to regard the course of human affairs principally in terms of dynamic law (every force has a counterforce, every imbalance is ultimately balanced), rather than in terms of a moral law, a divine plan, or even an evolutionary paradigm. Of course, the author being Dreiser, the trilogy has glimpses from other philosophic vantages too, some in keeping with the dominant mechanical perspective and others not. There is a good deal of Darwinism in the narrator's outlook, but it is the "hard" Darwinism of the struggle for dominance and survival rather than the "soft" Darwinism, more characteristic of American thought, of progress toward better, higher things. Appropriately to this framework, Dreiser concludes *The Financier* with the postlude parable of the Black Grouper, which demonstrates evolutionary survival through adaptation, deception, and predatoriness. There is no hint of progress or amelioration in this passage; life is as empty of values and purpose in the biological metaphor as it is in the physical. Totally or emotionally consistent with the biological and physical metaphors is the pervading sense of ultimate futility and disillusionment which the novels give. All Cowperwood's yearnings and striving, and all of the turmoil he precipitated finally end in almost nothing. Macbeth's witches pretentiously announce this to him at the end of *The Financier*: "Hail to you, Frank Cowperwood, master and no master, prince of a world of dreams whose reality was disillusion" (*Fin.*, 780). The philosophical pattern is similar to that in *Laughing Gas*, where the discovery of the mechanical essence of the universe reveals all human endeavor as ultimately futile, which suggests that possibly all life is illusion. That final point is only intimated in the Cowperwood trilogy in statements like that of the witches, but it is clear that that is one of the constituents of Dreiser's longest perspective on the events of the trilogy.

The last of the three volumes, *The Stoic*, has a slightly different emphasis due to the shift in Dreiser's philosophical proclivities in the thirty-odd year period during which he worried it along to near-completion. (He never quite finished it; his widow Helen finally had to put it together and have it published in 1947.) Inherently the least interesting novel of the trilogy, it is nevertheless curiously tinged with Dreiser's later religious preoccupations at the same time it reveals him still trying to find meaning in the situation of the embattled, now aging, and still polygamous financier in the universe of force. And finally, after Cowperwood's death and the dispersal of his fortune, his art collection, and his dreams in the litigation that followed, his true love, Berenice, motivated by their past relationship and by what seemed to be the philosophical lesson of Frank Cowperwood, turns to Hindu philosophy and humanitarian works done in his name. The universe of force is never denied in this spiritualized conclusion to the trilogy—in fact a force draws Berenice to India to find a guru ("Something appears to be drawing me like a magnet and I feel I shall not be deflected in any way").[75] The philosophy at which Berenice arrives views the universe as fundamentally spiritual but, like the universe of force, radically nonanthropocentric, ateleological, nonprogressive. Thus, in Dreiser's last attempt to find meaning in this welter of striving and disillusionment, Berenice's final humanitarianism counteracts the Social Darwinism that had so pervaded the trilogy, but her mystical metaphysic only serves to spiritualize the universe of force.

The trilogy is in some respects a landmark in American literature. It was a real achievement for Dreiser to have brought into the imaginative main stream of American culture the world of business, in which and by which so many Americans lived their daily practical lives; and to have depicted the give-and-take of business with such verisimilitude makes his achievement just that much greater. The originality of the trilogy comes from the viewpoint from which the whole welter is seen—not negatively from a moralistic, muckraking, or even humanistic viewpoint, but neutrally from a viewpoint congenial to if not inherent in the world being depicted. Thus, not only does the universe of force stand as the philosophical background, the indirect subject of the trilogy, but its mechanistic indifference infuses the unique and starkly amoral realism of the narrative point of view. It is the universe of force as viewed from the inside, as if the author were indeed at home there. And amoral though the realism is, each of the three novels gives a striking sense of man's limitations, as the once powerful Cowperwood is made powerless in the shifting equations of force.[76] There is a sense of tragic awe about this insight, a reminder of our humanness which adds to the novels' depth and impact.

In some respects, however, the trilogy is a failure, and they are important respects and not unrelated to the trilogy's originality and strength. Why does the whole Cowperwood saga seem more tedious than compelling? Why do we care so little what happens to Cowperwood? A confluence of factors, imaginative, philosophical, and technical, is involved. To begin with, it is very difficult for a writer to engage an audience by depicting a value-void universe from an essentially amoral point of view. It would be very difficult to locate what would matter to them in such a context, and to hang that in the balance, but if an artist had sufficient imaginative and technical resources it could be brought off, I feel. What Dreiser has done in this trilogy is to give us Cowperwood and his quantitative egotistical aspirations, virtually self-depicted, to care about. He asks us to set aside good-and-bad for a while in vicariously experiencing this life, but he offers us only winning-or-losing in its stead. It is almost as if we were offered an athletic competition instead of a drama; we can vicariously enjoy the conflict of great forces, the individual skill of the participants, the strategy and deception, the fate like the bounce of a ball, and the arbitrarily quintessential winning or losing, but absent is any sense that we as human beings have some stake in the game. Cowperwood's aspirations give us no more to care about. When, in *The Titan*, he is yearning and striving to become the man who exploits the public's need for natural gas and street railway transportation, when he is trying to hire a seducer for his faithful wife Aileen so he can be free to court his teen-aged idol Berenice, and at the same time keep Berenice distant from the other passing sexual affairs he is drawn into by his great magnetic force, it is very difficult to feel some loss, as Dreiser undoubtedly means us to, when some parts of his grand design fail. Our moral categories might well return, and we may feel he deserved his failure and precipitated it himself, which is precisely the sort of reaction Dreiser wanted to prevent in constructing the world of the trilogy around force rather than around what he felt were the outdated categories of good and evil. Finally, we might even feel the trilogy is not the high tragedy Dreiser intended, but a comedy of a selfish man's yearning for infinite gratification, and his ultimate frustration.

Dreiser's depiction of the titan doesn't help matters, either. Cowperwood's force and charm are merely posited, his behavior often seems petulant, and his apologies and explanations are trite and tedious:

> "Aileen," he said finally, coming up behind her, "can't you and I talk this thing over peacefully now? You don't want to do anything that you'll be sorry for. I don't want you to. I'm sorry. You don't really believe that I've ceased to love you, do you? I haven't you know. This thing isn't as bad as it looks. I should think you would have a little more sympathy with me after all we have been through together. You haven't any real evidence of wrong-doing on which to base any such outburst as this." (*Titan*, 155)

Cowperwood's magnificence is fudged. Dreiser's imagination and language failed him, and unfortunately produced a kind of superman who was petty at the core, thus reinforcing the reader's ambivalence. The final effect is less one of awe than one of confusion, as Dreiser, despite his great skill in depicting the realms of business and politics, lacked the art and the insight to successfully bring together amoral realism, the business-world hero, and the universe of force.

IN *The "Genius"* (1915) Dreiser attempted some of the same effects, but this time with a hero who was an artist and an intellectual of sorts. The book is richer and more vivid than any of the Cowperwood novels, especially in its depiction of motivation, subjective reflection, and personal relationships (some of the superior aspects of *An American Tragedy* first emerge in *The "Genius"*), but it leads the reader into some of the same sorts of ambivalences as does the trilogy. The hero, Eugene Witla, the genius in quotation marks, is presented by Dreiser as a man of great natural artistic talent, deep emotional stirrings, and considerable though somewhat undirected and undefined capacities. He comes across as more sensitive, more reflective, and more self-aware than Cowperwood, and without the tycoon's single-minded power drive, although in other respects (like their disdain for convention, their fickle and amoral amorousness, their weakness for eighteen-year-olds, their sense of special destiny) they are similar. Both heroes show signs of being self-justifications, self-depictions of Dreiser himself, and in the question of authorial perspective lie some of the problems with the novel's ambiguities.

The "Genius" is even based loosely on Dreiser's own experience in the way that the trilogy was based on Charles Tyson Yerkes's. Following its hero from young manhood to middle age, it parallels—substituting painting for writing as the hero's talent—Dreiser's marriage to the midwestern girl of his dreams, his first artistic success, his great crisis with psychological depression, his various love affairs with increasing strain on the marriage, his success as editor of a commerical magazine, his love affair with a beautiful eighteen-year-old, his loss of his job and his sweetheart through the actions of her enraged mother, his second great period of depression, and his reemergence as an artist of great significance. Witla even reads the same books Dreiser had read, experiences the same *Weltschmerz*, and follows approximately the same course of philosophical development (although here there seem to be some significant and perspective-yielding differences in Witla's proneness to rely on religion, as we shall see).

The universe of force is an important part of the conceptual background of the book. Early in his development the "genius" discerns that social ideals and the people who uphold them "meant nothing in the shifting, subtle forces of nature,"[77] and, in a gloomier frame of mind induced by romantic difficulties and a reading of the likes of Darwin and Tyndall he decides that "life was nothing save dark forces moving aimlessly" (157). As in the Cowperwood trilogy, motivation is seen as force-directed: the narrator explains that "the results of many experiments indicated that the apparently *willful* selection in these cases [of self-destructive behavior] is the inevitable action of definite chemical and physical laws which the individual organism can no more change than it can change the course of gravitation" (285); and especially the repetitious erotic motivation is again expressed in terms of force correlations: "She looked into his eyes and felt the impact of that emotional force which governed her when she was near him. There was something in the chemistry of her being which roused to blazing the ordinarily dormant forces of his sympathies" (177).

But despite this pseudoscientific aspect of *The "Genius,"* various mystical and superstitious ideas are also given credence by the characters and credence-implying function by the narrator. Fortune-tellers twice in the novel provide strikingly accurate foreknowledge for the characters and foreshadowing for the storyteller as well. (Witla's entire career is laid out before him—for a dollar—on page 253, and his wife Angela learns on page 684 that he was never to marry his eighteen-year-old sweetheart.) Astrology is also invoked, and on one occasion the good luck omen of seeing a cross-eyed boy accurately foretells to the hero (and foreshadows to the novel's audience) that the job interview to which he is hurrying is about to be monumentally successful (404). A kind of mystical thought transference occurs several times in the novel, of which the narrator offers the explanation that

One could almost accept the Brahmanistic dogma of a psychic body which sees and is seen where we dream all to be darkness. There is no other supposition on which to explain the facts of intuition. So many individuals have it. They know so well without knowing why they know. (366)

What are we to make of the novel's strange mixture of mechanistic material-ism and mystical idealism? Simply that Dreiser's own incompatible philosophi-cal enthusiasms, which are always close to expression in this nearly autobio-graphical work, come through in the novel as an incoherent narrative approach.

The problem of philosophical approach is magnified because the novel is to such a substantial extent the story of the hero's growth in philosophical un-derstanding. Unlike Frank Cowperwood, who as a boy learned for once and for all "how life was organized" in the drama of the lobster and the squid, Eugene Witla gropes, questions, reads, backslides, and, supposedly, *develops* in his view of the nature of things. The *"Genius"* is Dreiser's *Martin Eden* in respect to philosophical wisdom, and it is just as inadequate in that respect. But where London's wisdom was too narrowly and paradigmatically (and ob-soletely) Spencerian, Dreiser's is too diffuse and self-contradictory, though similarly obsolete. Eugene Witla early in his career has his eyes opened by the universe-of-force perspective. As he experiences setbacks in his life, his reading of Spencer, Darwin, and others haunts him with visions of man's helplessness and life's futility. In language close to that in which Dreiser described his own philosophical crisis in *Dawn*, he states of Witla that

He was an omnivorous reader now and a fairly logical thinker. He had already tackled Spencer's "First Principles," which had literally torn him up by the roots and set him adrift and from that he had gone back to Marcus Aurelius, Epictetus, Spinoza and Schopenhauer—men who ripped out all his private theories and made him wonder what life really was. He had walked the streets for a long time after reading some of these things, speculating on the play of forces, the decay of matter, the fact that thought forms had no more stability than cloud-forms. . . . Then came Darwin, Huxley, Tyndall, Lubbock. . . . He was still reading—poets, naturalists, es-sayists, but he was still gloomy. Life was nothing but dark forces moving aimlessly. (156–157)

The same ideas, then, which were first tokens of Witla's superior insight be-come symptoms of a morbid neuroticism, psychologically believable but still philosophically naive:

Neither in religion, philosophy, nor science was there any answer to the riddle of existence. . . . He figured life as a grim dark mystery, a sad, semi-conscious activity turning aimlessly in the dark. . . . Malevolence, life living on death, plain violence—these were the chief characteristics of existence. (251)

Out of these emotional and philosophical depths, Witla cries for the reassurance of some sort of spiritual or ideal element in nature, and, after his second breakdown, comes up with (not surprisingly, given the intellectual level of the book) Christian Science. Mary Baker Eddy and the idea that God is Love and that evil is man's illusion are preached to Witla extensively (and approvingly) near the end of the novel, and although he never becomes a Christian Scientist, he seems to get some of the reassurance he needs from its principles and from one of its practitioners. At this stage of his recovery he eagerly seizes on ideas of design in nature, of the action of God in cellular growth, and so forth—typical American popularizations of evolutionary philosophy and ones Dreiser himself would later cleave to—as if they were answers to his condition. And the narrator quotes at length a number of passages from essays in popularized science and philosophy along these lines which thrilled and revived Witla.

Yet there is another, a final stage to Witla's development. As the narrator explains, "If I were personally to define religion I would say that it is a bandage that man has invented to protect a soul made bloody by circumstances; an envelope to pocket him from the unescapable and unstable illimitable. . . . The need for religion is impermanent, like all else in life" (734). And so Witla moves beyond his religious phase, and he is ultimately pictured as the accomplished artist, his wife deceased and his sweetheart gone out of his world, seated before his fireplace, sadder but wiser, coming to terms with "the unescapable and unstable illimitable" by reading a passage (which Dreiser quotes at some length) from Herbert Spencer's *Facts and Comments*, affirming the unknowability of the ultimate universe. Then, standing out in the late November wind, musing under the constellations about the whereabouts of his deceased wife and about his own future,

> "Where in all this—in substance," he thought, rubbing his hand through his hair, "is Angela? Where in substance will be that which is me? What a sweet welter life is—how rich, how tender, how grim, how like a colorful symphony."
>
> Great art dreams welled up into his soul as he viewed the sparkling deeps of space. (736)

True, perhaps, to Dreiser's own experience, it was more the passage of time and the revival of his art that brought Witla out of his despondent *Weltschmerz*. The sought-after synthesis never arrives; the ultimate response to the universe is not philosophic but esthetic, resulting not in truth but in "great art dreams."

Although the *content* of the novel's philosophizing is shallow, incoherent, falsely and superficially "modern," disappointing to the educated reader, and demeaning to the stature of the protagonist, the function of that philosophizing makes good novelistic sense. The ultimate lesson of The *"Genius"* is a very sincere and valid one, one very close to the warp of Dreiser's own experience: emotions dominate ideas—a man's philosophy is a function of his state of mind. Whether we feel callousness and enmity from the great forces, or ideal and holy purpose, or merely the stimulation of an incomprehensible but awesomely beautiful welter, our comprehension, according to the novel, is a matter of our own personal and emotional adjustment to the universe of force.

DREISER'S other novels embody the universe of force in the same ways as the Cowperwood trilogy and The *"Genius,"* although less explicitly or to a lesser extent. In considering them it is worth restating that Dreiser's first allegiance as an artist was to experience and emotion rather than to any conceptual scheme, however awesome. And often it seems that what is basic to his sense of experience is his fatalism, for which the pseudoscientific determinism is only one form of expression, born of the novelist's need to get experience explained.

Sister Carrie is imbued with a certain amount of cosmic Spencerianism (as Dreiser understood that conceptual scheme in 1900) and some universe-of-force analysis of the motivations of individual characters and their effects on each other. At the outset Carrie is "A Waif Amid Forces"[78]—in another metaphor "a lone figure in a tossing, thoughtless sea"—and, we are lectured, "among the forces which sweep and play throughout the universe, untutored man is but a wisp in the wind" (83). One of the novel's most original features (along with its presentation of the success of a fallen woman) is its systematic deletion of conventional conceptions of volition and consequently of any sense of moral responsibility, and concepts of force sometimes help Dreiser achieve this effect. Chicago is "The Magnet Attracting" Carrie (1), and she too is "The Magnet," although early she was "more drawn than she drew" (84). Her seduction by Drouet is also presented as a matter of magnetic force: "They had been dawdling over the dishes, and their eyes had frequently met. Carrie could not help but feel the vibration of force which followed, which, indeed, was his gaze" (89). A vector effect is used to describe people's influence on each other in this novel too, as can be seen when the force of Hurstwood's eye-beam on Carrie outscores that of Drouet's—"Several times their eyes accidentally met, and there poured into hers such a flood of feeling as she had never before experienced"—and, partly as a consequence, "She instinctively felt that he was stronger and higher" than Drouet (121). It is thus mechanically inevitable that

Carrie will leave Drouet for Hurstwood. At times in the novel the narrator expresses the lack of free volition in terms other than those of pseudomechanics, as when Drouet plays the seducer because "he was drawn by his innate desire to act the old pursuing part" (85). At other times the narrator strains to bring the ordinary course of human events into some kind of scientific explanatory framework, as with his use of Elmer Gates's theory of "katastates" and "anastates," hypothetical chemicals in the blood that tended to decrease Hurstwood's capacities as he experienced reversals and to increase Carrie's capacities as she experienced successes (362). The explanation is as unnecessary as it is scientifically spurious; Carrie's success, predominantly a kind of fate-counterpoint to Hurstwood's decline, does seem to occur at least partly because of her own gumption, despite the "anastates" Dreiser calls upon in attempting to make it all a matter of mechanics.

Jennie Gerhardt (1911) is Dreiser's most didactically presented novel (as his narrator repeatedly tells us what to make of the characters and events of the novel and of life) but it has little to do with the universe of force (unlike *The Financier*, which was published in the following year), because its thematic center is in the contrast between social and natural values—even its plot grows essentially out of that contrast, unlike that of *Sister Carrie*. Jennie is not so much a waif amid forces as she is an avatar of the natural amid artificial and harmful ethical and social mores. Nevertheless, Dreiser occasionally uses ideas or language from the universe of force to make his points. Motivation and behavior that are aggressively erotic are in this novel (as in the Cowperwood trilogy) associated with "force." Lester Kane, who has some of Cowperwood's energy and avidity and some of Hurstwood's weakness before the forces of conventional society, is characterized by his force—"there were molten forces in him"[79]—and his attraction to Jennie is couched in terms of force correlation: "This strong, intellectual bear of a man, son of a wealthy manufacturer, stationed, so far as material conditions were concerned, in a world immensely superior to that in which Jennie moved, was, nevertheless, instinctively, magnetically, and chemically drawn to this poor serving-maid" (131). To these two main characters undergoing severe tribulations because of fate and society, the universe seems an immense impersonal machine, against which each individual establishes the values closest to his or her own personal propensities. Jennie is the most successful in arriving at a philosophy of life:

Admitting that she had been bad—locally it was important, perhaps, but in the sum of civilization, in the sum of big forces, what did it all amount to? They would be dead after a little while, she and Lester and all these people. Did anything matter except goodness—goodness of heart? What else was there that was real? (306)

Lester, having left Jennie for an advantageous marriage, comes to see on his deathbed the same force-universe, but with less reassurance:

". . . the individual doesn't count much in the situation. . . . All of us are more or less pawns. We're moved about like chessmen by circumstances over which we have no control. . . .

"After all, life is more or less of a farce," he went on a little bitterly. "It's a silly show. The best we can do is to hold our personality intact. It doesn't appear that integrity has much to do with it."

Jennie did not quite grasp what he was talking about. . . . (401)

Jennie Gerhardt, although with far less philosophizing than *The "Genius,"* comes to approximately the same conclusions about philosophizing: that whatever the forces of the universe are, each person tends to view them within the framework of his or her own personality, emotions, and fate.

A number of Dreiser's minor works use universe-of-force concepts substantively, but it would be repetitious to analyze them all here. The stories "Free" (*Free and Other Stories*, 1918) and "The Old Neighborhood" (*Chains*, 1927) concern thoughtful middle-aged protagonists who see themselves as surrounded by cosmic and social forces. The play *The Hand of the Potter* (1917) primarily concerns the deterministic forces of heredity and motive, as a halfwit accidentally murders a girl and suffers the consequences. Dreiser's autobiographical volumes *Dawn* (1931) and *A Book About Myself* (1922, reissued as *Newspaper Days*, 1931) also include a good many references to universe-of-force concepts (some of which were cited earlier in this chapter), although neither book has the literary quality or the importance in American literature to warrant a detailed analysis here.

An American Tragedy (1925), Dreiser's best and most important book, makes little explicit reference to the universe of force. There are occasional references to characters' inner forces, to the force of chemical erotic attraction or to social or cosmic forces; and beneath the narrative, fate and society seem to operate in the familiar mechanistic ways. But despite the novel's heavy diction and superior authorial tone, its situations develop in primary and secondary experiential terms—events occur the way they happened to Dreiser or the way he heard or read about them—rather than in terms of scientific or philosophical generalizations. It is rare for Dreiser to write in such consistently concrete terms; Pizer points toward a possible explanation in detailing Dreiser's method of composition of that novel:

Beginning with a documentary source, a powerful autobiographical confirmation of that source, and an elaborate "philosophical" explanation of his themes, he initally overdeveloped each of these interests. Having recognized the weakness of his early effort, he moved toward a more imaginative rendering that drew strength from documentary, autobiographical, and ideological roots but which was not confined by them. As always, Dreiser wrote diffusely at first. But aided by expert advisers and by his willingness to judge their advice on its merits, he produced a book which was not so much a combined effort as a distillation of his intent.[80]

The novel is certainly effective in this respect—universal and philosophically provocative without the tediousness of the Dreiserian explanations.

IN TERMS of fictional rhetoric, Dreiser could and did write novels without explicitly invoking the universe of force, but he often used its concepts to establish a cosmic frame of reference, to provide conceptual alternatives to conventional morality, or to explain or justify his characters' motivations and fates. Even then, the metaphysical explanations his fiction contains are often inconsistent, purely occasional, or less than essential. In the mind of Dreiser the fiction writer, the foreground of action—the basic and mundane needs and drives and ambitions, the intricacies of romance and infidelity, the poignant reactions to social rejection or acceptance—is prior to and determinant of the cosmic background of belief.

In terms of the author's beliefs, both stated and implied, however, there is no doubt that Dreiser was deeply moved by the revelations of the universe of force, and that his was an artist's reaction to them. Ultimately, there is a deep attitudinal difference between his apprehension of the universe of tropisms, katastates, and force-equations, and the apprehension of it by his scientific mentors. Loeb and Gates, Crile and Brill, like Joule, Helmholtz, and Spencer before them, might well feel reassured by the evidence of the universe's order and explainability, in which they have a great stake as scientists and philosophers; the novelist accepting such a naturalistic paradigm might, however, because of the very nature of the perceptive techniques of his craft, be less satisfied and complacent with such a state of universal affairs, as indeed Dreiser was. The individual, the humane, the intuitive response to the idea of a deterministic existence—even if that existence were thought to be in the long run determined benevolently—is likely to be gloomy or rebellious; the loss of individual significance through the loss of autonomy will likely, from the novelist's perspective, far outweigh the gain in the reassurance of the universe's rationality or benevolence. Thus, when Dreiser adopts theories like Spencer's or Loeb's, he does it pessimistically; and he consistently, almost obsessively, returns again and again in his thoughts and in his fiction to the situation of mechanically, chemically, impersonally caused behavior by which an individual does indeed lose his (or her) autonomy and significance. The universe of force essentially violates the sentient selves of his characters. Quite possibly then, the vision of the human situation which for any number of scientists was a great reassurance was for Dreiser the elemental anguish, like a perverse and persistent inspiration, out of which his art grew.

Dreiser saw life as force-determined, yet he loved its richness, variety, and color—including its tragic color. The universe of force was, in his literary vision of self and desire, a metaphor for that which limited individuality, coerced, determined, and ultimately defeated individual men (and indeed all individual earthly things), yet at the same time produced the richness and color of the earthly welter. The universe of force was deeply actual for him, and he felt toward it, as he felt toward life, a complex mixture of enthusiasm, anguish, and awe.

DENOUEMENT

FROM ITS literary apotheosis in the works of Theodore Dreiser, the universe of force had no substantial future in American culture. Its potential for yielding new or useful insights had essentially been played out. Physical scientists by the 1860s and 1870s had no real use for an expansive concept of force and had largely ceased to believe in it as an existential reality; life scientists, psychologists, and social scientists found it useful, metaphorically and literally, for a while longer, but likewise soon moved on to different and more productive conceptual frameworks. Philosophers, shortly after Spencer had erected the universe of force as a universally comprehensive and absolute system, tended, like the scientists, to be affected by crucial questions of epistemology and methodology, and they gravitated in the directions of phenomenalism, logical Positivism and, later, existentialism. Both the naive realism of the early force conservationists and the naive absolutism of the force metaphysicians went obsolete, and with them the odd and magnificent edifice of the universe of force.

As American literature of the 1920s and 1930s increasingly tended to take approaches that were relativistic, phenomenalistic, and psychological, literary naturalism of the sort practiced by Norris, London, and Dreiser also seemed to be played out. Naturalism's techniques of documentary realism may well have continued to influence such writers as Dos Passos, Steinbeck, and Richard Wright, and its involvement with scientific concepts and outlooks may have been carried on by the likes of Steinbeck, Mailer, and Pynchon, but the narrative point of view I have termed "naive omniscience" no longer seemed to be the way novelists chose to tell their stories, and the theme of cosmic determinism and the causal explanations in terms of force seemed out of date, reverberating distantly and melodramatically out of the pre-Freudian, pre-Joycean, pre-Depression past. Another age would have another set of terms and concepts, other descriptions and symbols of man's fears and travails, other possibilities for the creation of literary form; the universe of force was gone—its course run within the span of a single crucial century—and its traces were rather quickly covered over in the literary history of a differently preoccupied time.

The momentous dialogue between science and culture was largely begun on the conceptual grounds of the universe of force. Our principal legacy from the early days of that dialogue is twofold, as I see it: a feeling of alienation from a universe for which the only viable descriptions seem to be mechanistic and scientific, and, taking to heart the lessons of the early critics and absurdists of the universe of force, an opportunity for approaching reality from new, various, and self-aware intellectual perspectives, an opportunity that as yet has not been widely understood or fully explored.

NOTES

INTRODUCTION

1. *Characters and Events*, I (Henry Holt, 1929), 59–60.

PROLOGUE

1. *A New English Dictionary on Historical Principles*, ed. James A. H. Murray (Oxford Press, 1901), IV, 420. The full set of entries for *force* to which I refer in this discussion runs from p. 418 to p. 422.

1. NINETEENTH-CENTURY SCIENCE

1. Richard S. Westfall, *Force in Newton's Physics* (MacDonald, 1971), 2–47, 526–528.

2. Ibid., 56–90, 529–534.

3. Max Jammer, *Concepts of Force* (Harper and Bros., 1962), 166, 168–169.

4. Westfall, 283–322.

5. Quoted in ibid., 313, 311.

6. (Philosophical Library, 1961), 141–142.

7. Westfall, 439, 451.

8. Trans. Andrew Motte, rev. Florian Cajori (Univ. of California Press, 1946), xviii.

9. Marshall Clagett, ed., *Critical Problems in the History of Science* (Univ. of Wisconsin Press, 1959), 330–336.

10. Charles Coulston Gillispie, *The Edge of Objectivity* (Princeton Univ. Press, 1960), 352–405.

11. Edward Livingston Youmans, "Introduction," *The Correlation and Conservation of Force*, ed. E. L. Youmans (D. Appleton, 1890), xxviii; John Theodore Merz, *A History of European Thought in the Nineteenth Century*, 2 vols. (Wm. Blackwood and Sons, 1912), II, 111n.; Thomas S. Kuhn in Clagett, 336.

12. James Prescott Joule, *The Scientific Papers*, 2 vols. (Dawsons, 1963), I, 269. Parenthetical page numbers in the discussion of Joule refer to this volume.

13. *On the Correlation of Physical Forces, with other Contributions to Science* (n.p. [London], 1874), v.

14. *On the Correlation of Physical Forces*, 2nd ed. (n.p. [London], 1850), 99.

15. Ibid., 13–14.

16. "The Correlation of Physical Forces," in Youmans, 19 (my italics). Parenthetical page numbers in the discussion of Grove refer to this source.

17. *On the Correlation of Physical Forces*, 2nd ed., 93–94.

18. Ibid., 95.

19. Ibid., 99.

20. "The Conservation of Force: a Physical Memoir" [1847], in Russell Kahn, intro. and ed., *Selected Writings of Hermann von Helmholtz* (Wesleyan Univ. Press, 1971), 14.

21. "The Application of the Law of the Conservation of Force to Organic Phenomena" [1861], in Kahn, 109–110.

22. "Interaction of Natural Forces," trans. John Tyndall, in Youmans, 240. Parenthetical page numbers in the discussion of Helmholtz refer to this source.

23. *Popular Lectures on Scientific Subjects*, 1st series, trans. E. Atkinson (Longmans, Green, 1898), 326.

24. "The Forces of Inorganic Nature," in Youmans, 251–252.

25. "The Conservation of Force," in Youmans, 379.

26. *Popular Lectures*, 329.

27. Quoted in Ernst Cassirer, *The Problem of Knowledge*. trans. Wm. H. Woglom and Chas. W. Hendel (Yale Univ. Press, 1950), 86.

28. Merz, 404–405.

29. "The Force Behind Nature," *Popular Science Monthly*, XVI (March 1880), 619.

30. Quoted in Youmans, xxxii–xxxiii.

31. Quoted in J. B. Stallo, *The Concepts and Theories of Modern Physics*, ed. Percy W. Bridgman (Harvard Univ. Press, 1960), 53.

32. Youmans, 330–331.

33. *Fragments of Science* (A. L. Burt [1901?]), 15.

34. Quoted in Jammer, 235.

35. *Lectures on Some Recent Advances in Physical Science* (Macmillan [London], 1885), 344.

36. Ibid., 346.

37. Ibid., 16.

38. Merz, 98.

39. G. C. F[oster], in Youmans, 343n.

40. Gerd Buchdahl, "Science and Metaphysics," *The Nature of Metaphysics*, ed. D. F. Pears (Macmillan [London], 1957), 80.

41. Jammer, 220.

42. Cassirer, *The Problem*, 95.

43. *The Evolution of Physics* (Simon and Schuster, 1938), 33.

44. Jammer, 4.

45. "Alternative Interpretations of the History of Science," *Scientific Monthly*, LXXX, 2 (Feb. 1955), 113.

46. *Roots of Scientific Thought* (Basic Books, 1957), 479.

47. *The Rise of the New Physics* (Dover, 1951), 37.

48. Jammer, 248.

49. *Scientific Explanation* (Cambridge Univ. Press, 1953), 96.

50. *Determinism and Indeterminism in Modern Physics* (Yale Univ. Press, 1956), 21.

51. The quoted phrases are from *Determinism and Indeterminism*, 65; *Scientific Explanation*, 96; and Carnap's *Philosophical Foundations of Physics*, ed. Martin Gardner (Basic Books, 1966), 192.

2. HERBERT SPENCER

1. William Henry Hudson, *Herbert Spencer* (Archibald Constable, 1908), 10.

2. Herbert Spencer, *First Principles* (A. L. Burt [1880?]), 111. Parenthetical page numbers in the discussion of Spencer refer to this source.

3. *An Autobiography*, 2 vols. (D. Appleton, 1904), I, 538.

4. Spencer, "The Filiation of Ideas," in David Duncan, *Life and Letters of Herbert Spencer*, 2 vols. (D. Appleton, 1908), II, 322.

5. *An Autobiography*, I, 201.

6. Duncan, II, 285.

7. *An Autobiography*, I, 517.

8. Ibid., II, 15.

9. "The Filiation of Ideas," in Duncan, II, 328.

10. Ibid., 335.

11. *An Autobiography*, II, 86.

12. "The Filiation of Ideas," in Duncan, II, 328.

13. Hugh Elliot, *Herbert Spencer* (Greenwood Press, 1970), 249.

14. Darwin, quoted in Duncan, I, 113.

15. Elliot, 257, 262. See also Spencer's exchange with Huxley on this question in Duncan, I, 360.

16. *An Autobiography*, II, 115.

17. (Century, 1929), 231.

18. Boring, 231; Elliot, 273, 291.

19. *The Principles of Psychology*, 2 vols. (D. Appleton, 1897), II, 577.

20. Ibid., 610–611.

21. Joseph Maier, "Foreword," in Jay Rumney, *Herbert Spencer's Sociology* (Atherton Press, 1966), v.

22. Quoted in Robert L. Carneiro, *The Evolution of Society: Selections from Herbert Spencer's Principles of Sociology* (Univ. of Chicago Press, 1967), x.

23. *The Principles of Sociology* (D. Appleton, 1897), III, 61.

24. *An Autobiography*, II, 369–370.

25. Quoted in Hudson, 74.

26. Quoted in ibid., 66.

27. "The Unknowable," *Obiter Scripta*, ed. Justus Buchler and Benjamin Schwartz (Chas. Scribner's Sons, 1936), 163.

28. Elliot, 90.

29. *An Autobiography*, II, 198–199.

30. Ibid., I, ix, x.

31. *The Grammar of Science* (J. M. Dent, 1937), 277n.

32. *The Edge of Objectivity* (Princeton Univ. Press, 1960), 403.

33. *Evolution and Ethics and Other Essays* (D. Appleton, 1894), 131–132.

34. Duncan, I, 232.

35. *The Riddle of the Universe at the Close of the Nineteenth Century*, trans. Joseph McCabe (Harper and Bros., 1900), 4.

3. THE AMERICANIZATION

1. "The Philosophy of Herbert Spencer," *NAR*, C (April 1865), 454. Parenthetical page numbers in the discussion of Wright refer to this source.

2. Chauncey Wright, *Philosophical Writings: Representative Selections*, ed. Edw. H. Madden (Liberal Arts Press, 1958), 8–10.

3. Quoted by Madden in Wright, *Philosophical Writings*, xiv.

4. Ed. Percy W. Bridgman (Harvard Univ. Press, 1960), 3, 4. Parenthetical page numbers in the discussion of Stallo refer to this edition.

5. *Popular Science Monthly*, XII, 286–302. Reprinted in Peirce's *Collected Papers*, V, 248–271.

6. *The Thought and Character of William James*, 2 vols. (Little, Brown, 1935), I, 475.

7. "Herbert Spencer," *Atlantic Monthly*, XCIV (1904), 99–108. Parenthetical page numbers in the discussion of James refer to this source. The essay is also available in William James, *Memories and Studies* (Longmans, Green, 1911).

8. From *Journal of Speculative Philosophy* (1878) and *Nation* (1879), respectively; both reprinted in William James, *Collected Essays and Reviews* (Longmans, Green, 1920).

9. "Spencer's Definition of Mind as Correspondence," in ibid., 51–52.

10. "Spencer's *Data of Ethics*," ibid., 148.

11. "The Feeling of Effort," ibid., 213–214.

12. *An Autobiography*, 2 vols. (D. Appleton, 1904), I, 201.

13. Quoted in Milton Berman, *John Fiske: the Evolution of a Popularizer* (Harvard Univ. Press, 1961), 37.

14. See W. Stull Holt, "The Idea of Scientific History," *JHI*, I (June 1940), 352–362.

15. Buckle, quoted in Berman, 44.

16. "The Doctrine of Evolution," *A Century of Science and Other Essays* (Houghton, Mifflin, 1902), 40.

17. Berman, 146–147.

18. Ibid., 126.

19. Feb. 14, 1864, quoted in ibid., 54.

20. Spencer, letter to Fiske concerning his article "The Evolution of Language," *NAR* (Oct. 1963), cited by Berman, 45.

21. Quoted in Berman, 94.

22. *An Autobiography*, II, 477.

23. (Houghton, Mifflin, 1900), I, vii. Parenthetical page numbers in the discussion of Fiske refer to this edition.

24. "Edward Livingston Youmans," *A Century of Science and Other Essays* (Houghton, Mifflin, 1902), 73.

262

25. See "Sociology and Hero Worship," and "The Heroes of Industry," *Excursions of an Evolutionist* (Houghton, Mifflin, 1889).

26. Berman, 252.

27. *The Idea of God as Affected by Modern Knowledge* (Houghton, Mifflin, 1885), xxxi.

28. Ibid., xxi.

29. *The Destiny of Man, Viewed in the Light of his Origin* (Houghton, Mifflin, 1884), 32.

30. Ibid., 113, 112.

31. Ibid., 30.

32. Ibid., 114.

33. *The Idea of God*, xi.

34. Ibid., xvi.

35. *The Destiny of Man*, 117.

36. *The Idea of God*, 98.

37. Ibid., 166–167.

38. From *The Evolution of Christianity* (1892), quoted in Paul F. Boller, *American Thought in Transition* (Rand, McNally, 1969), 34–35.

39. (N.p., n.d. [Albany, N.Y., 1871]), 706. Parenthetical page numbers in the discussion of Martin refer to this source.

40. *The Autobiography of Joseph LeConte*, ed. Wm. Dallam Armes (D. Appleton, 1903), 335–337.

41. *Religion and Science* (D. Appleton, 1874), 277–278.

42. Ibid., 281.

43. *Evolution: Its Nature, Its Evidence and Its Relation to Religious Thought* (D. Appleton, 1891), 328.

44. *Religion and Science*, 281–282.

45. *Evolution: Its Nature*, 8.

46. *Primary Factors in Organic Evolution* (Open Court, 1896), 473. Parenthetical page references in the discussion of Cope refer to this source.

47. From Introduction to *The Origin of the Fittest*, quoted in Henry Fairfield Osborn, *Cope: Master Naturalist* (Princeton Univ. Press, 1931), 530.

48. From Cope's reply to Montgomery's review in *Open Court*, I (1887–1888), of his *Theology of Evolution*, quoted in Herbert W. Schneider, *A History of American Philosophy* (Columbia Univ. Press, 1946), 317.

49. Max Jammer, *Concepts of Force* (Harper and Bros., 1962), 150–151.

50. See Richard Hofstadter, "The Vogue of Spencer," *Social Darwinism in American Thought* (George Braziller, 1959), 31–50.

51. John Fiske, *A Century of Science*, 87–91; Berman, 54.

52. *The Holmes-Pollock Letters*, ed. Mark DeWolfe Howe, 2 vols. (Harvard Univ. Press, 1941), I, 58.

53. John Dewey, *Characters and Events*, ed. Joseph Ratner (Henry Holt, 1929), 59–60.

54. "Edward Livingston Youmans," *A Century of Science*, 79.

55. *Garrulities of an Octogenarian Editor* (Houghton, Mifflin, 1923), 301, 319.

56. Quoted in Boller, 48.

57. "Herbert Spencer," *Evolution, Popular Lectures and Discussions before the Brooklyn Ethical Association* (J. H. West, 1889), 1.

58. *Memories and Studies*, 126.

59. A list of the subscribers and an account of the proceedings were published as a pamphlet, *Herbert Spencer on the Americans and the Americans on Herbert Spencer*, ed. E. L. Youmans (D. Appleton, 1882).

60. *Herbert Spencer on the Americans*, 24.

61. See, for example, Minot J. Savage, "Agencies That Are Working a Revolution in Theology," *Arena*, I (Dec. 1889), 1–14; and B. O. Flower, "The Broadening Horizon of Civilization," *Arena*, V (May 1892), 775–780.

62. Frank L. Mott, "The Magazine Revolution and Popular Ideas in the Nineties," *Proceedings of the American Antiquarian Society*, LXIV (1954), 200.

63. Introduction, *Evolution, Popular Lectures and Discussions*, 19.

64. *Portrait of a Publisher* (D. Appleton, 1925), 48.

65. Hofstadter, 33.

66. Ibid., 22–23.

67. Donald Fleming, *John William Draper and the Religion of Science* (Octagon Books, 1972), 125.

68. Quoted in Max Fisch, "Evolution in American Philosophy," *Philosophical Review*, LVI (1947), 359.

69. I (Mar. 1870), 464–476.

70. *Evolution, Popular Lectures and Dicussions*, 7.

71. "Evolution as Related to Religious Thought," *Evolution, Popular Lectures and Discussions*, 330.

72. (D. Appleton, 1890), xli–xlii.

73. See Merle Curti, *The Growth of American Thought* (Harper & Row, 1964), 555–556, for effective documentation of the industrialists' social ideas.

74. Holt, *Garrulities*, 47, and Carnegie, quoted in Boller, 54.

75. *The Beginnings of Critical Realism in America 1860–1920*, Vol. 3 of *Main Currents in American Thought* (Harcourt, Brace, 1930), 318.

4. HENRY ADAMS

1. Ernest Samuels, *The Young Henry Adams* (Harvard Univ. Press, 1948), 133–135.

2. William H. Jordy, *Henry Adams: Scientific Historian* (Yale Univ. Press, 1952), 245–246.

3. Quoted in Samuels, *The Young Henry Adams*, 131–132.

4. Adams marked a passage that made this point in his copy (now in the Massachusetts Historical Society) of *The Positive Philosophy of Auguste Comte*, trans. and abridged by Harriet Martineau, 2 vols. (John Chapman, 1853), II, 50.

5. See Jordy, 172–182, for a detailed discussion of Adams's relation to geologic thought of his day.

6. Jordy, 74.

7. George Hochfield, *Henry Adams, an Introduction and Interpretation* (Holt, Rinehart and Winston, 1962); Peter Shaw, "Blood Is Thicker Than Irony: Henry Adams' *History*," *NEQ*, XL (June 1967), 163–187, and "The War of 1812 Could Not Take Place: Henry Adams's *History*," *YR*, LXII (Summer 1973), 544–556; Richard C. Vitzthum, *The American Compromise* (Univ. of Oklahoma Press, 1974).

8. To Samuel Jones Tilden, Jan. 24, 1883, in Harold Dean Cater, ed., *Henry Adams and his Friends: A Collection of Unpublished Letters* (Houghton, Mifflin, 1947), 125–126.

9. J. C. Levenson, *The Mind and Art of Henry Adams* (Houghton, Mifflin, 1957), 184.

10. Ernest Samuels, *Henry Adams: The Middle Years* (Harvard Univ. Press, 1958), 372, 374, 358.

11. Vitzthum, 156.

12. Aug. 9, 1890 (Massachusetts Historical Society Adams collection).

13. June 11, 1897, in Worthington Chauncey Ford, ed., *The Letters of Henry Adams 1892–1918*, 2 vols. (Houghton, Mifflin, 1938), II, 129.

14. Mar. 4, 1900, in Cater, 487.

15. [Sept.?] 1895, in Ford, II, 83.

16. Oct. 23, 1897, in Ford, II, 134n.

17. "The Tendency of History," in Henry Adams, *The Degradation of the Democratic Dogma*, ed. Brooks Adams (Capricorn, 1958), 124.

18. Ibid., 125.

19. Ibid., 127.

20. Ibid., 127–128.

21. For a sensible treatment of Henry's relationship to Brooks's book see Jordy, 131.

22. See Henry Adams, letter to Brooks Adams, [Sept.?], 1895, in Ford, II, 83–84.

23. Oct. 4, 1895 (MHS Adams Collection).

24. Brooks Adams, *The Law of Civilization and Decay* (Alfred A. Knopf, 1943), viii–ix.

25. Letter, Nov. 10, 1902, in Ford, II, 392n.

26. Nov. 11, 1897, in Ford, II, 136.

27. Ford, II, 290.

28. *Henry Adams: The Major Phase* (Harvard Univ. Press, 1964), 231.

29. Nov. 7, 1900, in Ford, II, 301.

30. *The Major Phase*, 236.

31. Letter to Brooks Adams, Aug. 10, 1902, in Ford, II, 391–392.

32. (Houghton, Mifflin, 1904), 32. Subsequent parenthetical page numbers in the discussion of this book refer to this edition.

33. (Random House, 1931), x. Subsequent parenthetical page numbers in the discussion of this book refer to this edition.

34. Letter, Feb. 28, 1908, in Cater, 614.

35. Feb. 17, 1908, in Ford, II, 490.

36. John J. Conder, *A Formula of His Own* (Univ. of Chicago Press, 1970), 120–123.

37. Adams's copy of *The Grammar of Science* (MHS Adams Collection), 118.

38. Ibid., 305.

39. Adams's copy of *Concepts and Theories of Physics* (MHS Adams Collection), 95.

40. Adams's copy of *Modern Views of Electricity* (MHS Adams Collection), 25.

41. Adams's copy of *La Physique Moderne, son évolution* (MHS Adams Collection), 308.

42. Letter to Barrett Wendell, Mar. 12, 1909, in Cater, 645.

43. Three vols., privately printed, Washington, 1908.

44. (Houghton, Mifflin, 1911).

45. Written in 1909 and 1910 respectively. First published in *The Degradation of the Democratic Dogma*, ed. Brooks Adams (Macmillan, 1919).

46. To H. A. Bumstead, Feb. 1, 1910, in Cater, 677.

47. Letter to John Franklin Jameson, Mar. 20, 1909, in Cater, 649–650.

48. Letter to Charles Milnes Gaskell, June 6, 1909, in Ford, II, 519.

49. Letter to Raphael Pumpelly, May 19, 1910, in Ford, II, 541.

50. Letter introducing *The Rule* to readers of the ms., dated Jan. 1, 1909, and included with George Cabot Lodge's copy of the ms., in Cater, 783.

51. Feb. 10, 1909, in Ford, II, 515n.

52. Letter to Henry Adams (MHS Adams Collection).

53. *The Degradation of the Democratic Dogma* (G. P. Putnam's, 1958), 285.

54. Ibid., 302.

55. Letter to Adams quoted in Jordy, 139–140n.

56. May 19, 1910, in Ford, II, 541.

57. Jan. 30, 1910, in ibid., 533.

58. Quoted in C. C. Gillispie, *The Edge of Objectivity* (Princeton Univ. Press, 1960), 403.

59. Letter to Raphael Pumpelly, May 19, 1910, in Ford, II, 542.

60. *Runaway Star: An Appreciation of Henry Adams* (Cornell Univ. Press, 1951), 201.

5. FRANK NORRIS

1. Quoted in Warren French, *Frank Norris* (Twayne, 1962), 24.

2. "A Plea for Romantic Fiction," in Donald Pizer, ed., *The Literary Criticism of Frank Norris* (Univ. of Texas Press, 1964), 75, 76, 78.

3. "Frank Norris's Weekly Letter," in Pizer, ibid., 75.

4. William B. Dillingham suggests one such application in *Frank Norris: Instinct and Art* (Houghton, Mifflin, 1969), 59; James K. Folsom makes a broader approach in "The Wheat and the Locomotive: Norris and Naturalistic Ethics," *American Literary Naturalism: A Reassessment*, ed. Yoshinobu Hakutani and Lewis Fried (Carl Winter [Heidelberg], 1975), 57–73.

5. "The Novel with a 'Purpose,' " in Pizer, *Criticism*, 90.

6. Ibid., 91.

7. General Notes on the Nature of the Work," trans. and quoted in Elliot M. Grant, *Émile Zola* (Twayne, 1966), 45.

8. "Differences between Balzac and Myself," *Émile Zola*, 45.

9. See especially his book *The Novels of Frank Norris* (Univ. of Indiana Press, 1966).

10. *Frank Norris: A Study* (Octagon Books, 1964), 102.

11. Franklin Walker, *Frank Norris: A Biography* (Russell and Russell, 1963), 85. See also Marchand, *Frank Norris: A Study*, 90; and Pizer, *Criticism*, 70.

12. Sources cited in this paragraph are Walcutt, *American Literary Naturalism, a Divided Stream* (Univ. of Minnesota Press, 1956), 155; Chase, *The American Novel and its Tradition* (Doubleday, 1957), 198; Marchand, 90, 127; Dillingham, 70; and Pizer, *Criticism*, 19.

13. Sources cited in this paragraph are Marchand, 173; and Pizer, *Criticism*, 102, and *Novels*, 22.

14. Walker, 58.

15. *Collected Writings* (Doubleday, Doran, 1928), 119. Parenthetical page numbers in the discussion of "Lauth" refer to this edition.

16. *Novels*, 18–19.

17. (Doubleday, Doran, 1928), 202. Parenthetical page numbers in the discussion of *Vandover* refer to this edition.

18. (Doubleday, Doran, 1928), 322, 329. Parenthetical page numbers in the discussion of *McTeague* refer to this edition.

19. Chase, 191.

20. Walcutt, 131.

21. Apr. 5, 1899, in Franklin Walker, ed., *The Letters of Frank Norris* (Book Club of Calif., 1956), 35.

22. [Mar. 1899?], in ibid., 34.

23. See Lars Ahnebrink, *The Influence of Émile Zola on Frank Norris* (Harvard Univ. Press, 1947), 41–49, for a number of striking parallels.

24. (Houghton, Mifflin, 1958), 123, 35–36. Parenthetical page numbers in the discussion of *The Octopus* refer to this edition.

25. For one of the best and earliest expressions of this viewpoint see Granville Hicks, *The Great Tradition* (Macmillan, 1933), 168–175.

26. The critical history of *The Octopus* is intelligently and conveniently set forth in Richard Davison, *Studies in The Octopus* (Chas. E. Merrill, 1969).

27. Walcutt, 156.

28. (Doubleday, Page, 1903), 419–420. Parenthetical page numbers in the discussion of *The Pit* refer to this edition.

6. JACK LONDON

1. *American Literary Naturalism: A Divided Stream* (Univ. of Minnesota Press, 1956), 92.

2. *Jack London and his Times* (Doubleday, Doran, 1939), 209.

3. Quoted in Charmian London, *The Book of Jack London*, 2 vols. (Century, 1921), I, 345.

4. "On the Writer's Philosophy of Life," *Editor*, X (Oct. 1899), 128.

5. March 15, 1900, in King Hendricks and Irving Shepard, eds., *Letters from Jack London* (Odyssey, 1965), 101.

6. "The Human Drift," *The Human Drift* (Macmillan, 1917), 24.

7. Mar. 1, 1900, in *Letters*, 96.

8. Quoted in Arthur Calder-Marshall, "Introduction," *The Bodley Head Jack London* (Bodley Head, 1963), I, 12.

9. London, letter to Ralph Kasper, June 25, 1914, in *Letters*, 425.

10. "What Life Means to Me," *Cosmopolitan Magazine*, XL (Mar. 1906), 528.

11. See Philip S. Foner, *Jack London: American Rebel* (The Citadel Press, 1947) for a thorough discussion of this important phase of London's life.

12. *The War of the Classes* (Macmillan, 1905), 217–218.

13. Charmian London, I, 297.

14. Jack London, *The Scarlet Plague* (Macmillan, 1915), 178–179.

15. Letter to Cloudesley Johns, Dec. 22, 1900, in *Letters*, 117.

16. (Grosset and Dunlap, 1902), 57–58.

17. (Macmillan, 1911), 6–7.

18. *The War of the Classes*, 243–244.

19. The review is reprinted in Foner, 507–511. The passage cited here is on 508–509.

20. "The Shrinkage of the Planet," *Revolution and Other Essays* (Macmillan, 1910), 154–155.

21. "The Shrinkage," 156–157.

22. *The People of the Abyss* (Macmillan, 1903), 256.

23. *The People*, 78–79.

24. Letter to Cloudesley Johns, Jan. 6, 1902, in *Letters*, 128.

25. "How I Became a Socialist," *The War of the Classes*, 267.

26. Letter to Philo M. Buck, Jr., Nov. 5, 1912, in *Letters*, 367.

27. Letter to Mary Austin, Nov. 5, 1915, in *Letters*, 463.

28. Letter to Charmian London, Dec. 6, 1904, quoted in Charmian London, II, 12.

29. (Grosset and Dunlap, 1906), 5–6. Subsequent parenthetical page numbers in the discussion of this book refer to this edition.

30. "Jack London's Symbolic Wilderness: Four Versions," *NCF*, XVII (1962), 151.

31. *The American Mind* (Yale Univ. Press, 1950), 110.

32. (Macmillan, 1903), iii. Subsequent parenthetical page numbers in the discussion of this book refer to this edition.

33. (Grosset and Dunlap, 1904), 44. Subsequent parenthetical page numbers in the discussion of this book refer to this edition.

34. Letter to Carrie Sterling, Sept. 15, 1905, in *Letters*, 180.

35. (Regent Press, 1908), 4. Subsequent parenthetical page numbers in the discussion of this book refer to this edition.

36. Open letter to Rev. Charles Brown, June 5, 1910, in *Letters*, 307.

37. (Macmillan, 1910), 77. Subsequent parenthetical page numbers in the discussion of this book refer to this edition.

38. (Grosset and Dunlap, 1908), 141. Subsequent parenthetical page numbers in the discussion of this book refer to this edition.

39. I, 11, 16.

40. I, 11–12.

41. This idea is effectively presented, though in a somewhat more extreme form, in Herbert Muller, *Modern Fiction: a Study of Values* (Funk and Wagnalls, 1937), 79–80.

7. THEODORE DREISER

1. *Dawn* (Horace Liveright, 1931), 370.

2. Larzer Ziff, *The American 1890's* (Viking, 1968), 337.

3. F. O. Matthiessen, *Theodore Dreiser* (Wm. Sloane, 1951), 59.

4. *Notes on Life*, ed. Marguerite Tjader and John J. McAleer (Univ. of Alabama Press, 1974).

5. *Letters of Theodore Dreiser*, ed. Robert H. Elias, 3 vols. (Univ. of Pennsylvania Press [1959]), I, 319.

6. *Letters*, I, 346.

7 Quoted in W. A. Swanberg, *Dreiser* (Scribner's, 1965), 432.

8. Robert Penn Warren, *Homage to Theodore Dreiser* (Random House, 1971), 90.

9. Vernon L. Parrington, *Main Currents of American Thought* (Harcourt, Brace, 1930), III, 356.

10. Irving Howe, "Dreiser and Tragedy: the Stature of Theodore Dreiser," *Dreiser: A Collection of Critical Essays*, ed. John Lydenberg (Prentice-Hall, 1971), 142.

11. *A Book About Myself* (Horace Liveright, 1922), 457–458.

12. Quoted in Frank Harris, *Contemporary Portraits*, second series (Frank Harris, 1919), 91.

13. *A Book About Myself*, 458.

14. *Ev'ry Month*, Sept. 1896, 5, 7.

15. *Ev'ry Month*, Feb. 1897, 3.

16. Ellen Moers, *The Two Dreisers* (Viking, 1969), 144.

17. For the idea of Dreiser's relationship to Gates, I am indebted to both Ellen Moers, 166–167, and Richard Lehan, *Theodore Dreiser* (Southern Illinois Univ. Press, 1969), 67–68. Both of these books have fuller explanations of the relationship than I attempt to offer here.

18. Moers, 258n.

19. Carl Snyder, *The World Machine* (Longmans, Green, 1907), 7.

20. Snyder, 465.

21. Swanberg, 187.

22. Jacques Loeb, *The Mechanistic Conception of Life* (Univ. of Chicago Press, 1912), Preface.

23. Ibid., 36.

24. Ibid., 30.

25. Ibid., 31.

26. George W. Crile, *Man, an Adaptive Mechanism* (Macmillan, 1916), vii.

27. Ibid., 20–21.

28. Charles Fort, *The Book of the Damned* (Boni and Liveright), 17.

29. Ibid., 131, 156.

30. See *Letters of Theodore Dreiser*, I, 343, and II, 531–533.

31. Fort, 11.

32. *Scientific Monthly*, XLI (July 1935), 5–18.

33. See, for example, Robert H. Elias, *Theodore Dreiser, Apostle of Nature* (Cornell Univ. Press, 1970); Donald Pizer, "Introduction," *Theodore Dreiser: A Selection of Uncollected Prose* (Wayne State Univ. Press, 1977); and works previously citied by Lehan, Matthiessen, Moers, and Swanberg.

34. Theodore Dreiser, *Hey-Rub-a-Dub-Dub!* (Boni and Liveright, 1920), 163.

35. Pizer, *Uncollected Prose*, 208n.

36. "The Essential Tragedy of Life," *Hey-Rub*, 248.

37. "Equation Inevitable," *Hey-Rub*, 166.

38. Theodore Dreiser, "The Freshness of the Universe," *The Color of a Great City* (Boni and Liveright, 1923), 238–240.

39. "Change," *Hey-Rub*, 19.

40. Theodore Dreiser, "What I Believe," *Forum*, LXXXII (Nov. 1929), 319.

41. For a full discussion of Dreiser's concept of "chemisms" see Moers, 256–264.

42. Swanberg, 375.

43. *Dawn*, 150. See also page 73 for a similar situation prompting a similar conclusion.

44. "Personality," *Hey-Rub*, 107.

45. "Equation Inevitable," *Hey-Rub*, 165.

46. Ibid., 174.

47. "The American Financier," *Hey-Rub*, 74, 83.

48. "The Reformer," *Hey-Rub*, 206, 207.

49. Pizer, *Uncollected Prose*, 22.

50. "Equation Inevitable," 162, 178.

51. Ibid., 168.

52. Ibid., 170.

53. Ibid., 166.

54. Theodore Dreiser, one-paragraph statement of belief, *Bookman*, 68 (Sept. 1928), 25.

55. "What I Believe," 319.

56. Ibid., 317, 280.

57. *Letters of Theodore Dreiser*, II, 474.

58. "What I Believe," 281.

59. Theodore Dreiser, "The Beauty of Life," *The Color of a Great City*, 171.

60. "What I Believe," 317.

61. *Letters of Theodore Dreiser*, III, 889.

62. Quoted by Marguerite Tjader, *Theodore Dreiser, a New Dimension* (Silvermine, 1965), 127.

63. Theodore Dreiser, "My Creator" (1943 ms.), quoted in Tjader, x.

64. Ziff, 336.

65. Theodore Dreiser, "The Scope of Fiction," *New Republic*, XXX (April 12, 1922), Spring Literary Supplement, 8–9.

66. Richard Poirer, *A World Elsewhere* (Oxford Univ. Press, 1966), 239.

67. Swanberg, 292, 295.

68. "The Scope of Fiction," 9.

69. Theodore Dreiser, *Plays of the Natural and the Supernatural* (John Lane, 1916), 89. Parenthetical page numbers in the discussion of this work refer to this edition.

70. Quoted in Matthiessen, 177.

71. Theodore Dreiser, *The Financier* (Harper and Bros., 1911), 254. Parenthetical page numbers in the discussion of this work refer to this edition.

72. See also John J. McAleer, *Theodore Dreiser: an Introduction and Interpretation* (Holt, Rinehart and Winston, 1968), 105, where the points are made that the characters in this novel are judged by their amount of force and that Cowperwood's sexual adventurousness is a sign of Dreiser's conception of him as a man of force.

73. *The Financier* (World, 1947), 136.

74. Theodore Dreiser, *The Titan* (John Lane, 1914), 124. Parenthetical page numbers in the discussion of this work refer to this edition.

75. Theodore Dreiser, *The Stoic* (Doubleday, 1947), 287.

76. This phenomenon is seen as one of the main features of Dreiser's fiction in Charles Child Walcutt, *American Literary Naturalism, a Divided Stream* (Univ. of Minnesota Press, 1956), 202–203. See also Warren, 19.

77. Theodore Dreiser, *The "Genius"* (World, 1946), 118. Parenthetical page numbers in the discussion of this work refer to this edition.

78. Theodore Dreiser, *Sister Carrie* (Doubleday, Page, 1900), 1. Parenthetical page numbers in the discussion of this work refer to this edition.

79. Theodore Dreiser, *Jennie Gerhardt* (Harper and Bros., 1911), 135. Parenthetical page numbers in the discussion of this work refer to this edition.

80. Donald Pizer, *The Novels of Theodore Dreiser* (Univ. of Minnesota Press, 1976), 232.

BIBLIOGRAPHY

The following is a selective list of works consulted in the preparation of this study. Works included here either were directly referred to in the text or indirectly provided some particularly valuable perspective. Entries designated with an asterisk indicate specific annotated copies of books in the Henry Adams collection of the Massachusetts Historical Society.

d'Abro, A. *The Rise of the New Physics.* 2 vols. [N.Y.?]: Dover Publications, 1951.

*Adams, Brooks. *The Law of Civilization and Decay.* London: Swan Sonnenschein, 1895.

*———. *The Law of Civilization and Decay.* New York: Macmillan, 1896.

Adams, Henry. *The Degradation of the Democratic Dogma,* ed. and intro. Brooks Adams. New York: G. P. Putnam's Sons, 1958.

———. *The Education of Henry Adams.* New York: Random House, 1931.

*———. *The Education of Henry Adams.* Washington: Privately printed, 1907.

———. *Letters of Henry Adams 1892–1918,* ed. Worthington Chauncey Ford. Boston: Houghton, Mifflin, 1938.

———. *Mont-Saint-Michel and Chartres.* New York: Houghton, Mifflin, 1904.

*———. *Mont-Saint-Michel and Chartres.* Boston: Houghton, Mifflin, 1903.

———. Unpublished letters and papers, Massachusetts Historical Society.

Adams, James Truslow. "Henry Adams and the New Physics," *YR,* XIX (Dec. 1929), 283–302.

Ahnebrink, Lars. *The Influence of Émile Zola on Frank Norris.* Cambridge, Mass.: Harvard Univ. Press, 1947.

Appleton-Century Co., D. *The House of Appleton-Century.* New York: D. Appleton-Century, 1936.

Baldwin, James Mark, ed. *Dictionary of Philosophy and Psychology.* New York: Macmillan, 1911.

Berman, Milton. *John Fiske: the Evolution of a Popularizer.* Cambridge, Mass.: Harvard Univ. Press, 1961.

Blackman, Richard P. "The Expense of Greatness: Three Emphases on Henry Adams," *The Expense of Greatness.* Gloucester, Mass.: Peter Smith, 1958, 253–276.

Blau, Joseph L. *Men and Movements in American Philosophy.* New York: Prentice-Hall, 1952.

Boller, Paul F., Jr. *American Thought in Transition: The Impact of Evolutionary Naturalism 1865–1900.* Chicago: Rand McNally, 1969.

Boring, Edwin G. *A History of Experimental Psychology.* New York: Century, 1929.

Braithwaite, R. B. *Scientific Explanation.* Cambridge, Eng.: Cambridge Univ. Press, 1953.

Brooklyn Ethical Association. *Evolution and Social Reform.* Boston: James H. West, 1890.

———. *Evolution in Science, Philosophy and Art: Popular Lectures and Discussions before the B.E.A.* New York: D. Appleton, 1891.

———. *Evolution: Popular Lectures and Discussions Before the B.E.A.* Boston: James H. West, 1889.

Buchdahl, Gerd. "Science and Metaphysics," in D. F. Pears, ed., *The Nature of Metaphysics.* London: Macmillan, 1957, 61–82.

Bumstead, Henry A. Unpublished critique of the first version of Henry Adams's *The Rule of Phase*, Massachusetts Historical Society.

Calder-Marshall, Arthur. Introduction to *The Bodley Head Jack London.* 4 vols. London: Bodley Head, 1963–1966.

Carnap, Rudolf. *Philosophical Foundations of Physics*, ed. Martin Gardner. New York: Basic Books, 1966.

Carneiro, Robert L., ed. and intro. *The Evolution of Society: Selections from Herbert Spencer's "Principles of Sociology."* Chicago: Univ. of Chicago Press, 1967.

Carpenter, William B. "The Force Behind Nature," *Popular Science Monthly*, XVI (March 1880), 614–625.

Cassirer, Ernst. *Determinism and Indeterminism in Modern Physics*, trans. O. Theodor Benfey. New Haven: Yale Univ. Press, 1956.

———. *The Problem of Knowledge*, trans. William H. Woglom and Charles W. Hendel. New Haven: Yale Univ. Press, 1950.

Cater, Harold Dean, ed. *Henry Adams and his Friends: A Collection of His Unpublished Letters.* Boston: Houghton, Mifflin, 1947.

Chase, Richard V. *The American Novel and Its Tradition.* New York: Doubleday, 1957.

Cohen, Robert S. "Alternative Interpretations of the History of Science," *Scientific Monthly*, LXXX, (Feb. 1955), 111–116.

Commager, Henry Steele. *The American Mind: An Interpretation of American Thought and Character since the 1880's.* New Haven: Yale Univ. Press, 1950.

*Comte, Auguste. *The Positive Philosophy of Auguste Comte*, trans. and condensed by Harriet Martineau. 2 vols. London: John Chapman, 1853.

Conder, John J. *A Formula of His Own: Henry Adams's Literary Experiment.* Chicago: Univ. of Chicago Press, 1970.

Cope, Edward Drinker. *The Primary Factors of Organic Evolution.* Chicago: Open Court, 1896.

Crile, George W. *Man—An Adaptive Mechanism.* New York: Macmillan, 1916.

Curti, Merle. *The Growth of American Thought.* New York: Harper and Row, 1964.

Dampier, Sir William Cecil. *A History of Science and its Relations with Philosophy and Religion*, 3rd ed. New York: Macmillan, 1943.

———. *The Recent Development of Physical Science.* Philadelphia: P. Blakiston's Son, 1924.

Davison, Richard Allan, ed. *The Merrill Studies in The Octopus.* Ohio: Chas. E. Merrill, 1969.

*Despaux, Arsène. *Cause des Énergies Attractives.* Paris: Ancienne Librarie Germer Baillière, 1902.

Dewey, John. *Characters and Events*, ed. Joseph Ratner. New York: Henry Holt, 1929.

Dillingham, William B. *Frank Norris: Instinct and Art.* Boston: Houghton, Mifflin, 1969.

Dreisch, Hans. *The Science and Philosophy of the Organism.* 2 vols. London: Adam and Charles Black, 1908.

Dreiser, Theodore. *A Book About Myself.* New York: Boni and Liveright, 1923.

————. *Chains: Lesser Novels and Stories.* New York: Boni and Liveright, 1927.

————. *The Color of a Great City.* New York: Boni and Liveright, 1923.

————. *Dawn.* New York: Horace Liveright, 1931.

————. *The Financier.* New York: Harper and Bros., 1911.

————. *The Financier* (rev. ed.). Cleveland: World, 1947.

————. *Free and Other Stories.* New York: Boni and Liveright, 1918.

————. *The "Genius."* Cleveland: World, 1946.

————. *The Hand of the Potter.* New York: Boni and Liveright, 1918.

————. *Hey-Rub-a-Dub-Dub!* New York: Boni and Liveright, 1920.

————. "If Force Transmutes," *Demorest's,* XXXV (Aug. 1899), 243.

————. Introduction to *McTeague* (*Works of Frank Norris,* VIII). New York: Doubleday, Doran, 1928.

————. *Jennie Gerhardt.* New York: World, 1946.

————. *Letters of Theodore Dreiser, a Selection,* ed. Robert H. Elias. 3 vols. Philadelphia: Univ. of Pennsylvania Press, [1959].

————. *Notes on Life,* ed. Marguerite Tjader and John J. McAleer. University, Ala: Univ. of Alabama Press, 1974.

————. *Plays of the Natural and the Supernatural.* New York: John Lane, 1916.

————. "Reflections," *Ev'ry Month,* monthly, 1896–1897.

————. *Sister Carrie.* New York: Doubleday, Page, 1900.

————. *The Stoic.* New York: Doubleday, 1947.

————. *The Titan.* New York: John Lane, 1914.

————. "What I Believe," *Forum,* LXXXII (Nov. 1929), 279–281, 317–320.

Drey, Sylvan. *The Moral and Religious Aspects of Herbert Spencer's Philosophy,* in Brooklyn Ethical Ass'n., Modern Science Essayist Series 1, no. 17. Boston: James H. West, 1889.

Duncan, David. *Life and Letters of Herbert Spencer.* 2 vols. New York: D. Appleton, 1908.

Einstein, Albert, and Leopold Infeld. *The Evolution of Physics.* New York: Simon and Schuster, 1938.

Elias, Robert H. *Theodore Dreiser: Apostle of Nature.* Ithaca, N.Y.: Cornell Univ. Press, 1970.

Elliot, Hugh. *Herbert Spencer.* Westport, Conn.: Greenwood Press, 1970.

*Findlay, Alex. *The Phase Rule and Its Applications,* 2nd ed. London: Longmans, Green, 1906.

Fisch, Max. "Evolution in American Philosophy," *Philosophical Review,* LVI (1947), 357–373.

Fiske, John. *A Century of Science, and Other Essays.* Boston: Houghton, Mifflin, 1902.

————. *The Destiny of Man, Viewed in the Light of his Origin.* Boston: Houghton, Mifflin, 1884.

————. *Edward Livingston Youmans, Interpreter of Science to the People.* New York: D. Appleton, 1894.

————. *Excursions of an Evolutionist.* Boston: Houghton, Mifflin, 1889.

————. *The Idea of God as Affected by Modern Knowledge.* Boston: Houghton, Mifflin, 1885.

————. *Outlines of Cosmic Philosophy*. 2 vols. Boston: Houghton, Mifflin, 1900.

Fleming, Donald. *John William Draper and the Religion of Science*. New York: Octagon Books, 1972.

Folsom, James K. "Mutation as Metaphor in *The Education of Henry Adams*," *ELH*, XXX (June 1963), 162–174.

Foner, Philip S. *Jack London: American Rebel*. New York: Citadel Press, 1947.

Fort, Charles. *The Book of the Damned*. New York: Boni and Liveright, 1919.

Frank, Philipp. "Metaphysical Interpretations of Science," *The British Journal for the Philosophy of Science*, I, i (May 1950), 60–74; and I, ii (Aug. 1950), 77–91.

French, Warren. *Frank Norris*. New York: Twayne, [1962].

Gillispie, Charles Coulston. *The Edge of Objectivity*. Princeton, N.J.: Princeton Univ. Press, 1960.

Grant, Elliott M. *Émile Zola*. New York: Twayne, 1966.

Grove, Sir William Robert. *On the Correlation of Physical Forces, the substance of a Course of Lectures, delivered in the London Institution in the year 1843*. 2nd ed. London, 1850.

*Haeckel, Ernst. *Les Énigmes de L'Universe*, trans. Camille Bos. Paris: Librairie C. Reinwald, 1902.

————. *The Riddle of the Universe at the Close of the Nineteenth Century*, trans. Joseph McCabe. New York: Harper, 1900.

Hakutani, Yoshinobu, and Lewis Fried, eds. *American Literary Naturalism: A Reassessment, Anglistische Forschungen*, Heft 109. Heidelberg: Carl Winter Universitätsverlag, 1975.

Helmholtz, Hermann von. *Popular Lectures on Scientific Subjects*, 1st series, trans., E. Atkinson. London: Longmans, Green, 1898.

————. *Selected Writings of Hermann von Helmholtz*, ed. Russell Kahl. Middletown, Conn.: Wesleyan Univ. Press, 1971.

Hemmings, F. J. W. *Émile Zola*. London: Oxford Univ. Press, 1953.

*Hertz, Heinrich. *Electric Waves*, trans. D. E. Jones, preface Lord Kelvin. London: Macmillan, 1893.

Hesse, Mary. *Forces and Fields*. New York: Philosophical Library, 1961.

Hochfield, George. *Henry Adams: An Introduction and Interpretation*. New York: Barnes and Noble, 1962.

Hofstadter, Richard. *Social Darwinism in American Thought*. New York: George Braziller, 1959.

Holt, Henry. *Garrulities of an Octogenarian Editor, with Other Essays Somewhat Biographical and Autobiographical*. Boston: Houghton, Mifflin, 1923.

Holt, W. Stull. "The Idea of Scientific History," *Journal of the History of Ideas*, I (June 1940), 352–362.

Hudson, William Henry. *Herbert Spencer*. London: Archibald Constable, 1908.

Hume, Robert A. "*The Education of Henry Adams*: A Critical Estimate," dissertation. Cornell Univ., 1940.

————. *Runaway Star: An Appreciation of Henry Adams*. Ithaca, N.Y.: Cornell Univ. Press, 1951.

James, William. *Collected Essays and Reviews*. New York: Longmans, Green, 1920.

————. "Herbert Spencer," *Atlantic Monthly*, XCIV (1904), 99–108.

————. *Memories and Studies*. New York: Longmans, Green, 1911.

Jammer, Max. *Concepts of Force*. New York: Harper, 1962.

Janes, Lewis George. *The Scope and Principles of Evolution Philosophy*, in Brooklyn Ethical Association, Evolution in Science and Art Series, 16. Boston: James H. West, n.d.

Jordy, William H. *Henry Adams: Scientific Historian*. New Haven: Yale Univ. Press, 1952.

Joule, James Prescott. *The Scientific Papers*. 2 vols. London: Dawsons, 1963.

Kazin, Alfred. *On Native Grounds*. New York: Doubleday, 1956.

——, and Charles Shapiro, eds. *The Stature of Theodore Dreiser*. Bloomington, Ind.: Indiana Univ. Press, 1955.

Kelvin, William Thomson, baron. *Popular Lectures and Addresses*. 2 vols. London and New York: Macmillan, 1894.

Kidd, Benjamin. *Social Evolution*. New York: Macmillan, 1895.

Koretz, Gene H. "Augustine's *Confessions* and *The Education of Henry Adams*," *Comparative Literature*, XII (Summer 1960), 193–206.

Kuhn, Thomas S. "Energy Conservation as an Example of Simultaneous Discovery," *Critical Problems in the History of Science*, ed. M. Clagett. Madison, Wis.: Univ. of Wisconsin Press, 1959, 321–356.

——. *The Structure of Scientific Revolutions*, 2nd ed. Chicago: Univ. of Chicago Press, 1970.

Labor, Earle. *Jack London*. New York: Twayne, 1974.

LeConte, Joseph. *The Autobiography of Joseph LeConte*, ed. William Dallam Armes. New York: D. Appleton, 1903.

——. *Evolution; Its Nature, Its Evidences, and Its Relation to Religious Thought*, 2nd ed. New York: D. Appleton, 1891.

——. "Instinct and Intelligence," *Popular Science Monthly*, VII (Oct. 1875), 653–664.

——. *Religion and Science*. New York: D. Appleton, 1874.

Levenson, J. C. *The Mind and Art of Henry Adams*. Boston: Houghton, Mifflin, 1957.

*Lodge, Oliver J. *Modern Views of Electricity*. New York: Macmillan, 1889.

Loeb, Jacques. *The Mechanistic Conception of Life*. Chicago: Univ. of Chicago Press, 1912.

London, Charmian. *The Book of Jack London*. 2 vols. New York: Century, 1921.

London, Jack. *Burning Daylight*. New York: Macmillan, 1910.

——. *The Call of the Wild and Other Stories*. New York: Dodd, Mead, 1960.

——. *The Cruise of the Snark*. New York: Macmillan, 1911.

——. *A Daughter of the Snows*. New York: Grosset and Dunlap, 1902.

——. *The Iron Heel*. New York: Grosset and Dunlap, 1908.

——. *Letters from Jack London*, ed. King Hendricks and Irving Shepard. New York: Odyssey, 1965.

——. *Martin Eden*. New York: Regent Press, 1908.

——. "On the Writer's Philosophy of Life," *Editor*, X (Oct. 1899), 125–129.

——. *The People of the Abyss*. New York: Macmillan, 1903.

——. *The Scarlet Plague*. New York: Macmillan, 1915.

——. *The Sea Wolf*. New York: Grosset and Dunlap, 1904.

——. *The War of the Classes*. New York: Macmillan, 1905.

——. *White Fang*. New York: Grosset and Dunlap, 1906.

——, and Anna Strunsky. *The Kempton-Wace Letters*. New York: Macmillan, 1903.

London, Joan. *Jack London and his Times*. New York: Doubleday, Doran, 1939.

Lydenberg, John. *Dreiser: A Collection of Critical Essays*. Englewood Cliffs, N.J.: Prentice-Hall, 1971.

Lyon, Melvin. *Symbol and Idea in Henry Adams*. Lincoln, Neb.; Univ. of Nebraska Press, 1970.

Mach, Ernst. *History and Root of the Principle of the Conservation of Energy*, trans. Philip E. B. Jourdain. Chicago: Open Court, 1911.

MacPherson, Hector. *Herbert Spencer: The Man and His Work*. New York: Doubleday, Page, 1900.

Madden, Edward H. *Chauncey Wright and The Foundations of Pragmatism*. Seattle: Univ. of Washington Press, 1963.

Marchand, Ernest. *Frank Norris: A Study*. New York: Octagon Books, 1964.

Margenau, Henry. *The Nature of Physical Reality*. New York: McGraw-Hill, 1950.

Martin, Benjamin. *The Natural Theology of the Doctrine of the Forces*. Proceedings of the University Convocation. [Albany, N.Y.]: [1871].

Matthiessen, F. O. *Theodore Dreiser*. [New York]: Wm. Sloane, 1951.

McAleer, John J. *Theodore Dreiser: An Introduction and Interpretation*. New York: Holt, Rinehart and Winston, 1968.

Merz, John Theodore. *A History of European Thought in the Nineteenth Century*. 2 vols. London: Wm. Blackwood, 1912.

Mindel, Joseph. "The Use of Metaphor: Henry Adams and the Symbols of Science," *JHI*, XXVI, no. 1 (1965), 89–102.

Moers, Ellen. *Two Dreisers*. New York: Viking, 1969.

Mott, Frank L. "The Magazine Revolution and Popular Ideas in the Nineties," *Proceedings of the American Antiquarian Society*, LXIV (1954), 195–214.

Muller, Herbert. *Modern Fiction: a Study in Values*. New York: Funk and Wagnalls, 1937.

Newton, Sir Isaac. *Principia Mathematica*, trans. Andrew Motte, rev. Florian Cajori. Berkeley, Calif.: Univ. of California Press, 1946.

Norris, Frank. *Collected Writings*. Vol. X, *Collected Works*. Garden City, N.Y.: Doubleday, Doran, 1928.

———. *The Letters of Frank Norris*, ed. Franklin Walker. San Francisco: Book Club of California, 1956.

———. *The Literary Criticism of Frank Norris*, ed. Donald Pizer. Austin, Tex.: Univ. of Texas Press, 1964.

———. *McTeague: A Story of San Francisco*. New York: Doubleday, Doran, 1928.

———. *The Octopus: a Story of California*. New York: Doubleday, Page, 1901.

———. *The Pit*. New York: Doubleday, Page, 1903.

———. *The Responsibilities of the Novelist, and other Literary Essays*. New York: Doubleday, Page, 1903.

———. *The Third Circle*. New York: John Lane, 1909.

———. *Vandover and the Brute*. New York: Doubleday, Doran, 1928.

Nye, Russell B. "John Fiske and His Cosmic Philosophy," *Michigan Academy of Science, Arts, Letters, Papers*, XXVIII (1942), 685–698.

Osborn, Henry Fairfield. *Cope: Master Naturalist*. Princeton, N.J.: Princeton Univ. Press, 1931.

Overton, Grant. *Portrait of a Publisher*. New York: D. Appleton, 1925.

Parrington, Vernon Louis. *The Beginnings of Critical Realism in America, 1860–1920*, Vol. 3 of *Main Currents in American Thought*. New York: Harcourt, Brace, 1930.

Pearson, Karl. *The Grammar of Science*. London: J. M. Dent, 1937.
*———. *The Grammar of Science*. London: Chas. and Adam Black, 1900.
Peirce, Charles Sanders. "How to Make Our Ideas Clear," *Collected Papers*, V, 248–271.
Perry, Ralph Barton. *The Thought and Character of William James*. 2 vols. Boston: Little, Brown, 1935.
Persons, Stow. *Evolutionary Thought in America*. New Haven: Yale Univ. Press, 1950.
Pizer, Donald. *The Novels of Frank Norris*. Bloomington, Ind.: Indiana Univ. Press, 1966.
———. *The Novels of Theodore Dreiser*. Minneapolis: Univ. of Minnesota Press, 1976.
———. "The Problem of Philosophy in the Novel," *Bucknell Review* XVIII (Spring 1970), 53–62.
———, ed. *Theodore Dreiser: A Selection of Uncollected Prose*. Detroit: Wayne State Univ. Press, 1977.
*Poincaré, H.[enri]. *La Science et l'Hypothèse*. Paris: Ernest Flammarion, n.d.
———. *Science and Hypothesis*, n. trans. [New York]: Dover Publications, [1952].
*Poincaré, Lucien. *La Physique Moderne, son évolution*. Paris: Ernest Flammarion, 1906.
Poirer, Richard. *A World Elsewhere: The Place of Style in American Literature*. New York: Oxford Univ. Press, 1966.
Ratner, Sidney. "Evolution and the Rise of the Scientific Spirit in America," *Philosophy of Science*, III (Jan. 1936), 104–122.
Richmond, A. B. "Is There a To-Morrow for the Human Race?" *Arena*, I (March 1890), 464–476.
Roelofs, Gerrit H. "Henry Adams: Pessimism and the Intelligent Use of Doom," *ELH*, XVII (Sept. 1950), 214–239.
Rowe, John Carlos. *Henry Adams and Henry James*. Ithaca: Cornell Univ. Press, 1976.
Royce, Josiah. *Herbert Spencer, An Estimate and Review; Together with a Chapter of Personal Reminiscences by James Collier*. New York: Fox, Duffield, 1904.
Rumney, Jay. *Herbert Spencer's Sociology*. New York: Atherton Press, 1966.
Samuels, Ernest. *Henry Adams: The Major Phase*. Cambridge, Mass.: Harvard Univ. Press, 1964.
———. *Henry Adams: The Middle Years*. Cambridge, Mass.: Harvard Univ. Press, 1958.
———. *The Young Henry Adams*. Cambridge, Mass.: Harvard Univ. Press, 1948.
Santayana, George. "The Unknowable," *Obiter Scripta*, ed. Justus Buchler and Benjamin Schwartz. New York: Chas. Scribner's Sons, 1936, 162–188.
Sarton, George. "The Discovery of the Law of Conservation of Energy," *Isis*, XIII, i (1929), 18–44.
Savage, Minot J. "Agencies That Are Working a Revolution in Theology," *Arena*, I (Dec. 1889), 1–14.
———. *The Religion of Evolution*. Boston: Lockwood, Brooks, 1876.
Schneider, Herbert W. *A History of American Philosophy*. New York: Columbia Univ. Press, 1946.
Shaw, Peter. "Blood is Thicker Than Irony: Henry Adams' *History*," *NEQ*, XL (June 1967), 163–187.
———. "The Success of Henry Adams," *YR*, LIX (Autumn 1969), 71–78.

———. "The War of 1812 Could Not Take Place: Henry Adams's *History*," YR, LXII (Summer 1973), 544–556.

Snyder, Carl. *The World Machine; The First Phase, The Cosmic Mechanism.* London: Longmans, Green, 1907.

Spencer, Herbert. *An Autobiography.* 2 vols. New York: D. Appleton, 1904.

———. *Essays: Scientific, Political and Speculative.* New York: D. Appleton, 1891.

———. *First Principles.* New York: A. L. Burt, [1880?].

———. *The Principles of Biology.* 2 vols. New York: D. Appleton, 1866.

———. *The Principles of Ethics.* 2 vols. New York: D. Appleton, 1892.

———. *The Principles of Psychology.* 2 vols. New York: D. Appleton, 1897.

———. *The Principles of Sociology.* 3 vols. New York: D. Appleton, 1897.

Spiller, Robert E., et al. *Literary History of the United States.* New York: Macmillan, 1953.

Stallo, J. B. *The Concepts and Theories of Modern Physics,* ed. Percy W. Bridgman. Cambridge, Mass.: Harvard Univ. Press, 1960.

*———. *La Matière et la Physique Moderne,* with a preface, "On the Atomic Theory" by C. Friedel. Paris: Ancienne Librarie Germer Baillière, 1899.

*Stewart, Balfour. *La Conservation de l'Énergie,* n. trans., with appendix: "La Nature de la Force" by P. de Saint-Robert. Paris: Ancienne Librarie Germer Baillière, 1899.

———. *The Conservation of Energy.* London: Kegan, Paul, Trench, Trübner, 1890.

Swanberg, W. A. *Dreiser.* New York: Chas. Scribner's Sons, 1965.

Tait, Peter Guthrie. *Lectures on Some Recent Advances in Physical Science.* London: Macmillan, 1885.

———. "On Force," *Nature,* XVII (1869), 459.

Theobald, D. W. *The Concept of Energy.* London: E. and F. N. Spon, 1966.

*Trowbridge, John. *What Is Electricity?* New York: D. Appleton, 1896.

Tyndall, John. *Fragments of Science.* New York: A. L. Burt, n.d. [1901].

Vitzthum, Richard C. *The American Compromise.* Norman, Okla.: Univ. of Oklahoma Press, 1974.

Wagner, Vern. *The Suspension of Henry Adams.* Detroit: Wayne State Univ. Press, 1969.

Walcutt, Charles C. *American Literary Naturalism, A Divided Stream.* Minneapolis: Univ. of Minnesota Press, 1956.

Walker, Franklin. *Frank Norris: A Biography.* New York: Russell and Russell, 1963.

*Wallace, Alfred R. *Man's Place in the Universe.* London: Chapman and Hall, 1903.

Warren, Robert Penn. *Homage to Theodore Dreiser.* New York: Random House, 1971.

Wasser, Henry. *The Scientific Thought of Henry Adams.* Thessaloniki, 1956.

Westfall, Richard S. *Force in Newton's Physics.* London: MacDonald, 1971.

Wiener, Philip P., and Aaron Noland. *Roots of Scientific Thought.* New York: Basic Books, 1957.

Wright, Chauncey. *Philosophical Writings: Representative Selections,* ed. Edward H. Madden. New York: Liberal Arts, 1958.

———. "The Philosophy of Herbert Spencer," *NAR,* L (April 1865), 423–476.

Youmans, Edward L., ed. and intro. *The Correlation and Conservation of Forces.* New York: D. Appleton, 1890.

———. *An Exposition of the Development Hypothesis.* [No publisher, place or date (1871?)] ("Written expressly for 'Johnson's Natural History'").

[————]. *Herbert Spencer on the Americans and the Americans on Herbert Spencer.* New York: D. Appleton, 1883.

————. "Spencer's Reconciliation of Science and Religion," *The Christian Examiner,* LXXII, 5th series, Vol. 10 (May 1862), 337–352.

Ziff, Larzer. *The American 1890's.* New York: Viking, 1966.

Zilsel, Edgar. "Physics and the Problem of Historico-Sociological Laws," *Philosophy of Science,* VIII (1941), 567–579.

INDEX

Ronald E. Martin is Professor of English and of Life and Health Sciences, and is Director of the Center for Science and Culture, University of Delaware. He is author of *The Fiction of Joseph Hergesheimer.*